The
English Common ⌐ ⌐r

The
English Common Reader

A Social History
of the Mass Reading Public, 1800–1900

SECOND EDITION

BY RICHARD D. ALTICK

WITH A FOREWORD BY JONATHAN ROSE

Ohio State University Press
Columbus

Library of Congress Cataloging-in-Publication Data

Altick, Richard Daniel, 1915–
    The English common reader : a social history of the mass reading public,
  1800–1900 / by Richard D. Altick ; with a new foreword by Jonathan Rose.
  — 2nd ed.
      p.   cm.
    Includes bibliographical references and index.
    ISBN 0–8142–0793–6 (cl : alk. paper). — ISBN 0–8142–0794–4 (pa : alk. paper).
    1. Books and reading—Great Britain—History—19th century.
  I. Title.
    Z1003.5.G7A53   1998
    028′.9′0941—dc21   98–19581
                                                   CIP

Cover design by Gore Studio Inc.
Typeset in Century Schoolbook.
Printed by Cushing-Malloy, Inc.

The paper used in this publication meets the minimum requirements of the American
National Standard for Information Sciences—Permanence of Paper for Printed
Library Materials. ANSI Z39.49-1992.

9 8 7 6 5 4 3 2

For Helen, Anne, and Elizabeth

Contents

BIBLIOGRAPHY

SUPPLEMENTARY BIBLIOGRAPHY

INDEX

{ *Foreword*

Richard D. Altick has been the most original
Victorian scholar of his generation, for two obvious reasons. First,
he had no formal graduate training in Victorian literature and
could therefore approach the subject with an unbridled mind. Second, he signed on to none of the critical fashions, from New Criticism to Postcolonialism, that cycled through his long professorial
career. One can only do truly creative work if one steers clear of
the avant garde, and because Altick followed his own beacon, he
became a pioneer on several academic frontiers, always a few
steps ahead of "the cutting edge." The better part of his scholarship converged on that very new field now known as the history
of the book: the social, economic, and cultural history of print.
Today it is the most innovative and rapidly growing branch of historiography, but when we look back to *The English Common
Reader*, we realize that Altick was there first.

Book history is generally presumed to have a French pedigree,
and so it does—on one side of the family tree. The sociological
historians of the *Annales* school developed quantitative methods
for the study of ordinary people and everyday life, and some of
them applied those techniques to the history of ordinary readers and everyday books, starting in 1958 with Lucien Febvre and
Henri-Jean Martin's *L'Apparition du livre*. Their findings were
fascinating—but *The English Common Reader* had already, and
quite independently, innovated much the same approach to literary studies. A few years earlier still, Altick had laid down the basic rationale behind what would become book history: "From the
very beginnings of publishing as a profit-making enterprise, the
publisher's estimate of the size of a book's potential audience, its
willingness to pay the price he will ask, and above all its current
tastes, has been the major consideration in his decision whether

or not to send the manuscript on to the typesetter. The whole history of literature in the past few centuries is, in a sense, the aggregate history of such decisions."[1]

In 1982 Robert Darnton, working within the *annaliste* tradition, would sketch out a blueprint for researchers in his manifesto "What Is the History of Books?" The objective, he argued, should be to trace the life cycle of books through a "communications circuit," from author to publisher to printer to shipper to bookseller to reader, while at all points factoring in the political, social, economic, and intellectual context.[2] Yet a glance at Altick's table of contents makes it clear that he was actually carrying out Darnton's program a quarter-century earlier. Models like Darnton's are useful for guiding students, for establishing a common agenda for the field, for alerting researchers to the kinds of issues they ought to be addressing. Altick, however, was not much concerned with theoretical models, because he never really needed them. He exemplified the scholar who is so thoroughly familiar with the literature and the archives that he knows instinctively what questions to ask and how they can be answered. Forty years ago Altick realized that a history of reading would require background research into primary and adult education, textbooks, libraries, publishing, book distribution, popular religion, leisure, artificial illumination, housing, and (of course) eyeglasses: and these are precisely the subhistories that today engage the most sophisticated scholars of the book.

In 1957 Altick knew well that he was inventing a new academic discipline, and said so. "There is room for literally hundreds of studies of topics which are here merely sketched," he wrote in the first edition of *The English Common Reader.* His aim was "to provide a preliminary map of the vast territory, still virtually unexplored, which awaits the researcher" (pp. 8–9). In fact, he did not wait for others to follow: most of his career would be devoted to chronicling the mundane varieties of print culture that academics before him had not considered worthy of study. He wrote up the

---

[1] Richard D. Altick, "English Publishing and the Mass Audience in 1852," in *Writers, Readers, and Occasions: Selected Essays on Victorian Literature and Life* (Columbus, 1989), p. 141.

[2] Robert Darnton, "What Is the History of Books?" in *The Kiss of Lamourette* (New York, 1990), esp. pp. 107–13.

history of everything from literary biography[3] to newspaper crime reports[4] to cheap editions of the classics. There was a fascinating literary critique of a Victorian tobacco trade journal, as well as an innovative and still useful sociological profile of authors in modern Britain.[5] D. F. McKenzie, in his 1985 Panizzi Lectures, would urge bibliographers to extend their attention to nonprint media such as the cinema,[6] but here too Altick was out in front. Seven years earlier, in *The Shows of London*—what was in effect a companion volume to *The English Common Reader*—he had compiled the first systematic history of the ancestors of television: the popular museums, exhibitions, waxworks, sideshows, and dioramas that entertained the masses before moving pictures. By 1985 he was exploring the interaction of print and image at yet another border crossing: *Paintings from Books: Art and Literature in Britain, 1760–1900.*

Altick has lately returned to popular print and its readers in a history of the first decade of *Punch,* a project he characterized as an indulgence in "serious fun."[7] Arguably, that has been the motive behind all his research. The intrinsic joy of literary detective work, which he described so grippingly in *The Scholar Adventurers* (1950), impelled him to take on one groundbreaking project after another. Like a backyard engineer, he was continually inventing wonderful things, even if his neighbors did not immediately appreciate their possibilities. As recently as 1988 he gently complained that academics were not following up the work he had begun in *The English Common Reader.*

But in fact, by then the climate was beginning to change. As an interdisciplinary pursuit that engaged historians, librarians, and literary scholars alike, book history was at last taking off. Eliza-

[3] Richard D. Altick, *Lives and Letters: A History of Literary Biography in England and America* (New York, 1965).

[4] Richard D. Altick, *Victorian Studies in Scarlet* (New York, 1970), and *Deadly Encounters: Two Victorian Sensations* (Philadelphia, 1986).

[5] "From Aldine to Everyman: Cheap Reprint Series of the English Classics, 1830–1906" (1958), "*Cope's Tobacco Plant:* An Episode in Victorian Journalism" (1951), and "The Sociology of Authorship: The Social Origins, Education, and Occupations of 1,100 British Writers, 1800–1935" (1962) have all been republished in Altick, *Writers, Readers, and Occasions.*

[6] D. F. McKenzie, *Bibliography and the Sociology of Texts* (London, 1986).

[7] Richard D. Altick, *Punch: The Lively Youth of a British Institution, 1841–1851* (Columbus, 1997), p. xv.

beth Eisenstein's *The Printing Press as an Agent of Change* and Robert Darnton's *The Business of Enlightenment: A Publishing History of the Encyclopédie, 1775–1800* had both appeared in 1979, and both had done much to make the field visible in the academic world. Scholars were now beginning to explore common readers in other societies and other historical periods: Jeffrey Brooks in *When Russia Learned to Read: Literacy and Popular Literature, 1861–1917* (1985), James Smith Allen in *In the Public Eye: A History of Reading in Modern France* (1991), Martyn Lyons and Lucy Taska in *Australian Readers Remember: An Oral History of Reading, 1890–1930* (1992), Ronald J. Zboray in *A Fictive People: Antebellum Economic Development and the American Reading Public* (1993), to give only a few prominent examples. *The English Common Reader* directly inspired the foundation of the Society for the History of Authorship, Reading and Publishing in 1991. Within six years, SHARP would attract a thousand members in twenty countries.[8]

Although book historians are now exploring every link in Darnton's communications circuit, one could argue that all their researches into authorship, printing, publishing, distribution, and literary property lead ultimately to the reader. No book can play any meaningful role in history until somebody reads it, and we cannot know what influence a given book has unless we can somehow enter the minds of its readers. This promises to become one of the most important questions confronting historians of the near future. It will certainly not be easy to answer. Altick emphatically disclaimed any attempt to explore reading tastes or readers' responses, if only because the documents for such a study were mostly unknown to scholars in 1957. Since then, however, we have recovered the primary sources that Altick lacked: the memoirs and diaries of ordinary people, school records, library borrowing registers, marginalia, social surveys, oral interviews, letters to the editor (especially those the editor chose not to publish), as well as a Reading Experience Database sponsored by the Brit-

---

[8] For an overview of the recent and remarkable growth of the field, see Jonathan Rose, "The History of Books: Revised and Enlarged," *Studies on Voltaire and the Eighteenth Century* (1998).

ish Library and the Open University. With those resources, we are proceeding to fill in the white spaces on Altick's outline map.[9]

It has been said that a scholarly discipline achieves maturity when it is discovered by popularizers, in which case Altick's moment arrived in 1996, when Alberto Manguel produced *A History of Reading* for a general audience. Significantly, most everything Richard Altick wrote was accessible to the common reader, even while his profession withdrew into jargon and hyperspecialization. Significantly, one of his earliest monographs was a joint biography of Charles and Mary Cowden Clarke, who popularized Chaucer and Shakespeare among the Victorian working classes.[10] It was inevitable that Altick would write the history of their audience: the unknown autodidacts who pursued knowledge under incredible difficulties. In the Great Depression, while working the night shift at a Pennsylvania filling station, Altick himself had read Whitman, Gissing, G. K. Chesterton, E. M. Forster, Xenophon in Greek and, amid the gasoline fumes, Max Beerbohm's "In Defence of Cosmetics." As he announced in his *Preface to Critical Reading* (1946), his mission was to enable everyone in a democratic society to read intelligently. There you have the agenda of *The English Common Reader.* It is, after all, the only political ideology that a humane scholar of letters can work with.

JONATHAN ROSE

[9] Roger Chartier offers a concise bibliography of the history of reading in "Histoire de la Lecture: Sélection bibliographique," *In Octavo*, no. 3 (Spring 1993): supplement.

[10] Richard D. Altick, *The Cowden Clarkes* (London, 1948).

Preface to the Second Edition

This fresh edition of *The English Common Reader* appears at a moment when the future of the book and of the reading habit is clouded by contradictory signs. On the one hand, at least in the United States, the proliferation of chains of mega-bookstores, outdoing one another in enticing potential patrons to come and browse in comfort, seems to suggest that despite the competition of television, computer games, and other up-to-date means of filling leisure, books and magazines still appeal to the mass market of our own day as they did in the long period covered by the present volume. The people who enter those bright, spacious, and well-stocked treasuries of the printed word come, after all, for more than a cup of coffee, just as Londoners in the time of *The Spectator* and *The Tatler* dropped into coffeehouses to read the newspapers and current periodicals. On the other hand, the advent of electronic texts, to be read from a screen rather than a paper page, has constantly inspired portentous prophecies that the *Bücherdämmerung*—the day of doom for the printed word— is approaching, though the precise date of its arrival has not been ascertained.

Whatever the future may hold, it is now clear that the publication of this book in 1957—"the first large-scale work on the reading public as a social phenomenon," as I described it—coincided with the beginnings of a kind of socio-historical study that has, since then, become a growth industry.[1] The amount of research done on the printed word as a cultural object and reading as a private act enlarged into a social activity is well attested by the

---

[1] For convenient overviews of the directions research has taken down to the mid-1990s, see the complementary introductions to Jordan and Patten, *Literature in the Marketplace* (1995), and Raven, Small, and Tadmor, *The Practice and Representation of Reading in England* (1996).

size of the supplementary bibliography appended to the original one. (A few scattered nineteenth-century references, absent from the original list, have been included.) Apart from the new bibliography, this edition is identical with the first. A few passages might have been altered or added in the light of more recent publications, but not enough to justify its presentation as a "revised edition." To offer it as being simply of historical interest would be unduly disparaging, underestimating the usefulness its backward look, with its running subtext of suggestions for further exploration, seems to have had—and, I am assured, still has—to subsequent workers in the field. As it stands, however, it fairly reflects the state of knowledge forty years ago and can still serve as a reliable introduction to the subject.

Anyone attempting to write a book like this from scratch would have to assimilate a great body of new information and fresh perceptions, even if it were limited, as the present one is, to the emergence of a reading public in England, Wales, Scotland, and Ireland, without taking account of parallel developments in western Europe and even in Russia—the national heritage stemming from William Caxton of Westminster rather than the more diffuse legacy of Johann Gutenberg of Mainz. One of the most striking aspects of the recent surge of interest in the history of print culture, indeed, is that it is not only interdisciplinary, as is suggested by the catch-all term "sociology of literature," but wider in both chronological and geographic scope. Increased attention has been paid to the incidence of literacy and reading in Britain in the centuries before 1800, thus filling in the inevitably sketchy narrative given in the first three chapters of this book. A more comprehensive bibliography would highlight such seminal works as Lucien Febvre and Henri-Jean Martin's *L'Apparition du livre* (Paris, 1958; English translation, *The Coming of the Book: The Impact of Printing 1450–1800,* 1976) and Elizabeth Eisenstein's two-volume *The Printing Press as an Agent of Change: Communications and Cultural Transformations in Early-Modern Europe* (1979), as well as Robert Darnton's groundbreaking works on the French book trade and readership in the Age of Enlightenment.

About the time that this book was published, social historians, prompted in part by the French *Annales* school of historiography, began seriously to delve into the broad but hitherto neglected—

because depreciated—field of popular culture, including the use, content, control, and eventually the commercialization of leisure-time activities. An equally influential book, in this field, was Peter Burke's *Popular Culture in Early Modern Europe* (1978). Another, closely related, branch of interest has been the history of literacy before and during the Industrial Revolution, students of which have questioned and often discredited the traditional methods of measurement and in the process generated considerable controversy. The ability to read presupposed (putting aside the problematic element of self-teaching) some small amount of classroom experience, and the history of elementary and adult education, from the English Renaissance downward, has been more intensively examined than ever before.

The book, regarded as an object, claimed wider attention not only as the physical manifestation of a cultural force of incalculable power but as a commercially valuable commodity supplied to an ever-growing consumer society. It will be noted from the new bibliography that few histories of individual publishing houses have appeared in recent decades despite the new availability of old firms' archives in research libraries and on film, one possible reason being the loss of distinctive identity as well-established houses were bought out or merged into conglomerates. The new concern has been with the production and distribution mechanisms of "the trade" at large, one cog in the economic-cultural machine. The history of one other supplier of reading matter to the masses of people, the public library, has come in for closer scrutiny, largely by librarians themselves—a textbook instance, as it were, of the way a movement in one or another sphere of society, initially of little consequence, seeks to dignify itself by reviewing its humble, inchoate origins once it has been institutionalized and its workers (justifiably) have come to regard themselves as members of a profession.

Like much scholarship in the latter half of the twentieth century, the study of the history of the book and its readers has been in large part a communal effort in the form of specialized periodicals (*Publishing History, Library History, History of Education,* et al.) and groups. A Center for the Book was founded at the Library of Congress, soon joined by the international Society for the History of Authorship, Reading and Publishing (SHARP) and the

Cambridge (England) Project for the Book. These and other bodies have sponsored conferences for the presentation of papers that were collected into volumes, a dozen of which are listed in the bibliography. A number of scholarly publishers in the United States and abroad, notably the Cambridge University Press, have launched series dedicated to the history of the printed word and of reading.

Some of the research on audiences and their expressed or implicit tastes (evidenced, for example, by the contents of circulating libraries and publishers' sales figures) has had the incidental effect of supplying a limited amount of factual underpinning for the structures of the reader-response school of theoretical and explicatory criticism founded in the 1970s by Wayne Booth, Stanley Fish, and Wolfgang Iser. More recently, Jerome J. McGann has devised a literary application of book-trade history in his concept of the "socialized text," an approach to editing which stresses the influences that shaped a text after publishers and printers—and ultimately reviewers and readers—took it over from its author.

These are among the immediate benefits that research in the history of the reading public has conferred on various kinds of literary studies. Speculations on the future of the book are not new, and they come and go (who now reads Marshall McLuhan?), but its past is permanent, ineffaceably though sometimes enigmatically inscribed on the historical record. Learning more about it can only strengthen our appreciation of the crucial role it has played in the making of western civilization for five and one-half centuries.

R.D.A.

December 1997

Preface

In the ten years during which this book was under construction, I incurred many debts, of which this note is an all too inadequate acknowledgment. I must express my gratitude to my colleagues on the faculty of the Ohio State University, as well as to members of the university administration, for their deeds of practical assistance. Dean James F. Fullington and his successor as chairman of the Department of English, Professor Robert M. Estrich, whose interest in my work has been unflagging, lightened my teaching load at various times and provided me with a series of research assistants. In addition, through their good offices the university relieved me entirely from teaching duties for two three-month periods at crucial junctures in my writing. To the university's Research Foundation and its Graduate School I am obliged for several grants-in-aid. Mr. Conrad E. Tanzy, the most recent of my assistants, dispatched with energy and good humor the considerable task of combing errors from my pages; and Mrs. Ruth Townsend transformed the chaos of my penultimate draft into the order of the final typescript. The constant and varied demands I made upon the staff of the Ohio State University Library, where most of my research was done, were met with unfailing courtesy, particularly in the inter-library loan and reference departments.

The resources of two other great libraries proved more than equal to the peculiarly wide-ranging nature of my research: the Widener Library at Harvard and the Newberry Library. I am indebted to the Board of Trustees of the latter institution for a fellowship which enabled me to live in Chicago while using the Newberry's remarkable collections for several months in 1952, and to the librarian, Dr. Stanley Pargellis, and his staff for their great helpfulness.

A number of my friends have read portions of my manuscript and given me the benefit of their special knowledge in certain fields. In particular I must thank Professor John Harold Wilson, who plowed through the whole book, and Professor Oscar Maurer, of the University of Texas, who read the chapters on periodicals. And I owe a special debt to the numerous scholars in the field of nineteenth-century English literature and social history who, in conversation and correspondence, helped sustain my conviction that the project was worth carrying forward.

My wife, Helen, has figured in the prefatory paragraphs of my earlier books, but now my gratitude is infinitely greater; not least because she, along with our two daughters, endured with cheerful fortitude the many trials incident to having an author in the house.

R. D. A.

{

Introduction

I. This volume is an attempt to study, from the historian's viewpoint, the place of reading in an industrial and increasingly democratic society. It is the story of how, through numberless tribulations, and against what sometimes appeared to be hopeless odds, there took root and eventually flourished in nineteenth-century England a revolutionary social concept: that of the democracy of print.

Despite its enormous importance in social and cultural history, the growth of the mass reading public in England has never been systematically analyzed and documented.[1] The complexity of the development, in which much of its fascination lies, seemingly has not even been recognized. Everybody knows that in the nineteenth century the number of English readers, and therefore the productions of the press, multiplied spectacularly. By and large, however, the phenomenon has been taken for granted; the whys and hows have not been inquired into.

Historians who have glanced at the development of the mass reading public have drawn for the most part upon two kinds of data: anecdotes and the records of best-selling books and popular

---

[1] In the second half of his little book, *The Old Printer and the Modern Press* (1854), Charles Knight attempted something of the sort, without, however, exploring the ramifications of the subject. Modest though it is, and ending just at the time when the mass public was entering upon its greatest period of expansion, Knight's has remained the only connected narrative of the English common reader. R. K. Webb's recent monograph, *The British Working Class Reader*, deals with only a small segment of the subject treated in the present volume, though within its chosen scope it is authoritative and refreshingly corrective of received opinion.

NOTE.—Full bibliographical information concerning most of the references given in the footnotes in abbreviated form will be found in the Bibliography. The exceptions are references to books and articles which are drawn upon infrequently and which as a whole are not of sufficient importance to merit inclusion in the Bibliography. Full citations for these are given on their first occurrence in each chapter. The place of publication, unless otherwise stated, is London.

periodicals. The present writer, as many passages in the following
chapters will show, is not one to scorn either kind of information.
The anecdote is often a valuable microcosm of history. Our knowledge would be so much the poorer if we did not have Coleridge's
anecdote of how, when soliciting subscriptions for his periodical the
Watchman, he tackled a Calvinist tallow-chandler in Birmingham.
After listening silently to Coleridge's sales talk, which, if it was
anything like his later philosophical monologues, must have been
an impressive performance, the chandler asked how much the
Watchman would cost. Fourpence, said Coleridge; thirty-two pages
an issue, large octavo, closely printed. "Thirty and two pages!"
exclaimed his prospect. "Bless me! why except what I does in a
family way on the Sabbath, that's more than I ever reads, Sir!
all the year round."[2]

Nor is it irrelevant to recall the many stories of Scott's fame
among all classes of society—for example, of a London workman
accosting Charles Lamb to point in awe to the author of *Waverley*
crossing the street.[3] We hear of the old charwoman who never
missed a subscription tea conducted on the first Monday of every
month at a snuff shop over which she lodged, when the landlord
read the newest number of *Dombey and Son* to his assembled
guests.[4] And of the vagrant in Covent Garden who, according to
Thackeray's daughter, plucked at Tennyson's sleeve, saying,
"Look here, sir, here am I. I've been drunk for six days out of the
seven, but if you will shake me by the hand, I'm damned if I ever
get drunk again."[5] And of the three hundred soldiers in the Boer
War who, after listening to Violet Hunt lecture on poetry, stayed
to take down from dictation, in pocket Testaments and on the
backs of envelopes, lines from Browning's "Epilogue to *Asolando*"
which had caused a stir when she quoted them in the course of her
talk.[6]

Similarly, it is useful to know that the sale in monthly parts of
Dickens' novels averaged about 40,000 copies and that, from the

[2] *Biographia Literaria*, chap. x.

[3] Lamb, *Letters*, ed. E. V. Lucas (New Haven, 1935), III, 344–45.

[4] Johnson, *Charles Dickens*, II, 613.

[5] Anne Thackeray Ritchie, *Records of Tennyson, Ruskin, Browning* (New York, 1892), p. 52.

[6] *Spectator*, LXXXIX (1902), 607.

fifties onward, popular papers like the *Family Herald* and the *London Journal* had circulations reaching into six figures. Such statistics are indispensable indications of popular taste and of the steady expansion of the audience for printed matter. But even if we collect as many figures as we can, we are still left with only a superficial impression of our subject. To describe and measure the spread of reading by such means is relatively easy. To account for it, and to fix it against the panoramic background of nineteenth-century English history, is a more complex task.

For the mass reading public had its roots deep in the total history of the period. Far from being an isolated phenomenon, it was the resultant of many forces, most of which—political, religious, economic, technological—seem on first glance to have little bearing on the growth of the reading habit. But once we have exposed the hidden tendrils of association, we discover that few major tendencies in nineteenth-century English social life were without their effect. Some stimulated the taste for reading; some inhibited it; some, paradoxically, did both. Hence, to understand how the common Englishman came to be a reader, we must first review the dominant social and political attitudes of the time and recall how they often masqueraded as religious piety. We must explore the prejudices, inherited from earlier centuries and intensified by the panic of the French Revolution, which stood in the way of decent education and cheap literature for the common people and which strewed the path of innovations like mechanics' institutes and free libraries with disheartening obstacles.

The history of the mass reading audience is, in fact, the history of English democracy seen from a new angle. In 1840 Carlyle wrote to John Sterling, "Books are written by martyr-men, not for rich men alone but for all men. If we consider it, every human being has, by the nature of the case, a *right* to hear what other wise human beings have spoken to him. It is one of the Rights of Men; a very cruel injustice if you deny it to a man!"[7] The struggle for political democracy, it is true, normally did not stress the right of the common man to read, though, at the time Carlyle wrote, the moral-force Chartists, led by William Lovett, had adopted this as one of their great principles. The ordinary man had more immediate necessities to contend for, such as steady employment, better

[7] *New Letters of Carlyle*, ed. Alexander Carlyle (1904), I, 212.

wages and working conditions, the right to organize unions, and parliamentary representation. But beneath the surface the issue was there, all the same. It was increasingly crucial because under the conditions of industrial life the ability to read was acquiring an importance it had never had before. The popular cultural tradition, which had brought amusement and emotional outlets to previous generations, had largely been erased. The long hours and the monotony of work in factory and shop, the dismal surroundings in which people were condemned to spend such leisure as they had, the regimentation of industrial society with its consequent crushing of individuality, made it imperative that the English millions should have some new way of escape and relaxation, some new and plentiful means of engaging their minds and imaginations. Books and periodicals were the obvious answer. But the goal was no easier to win than that of political and economic justice—and for the same reasons.

The many threads which in sum constitute the history of the English common reader are therefore woven deep in the fabric of nineteenth-century annals. And just as the various attitudes and movements of the age fatefully molded the audience for print that eventually emerged, so did that public, in turn, affect the progress of the age itself. Is it possible, for instance, to understand how the balance of political power shifted from a small oligarchy to a popular electorate without reviewing the spread of reading? Behind the Reform Bills of 1832 and 1867, which were formal landmarks in the political transformation of England, lay the press and its steadily enlarging public. Despite the high prices necessitated by taxation —itself a political issue of great moment—the newspaper press, shaking off the venality that had been its shame under Pitt, became a forthright, independent mouthpiece of middle-class opinion and eventually brought about the transfer of power to that class during the early Victorian era. At the same time the philippics of Cobbett in his *Political Register* and the brutal parodies of William Hone, which aroused the workingman from his political apathy, paved the way for a radical press that endured persecution and suppression to undermine, in turn, the foundations of middle-class rule. The hard-hitting political commentary of mass-circulation weekly newspapers conducted by men like Edward Lloyd and G. W. M. Reynolds helped build up the pressure which, after the middle of the century, forced the governing class to concede more and more power to the artisan and laborer.

No less important was the effect the spread of reading had upon the social habits of the Victorian era. Never before in English history had so many people read so much. In the middle class, the reading circle was the most familiar and beloved of domestic institutions; and as cheap printed matter became more accessible, hardly a family in Britain was without its little shelf of books and its sheaf of current periodicals, whether church papers or the latest hair-raising episodes concocted by Holywell Street hacks. Though in the first half of the century there was deep (and not wholly idle) apprehension that making the "lower ranks" of society literate would breed all sorts of disorder and debauchery, in the long run the proliferation of reading matter proved to have been the oil that was needed to quiet the troubled waters. If the common man did not necessarily become wiser after he had an abundant supply of printed matter at his command, he was certainly kept amused. The comparative tranquillity of Victorian society after mid-century was due in no small part to the growth of the popular press.

Above all, the democratizing of reading led to a far-reaching revolution in English culture. No longer were books and periodicals written chiefly for the comfortable few; more and more, as the century progressed, it was the ill-educated mass audience with pennies in its pocket that called the tune to which writers and editors danced. In 1858 Wilkie Collins, announcing his personal discovery of "the unknown public" which bought huge quantities of cheap fiction papers, wrote: "The Unknown Public is, in a literary sense, hardly beginning, as yet, to learn to read. The members of it are evidently, in the mass, from no fault of theirs, still ignorant of almost everything which is generally known and understood among readers whom circumstances have placed, socially and intellectually, in the rank above them. . . . The future of English fiction may rest with this Unknown Public, which is now waiting to be taught the difference between a good book and a bad. It is probably a question of time only. The largest audience for periodical literature, in this age of periodicals, must obey the universal law of progress, and must, sooner or later, learn to discriminate. When that period comes, the readers who rank by millions, will be the readers who give the widest reputations, who return the

richest rewards, and who will, therefore, command the service of
the best writers of their time. A great, an unparalleled prospect
awaits, perhaps, the coming generation of English novelists. To
the penny journals of the present time belongs the credit of having
discovered a new public. When that public shall discover its need
of a great writer, the great writer will have such an audience as
has never yet been known."[8]

This is the voice of prophecy indeed, though most people will
feel that it is tinged with what, in the event, has proved an un-
warranted optimism. The impact of the mass public upon modern English literature—taking the term in the widest possible
sense—is incalculable. Though a great deal has been said on the
subject between Collins' day and our own, no truly serious study
has yet been made of it. The widely held opinion that the coming
of the democratic audience vulgarized literature may well be correct, but to test it is no part of our design. For (and this sentence
ideally should be printed in bold red letters, to forestall unfounded
expectations) this volume is not intended to be an examination of
nineteenth-century literary taste, or of the effect the new mass
public had upon the practice of contemporary writers. Inevitably,
the problem of taste will be touched upon now and again, in connection with other topics. But our present design is not to analyze
the popular literature of the period as such. Instead, one of the
main purposes of this book is to provide some of the information
that obviously must be taken into account before anyone can
safely interpret the popular taste of an age—information, that is,
on the social composition, educational experience, and general
character of the public whose taste is to undergo scrutiny. The
lack of such knowledge inevitably makes discussion of the audience' formative influence upon literature little more than idle
speculation.

Since the term "reading public" has always been used elasti-
cally, attention must be called to the qualifying word "mass" in
the subtitle. The reading public studied in this book is the one
composed of what the Victorians were fond of calling "the million." It is *not* the relatively small, intellectually and socially superior audience for which most of the great nineteenth-century
authors wrote—the readers of the quarterly reviews, the people

<hr>

[8] Collins, "The Unknown Public," p. 222.

whom writers like Macaulay, the Brontës, Meredith, George Eliot, and John Stuart Mill had in mind. Here we are concerned primarily with the experience of that overwhelmingly more numerous portion of the English people who became day-by-day readers for the first time in this period, as literacy spread and printed matter became cheaper. The "common reader" studied in these pages may be a member of the working class, or he may belong to the ever expanding bourgeoisie. In preceding centuries, as the opening chapters will show, some hand-workers and some members of the lower-middle class had been readers; but not until the nineteenth century did the appetite for print permeate both classes to the extent that it became a major social phenomenon.

One or two biases on the part of the author may as well be admitted at the outset. One is that genuine democracy resides not alone in the possession of certain social, political, and economic advantages but in the unqualified freedom of all men and women to enjoy the fruits of a country's culture, among which books have a place of high, if not supreme, importance. This is a concept which, though it was increasingly voiced in the course of the nineteenth century, especially by those thinkers who like Carlyle were most devoted to the idea of human dignity, was not widely accepted until near our own time. And as the currents of antidemocratic thought surge through the mid-twentieth-century world, that concept is again being denied, at least by implication.

Twenty-five years ago an American journalist, R. L. Duffus, put the matter so eloquently and succinctly that a direct quotation may well serve to express the credo underlying this volume:

"It may be that only a small minority are capable of that exhilarating and strenuous pursuit of truth and beauty which great literature demands. It may be that even those who strive for 'culture' for snobbish and unworthy reasons are not much more numerous, and that underneath these layers of the truly cultured and their pathetic imitators lies a barbaric mass which can never be deeply penetrated by civilization. If these things are true, the cultural missionary, whether in literature, in the arts, or in the sciences, might as well pack his trunk and sail for home. I do not think they are true.

"Undoubtedly there will always be variations in the ability to appreciate, just as there are variations in the ability to create.

Great readers will not be as scarce as great writers, but they will be a chosen company. There are ideas so subtle that the democratic mass is shut off from them. But I do not believe these ideas are as numerous as is sometimes assumed. I believe that the failure of the democratic majority to accept intellectual and aesthetic ideals is due rather to a lack of will to do so than to a lack of ability. And I believe that the lack of will is due to false and imperfect systems of education and to other conditions in the environment which can be altered. The culturability of mankind—if I may invent a word—ought not to be judged by its response to stimuli which until yesterday were enjoyed almost wholly by a leisure class. Only an abysmal ignorance of human nature can account for such assumptions."[9]

Of course not all men want to read; not all men, for that matter, have any conscious interest in achieving or preserving political democracy. Nothing that education can do, probably, will ever induce some people to become habitual readers. On the other hand, it is a basic assumption of this book that among the masses of people in the nineteenth century there were, just as there are today, hundreds of thousands and indeed millions whom force of circumstance alone barred from the stimulating and solacing influences of books.

II. Though this is the first large-scale work on the reading public as a social phenomenon, the writer hopes and believes it will not be the last. As has been suggested, our knowledge of the subtle relationships between literature and society is still scanty. We are beginning to understand the effect of general social conditions upon the production of literature; but the role of the reader—the consumer—has been largely neglected. Such commentary as exists on the topic is offhand and impressionistic. The present book does not pretend to be exhaustive in any one of the many areas it touches. There is room for literally hundreds of studies of topics which are here merely sketched. No manuscript sources have been used, and only a few selected periodicals, out of all that nineteenth-century England produced, have been gone through systematically. Future students who concentrate on a single aspect of the reading public and its social and cultural im-

[9] R. L. Duffus, *Books: Their Place in a Democracy* (Boston, 1930), pp. xi–xii.

plications will bring to light much information unknown to the present writer, and sometimes they may be obliged to modify his generalizations. Though the purpose of this book is first of all to present a body of data and ideas which are useful and significant in themselves, hardly less dominant is the desire to provide a preliminary map of the vast territory, still virtually unexplored, which awaits the researcher.

Some readers undoubtedly will regret the omission of certain topics which bear more or less directly on the main theme of the book. But a line had to be drawn somewhere, else the book would never have been finished. Much could be said, for example, on the contribution that juvenile literature made to the early instilling of a taste for reading. Apart from the praiseworthy efforts of John Newbery in the eighteenth century, little attempt was made to provide children with reading matter designed especially for them until Maria Edgeworth, Mrs. Sherwood, and the Sunday-school tract writers sharpened their pens early in the nineteenth century. Then came the deluge; but that story requires a volume to itself.

Another relevant topic that has been reluctantly omitted is the many-faceted one of the relationship between public and author. The books of Alexandre Beljame and A. S. Collins, as well as a few more recent articles, have described the changing economic status of the author from the Restoration down to the beginning of the Victorian era, but a great deal more needs to be written on the subject, especially from the age of Scott on. To what extent, for instance, did the authors' improved bargaining position, resulting from the increased demand for their wares, delay the cheapening of books and periodicals? What effect had the gradual substitution of the royalty system for the older practice of buying a literary property outright? The transformation of the economic basis of authorship and publishing in the nineteenth century—the degree to which it was caused by the rise of a mass public and, in turn, its effect upon that public—calls for much study.

There has not been space enough to do justice to Scotland's remarkable contribution to the expansion of the English reading public. That contribution, made through the example of Scottish institutions and the enterprise of individual Scotsmen, was much greater than the actual size of the Scottish population would suggest. The reading habit was democratized above the border long before it was farther south, thanks to the strong Calvinist tradition of Bible study and the consequent emphasis upon schooling for all. Despite terrible poverty, in the eighteenth century the Scottish educational system was responsible for an incidence of literacy and book-reading strikingly greater than that in England. From Scotland, too, came the circulating library, and the cheap reprints which eventually led to the breaking of the London publishers' price-inflating monopoly on older books. And in the nineteenth century it was Scotsmen especially—Lord Brougham, Archibald Constable, the Chambers brothers, Samuel Brown of "itinerating library" fame—who in various ways helped enlarge the English reading audience.

Although the main body of the book is concerned with nineteenth-century developments, it has seemed advisable to devote the first three chapters to the prior history of the English reading public. This would not have been necessary were there any account to which the reader could be referred; but in the absence of such an account, written from approximately the same viewpoint as the one adopted in the present volume, the author has supplied one for the sake of historical continuity. In thus venturing outside his accredited "field," he has adopted a smaller scale of treatment and has relied heavily upon secondary sources rather than upon the contemporary materials on which his treatment of the nineteenth century is based. It is hoped, however, that those who possess an intimate knowledge of the centuries between Caxton and Tom Paine will find the first chapters to be a reasonably authentic narrative.

Extensive research in the many contiguous areas of history covered by a study such as this is not easy; the bibliographical jungle to be explored is enormous, and the existing maps are sketchy. Ponderous volumes of reports by parliamentary investigating committees and royal commissions; the windy expanses of *Hansard's Parliamentary Debates;* league-long files of professional librarians' periodicals, book-trade journals, proceedings of statistical societies; official histories of publishing firms, so filled with decorous anecdotes and homage to the departed great, so devoid of solid information; solemn studies of political radicalism, economic conditions, religious philanthropy, the contentious history of English education; biographies by the hundreds—these are the dusty despair of the scholar quite as often as they are his delight.

Every social historian probably is sustained at his work by a sense, more or less peculiar to his occupation, of vicarious yet intimate contact with human beings in the simple process of being human. In the books that pass across his study table he feels the strong current of life as it was lived, not by the exceptional man, the statesman or the general or the artist, but by the humble millions who fade into the merciless anonymity of an epoch's history. To one intent upon tracing the development of the reading public, this sense is especially inspiring; for behind all the fine-print statistical tables, behind the orotund periods of the parliamentary debater, behind the squabbles over education and working hours and free libraries, shines the image of the ordinary man or woman at what is surely one of the happiest and most rewarding of human pursuits—the reading of the printed word.

If the living presence of the common reader has survived transference from the "sources" into these pages, then the moving human significance—the poignant, inspiring qualities—of the story to be told needs no further gloss.

Unemployed, dispossessed workmen gathering in alehouses to read radical papers that spell out the reasons for their misery and suggest desperate remedies. A rheumatic London crossing-sweeper crawling back to his cold, squalid room to pore over a copy of *Reynolds' Miscellany*.[10] Twenty men and women gathering in a locksmith's shop to listen to the newest number of the *Pickwick Papers*, borrowed from a circulating library at 2*d.* a day.[11] A Cockney fishmonger smoking his pipe, late at night, over three prized books—the *European Magazine* for 1761, *Tristram Shandy*, and *Gil Blas*.[12] A schoolboy putting down his penny for John Dicks's latest issue of a paper-covered play. A laborer meeting the hawker on Sunday morning to buy his Sabbath entertainment, a copy of the *Illustrated Times*, full of red-blooded murder. Apprentices trading well-thumbed numbers of *Cassell's Popular Educator*. . . .

This book, then, is about people: humble people for the most part, mechanics, clerks, shopmen, domestic servants, land workers, and their families; people who lived in the endless rows of jerry-

---

[10] Mayhew, *London Labour and the London Poor*, II, 538.

[11] Johnson, *Charles Dickens*, I, 155.

[12] William Hazlitt, "On Londoners and Country People," *Works*, ed. P. P. Howe (1932), XII, 74.

built city houses and along the village street. Numbering in mere thousands at first, then hundreds of thousands, then millions, they read because they wanted to find political salvation, or to discover the keys to the kingdom of heaven, or to make more money, or to exercise the emotions and imaginative cravings that were stifled in an England whose green and pleasant land was being built over with red-brick factories. Here, in short, is the story of the common reader, nameless but exceedingly numerous—how he came into being, and why; and what his fortunes were in an age of profound social change.

THE BACKGROUND
1477–1800

CHAPTER 1

From Caxton to the Eighteenth Century

I. William Caxton set up his printing press in Westminster at a fortunate moment in history. Already the great cultural revolution with which his name is associated was under way. Though most Englishmen still depended upon their ears for their share of the common cultural heritage, or upon their ability to interpret the pictures and statuary they saw in the churches, by 1477 there were substantial hints that in the future the art of reading would have a greater role in their lives. The demand for manuscripts was increasing. Caxton had not yet begun business when John Shirley, a dealer in manuscripts, started to lend out copies of the works of such authors as Chaucer and Lydgate in a sort of primitive circulating-library arrangement. In fifteenth-century inventories and wills, too, one finds mention of books, as if the rising class of country gentlemen and city merchants felt that the possession of a few manuscript volumes would provide them with a certain cachet.[1] The demand threatened soon to exceed the supply—unless, as actually happened, a means were discovered of duplicating books so that, instead of but a single manuscript, there could be hundreds and even thousands of printed copies.

We do not know how large the literate public was in Caxton's time, or in the century that followed. Only a few unsatisfactory scraps of evidence survive. Of 116 witnesses before the consistory court in 1467–76, some 40 per cent were recorded as literate.[2] In 1533 Sir Thomas More said that "farre more than fowre partes of

[1] Bennett, "The Author and His Public in the Fourteenth and Fifteenth Centuries," pp. 19–23. This and the other studies by Bennett (see Bibliography) are the fullest sources for the reading public in Caxton's time and the first century afterward.

[2] Sylvia L. Thrupp, *The Merchant Class of Medieval London, 1300–1500* (Chicago, 1948), p. 156.

15

all the whole divided into tenne coulde never reade englishe yet,"[3] an obscure statement which may possibly be interpreted as implying a literacy rate of 50 per cent or so. In 1547, on the other hand, Stephen Gardiner, Bishop of Winchester, observed that "not the hundredth part of the realme" could read.[4] One modern estimate is that in Shakespeare's London between a third and a half of the people were literate.[5] It is at least certain that the growing commercial life of the nation required men of the merchant class to read and write English in order to transact business, keep records, and interpret legal documents. Some guilds set literacy as a condition of membership. Even women were becoming literate, and servants as well, if their circumstances required and permitted it.[6] Indeed, a recent historian has asserted that in Elizabethan times "there was a higher level of literacy among women than at any other time until the later nineteenth century."[7]

Opportunities for education, at least to the extent of learning to read the vernacular, increased in the fifteenth and sixteenth centuries and were available to a fairly wide diversity of classes. A youth from even the lowest stratum of freemen had always had the chance of following Chaucer's clerk to the university as a mendicant student. The ideal of extending education to the "poor" was affirmed in the foundation statutes of the grammar schools. The phrase *pauperes et indigentes scholares* in such statutes, it appears, was not simply designed to insure to the school the legal privileges of a charitable institution but means that boys of relatively humble station (say the equivalent of the modern lower-middle class) really were enrolled in some numbers.

No longer, in any event, was education limited, as it had been in the Middle Ages, to those destined for the religious life. Even if the prospects were that they would take up their father's occupation, the children of small tradesmen, farm laborers, and domestic servants had some opportunity to learn to read English. For them,

---

[3] Quoted by Adamson, "Literacy in England in the Fifteenth and Sixteenth Centuries," p. 45.

[4] Bennett, *English Books and Readers*, p. 28.

[5] Albert C. Baugh, *A History of the English Language* (New York, 1935), p. 246.

[6] Bennett, "The Author and His Public," pp. 18–19.

[7] A. L. Rowse, *The England of Elizabeth: The Structure of Society* (1950), p. 503.

by Henry VIII's time, were provided petty schools, ABC schools, and song schools for the training of choirboys.[8]

These schools were all under the control of the church, and it used to be thought that Henry VIII's expropriation of ecclesiastical property, some of the income from which had been earmarked for teaching purposes, dealt a severe blow to English education. Today, however, it is believed that the dissolution of the churchly establishments did not interfere too much, at least in the long run, with the spread of learning. In time, new schools sprang up to replace those that were wiped out. A favorite practice among those who profited by the nation's prosperity was to endow grammar (that is, classical) schools. Almost every town of any size had at least one such school; in 1600 there were about 360 of them.[9] In addition, many noblemen and other large landowners founded and supported schools for the children of the neighborhood. Some of these were limited to elementary instruction; others, like the one at Stratford-on-Avon which Sir Hugh Clopton re-endowed in 1553, provided an excellent Latin education.

Therefore, since there was as yet little sign of the social exclusiveness that later was to reserve grammar-school and university education largely for children of noble or gentle birth, it was possible for bright boys from the artisan and tradesman class to acquire a thorough schooling. This is suggested by the number of Elizabethan writers who sprang from that station. To mention only a few: Peele was the son of a salter; Marlowe, of a cobbler; Munday, of a draper; Chettle, of a dyer; Herrick, of a goldsmith; Gabriel Harvey, of a ropemaker; Donne, of an ironmonger.[10]

A classical education was, however, the lot of only a minority of those who went to school at all. More numerous were the boys who received an abbreviated education in primary or petty schools. These schools were open not only to those destined to go on to the Latin curriculum but also to those who would begin their apprenticeship immediately after learning to read. While parish clergy-

[8] Material on Tudor and Stuart schools has been derived from Adamson's article (n. 3 above); Curtis, *History of Education in Great Britain*, chap. ii; Wright, *Middle-Class Culture in Elizabethan England*, chap. iii; Rowse, *The England of Elizabeth*, chap. xii; and general histories of the period. These draw upon specialized earlier studies of the subject, notably those by A. F. Leach.

[9] Rowse, p. 496.

[10] Wright, pp. 17–18.

men still could be found teaching children their letters, by the middle of the sixteenth century the church's monopoly over elementary education was forever ended. From the humble hand-laborer in a remote parish teaching a few pupils the ABC's, to the professional schoolmaster in the town, laymen became teachers. Their "private adventure" schools made literacy available to a wide range of society. In addition, a growing number of craft guilds established schools for their members' children.

By the latter part of the sixteenth century the people who could read only English had become so numerous as to require more and more books to be printed in the vernacular. Contemporary writers, apologizing for their use of what was still considered an inferior language, frequently alluded to the "unskilfull," the "unacquainted with the latine tounge," the "unlettered," who nevertheless should share in the age's knowledge. The very fact that this was the great age of translations proves the existence of a sizable audience who knew only English. The translator of a Latin theological work in 1599 remarked that he "brought into the artificer's shop, [that] which was before in the studies and closets of the learned alone."[11]

In the country, where most of the people lived, the proportion of literates probably was much smaller than in the towns, partly because there were fewer schools, partly because the conditions of rural life made illiteracy less of a handicap. Most cottagers were wholly indifferent to education, or could not spare their children from labor in field or cottage for even a year or two. Furthermore, by no means all the children who learned to read ever exercised their talent in later life. The boys soon went to the plow or the craftsman's shop, and the girls (of whom there were at least a sprinkling in some of the ABC schools) to the spinning wheel and the rearing of families; and having neither books nor any necessity for them, they lost such small gift as they had once possessed.

When all allowances have been made, however, it seems likely that in the Tudor and Stuart eras the ability to read was more democratically distributed among the English people than it would again be until at least the end of the eighteenth century. But, since there is a vital distinction between the simple possession of literacy and its active, continual exercise, it does not follow that the read-

[11] Richard F. Jones, *The Triumph of the English Language* (Stanford, Calif., 1953), pp. 36 ff.

ing public in the late sixteenth and early seventeenth centuries was either as large or socially as diversified as the apparent extent of literacy in the nation might suggest. Books were not easy to acquire. Their production was artificially limited in several ways. One was the restriction on the number of printers. In 1586, partly to satisfy the printers already in business and partly to ease the ecclesiastical authorities' alarm over the spread of controversial and polemic books, the Star Chamber forbade the establishment of any new press until a vacancy occurred among the already existing ones (twenty-two commercial presses, in addition to the Queen's Printer and the two university presses).[12] Again, to make work for the increasing number of journeymen and apprentices, the Stationers' Company in 1587 limited to 1,250 or 1,500 the number of copies of a book that could be produced from one setting of type, although, in the interests of public morality and enlightenment, "grammers, Accidences, prymers, and Catechisms" were allowed four impressions annually, of 2,500 to 3,000 copies each.[13] How prices would have been affected had a printer been free to issue as many copies as he foresaw a sale for, we can only speculate.

The book trade was also restricted, at the expense of the reader, by "privilege"—the vested right accorded to certain booksellers in the printing and sale of specified categories of books. As early as 1559 such patents had been granted, and although in the 1580's some individual patentees transferred their monopolies to the Stationers' Company, the practice continued unabated to the end of the Queen's reign. Her successors, James I and Charles I, between them allowed forty-three new patents.[14] The effect this monopoly had upon prices is illustrated by the fact that the London booksellers sold *Aesop's Fables* at 4d. a sheet[15] and Ovid's

[12] Plant, *The English Book Trade*, p. 83.

[13] *Ibid.*, pp. 92–93. Occasionally a printer evaded this regulation by setting aside his types after the legal maximum of copies had been struck off, and then reusing them after a prudent interval for a "new edition." But type was too scarce to make this a frequent procedure.

[14] *Ibid.*, pp. 100–14.

[15] A "sheet" is a piece of paper one side of which is printed in a single operation. After both sides have been printed, it is folded once or several times to form one unit of the prospective book. The practice of selling books at retail in individual sheets—that is, a small section at a time—was a common means of "cheapening" literature during the nineteenth century.

Epistles at 8*d*., while in Cambridge the same books, issued by the university press (which was unaffected by "privilege"), cost respectively 3*d*. and 5*d*. a sheet. The university authorities bitterly resented the refusal by members of the Stationers' Company to sell these cheaper books, and in 1621 they obtained a royal injunction against the company's boycott of the Cambridge edition of Lily's *Grammar*.[16] Thus, although there might be a brisk demand for books of a certain kind, the number available was limited to those that the privileged bookseller desired or was able to produce in his own shop. There could be no competition and no healthy multiplication of such books.

The crescendo of public events in the first part of the seventeenth century, as well as the spread of the reading habit on other grounds among the middle class, increased the demand for books. Gradually the Tudor restrictions were lifted, and the market became better supplied. When the Court of the Star Chamber was abolished in 1641, the number of London printers ceased to be limited, and by 1660 there were about sixty printing houses in the city. Although the Licensing Act of 1662 reaffirmed the old regulation, it was for the most part ineffectual.[17] The day when the availability of books could be governed by that kind of maneuver was past, and in the future the government would have to find other ways of regulating the press.

In 1635, the restrictions on the number of copies to be issued from a single setting of type were liberalized to 1,500 or 2,000 for ordinary books, and to 3,000 for books in brevier type and 5,000 in nonpareil.[18] These ceilings were probably adequate for the market. In 1652, during a squabble between members of the Stationers' Company, one party alleged that the usual impression of a book was 1,500 copies, while the other asserted that the figure was too high.[19] Apart from staple items like almanacs (Partridge's *Anglicus* sold 13,500 in 1646, 17,000 in 1647, and 18,500 in 1648) and Lily's imperishable *Grammar* (20,000 copies a year in mid-century), a

[16] S. C. Roberts, *A History of the Cambridge University Press* (Cambridge, 1921), pp. 34–38.

[17] Plant, pp. 84–85.

[18] *Ibid.*, p. 93; W. W. Greg, *Some Aspects and Problems of London Publishing between 1550 and 1650* (Oxford, 1956), p. 16.

[19] Communication by Alcuin Shields, O.F.M., *Times Literary Supplement*, February 22, 1952, p. 141.

book would have had to be very popular indeed to sell as many as 5,000 copies in two years, as did the combined edition of Quarles's *Emblems and Hieroglyphikes* in 1639–40.[20] *Paradise Lost* sold 1,300 copies in two years. No edition, according to Milton's agreement with his bookseller, was to consist of more than 1,500 copies.[21]

Our information on the prices of new books in the sixteenth and seventeenth centuries is sketchy.[22] In the earlier part of the sixteenth century, the average cost of a book was between two and three sheets for a penny.[23] On this basis, in 1520, Luther's *De potestate papae* cost 3*d.*, the ABC's a penny or 2*d.*, broadside ballads a halfpenny, Christmas carols 1*d.* or 2*d.*, and the book of Robin Hood, 2*d.*[24] In 1541, by royal proclamation, the price of Coverdale's Great Bible was fixed at 10*s.* unbound, 12*s.* bound.

Debasement of the coinage resulted in the doubling of commodity prices between 1540 and 1550, and books shared in the inflation. The cost of a psalter rose from 10*d.* in 1548 to 2*s.*4*d.* in 1563. But after this increase, the prices of books remained remarkably constant down to 1635, despite another 100 per cent rise in the general price index during that period. In the golden age of Elizabethan literature, Holinshed's *Chronicles* cost £1 6*s.* bound, *Euphues* 2*s.* unbound, Camden's *Britannia* 2*s.*6*d.*, North's *Plutarch* 14*s.* bound, Spenser's *Shepheardes Calender* 1*s.*, Sidney's *Arcadia* 9*s.* bound, and Hakluyt's *Voyages* 9*s.* unbound. Quarto plays, such as Shakespeare's, were 4*d.* or, more usually, 6*d.*[25]

During the Elizabethan and Jacobean periods, therefore, books

---

[20] Stanley Gardner, *Times Literary Supplement*, March 7, 1952, p. 173. This letter and an accompanying one by H. John McLachlan provide much information, garnered from contemporary sources, on the number of copies printed at a single impression in the seventeenth century.

[21] David Masson, *The Life of John Milton* (1894), VI, 510, 628.

[22] Only after the Restoration did booksellers begin to adopt fixed prices; until then, they asked whatever the customer could be induced to pay. Hence such figures as we have for the period before 1660 are for individual transactions, and they may or may not represent the average selling price. Nor are the records always clear as to whether the price given is for a volume in its bound or unbound state. Binding could as much as double the price of a book.

[23] Bennett, *English Books and Readers*, p. 233.

[24] *The Day-Book of John Dorne, Bookseller in Oxford, A.D. 1520*, ed. F. Madan, *Collecteana*, Ser. 1, Part III (Oxford Historical Society, 1885).

[25] Johnson, "Notes on English Retail Book-Prices, 1550–1640" (the most detailed survey of the subject, as Bennett's *English Books and Readers* is for the period just preceding); Plant, p. 240.

were not too expensive when compared with other commodities. But that does not mean that they were easily accessible to a great many would-be readers, for one of the basic facts of English economic history at this time is that wages lagged far behind prices. The ordinary man could afford only the cheapest of books, and not many of these. When an unbound copy of *Hamlet* was selling for 6*d*., master artisans and handicraftsmen in London—carpenters, joiners, cobblers, smiths—earned about 16*d*. a day. Shopkeepers made about the same. Thus a man who had seen *Hamlet* at the Globe and wanted to read it at his leisure would have had to spend between a quarter and a half of his day's earnings. With that same sixpence he could have bought two dinners or gone back to the Globe (if he were content to stand in the pit) for six more performances.[26]

Even professional men, who would have been more likely to be habitual readers, did not have enough money to buy many books. An ordinary clergyman made between £10 and £20 a year, which means that the purchase of Sidney's *Arcadia* or Hakluyt's *Voyages* would have required the sacrifice of one or two whole weeks' income. A schoolmaster, making, say, £6 9*s*. a year, would have had to spend the equivalent of about three weeks' income.[27]

About 1635, for a reason not yet clear, book prices rose by some 40 per cent.[28] Incomes, however, were rising as well, so that books were relatively no more expensive by the Restoration than they had been in Shakespeare's time. In 1668 folios, meant for the wealthy trade, were priced from 5*s*. to 16*s*., the majority from 7*s*. to 10*s*. Most newly published books in octavo, the commonest size, ranged from 1*s*. to 4*s*. bound. Unbound plays were regularly published at 1*s*., and sermons, controversial pamphlets, accounts of trials, and other "timely" items of restricted length as a rule were 6*d*. The smallest books (12mo) usually were 1*s*.6*d*.[29] During this

[26] Alfred Harbage, *Shakespeare's Audience* (New York, 1941), pp. 55–62. J. E. Thorold Rogers, *A History of Agriculture and Prices in England [1259–1793]* (Oxford, 1866–1902), Vols. V and VI, gives masses of figures for sixteenth- and seventeenth-century wages and commodity prices. The prices, unfortunately, are almost always wholesale; very few retail prices are available. Figures for London wages are only approximate, since few city wages for these centuries are known to economic historians. They are reckoned on the assumption that the pay scale in London was at least a third higher than in the country. It may sometimes have been double the country rate.

[27] Plant, p. 42.   [28] Johnson, p. 93.

[29] Based on advertised prices for books published in 1668–69: *Term Catalogues, 1668–1709*, ed. Edward Arber (1903–1906), I, 1–7.

general period (there were, of course, variations from year to year) butter sold for 6*d.* a pound, coffee 3*s.* a pound, sugar 6*d.* a pound, and canary wine 7*s.* a gallon.[30] Pepys laid out 24*s.* for a "nightgown" (i.e., dressing robe) for his wife, and 2*s.* for a pair of kid gloves. Admission to the gallery of a theater where Nell Gwyn was playing cost 12*d.* or 18*d.*, although a citizen out on the town might pay as much as 2*s.*6*d.* to go into the pit.[31] In 1688 the average income of lesser clergymen was estimated at a little less than a pound a week; that of farmers, 16*s.*4*d.*; of shopkeepers, 17*s.*4*d.*; and of artisans and handicraftsmen, 14*s.*7*d.*[32]

Between this time and the first quarter of the eighteenth century, book prices again rose. Whatever the strictly economic reasons behind the increase, it was also a natural development in a period when the reading public was contracting instead of expanding. The demand for books, like the writing of them, was limited to a narrower social group. Whether the higher prices charged for books were a contributory cause or merely a symptom of the change, we cannot tell. But as the seventeenth century drew to a close, it is at least plain that books were dearer and readers were fewer.

Books, then, were the possession chiefly of the more prosperous members of the middle class in the sixteenth and seventeenth centuries, as well as of that permanent nucleus of well-educated upper-class readers whose existence will be constantly assumed, though seldom mentioned, in this volume. Among them were the keepers of fair-sized shops and master artisans who, like Simon Eyre in Dekker's comedy *The Shoemaker's Holiday*, had achieved the dignity of being employers of labor. Here and there, members of the class carried their bookishness to the point of becoming collectors on a modest scale. As early as 1575 a London mercer, writing to another, described the library of one Captain Cox, a Coventry mason. Eighty years later we find an undersheriff of London giving

[30] From household accounts of the Russell family at Woburn: Gladys S. Thomson, *Life in a Noble Household, 1641–1700* (1937), pp. 137, 166–67, 198. This volume gives hundreds of figures for food, clothing, and other expenses in the middle and late seventeenth century.

[31] Pepys, *Diary*, under dates of September 7 and 8, 1667, and January 1, 1667/68. Pepys's entries for April 13–17, 1668, contain many records of everyday expenses such as cab fare and meals.

[32] Gregory King's estimate of the annual incomes of the various classes of society; frequently reprinted, e.g., in G. N. Clark, *The Later Stuarts* (Oxford, 1934), p. 25.

up his office to be free to make his daily round of the bookstalls, and a turner in Eastcheap lining his "studdy" with books.[33]

Since the printing trade was concentrated in London and transportation and communication were still primitive, there was little commerce in books in the provinces. Only occasionally are books mentioned in yeomen's wills. Most men of that class seem to have read little, or in any event to have owned so few books that it was not worthwhile to include them in the inventories of their personal effects.[34]

II. The people of the Tudor and Stuart eras read books for reasons which would have made excellent sense to their Victorian descendants. John Stuart Mill, in his inaugural address at the University of St. Andrews in 1867, spoke of "the two influences which have chiefly shaped the British character since the days of the Stuarts: commercial money-getting business, and religious Puritanism." These influences affected reading tastes in Milton's time as profoundly as in Mill's. Their tendency was to discourage popular interest in most forms of imaginative literature. "Business," said Mill, "demanding the whole of the faculties, and whether pursued from duty or the love of gain, regarding as a loss of time whatever does not conduce directly to the end; Puritanism, which looking upon every feeling of human nature, except fear and reverence for God, as a snare, if not as partaking of sin, looked coldly, if not disapprovingly, on the cultivation of the sentiments."[35]

Protestantism, in the phrase of Élie Halévy, is a "book religion."[36] From the time it began to transform English life in the sixteenth century it laid emphasis upon the practice of private reading. With the appearance in 1540 of the Great Bible (Coverdale's revised translation), the first English Bible to be authorized by the Crown, Henry VIII ordered a copy to be placed in every church. "Every body that could," wrote Strype, the early biogra-

[33] Wright, *Middle-Class Culture*, pp. 76 n., 84–85. On other Elizabethan book collectors, see Phoebe Sheavyn, *The Literary Profession in the Elizabethan Age* (Manchester, 1909), pp. 150–51, and Raymond Irwin in *Library Association Record*, LVI (1954), 195–201.

[34] Sheavyn, p. 149; Mildred L. Campbell, *The English Yeoman under Elizabeth and the Early Stuarts* (New Haven, 1942), pp. 266–68.

[35] *Inaugural Address Delivered to the University of St. Andrews* (1867), p. 89.

[36] *History of the English People in 1815*, p. 457.

pher of Cranmer, "bought the book, or busily read it, or got others to read it to them, if they could not themselves; and divers more elderly people learned to read on purpose. And even little boys flocked among the rest to hear portions of the holy Scripture read. . . . When the King had allowed the Bible to be set forth to be read in all churches, immediately several poor men in the town of Chelmsford in Essex . . . bought the New Testament, and on Sundays sat reading it in the lower end of the Church."[37] But this novel freedom to read the Bible was short-lived. In 1543 the Reformed Parliament forbade it to all women (except those of high birth), artificers, apprentices, journeymen, servingmen, husbandmen, and laborers—an evidence of the social distribution of literacy even at that early date.

However, with the accession of Mary, though the practice of displaying Bibles in the churches was condemned, no attempt was made to interfere with individual reading. Under Elizabeth I, Bibles were restored to the churches, and the idea that men had to be "authorised and licensed" to read Scripture for themselves was quietly dropped.[38] But only under the Puritans did Scripture become the veritable foundation of Christian faith, achieving, along with the surrounding literature of religion, a place in men's lives that was inconceivable in pre-Reformation England.

It was not, however, only the Protestant, and especially the Puritan, emphasis upon private Bible-reading as a way to religious truth and thus to personal salvation which stimulated the spread of reading. The religious controversies that reached a climax in the Civil War played their part as well. They reached into the minds, and even more the passionate emotions, of great numbers of ordinary people, who were as stirred by them as later generations would be by purely political furor. And the controversies were carried on by floods of tracts and pamphlets, arguments and replies and rejoinders and counterrejoinders—printed matter which found a seemingly limitless market among all classes that could read.[39] With the establishment of the Commonwealth, "everybody with views to express, from Milton down to the most insignificant

[37] Quoted by David Daiches, *The King James Version of the English Bible* (Chicago, 1941), pp. 38–39.

[38] *Ibid., passim.*

[39] David Mathew, *The Social Structure in Caroline England* (Oxford, 1948), p. 95.

crank or fanatic, took a hand."[40] The London bookseller George
Thomason collected some 23,000 books and pamphlets printed
between 1641 and 1662.

On the secular side of life, men's interest in books stemmed from
motives strikingly prophetic of nineteenth-century utilitarianism.
Readers were increasingly concerned to obtain books of practical
guidance and information.[41] With the simultaneous spread of a
new economy, which required a degree of knowledge unnecessary
under the old feudal system, and of a humanism which brought
vast new areas of worldly interest to men's attention, books became instruments of utility. Through them, men could learn the
things they needed to know as businessmen and functionaries in
civil government and could share in the humane learning of the
Renaissance. Reading was inextricably associated with "improvement," with cultivation of the prudential virtues and the more
easily acquired amenities of conduct. The books most in request
were those which either showed the way to a morality acceptable
in the eyes both of God and of Mammon or brought the ideals of
humanistic conduct down to the level of the common man. Thus—
to adopt the categories described in Louis Wright's encyclopedic
account of middle-class reading in the age—the demand was for
handbooks of improvement, lessons in diligence and thrift, instruction in domestic relations, guides to godliness, popularized histories
(always with useful lessons), translations, travel books, and books
on science.

These were the books that the sober, ambitious citizen read.
Other kinds were available, as we shall note in a moment; but,
though they might be admitted to a Simon Eyre's shelf, they
owed their presence there to stealth or rationalization, or both.
For the spirit of the time was strongly against books of any lighter
quality than the types just mentioned. Over the whole age, affect-
ing even those who were staunchest in their allegiance to orthodox
Anglicanism, hung the fervent Puritan opposition to polite letters
as un-Christian, frivolous, and demoralizing. From the 1580's to
the Root and Branch petition of 1640, which attacked the preva-
lence of "lascivious, idle, and unprofitable Books and Pamphlets,
Play-Books and Ballads," the Puritan divines ceaselessly denounced the reading of books which offered no more than idle en-

[40] Esmé Wingfield-Stratford, *The History of British Civilization* (1928), I, 563.
[41] Bennett, "Caxton and His Public," *passim*.

tertainment. We shall hear their voices again—though the rhetorical splendor of Puritan pulpit utterance will be sadly missing—when we look into the effect of evangelicalism, the neo-Puritanism of the industrial age, upon the reading habits of the nineteenth century.

Even the courtesy books, interpreters of humanistic standards of conduct to the middle-class citizen, frowned upon the reading of plays and romances. At best, reading was only a minor one among the many polite activities one might pursue; but if one did read, it should always be with at least a moderately serious purpose.[42]

But the demands of the imagination and the feelings are too strong to be consistently denied. At their disposal always is man's inexhaustible talent for rationalization, and the extent to which it was employed is suggested by the popularity of lighter forms of literature—jestbooks, chapbooks, ballads, and the fiction that Thomas Nashe and Thomas Deloney devised expressly for the common reader. Usually the Elizabethan or Jacobean reader could find a plausible reason for dipping into such dubious books. The reading of jestbooks could be, and was, justified on the ground that they were pills to purge melancholy and thus (since the Elizabethans were firm believers in psychosomatic medicine) could improve one's physical health. Similarly, because the reading of history was recommended as perfectly safe and useful, it was possible to take up with a clear conscience any book, however fantastic, that had the word "history" displayed on its title page.[43] Thus innumerable chapbooks and debased romances found their way into the hands of pious purchasers. Nor did the factual truth of the travel books have to be scrutinized too carefully. So long as they had an air of genuineness—so long as their authors did not candidly admit that they were spinning tales—they could be read as improving literature, no matter how outrageous their romancing. In such ways as these the reading regimen of the sixteenth- and seventeenth-century public had, despite its surface appearance of austerity, a full seasoning of imagination and escapism.[44]

[42] See John E. Mason, *Gentlefolk in the Making* (Philadelphia, 1935).

[43] Wright, pp. 102–103, 301.

[44] Pepys permitted himself to read Helot's *L'Escole des Filles* before throwing it into the fire on the ground that, though it was a "mighty lewd book," yet it was "not amiss for a sober man once to read over to inform himself in the villainy of the world" (*Diary*, entry for February 9, 1667/68). The rationalization is thoroughly in the spirit of his class and time.

Even among the strictest of Puritans, whose reading dealt exclusively and unambiguously with the concerns of the soul, imaginative stimulation and satisfaction were by no means lacking. The Bible is unequaled, among all the books of the world, for the variety and splendor of its imaginative and emotional appeal. Between a single pair of covers it offers the cosmic dramas of creation and the Last Judgment, the human pathos of Ruth and the tragedy of Samson; the wars of the Hebrews, the destruction of the Babylonians, the simple charm of the nativity story, the wonder of the miracles, the supreme climax of the Crucifixion and the Resurrection.

Furthermore, as William Haller has pointed out in his study of Puritanism, the Puritan preachers offered in their sermons, which in printed form had a wide circulation, a very acceptable substitute for the forbidden drama. "They were to discover that their listeners . . . took a livelier interest in sin itself than in its categories, in the psychology of spiritual struggle than in the abstract analysis of moral behavior or even the satirical exposure of vice and folly. . . . So they set out to describe the warfare of the spirit, to portray the drama of the inner life, to expound the psychology of sin and redemption."[45] Between the Bible itself, and such works as Foxe's *Book of Martyrs*, and these exceedingly dramatic presentations of the conflict of good and evil, the reading hours of even the most rigorous Puritans were seldom dull.

Of another segment of the reading public, which had few such scruples as affected the book choice of the sober middle class, we have little record except that of the books it preferred. This was the lowest stratum of the literate population: the casual, unpurposeful readers, those who, in the phrase of Heming and Condell's dedication in the 1623 Shakespeare folio, "can but spell." It was among these people—apprentices, common laborers, peasants, rivermen, and the rest—that the printers of broadside ballads and chapbooks found their chief market. The ballads were the precursors of a later era's sensational newspapers: never was a celebrated highwayman executed or a catastrophe visited upon a hapless town but the event was described in crude language and cruder woodcuts. They were, as well, the poor man's history: John Aubrey's nurse could recite the whole chronicle of England, from

[45] William Haller, *The Rise of Puritanism* (New York, 1938), pp. 32–33.

the Conquest to Charles I, in ballads.[46] The chapbooks, vulgarized versions of old chivalric tales, were his fiction—as Milton put it, "the countryman's *Arcadias*, and his *Monte Mayors*."[47]

This popular printed literature ran as a continuous thread, however seldom seen in the formal historical records, from Elizabeth's time to Victoria's. The descendants of Autolycus were to be found trudging with their packs along every rural road; in the end they would be acquiring fresh stock from the thriving establishment of Jemmy Catnach in London's unsavory Seven Dials. The fact that ballads and chapbooks did not vanish from the English scene until the advent of penny periodicals is assurance enough that the tradition of reading among the poor, in town and country, never wholly disappeared.

But the size of this public fluctuated with the vicissitudes of popular education, and we cannot know how large it was, in Tudor times or later. Though it is pleasant to envision the Elizabethan cottage with its faded and tattered ballads on the wall, and the cottager crouching over the feeble fire spelling out the words of a chapbook of Sir Thopas or an account of a late horrid crime and the ensuing visitation of justice on the malefactor, it would be a mistake to imagine that reading had any but the most incidental place in the life of the masses. For most of them—the fact is inescapable—were illiterate; and, impressive though the spread of reading was among the middle class in these first centuries of printing, it made little headway among the humble in either town or country. Their life still was lived according to the immemorial pattern. The recreations that occasionally lightened their hard lives were those which had been traditional centuries before Caxton—the rude games, the maypole dances, the harvest celebrations, and the other festivals that marked the progress of the seasons. Songs and stories were handed down by word of mouth from generation to generation, with never a page of print intervening. The life of the imagination and the feelings was still attuned to the ear rather than to the eye. The popular tradition, rich in folk heroes and broad humor and proverbial wisdom and memorable events, a strange and fascinating mixture of local legend and the lore of the Bible and the classics and medieval tale, was part of the very soil, and there was as yet no need for the printed word to supplant it.

[46] *Aubrey's Brief Lives*, ed. O. L. Dick (1949), p. xxix.
[47] *Areopagitica*.

CHAPTER 2 { *The Eighteenth Century*

I. If, speculating from such little information as we have, we tried to chart the growth of the reading public in the first three centuries after Caxton, the line would climb slowly for the first hundred years. During the Elizabethan period its rate of ascent would considerably quicken. The line would reach a peak during the Civil War and Commonwealth, when interest in reading was powerfully stimulated by public excitements. But during the Restoration it would drop, because of the lessening of popular turmoil, the damage the war had done to the educational system, and the aristocratic domination of current literature in the age of Dryden. A fresh ascent would begin in the early eighteenth century, the time of Addison and Steele, and thereafter the line would climb steadily.

This chart, be it noted, represents the number of people that *did* read, not the larger number of those who *could* read. A graph of the literacy rate would probably follow the same general pattern down to the latter part of the seventeenth century, when it too would decline sharply. But its recovery during the eighteenth century was much slower; indeed, it is quite possible that the percentage of literates decreased still further. At least we may be fairly sure that by 1780 the national literacy rate was scarcely higher than it had been during the Elizabethan period.

Between 1700 and 1801 the population of England and Wales increased from an estimated 5,500,000 to an official 8,893,000.[1] The greatest growth occurred, as always, in the lower reaches of society. And by this time the attitude toward the education of the working class had radically changed. During the Tudor period

[1] Basil Williams, *The Whig Supremacy* (Oxford, 1939), p. 119; Porter, *The Progress of the Nation* (1912), p. 3.

educational opportunity had been reasonably democratic, for the medieval belief persisted that all men, regardless of worldly station, were bound together in one society under God. Its social status bulwarked by feudal privileges, the upper class could afford to tolerate a certain amount of ambition on the part of the inferior. But with altering economic conditions, with the rise of the mercantile middle class, which forced the extremes of society farther apart, and with the gradual weakening of feudal privileges, the upper class urgently needed to shore up its own position. The essential tolerance that had eased its relations with the lower class gave way to condescension and even contempt. "Disraeli's two nations," it has been said, "sprang originally not out of the industrial revolution but out of the breach between peasant and squire-archy"[2]—and, it could be added, between town laborer and citizen. By the end of the seventeenth century the old idea of "degree" had hardened into a rigid pattern of social attitudes, and everywhere there was an intensified awareness of status.

On the upper levels of English education, this changed social atmosphere was reflected in the growing restriction of the public schools and universities to sons of the gentry and the nobility (though boys of lower station were never entirely excluded). On the elementary level, the opportunity for children of the poor to learn to read was sharply curtailed. The Civil War and its aftermath dislocated the system of endowed primary schools that had spread literacy among a certain portion of the common people. After the restoration of the monarchy, also, one great aim of public policy was to prevent a repetition of the late upheaval. Since the power of the press had been so dramatically revealed during the Puritan regime, one vital way of insuring the nation's stability was to keep the masses ignorant of their letters. Such a course also had its practical advantage, because it would guarantee a perpetual supply of cheap labor in an increasingly industrial economy.

Soame Jenyns spoke for many men of his century when he maintained in 1757 that ignorance was "the appointed lot of all born to poverty and the drudgeries of life, . . . the only opiate capable of

---

[2] Mack, *Public Schools and British Opinion*, I, 23. Mack, like Wingfield-Stratford (*History of British Civilization*, I, 377-78, 426), emphasizes that the hardening of the concept of "degree" was already under way in the Renaissance. But the nadir of democratic sympathies was reached in the late seventeenth and early eighteenth centuries.

infusing that sensibility, which can enable them to endure the miseries of the one and the fatigues of the other . . . a cordial, administered by the gracious hand of providence, of which they ought never to be deprived by an ill-judged and improper education."[3] To encourage the poor man to read and think, and thus to become more conscious of his misery, would be to fly in the face of divine intention, "the great law of subordination," as Defoe had described it.[4] To tempt the poor to rise by their own bootstraps was not merely impolitic but sinful. Neglect degree, and chaos was sure to come again.

Yet something could be said for a less uncompromising approach; for, as the founders of the Society for Promoting Christian Knowledge in 1699 argued, how could the masses be taught their duty except in schools? How else could the necessity for piety, morality, industry, and unquestioning loyalty to the Protestant faith be impressed upon them?

This was the mission of the charity schools set up by the S.P.C.K. in the first half of the eighteenth century.[5] The projectors, agreeing with the total-ignorance party that even a little learning, of the wrong sort, could be a dangerous thing, looked upon education for the poor exclusively as a means of insuring that they would forever know their place. "It is but a cheap education that we would desire for them," pleaded Griffith Jones, the founder of Welsh primary education, in phrases that were echoed in every charity-school sermon and prospectus; "only the moral and religious branches of it, which indeed is the most necessary and indispensable part. The sole design of this charity is to inculcate upon such . . . as can be prevailed on to learn, the knowledge and practice, the principles and duties of the Christian Religion; and to

---

[3] Jenyns, *Free Inquiry into the Nature and Origin of Evil,* quoted in Johnson's review: Samuel Johnson, *Works* (Literary Club edition, Troy, N.Y., 1903), XIII, 226. In this review, to his everlasting credit, Dr. Johnson lost no time putting Jenyns in *his* place: "The privileges of education may, sometimes, be improperly bestowed, but I shall always fear to withhold them, lest I should be yielding to the suggestions of pride, while I persuade myself that I am following the maxims of policy; and, under the appearance of salutary restraints, should be indulging the lust of dominion, and that malevolence which delights in seeing others depressed" (*ibid.,* XIII, 230–31). This was wisdom that the managers of popular education in the early nineteenth century could well have used.

[4] Quoted in Jones, *The Charity School Movement,* p. 4.

[5] Unless otherwise noted, material on the S.P.C.K. schools is from Jones, *The Charity School Movement*—the standard work on the subject.

make them good people, useful members of society, faithful servants of God and men and heirs of eternal life."[6] The sole intention
was to enable the child to read the Bible, the catechism, and such
other works of approved piety as might come his way. Until widespread alarm over the so-called "literary curriculum" forced the
charity schools to replace it with one concentrating on the manual
skills, "reading and repetition" were the chief, and in many cases
the only, subjects taught.

There was no possibility of introducing reading matter more
suitable for the pupils' tender years and their human inclinations.
Children's stories were unknown in these schools. It was the Bible
and religious literature or nothing. Charles Hoole's ideal, expressed in his proposal for a Latin-less "petty school" in 1660, had
no place in such a scheme. The children, Hoole had suggested, were
to "be benefited in reading orthodoxall catechisms and other books
that may instruct them in the duties of a Christian, . . . and ever
afterward in other delightful books of English History, as *The History of Queen Elizabeth*, or poetry, as Herbert's *Poems*, Quarles'
Emblems: and by this means they will gain such a habit and delight in reading as to make it their chief recreation when liberty is
afforded them. And their acquaintance with good books will (by
God's blessing) be a means to sweeten their (otherwise) sour natures, that they may live comfortably towards themselves, and
amiably converse with other persons."[7] Such a concept of popular
education struck horror into the souls of those committed to eighteenth-century social theory. It promised sloth, debauchery, and
the assumption of superior airs on the part of the people—followed, as the day the night, by irreligion and revolution.

It was this fear of teaching too much, coupled with an exclusively disciplinary motive, that distinguished the charity schools
of Queen Anne's reign from the various kinds of schools in which
Elizabethan children had learned to read. That is why the
S.P.C.K. schools were probably far less effective instruments of
popular education. In other respects they may have been no worse
than their predecessors; the badness of eighteenth-century charity
schools is well documented, while that of Elizabethan schools is

[6] Quoted in Birchenough, *History of Elementary Education*, p. 251.

[7] Quoted in J. W. Adamson, *Pioneers of Modern Education* (Cambridge, 1921), pp. 162–63.

mercifully obscured in the haze of a more remote past. A few
S.P.C.K. schools, to be sure, were as good as any that had ever
been open to the poorer classes—well housed and appointed, according to the standard of the times, with their masters paid almost as much as clergymen. But the great majority were dreadful.
Commonly the teachers were themselves barely literate; they were
recruited from the motley ranks of the crippled, the diseased, the
chronically unsuccessful in other lines of work; they were paid less
than honest day laborers; and, lacking any sense of mission and
any temperamental fitness for their job, they earned their pittance
chiefly by obeying the managers' injunction to teach the children,
by birch rod and word of mouth, the principles of "humility,"
"placid obedience," and "a due reverence for their superiors."

For children on a slightly higher plane of society, there were endowed elementary schools, of which at least 1,100 were set up in
the course of the eighteenth century,[8] as well as establishments
which had started out as grammar schools but had degenerated in
the course of the years into mere elementary schools, and countless
dame schools. These schools—the endowed ones sometimes, the
dame schools always—charged fees, if only a penny or two a week.
The education they offered was hardly better than that in the
charity schools, the principal difference being that the children
were not subjected to as stringent a course of instruction in keeping their place. It may be reckoned an advantage that they learned
to read without too many strings attached.

We do not know how many eighteenth-century children went
to school. The records of the S.P.C.K. schools are untrustworthy.
In 1723 there were said to be 1,329 such schools, with 23,421 scholars. But since precisely the same figures were returned year after
year down to 1799, we may suspect a certain statistical lethargy
which dooms any latter-day attempt to get at the facts.[9] At any
rate, the charity schools' contribution toward popular literacy declined sharply after the first third of the century. They became a
hapless pawn in the political struggle between High and Low
Church; Mandeville, for example, attacked the whole S.P.C.K.
movement in his *Essay on Charity and Charity Schools* (1723).
Faced with formidable opposition from those who disapproved of

[8] Jones, p. 25.

[9] *Ibid.*, p. 24. Further figures are on pp. 57, 61, 65, 72.

any education whatsoever for the poor, the projectors' initial enthusiasm cooled and the subscribers' purse-strings tightened. At the same time educational fervor noticeably decreased among the parents themselves, who from the beginning had been caught between the parson's insistence that they send their children to school and the employer's aversion to hiring sophisticated workers. Since the few pennies a day that a child's labor could add to the meager family income were of far greater moment than a smattering of book-learning, parents sacrificed whatever ambition they may have had for their children.

Few ordinary laborers could read at any time in the century. In 1700 the nascent S.P.C.K. arranged to pass out a tract called *Kind Cautions against Swearing* among hackney coachmen and seamen, but this is better evidence of the reformers' lack of realism than of the incidence of literacy.[10] About the same time Charles Leslie, in his paper the *Rehearsal*, said that "the greatest part of the *people* [in London?] do not read *books;* most of them cannot *read* at all, but," he added, "they will gather about one that can *read*, and listen to an *Observator* or *Review* (as I have seen them in the streets)."[11] The very fact that reading aloud was so common in the century points to a low literacy rate among the masses; one recalls Sir John Herschel's famous—and, one fears, somewhat romanticized—story of the village blacksmith reading *Pamela*, volume by volume, to an enraptured company of his neighbors.[12]

II. The largest single group of lower-class readers was the Wesleyans, who numbered over 56,000 by 1789.[13] Among them, reading had the same importance that it had among the Presbyterians north of the border. All Wesleyans were expected to read as much as their leisure allowed. "Reading Christians," John Wesley himself once wrote, "will be knowing Christians,"[14] and he urged his preachers to spend at least five hours

---

[10] Clarke, *Short History of S.P.C.K.*, p. 20.

[11] Quoted in Taylor, *Early Opposition to the English Novel*, p. 4.

[12] "Address," pp. 11–12. For an interesting history of the anecdote from Herschel to the present day, see A. D. McKillop, "Wedding Bells for Pamela," *Philological Quarterly*, XXVIII (1949), 323–25.

[13] Edwards, *After Wesley*, p. 143.

[14] Quoted in Thomas W. Herbert, *John Wesley as Editor and Author* (Princeton, 1940), p. 4. In addition to Herbert's valuable account, the following studies have been drawn

every day in reading "the most useful books." From 1740 onward, the Methodist Book Room in London was a busy headquarters from which were distributed the almost innumerable pieces of Wesleyan literature. Every chapel had its display of pamphlets and books for sale; all itinerant preachers carried a supply of cheap reading matter with them. To critics who commented upon the profit resulting from this steady traffic in the printed word—Wesley, it is said, cleared between £30,000 and £40,000 on the sale of his books[15]—the founder of Methodism replied that "books, to be of value, had to be read; and . . . that people would read books for which they paid—however small the price."[16] This argument is not as ingenuous as it seems; quite probably Wesley's publications, for which a small fee was charged, were more respected by the people to whom they were addressed than the free tracts which were to be broadcast the length and breadth of England from Hannah More's time onward.

Wesley himself was a pioneer popularizer of literature. In 1743 he condensed—a better word would be "transformed"—*Pilgrim's Progress* into a pocket-size booklet selling for 4d. The primer-like sentences of this new version, as well as some of the theology, were Wesley's, not Bunyan's. Twenty years later he performed a similar operation on *Paradise Lost*,[17] and still later he produced a simplified version of Young's *Night Thoughts* and an abridgment of Brooke's *Fool of Quality*, renamed *The History of Henry, Earl of Moreland*. His anthology of poetry, the *Collection of Moral and Sacred Poems* (1744), was an attempt to provide a course in polite literature that would relieve the cultural narrowness of Methodist readers at no cost to their piety or morality. It was a forerunner of the many winnowed anthologies of the next century and a half.

In all these books Wesley compressed, abridged, rewrote, wherever he felt necessary—partly in order to expunge non-Wesleyan

---

upon for the present discussion of Wesleyanism and reading: Richard Green, *The Works of John and Charles Wesley: A Bibliography* (1906); Bready, *England: Before and after Wesley;* T. B. Shepherd, *Methodism and the Literature of the Eighteenth Century* (1940); Whiteley, *Wesley's England;* Warner, *The Wesleyan Movement in the Industrial Revolution.*

[15] Shepherd, p. 63.   [16] Bready, p. 220.

[17] On Wesley's Milton, see Oscar Sherwin, "Milton for the Masses," *Modern Language Quarterly*, XII (1951), 267–85.

ideas and highlight Wesleyan ones, but, more importantly, to bring Milton, Bunyan, and other writers down to the level of common understanding. He had no illusions as to the capacities of his followers, who were poorly educated and had little if any prior experience in reading.[18] In his own voluminous writings, he tried to adopt a style suitable to the limitations of his audience. He was the inveterate enemy of what he termed "the superfluity of words"; his ideal was to clothe thoughts "in the plainest dress: simply and nakedly expressed, in the most clear, easy and intelligible manner."[19]

Thus the growth of Wesleyanism was a noteworthy milestone in the spread of reading among the masses. The new sect preached the spiritual necessity of reading; it circulated books and leaflets in great quantities; and it fostered a style of writing that was especially fitted for the novice reader. But the example of the book-reading Methodists was not followed by their unconverted neighbors. Actually, the association of serious reading with what the non-Methodist world took to be sheer fanaticism may well have slowed the general spread of interest in books. There has always been a popular belief that more than casual attention to books is either a symptom or a cause of madness, and the fact that Wesley's followers were addicted to the printed page did nothing to allay the suspicion.

Furthermore, even within its own circle, Wesleyanism did not add perceptibly to the audience for general literature. Despite Wesley's own relatively liberal attitude toward belles-lettres (he was a widely read man, who interlarded his sermons and tracts with countless allusions and quotations) the movement as a whole disapproved of any but religious and moralistic reading. The long list of books James Lackington and a fellow apprentice, both of them fanatical Methodists, collected in their adolescent zeal for reading reveals the narrowness of Wesleyan interests. It included many of Bunyan's works; the exegetical volumes of approved di-

---

[18] A clue to the state of literacy among Wesley's followers (and thus, inferentially, of the working class in general) is found in the fact that he compiled and published two elementary tools for the new reader: a *Short English Grammar* in 9 pages and a *Complete* [!] *English Dictionary* in 144 pages—the latter being intended, in Wesley's words, "to assist persons of common sense and no learning to understand the best English authors" (Green, pp. 55, 80–81; the quotation from Wesley is given in Quinlan, *Victorian Prelude*, p. 29).

[19] Quoted in Shepherd, p. 84.

vines; and such items, sufficiently described by their titles, as *Divine Breathings of a Devout Soul*, Collings' *Divine Cordial for the Soul*, *Heaven Taken by Storm*, Young's *Short and Sure Guide to Salvation*, Baxter's *Call to the Unconverted*, and the same author's *Shove for a Heavy-arsed Christian*. Only "a few of a better sort" of books were included in what Lackington and his friend considered at the time to be "a very good library": Gay's *Fables*, Pomfret's *Poems*, *Paradise Lost*, Hobbes's *Homer*, and Walker's *Epictetus*.[20]

Therefore such little reading as the common non-Wesleyan people of the countryside did was confined to the immemorial fare of the cottage shelf: the Bible and Prayer Book, perhaps a history of England published in numbers, an almanac or two, chapbooks, and sixpenny romances. The peasant father of the poet John Clare, though barely able to read, doted on such penny treasures as *Nixon's Prophesies*, *Mother Bunches Fairy Tales*, and *Mother Shipton's Legacy*, and late in the century Clare himself learned to read from chapbooks like *Cinderella*, *Little Red Riding Hood*, and *Jack and the Beanstalk*.[21] The popularity of these little books was not confined, of course, to the lower classes. They were the beloved pabulum of children belonging to the educated class as well; Wordsworth, Coleridge, Scott, and Lamb pored over them in childhood.[22]

More sophisticated reading matter was seldom encountered in the ordinary course of a country life. Thomas Holcroft, for instance, a stable boy at Newmarket in the 1760's, having learned to read from the Bible and two chapbooks, saw almost no books for six or seven years thereafter and kept his skill alive principally by reading the ballads pasted on the walls of cottages and alehouses. Then, having turned shoemaker, he had for shopmate a youth who divided his leisure between cock-feeding and reading. His friend lent him *Gulliver's Travels* and the *Spectator*, and Holcroft's literary education began.[23]

[20] Lackington, *Memoirs*, pp. 98–99.

[21] *Sketches in the Life of John Clare*, ed. Edmund Blunden (1931), pp. 46, 51–52.

[22] See J. L. Lowes, *The Road to Xanadu* (Boston, 1927), pp. 459–61, and the Appendix ("The Popularity of Elizabethan Prose Fiction in the Eighteenth Century") in Earl R. Wasserman, *Elizabethan Poetry in the Eighteenth Century* (Urbana, Ill., 1947). These are meaty discussions of chapbook literature in the late eighteenth century.

[23] William Hazlitt, *Life of Thomas Holcroft*, *Works*, ed. P. P. Howe (1932), III, 4–5, 41–42.

To boys who had access to so few books, the ones they did meet with were extraordinarily precious. On his way to find a job at Kew, William Cobbett, the fourteen-year-old son of a farmer-inn-keeper, saw in a Richmond bookseller's window a copy of *A Tale of a Tub.* It cost him 3*d.*, his entire capital, and in the shade of a haystack in a corner of Kew Gardens he began to read. "The book," he recalled, "was so different from any thing that I had ever read before: it was something so *new* to my mind, that, though I could not at all understand some of it, it delighted me beyond description; and it produced what I have always consid-ered a sort of birth of intellect. I read on till it was dark, without any thought about supper or bed. When I could see no longer, I put my little book in my pocket, and tumbled down by the side of the stack, where I slept till the birds in Kew Gardens awaked me in the morning; when I started to Kew, reading my little book."[24]

The burden of evidence, then, hardly supports the statement made in the 1790's by James Lackington, who had turned from shoemaking to bookselling, that even "the poorer sort of farmers, and even the poor country people in general, . . . shorten the winter nights by hearing their sons and daughters read tales, ro-mances, etc. and on entering their houses, you may see *Tom Jones, Roderic Random*, and other entertaining books, stuck up on their bacon-racks, &c. If John goes to town with a load of hay, he is charged to be sure not to forget to bring home 'Peregrine Pickle's Adventures;' and when Dolly is sent to market to sell her eggs, she is commissioned to purchase 'The History of Pamela Andrews.' In short," Lackington concluded, "all ranks and degrees now READ."[25]

This passage, often quoted to prove the extent to which reading was democratized in the late eighteenth century, is, to put it mildly, debatable. One need not contest Lackington's assertion that countrypeople listened to someone reading on winter nights, though the statement should be heavily qualified; only a minority of rural families had a single literate in their midst, and few of those that did could obtain books. *Tom Jones, Roderick Random, Peregrine Pickle*, and *Pamela* must have been rare sights indeed in humble English cottages. To be ruthlessly prosaic about it, any one of those novels would have cost several times as much as Dolly got for her basket of eggs, unless she was lucky enough to find a

---

[24] Quoted in Cole, *Life of Cobbett*, p. 17.   [25] *Memoirs*, p. 257.

secondhand copy. As for the sweeping finale, "all ranks and degrees now READ," that is sheer fantasy.

Lackington would have been on slightly safer ground had he chosen his illustration from city rather than country life. Thanks to the greater provision of schools in the towns, the more pressing need for literacy under urban conditions, and the easier availability of printed matter, people on the social level of artisans and domestic servants could read, though even in this class literates may have been in the minority. Numerous visitors to London were impressed by the spectacle of artisans reading newspapers. About 1730 Montesquieu saw a slater having his paper delivered to him on the roof where he was working; twenty years later another French traveler recorded that "workmen habitually begin the day by going to the coffee-houses in order to read the latest news"; and in 1775 Dr. Thomas Campbell, an Irishman, found it worthy of note that while he was in the Chapter Coffee House "a whitesmith in his apron & some of his saws under his arm, came in, sat down & called for his glass of punch & the paper, both of which he used with as much ease as a Lord."[26] Although the available records suggest that newspapers were the favorite reading matter of artisans themselves, their wives took up books—especially, as we shall note later on, novels. In the 1780's a German visitor to London wrote that his landlady, a tailor's widow, "reads her Milton; and tells me, that her late husband first fell in love with her, on this very account; because she read Milton with such proper emphasis. This single instance perhaps would prove but little; but I have conversed with several people of the lower class, who all knew their national authors, and who all have read many, if not all of them."[27]

But, as Lackington said in another place, the barriers in the way of liberal indulgence in the taste for reading were formidable. Not merely were books themselves scarce except as the circulating library supplied them; shops in which to browse and people to give advice both were hard for the common reader to find. Lackington and a friend, journeymen cobblers at Bristol in the late sixties,

[26] Montesquieu, "Notes sur l'Angleterre," *Œuvres Complètes*, ed. Édouard Laboulaye (Paris, 1879), VII, 189; M. de Saussure, *A Foreign View of England in the Reigns of George I and II*, quoted in Dobbs, *Education and Social Movements*, p. 102; *Dr. Campbell's Diary of a Visit to England in 1775*, ed. J. L. Clifford (Cambridge, 1947), p. 58.

[27] Carl P. Moritz, *Travels in England* (1924), p. 43.

must have had counterparts enough among the literate young men of their class: they wanted to read books, "but," wrote Lackington long afterward, "so ignorant were we on the subject, that neither of us knew what books were fit for our perusal, nor what to enquire for, as we had scarce ever heard or seen even any *title pages*, except a few of the religious sort, which at that time we had no relish for. . . . [Hence] we were ashamed to go into the booksellers' shops; and . . . there are thousands now in England in the very same situation: many, very many have come to my shop, who have discovered an enquiring mind, but were totally at a loss what to ask for, and who had no friend to direct them."[28]

Taking the English people as a whole, therefore, the available information scarcely substantiates the eighteenth century's well-known complacence over its "diffusion of learning." "General literature," Dr. Johnson observed in 1779, "now pervades the nation through all its ranks"; every house, he said, was "supplied with a closet of knowledge."[29] Such remarks were made, we must remember, in a very restricted social context. To Johnson and his contemporaries the ranks of civilized society ended with the middle class; below it lay the broad, unregarded expanses of the working class, which no correct Englishman could conceive as sharing in the nation's culture. Charles Knight, the Victorian pioneer of cheap literature, deflated the balloon of post-Augustan self-satisfaction quite justly when he observed that "There appears to have been a sort of tacit agreement amongst all who spoke of public enlightenment in the days of George III to put out of view the great body of 'the nation' who paid for their bread by their weekly wages."[30]

III. Hence it was among the middle class, rather than among the working people, that the taste for reading made headway during the eighteenth century. It had a great distance to go, partly because at the beginning of the century the middle class as a whole was in the deplorable cultural condition that Macaulay attributed, though with some exaggeration, to the country gentry of James II's day and partly because with the development of a mercantile economy the class itself grew swiftly. What sort of schooling did these people have, and to what ex-

[28] *Memoirs*, p. 92.   [29] "Milton," *Lives of the Poets* (World's Classics ed.), I, 103–104.
[30] *The Old Printer and the Modern Press*, pp. 226–27.

tent did formal education affect their interest in reading? There were, first of all, the endowed grammar schools and the numerous private-venture classical schools which supplemented them.[31] These schools adhered to the Latin curriculum which had persisted almost unchanged since Tudor times. To the majority of boys (most of whom went directly into commerce or the professions, rather than proceeding to the university) they gave only a stock of classical tags handy for any occasion and a firm distaste for the ancient literary works in which they were embalmed. No attempt was made to encourage reading as a pastime for adult Englishmen, and works in the vernacular, which was still looked upon more or less as a second-class language, were neglected.

From the middle of the seventeenth century the hallowed grammar-school program came under heavy fire from the Puritans, who found that its exclusive emphasis upon the writings of pagan authors was the very denial of Christian piety—to say nothing of a waste of time at an age when a youth's energies should be devoted to equipping himself, as a prospective businessman, for harvesting the material evidences of God's favor. To the Puritans' support came the authority of Bacon, Comenius, and Locke, each of whom, in his own way, decried the futility of scholastic disciplines and extolled the value of "modern," or practical, subjects.

In 1662 the Act of Uniformity, reinforced three years later by the Five Mile Act—both laws being part of the Clarendon Code, designed to eradicate religious dissent—barred all non-Anglicans from teaching in the schools and universities. The result was the setting up of numerous "academies" conducted by and for dissenters. However, these academies, which provided the equivalent of not only a grammar-school but also a university education, did not for many years radically alter the schooling given to England's future tradesmen and merchants.[32] The majority gave no more at-

[31] The private-venture schools have left hardly any record. A recent investigator, basing his guess upon an examination of the admission lists of certain Cambridge colleges, has suggested that "on the average there were at least 200 private classical schools at any time throughout the century. In the middle of the century the number rose to about 300, decreasing to about 100 at the end of the century" (Nicholas Hans, *New Trends in English Education in the Eighteenth Century* [1951], p. 119).

[32] The following account is derived chiefly from Adamson, *Pioneers of Modern Education,* and the same author's *English Education, 1789–1902;* Irene Parker, *Dissenting Academies in England* (Cambridge, 1914); and Herbert McLachlan, *English Education under the Test Acts* (Manchester, 1931).

tention to English books than did the Anglican institutions, which is to say they gave none at all. But here and there the seeds of a great change were sown. An occasional teacher, like Charles Morton, Defoe's master at Newington, and later Philip Doddridge at Northampton Academy, lectured in English rather than Latin. As a natural consequence, illustrative passages were chosen from English books instead of from the ancient classics. When Joseph Priestley wrote his *Rudiments of English Grammar* (1761), he added an appendix containing extracts from Addison, Young, Pope, Bolingbroke, Hume, Swift, and other modern English writers.

At the same time the study of elocution and oratory slowly began to turn to English books. Dr. John Taylor, the divinity tutor at Warrington in the time of Priestley, having heard his pupils deliver original Latin essays and sermon outlines, would then have them read passages from such poets as Milton, Pope, Thomson, Young, and Akenside. The popularity of courses in elocution was responsible in no small measure for the development of a larger audience for polite literature. William Enfield's famous *Speaker*, originally compiled for his classes at Warrington Academy, went through many editions and was probably the most influential of all the early textbook anthologies of English prose and verse.[33]

The extent to which English literature was introduced into the later eighteenth-century academies is best measured by the number of poetical anthologies and "beauties" volumes published and reprinted during those decades. Addison had pointed the way in his *Spectator* series on Milton, and the practice of collecting elegant extracts from great authors for study and imitation was encouraged by the Frenchman Rollin, whose influential treatise, translated as *The Method of Teaching and Studying the Belles Lettres*, was widely read by contemporary educators.[34] The result was that virtually every English author of great contemporary repute was ransacked for passages suitable for classroom analysis: Shakespeare, of course, and Fielding (whose "beauties" were several times reprinted in the single year 1782), Sterne (eleven editions between 1782 and 1790), Dr. Johnson, the *Spectator*, *Guardian*, and *Tatler*, and so on. Thanks to the use of these anthologies during

[33] McLachlan, pp. 21, 216, 222.

[34] Gardiner, *English Girlhood at School*, pp. 405–407.

their school days, middle-class Englishmen enjoyed at least a nodding acquaintance with some of the luminaries of their national literature.

Though these developments represented a hopeful departure from the cut-and-dried classical grind, their basic motivation was still narrow. The dissenting academies and the private-venture schools modeled on them[35] reflected and in turn gave greater currency to the middle-class ethos so characteristic of the century—an ethos admirable in many ways but illiberal in others. In his *Miscellaneous Observations Relating to Education* (1778), Joseph Priestley, one of the most advanced and influential educational theorists of the time, said nothing about cultivating the imagination or the aesthetic sense. Although he provided for the reading of good literature, both modern and classical, it was not as an end in itself but always with a more or less extraneous purpose, such as that of encouraging morality or enlarging worldly knowledge. It is true that there was sometimes a conscious effort to study literature as art; under a master like Andrew Kippis at Hoxton Academy,[36] "the belles-lettres" was a means of kindling genuine interest in the aesthetic values of literature and in reading as a pastime adaptable even to the life of a middle-class tradesman. But only occasionally and hesitantly, in the second half of the century, do we find the element of sheer pleasure, of diversion, appearing in explanations of why men should read books.

However unsatisfactory its quasi-utilitarian bias seems to us today, the later eighteenth-century academy unquestionably helped spread the reading habit among the class it served. It produced a great part of the audience, soberly concerned for private morality and an improved society, which sought guidance from the periodical essayists as their work was reprinted time after time. And an important by-product of the courses in belles-lettres and elocution was a widened public for poetry and drama. Those who bought the new cheap series of British classics in the last quarter of the eighteenth century included many men who had first learned

[35] It has been estimated that in the 1780's and 1790's there were about two hundred such schools in the whole country, two-thirds of them being in London or its vicinity. Their pupils were the children of teachers, artists, merchants, farmers, and skilled craftsmen (Hans, p. 69).

[36] McLachlan, p. 123.

the delights of reading at Warrington Academy, Hoxton, Kibworth, or Northampton.

Boarding schools for girls of the upper and upper-middle classes had sprung up early in the seventeenth century as the successors to the pre-Reformation nunneries in which girls of that social level had been educated. When prospering and socially ambitious tradesmen began to send their daughters to them, the educational value of these schools declined. Since nothing was expected of them beyond providing superficial instruction in the "fashionable accomplishments, most eighteenth-century female academies were useless in any cultural sense.[37] The mistresses were ignorant and often shadowed by their past. But by spreading literacy among the women of a class which had previously been indifferent to female education, even these schools helped increase the eighteenth-century reading public. As more and more women were relieved of domestic chores, they had time on their hands; and as certain other customary means of occupying it, needlework for instance, were no longer regarded as quite genteel, they were forced to fight ennui with books.

Down to almost the middle of the century, however, there was comparatively little for the literate but uneducated woman to read. Old-fashioned romances like *The Grand Cyrus* and *Astraea*, however lengthy, could not solace her indefinitely, and when she finished them she had nothing further to occupy her unless (improbably) she could force a taste for the sort of books Addison noted (in *Spectator* 37) on Leonora's shelves—Culpepper's *Midwifery*, Newton's works, *The Countess of Pembroke's Arcadia*, and Locke on human understanding. The time was ripe for a Richardson, and when *Pamela* appeared (1740–41) its success and that of the novels that followed it revealed the extent of the female audience which for several decades had been waiting for something to read. From that time onward, as the mounting flood of sentimental novels attests, women played an important part in the history of the English reading audience.

What other factors stimulated the taste for reading in the eighteenth century? For one thing, there was the steadily growing need for information and guidance in everyday affairs. As the middle class acquired ever greater economic importance and civic respon-

[37] On this subject, see Gardiner, chaps. xv–xviii.

sibility, and as the body of practical knowledge grew under the influence of the Enlightenment, books of utility were more important in ordinary life than they had been even a century earlier. The London merchant needed to keep up with developing possibilities in foreign markets and new trade products; the country squire had to have his lawbooks; the prosperous farmer had to know the latest developments in agriculture and stock-breeding. To what extent this practical necessity stimulated the habit of reading for pleasure cannot of course be decided. But at the very least it kept men's literacy in good repair and accustomed them to the everyday presence of books.

The contribution of Addison and Steele to eighteenth-century interest in reading is so well known as scarcely to need retelling here. Addison achieved his announced purpose (*Spectator* 10) of "bringing philosophy out of closets and libraries, schools and colleges, to dwell in clubs and assemblies, at tea-tables and in coffee-houses"— in a word, he performed the worthy but too often undervalued role of popularizer. He and Steele possessed a combination of qualities which, in retrospect, were exactly calculated to win the middle class to reading: a tolerant humor beneath which rested moral principles as solid as any citizen could wish; a learning that never smelled of the lamp; a relish for life that was never tinged with Restoration profligacy; a prose style that was simple yet never condescending. The essays of the *Spectator* and the *Tatler* were made to order both for the man to whom the other reading matter of the age seemed either forbiddingly profane or portentously dull and for him who simply had never been accustomed to read.

The early periodical essay enlarged the specifically literary interest of the middle-class public. Addison and Steele eased into their discourses brief, agreeable passages on polite literature and its pleasures and rewards. The thousands who read the *Spectator* as it was first issued, and the thousands more who knew it in its many collected editions, were thus encouraged to read more extensively and profitably than before. The way cleared, literary material now entered the other periodicals that appeared during the century. Long before 1750, newspapers began to print general essays, often discussing books and authors; and in 1757 the *London Chronicle*, probably on Dr. Johnson's suggestion, started to review books, so that the man who looked at a paper in the first instance for the advertisements and "intelligence" found himself being brought up to date on current publications as well. Magazines performed the same function, especially as the volume of purely political discussion which had filled their columns during the early years of Walpole's administration subsided. In the late thirties literary essays and criticisms began to appear in the *Gentleman's Magazine*, and by the fifties notices of current books were a regular feature of the magazine.[38] Thus interest in books was more widely diffused than ever before; newspapers, magazines, and reviews brought literary topics to the attention of tens of thousands whose fathers had been indifferent to such matters.

Individual magazines and reviews did not have large editions. For example, in 1746, when the population of England was perhaps six or seven million, the *Gentleman's Magazine* had a circulation of 3,000.[39] The great influence these periodicals had upon the eighteenth-century reading habit was due not to large circulations but to the increase in the number of individual magazines and reviews and to their presence in the coffeehouses, where they found most of their readers. The number of coffee-drinkers who pored over a single copy of the *Gentleman's Magazine* or the *Critical Review* in the course of a month ran into many scores.

The large figures formerly given for the *Spectator* (14,000 according to some authorities, 20,000 according to at least one) are now discredited; the print order probably was nearer 3,000 or 4,000 an issue.[40] Among the newspapers published in 1704, the *London Gazette* printed 6,000 an issue and the others considerably fewer; Defoe's *Review* had an edition of but 400. It has been calculated

[38] C. Lennart Carlson, *The First Magazine: A History of "The Gentleman's Magazine"* (Providence, R.I., 1938), pp. 126, 137, 149–50.

[39] *Ibid.*, p. 62. The figure of 3,000, given by the editor himself, perhaps is nearer the truth than Dr. Johnson's statement that the magazine's circulation went as high as 10,000 at mid-century (Boswell, *Life of Johnson* [Hill-Powell ed.], III, 322). Johnson may, however, have been referring to the *total* sale, which often included several reprinted editions. In 1769 Boswell recorded in his journal that the *London Magazine* circulated 4,000 (*Boswell in Search of a Wife*, ed. Frank Brady and Frederick A. Pottle [New York, 1956], p. 289). Sir Richard Phillips alleged that "for many years previously to 1790" the *Town and Country Magazine* sold 15,000 copies a month, and the *Lady's Magazine* 16,000 (Sydney, *England and the English in the Eighteenth Century*, II, 137). But compare the much lower circulation figures for several leading periodicals at the very end of the eighteenth century, given in Appendix C.

[40] Donald F. Bond, "The First Printing of *The Spectator*," *Modern Philology*, XLVII (1950), 166–67. In this article reference is made to previous higher estimates of the paper's circulation.

that in that year 7,600 copies of newspapers were printed on Monday, 8,400 on Tuesday, 2,600 on Wednesday, 14,000 on Thursday, 1,600 on Friday, and 9,600 on Saturday—an average daily sale of 7,300.[41]

Newspaper circulation grew steadily throughout the century. By 1780 the annual sale of newspaper stamps (14,100,000) was almost double what it had been in 1753, and at the time of Britain's entry into war with France (1793) it was 17,000,000.[42] The reason again was not that individual papers had larger sales but rather that many more papers were being issued. In 1768, the *Public Advertiser*'s average was 2,800 or 2,900 daily, and even when it was making journalistic history by printing the letters of Junius (1769–71) its average circulation was no more than 3,400. At the very end of the century, in the midst of sensations that far eclipsed even the Junius controversy, the *Times* circulated 4,700 or 4,800 per issue.[43]

Newspapers were common only in the larger towns. Though some were issued in the provinces, their circulation and influence were limited. A few London papers were sent into the country, increasingly so as the appetite for news grew under the stress of events, and these passed from hand to hand. The ordinary man outside London, nevertheless, was not a newspaper reader. The newspaper was still far from being the indispensable adjunct to everyday life it later became. The few columns of news it contained were almost swallowed by advertisements. As an instrument of free public opinion it was impotent, for every paper was on the payroll either of the government or of the opposition.

Because of the stamp duty, newspapers were priced beyond the reach of most would-be buyers. The original duty (1712) was a penny on every whole sheet. Increases in 1776, 1789, and 1797 brought the tax to $3\frac{1}{2}d.$, so that by the end of the century the price of newspapers was a forbidding 6d.[44] Since the papers were to be seen in coffeehouses, however, they, like the magazines, were of great service in expanding interest in the printed word. They were

[41] Sutherland, "The Circulation of Newspapers and Literary Periodicals, 1700–1730," p. 111.

[42] Timperley, *Encyclopaedia of Literary and Typographical Anecdote*, p. 806.

[43] Smith, "The Newspaper," pp. 332–33.

[44] *Ibid.*, pp. 362–64. For a convenient summary of the taxes laid upon newspapers, advertisements, and pamphlets, 1712–1815, see Aspinall, *Politics and the Press*, p. 16.

read by many persons who had neither the time nor the endurance to read a whole book but who found casual interest in the news, the advertisements, and the capsule literary material.

IV. Edmund Burke is reported to have estimated that about 1790 the English reading public included some 80,000 persons.[45] All that can be said of his guess is that it is interesting. To judge from the size of editions and the relative infrequency with which new editions of a popular book were called for, the book-*buying* audience in eighteenth-century England was very small. The most famous instance of "best-sellerism," apart from the sales of pamphlets with sensational immediate interest, was the reception given to the novels of the period 1740–53. How large, then, was the buyers' market for newly published books of great appeal?

The population of England in 1750, as has been said, was between six and seven million. *Pamela* (1740) sold five editions (size unknown) in a year, *Joseph Andrews* (1742) three editions, totaling 6,500 copies, in thirteen months. *Roderick Random* (1748) circulated 5,000 in the first year. The second printing of *Clarissa Harlowe* (1749), 3,000 copies, lasted about two years. In three years Smollett's translation of *Gil Blas* (1748) went through three editions totaling 6,000 copies. Fielding's *Amelia* (1751) sold out its first edition of 5,000 copies in a week or less—an amazing performance which Dr. Johnson improved somewhat when he told Mrs. Piozzi that it was "perhaps the only book, which being printed off betimes one morning, a new edition was called for before night"— but the second edition lasted indefinitely. The first edition of *Sir Charles Grandison* (1753) was 4,000 copies; the third, called for within four months, amounted to 2,500.[46]

---

[45] Preface to the first volume of the *Penny Magazine* (1832). Efforts to locate the statement in Burke's own writings or speeches have been fruitless.

[46] Figures for *Pamela, Clarissa Harlowe,* and *Sir Charles Grandison* are from Alan D. McKillop, *Samuel Richardson, Printer and Novelist* (Chapel Hill, 1936), pp. 43, 154, 215 n.; for *Joseph Andrews* and *Amelia,* from Wilbur L. Cross, *The History of Henry Fielding* (New Haven, 1918), I, 316, 352, 355; II, 304; for *Roderick Random* and *Gil Blas,* from Lewis M. Knapp, "Smollett's Works as Printed by William Strahan," *Library,* Ser. 4, XIII (1932), 284–85. Most of the figures in this passage are well authenticated, something which cannot be said for many of the sales and circulation figures that will occur in other parts of this book. It is probably advisable at this point to emphasize that data on book and periodical sales have to be gathered from a wide variety of sources, whose reliability is in many cases dubious. Whether or not they are literally true, however, they are interesting

Thus single editions of the novels of Richardson, Fielding, and Smollett seldom exceeded 4,000 copies, and four or five editions, totaling less than 9,000 copies, were all the market could absorb of even the most talked-of novel in a single year. The novel-reading audience expanded steadily in the wake of the first masters, but its growth was reflected by the proliferation of individual novels and the increased patronage of the circulating libraries rather than by any increase in the sales of specific titles. The second edition of Smollett's *Count Fathom* (1771) was 1,000 copies.[47] Only when an author's star was in the ascendant did a publisher venture to order 2,000 copies in a first edition, as was the case with Fanny Burney's *Cecilia*. The usual first printing of a novel at this time, Fanny's sister was told, was 500.[48] The first printing for a work of non-fiction normally ranged from 500 to 1,000 or at the most 2,000. Johnson's *Dictionary* had an edition of 2,000, *Rasselas* 1,500, and the collected *Rambler* 1,250. (Ten editions of the *Rambler*, all of the same size, were sold between 1750 and 1784.) In 1776–77 the three editions of Gibbon's *Decline and Fall* (Volume I) that were required in fourteen months totaled 3,500 copies.[49]

If we are to believe the group of London booksellers who addressed a "humble representation" to Parliament in 1774, an ordinary edition of a work of standard literature lasted for years, even a lifetime. After its initial popularity had worn off, a 12mo edition of a novel like *Clarissa, Pamela, Grandison*, or *Tom Jones* might remain in stock for four to six years. Johnson's folio *Dictionary* lasted eight years, the octavo edition half as long; unsold copies of various editions of Shakespeare gathered dust for periods ranging from six to forty-eight years. Two separate editions of *The Faerie Queene* lasted sixteen and eighteen years.[50]

---

as approximations, suggesting the order of magnitude in which various epochs thought. No attempt usually is made in the text to indicate the author's own evaluation of the figures given, but all such data are duly documented for the reader's convenience. See further the prefatory comments to Appendixes B and C.

[47] Knapp, p. 288.

[48] Fanny Burney, *Early Diary*, ed. A. R. Ellis (1907), II, 307.

[49] R. A. Austen Leigh, "William Strahan and His Ledgers," *Library*, Ser. 4, III (1923), 280, 283–84; Collins, *Authorship in the Days of Johnson*, pp. 254–55. On pp. 250–55 Collins collects other sales figures for the period.

[50] *Publishers' Circular*, August 1, 15, 1889, pp. 884–85, 938–39. The pamphlet upon which this two-part article is based is an important document for eighteenth-century book-trade economics.

In this document, the London publishers were trying to prove that current prices were as reasonable as anyone could expect. Since, they argued, turnover was slow even at such prices, they could not possibly issue still cheaper editions to compete with the Edinburgh publishers who were doing just that. The question is: Were books really cheap in this period?

Down to about 1780, book prices were fairly constant. Full-length quartos and folios sold at between 10s. and 12s.; octavos were 5s. or 6s. Books in small octavo or 12mo—essays and novels, for instance—were 2s., 2s.6d., or 3s. The first four volumes of *Tristram Shandy* cost 2s.6d. each, the last five, 2s. During the seventies novels were issued in three forms: bound at 3s. per volume, in paper wrappers at 2s.6d., and in sheets for country libraries at 2s. Pamphlets of less than fifty pages were 6d., but if longer, 1s. or 1s.6d.[51]

General commodity prices and wages rose during the century, but so slowly that one can make approximate generalizations for the whole period before 1790. Shopmen out of their apprenticeship earned from 4s. to 16s. a week, plus board; the average wage was around 8s. Clerks in merchants' offices earned about £1 a week. Ushers in schools received 4s. to 8s. a week and board, London journeymen from 15s. to 20s. In the country, wages varied, as always, with the region, but they were uniformly below those prevailing in London. Craftworkers earned 10s. or 12s. a week in the west and north, only 6s.6d. in the east.[52]

Books, therefore, except for pirated works and, especially after 1774, reprints of standard authors, could seldom be purchased except by the relatively well-to-do. If a man in the lower bracket of the white-neckcloth class—an usher at a school, for instance, or a merchant's clerk—had a taste for owning books, he would have had to choose between buying a newly published quarto volume and a good pair of breeches (each cost from 10s. to 12s.), or between a volume of essays and a month's supply of tea and sugar

[51] See the *Publishers' Circular* as just cited for prices of scores of titles; also Plant, *The English Book Trade*, p. 245; Chapman, "Authors and Booksellers," pp. 318–19; J. M. S. Tompkins, *The Popular Novel in England, 1770–1800* (1932), pp. 10–12; and Sutherland, *A Preface to Eighteenth Century Poetry*, p. 46.

[52] Wages and commodity prices in this passage are from Cole and Postgate, *The Common People*, pp. 71–84, and Elizabeth W. Gilboy, *Wages in Eighteenth Century England* (Cambridge, Mass., 1934), *passim*.

for his family of six (*2s.6d.*). If a man bought a shilling pamphlet he sacrificed a month's supply of candles. A woman in one of the London trades during the 1770's could have bought a three-volume novel in paper covers only with the proceeds of a week's work. To purchase the *Spectator* in a dozen little 12mo volumes (16*s.*) would have cost an Oxfordshire carpenter eight days' toil; to acquire the 1743 version of the *Dunciad* at 7*s.6d.* would have taken almost a full two weeks' salary of a ten-pound-a-year school usher.

If the prices of new books were high before 1780, they were prohibitive afterward to all but the rich. Quartos jumped from 10*s.* or 12*s.* to a guinea; Boswell's *Life of Johnson*, for instance, cost £2 2*s.* the two-volume set. Octavos likewise doubled in price, and 12mos rose from 3*s.* to 4*s.*[53] Publishers generally preferred to issue sumptuous books in small editions, at high prices, rather than to produce more modest volumes in larger quantity. Benjamin Franklin was only one of many who complained of the practice: so lavish was the use of white space between lines, wide margins, and other wasteful devices that to him "the selling of paper seems now [1785] the object, and printing on it only the pretence."[54] The *Gentleman's Magazine* in 1794 remarked, "Science [i.e., learning in general] now seldom makes her appearance without the expensive foppery of gilding, lettering, and unnecessary engravings, hot pressing and an extent of margin as extravagant as a court lady's train. The inferior orders of society can scarce get a sight of her. . . ."[55] Ironically, as a climax to a century that prided itself on its unprecedented diffusion of learning, newly published books were priced completely out of the ordinary man's reach. Books of older authors, for a reason we shall come to in a moment, were somewhat cheaper.

Down to 1774, the prosperity of the pirates is the best evidence we have that the demand for books was greater than the supply provided by the regular booksellers. Defoe's *Jure divino*, for instance, originally issued in folio at 10*s.*, soon reappeared in an

---

[53] [Charles Knight?], "The Market of Literature," p. 4. The figures given in this article for book prices and the size of editions in various epochs have been closely substantiated by modern research.

[54] Franklin to Benjamin Vaughan, April 21, 1785; *Writings of Benjamin Franklin*, ed. A. H. Smyth (New York, 1906), IX, 305.

[55] *Gentleman's Magazine*, LXIV (1794), 47.

unauthorized octavo at 5*s*., which in turn was undercut by a chap-book at 6*d*. In 1729 the 6*s*.6*d*. quarto of the *Dunciad variorum* was pirated at 2*s*.[56] There were innumerable other examples of such practices—the bibliographies of eighteenth-century authors are full of unauthorized Irish and Scottish reprints—and to some extent it satisfied the poor man's hunger for books. But it was always a risky business, enlivened by litigation, and the supply of cheapened books could never be relied upon.

The pirates justified themselves by asserting that the regular booksellers were attempting to enforce a concept of copyright that had sanction neither in morality nor in law. Since Elizabethan times it had been a working fiction in common law, never reduced to formal statute, that a copyright could remain the property of a bookseller in perpetuity. The Copyright Act of 1709, however, limited copyright in books already published to twenty-one years, and in future books to a maximum of twenty-eight. When rival publishers issued editions of works whose copyright had expired under this act, the owners nevertheless sought, and usually obtained, restraining injunctions. Once a work was in copyright, the courts said, it remained so forever, the Act of 1709 notwithstanding. Thus protected, the copyright holders could charge as much as the market would stand.

Repeated injunctions, however, failed to discourage the pirates, a sure sign that their business paid despite the expense of constant lawsuits. By mid-century the pirates in Scotland, where there was an insistent demand for cheap books and, thanks to low labor costs, easy means of fulfilling it, became especially troublesome to the organized London trade. Among the chief offenders was Alexander Donaldson, the "bold Robin Hood" to whom Boswell's uncle drank a genial health in 1763.[57] In 1774 Donaldson appealed to the House of Lords a Chancery decision forbidding him to publish or sell Thomson's *Seasons*, a book which, under the law, had moved into the public domain. In one of the most momentous decisions in book-trade history (*Donaldson* v. *Beckett*) the concept of perpetual copyright was finally killed; copyright, the Lords held, ended when the Act of 1709 said it did. Now, for the first time, any

---

[56] Sutherland, *A Preface to Eighteenth Century Poetry*, pp. 46–47.

[57] *Boswell's London Journal*, ed. Frederick A. Pottle (New York, 1950), pp. 312–13.

book whose copyright had expired could be reprinted as cheaply as a publisher was able, without fear of legal complications. The consequences to the mass reading public are almost incalculable.[58]

The first noteworthy result of the 1774 decision was the launching by John Bell, "the most resourceful and inventive bookseller of his generation,"[59] of the famous series of Poets of Great Britain Complete from Chaucer to Churchill (109 volumes, 1776–92?) at 1s.6d. a volume, and Bell's British Theatre (21 volumes, 1776–78?) in 6d. weekly parts. Beginning in 1791, both of these series were reissued, along with Bell's Shakespeare (originally published in 1774), at 1s.6d. a volume, or 6d. on coarse paper. In the closing years of the century John Cooke issued his editions of the British poets, prose writers, and dramatists in 6d. weekly numbers, and John Harrison, who in the 1780's had had great success with his *Novelist's Magazine* (a "select library" of fiction, published in weekly parts), competed with his own series of British classics.[60]

These were the first memorable cheap reprint series. The delight with which they were received by impecunious booklovers is almost legendary. Cooke's editions especially won the affection of young students who could afford hardly more than a weekly sixpence for good reading. William Hone, John Clare, Henry Kirke White, Thomas Carter, Leigh Hunt, and William Hazlitt all left records of their purchases.[61] "How I loved those little sixpenny numbers containing whole poets!" Hunt exclaimed late in life. "I doated on their size; I doated on their type, on their ornaments, on their wrappers containing lists of other poets, and on the engravings from Kirk. I bought them over and over again, and used to get up select sets, which disappeared like buttered crumpets; for I could resist neither giving them away, nor possessing them. When the master tormented me, when I used to hate and loathe the sight of Homer, and Demosthenes, and Cicero, I would comfort

[58] This account of the death of perpetual copyright is derived chiefly from A. S. Collins, "Some Aspects of Copyright from 1700 to 1780," *Library*, Ser. 4, VII (1926), 67–81.

[59] Stanley Morison, *John Bell (1745–1831)* (Cambridge, 1930), p. 88. This is the standard source on Bell.

[60] On Harrison, see Thomas Rees and John Britton, *Reminiscences of Literary London from 1779 to 1853* (New York, 1896), pp. 21–23.

[61] F. W. Hackwood, *William Hone: His Life and Times* (1912), p. 47; J. W. and Anne Tibble, *John Clare: A Life* (New York, 1932), p. 175; *Remains of Henry Kirke White* (10th ed., 1823), I, 6; Carter, *Memoirs of a Working Man*, p. 97 n.

myself with thinking of the sixpence in my pocket, with which I should go out to Paternoster-row, when the school was over, and buy another number of an English poet."[62]

Hazlitt remembered Cooke's *Tom Jones* with particular affection: "I had hitherto read only in schoolbooks, and a tiresome ecclesiastical history (with the exception of Mrs. Radcliffe's *Romance of the Forest*): but this had a different relish with it,—'sweet in the mouth,' though not 'bitter in the belly.' . . . My heart had palpitated at the thoughts of a boarding-school ball, or gala-day at Midsummer or Christmas: but the world I had found out in Cooke's edition of the British Novelists was to me a dance through life, a perpetual gala-day."[63]

There is apparently no evidence of how large the Cooke, Bell, and Harrison editions were; but copies passed from hand to hand, making converts to good literature wherever they went, well down into the Victorian era. Almost a full century after they appeared, Augustine Birrell wrote: "You never see on a stall one of Cooke's books but it is soiled by honest usage, its odour . . . speaks of the thousand thumbs that have turned over its pages with delight. Cooke made an immense fortune, and deserved to do so. He believed both in genius and his country. He gave people cheap books, and they bought them gladly."[64]

These reprint series simply adapted to new conditions, with the immense advantage of having the whole public domain of literature to draw from, the old principle of number-publication. As early as 1692 Richard Bentley—"Novel Bentley" as the bookseller John Dunton called him, not foreseeing that there was to be a much more famous one in Victoria's reign—published a collection of fifty "modern novels" in serial form. In the 1720's another fiction series, the *Monthly Amusement*, offered a novel complete in each shilling number.[65] These numbers, however, lacked the distinctive characteristic of their descendants in that each contained a complete work. As the century progressed, number-publishing

[62] *Autobiography* (New York, 1855), I, 91–92.

[63] *The Plain Speaker, Works*, ed. Howe, XII, 222–23.

[64] Augustine Birrell, "Books Old and New," *Essays about Men, Women, and Books* (New York, 1899), p. 143.

[65] John Carter, "The Typography of the Cheap Reprint Series," *Typography*, No. 7 (1938), p. 37.

tended more and more to slice large works into instalments at 6*d.* or 12*d.* each.[66]

History-on-the-instalment-plan had a special vogue in mid-century. What Hume took to be their "quackish air"[67] went unnoticed by the 10,000, or possibly 20,000, readers who bought the 6*d.* weekly numbers of Smollett's *History of England*. According to a story circulated long afterward, this startling sale was due in great part to the promotional scheme employed by the publishers, who tipped every parish clerk in the kingdom a half-crown to scatter their prospectuses in the pews.[68]

Favorite among the works selected for issue in this form were annotated and illustrated Bibles, histories of England and London, Foxe's *Book of Martyrs*, lives of Christ, and the writings of Flavius Josephus. Some of these were not especially light reading, but number-publications were probably bought quite as much for their pictures as for their text. The horrifying illustrations in the *Book of Martyrs* cost many an impressionable English child his sleep. Some number-publishers, like Alexander Hogg late in the century, were masters of the inflated title page, by which they guaranteed the wonders to come in subsequent instalments. "In announcing the embellishments of these publications, language failed; and the terms, 'beautiful,' 'elegant,' 'superb,' and even 'magnificent,' became too poor to express their extreme merit."[69] The number-men, indeed, were remarkable in their time for their command of tricks of the trade. When the sale of a certain work showed signs of falling off, they promptly renamed it and started it, refreshed, on a new career. However easygoing their business ethics, the number-publishers introduced reading matter into many homes which had

[66] By 1734 the custom was so widespread that it earned a blast from a writer in the *Grub Street Journal:* "You have Bayle's *Dictionary*, and Rapin's *History* from two places. The Bible can't escape, I bought, the other Day, three Pennyworth of the Gospel, made easy and familiar to Porters, Carmen, and Chimney-Sweepers. . . . What an Age of Wit and Learning is this! In which so many Persons in the lowest Stations of Life, are more intent upon cultivating their Minds, than upon feeding and cloathing their Bodies" (quoted in *Gentleman's Magazine*, IV [1734], 489).

[67] David Hume, *Letters*, ed. J. Y. T. Greig (Oxford, 1932), I, 359.

[68] This story, along with the figure of 20,000 weekly sales, seems not to have been traced before 1827, when it appeared in Goodhugh's *English Gentleman's Library Manual*. Smollett himself, in a letter written while the *History* was being issued in 6*d.* numbers, put its circulation at over 10,000 (Lewis M. Knapp, *Tobias Smollett: Doctor of Men and Manners* [Princeton, 1949], pp. 187, 192).

[69] Timperley, *Encyclopaedia of Literary and Typographical Anecdote*, p. 838.

never before had it. Among those who could already read, they stimulated the habit, and among those who could not, they provided incentive to do so. Looking back from the dawn of the true age of popular literature in the 1830's (and somewhat careless of his metaphors), Timperley, the encyclopedist of the English printing and publishing trade, observed: "However it may be customary to kick the ladder down when we find we no longer want it, these sort of publications must be confessed to have greatly contributed to lay the foundation of that literary taste and thirst for knowledge, which now pervades all classes."[70]

V. Except in London, Edinburgh, and a few other towns, there were no shops devoted exclusively to books. Many of the so-called booksellers of the period stocked books only as one of several lines. Some also handled "general stationery," as capacious a category as the American "notions." Others sold such goods as patent medicines: the famous children's publisher John Newbery, for instance, was the proprietor of that universal remedy, Dr. James's Powders. Hence, in all but the relatively few shops dedicated to books alone, the selection of reading matter was small and unattractive. Nor was the typical eighteenth-century bookseller interested in enlarging his trade. He was content merely to serve the customers who came to his door.

The great exception was Lackington, who, by cheerfully violating all the traditions of the trade, set an example of aggressive enterprise which was destined to benefit the common reader of future generations as well as of his own. The son of a journeyman shoemaker who drank himself to death, and himself an ex-shoemaker, random amorist, and converted Methodist, Lackington started a bookshop in London in 1774, with capital borrowed from a fund the Wesleyans maintained for such purposes. He bought up large quantities of books at the auctions where publishers periodically unloaded their slow-moving stock, and then, instead of sending half or three-quarters of his purchases to the trunk-makers, who used the paper for linings, and selling what remained at their full price, he offered all he acquired at half or even a quarter of the published price. This unheard-of and, to his colleagues, immoral procedure brought down on him the wrath of the trade; but this

[70] *Ibid.*

was more than compensated for by the business he did with the bargain-hunting public. Within a short time he was the most lavish buyer of remainders in London. At one time, he boasted, he had in stock 10,000 copies of Watts's *Psalms*, and an equal number of his *Hymns;* at a single afternoon's auction he bought £5,000 worth of books.

Lackington earned the increased hostility of the orthodox booksellers, and the further gratitude of readers, by cutting prices on new books, thus initiating the "underselling" practice that was to breed animosity in the trade for the next hundred years. These steps, as well as his dealing in secondhand books sent up from the country, resulted in well-deserved prosperity. In 1791 and 1792, he says in his engagingly candid memoirs, he had an annual turnover of 100,000 volumes and a profit of £4,000 and £5,000.[71]

Lackington's "Temple of the Muses" in Finsbury Square was one of the sights of London. A large block of houses had been turned into a shop, the whole surmounted by a dome and flagpole. Over the main entrance appeared the sign, whose proud claim no one evidently challenged, CHEAPEST BOOKSELLERS IN THE WORLD. Reportedly, the interior was so spacious that a coach-and-six could be driven clear around it. In the center was a counter behind which the clerks waited on the fine ladies and country gentlemen who clustered about. At one side, a staircase led to the "Lounging Rooms" and to a series of circular galleries under the dome. Around each of these galleries ran crowded shelves; the higher the shelves, the shabbier the bindings, and the lower the price.[72]

Nothing like the "Temple of the Muses," with its cut prices, its strict cash-and-carry policy, and its disdain of haggling, had ever been seen in the book world. Lackington's own statement may be colored by the self-satisfaction that informs all his writing, but it is probably not far from the truth: "Thousands . . . have been effectually prevented from purchasing (though anxious so to do) whose circumstances in life would not permit them to pay the full price, and thus were totally excluded from the advantage of improving their understandings, and enjoying a rational entertainment. And you may be assured, that it affords me the most pleasing satisfaction, independent of the emoluments which have

[71] All the foregoing material is from Lackington, *Memoirs*, pp. 220–39, 279, 285.
[72] Charles Knight, *Shadows of the Old Booksellers* (New York, 1927), pp. 251–52.

accrued to me from this plan, when I reflect what prodigious numbers in inferior or *reduced* situations of life, have been essentially benefited in consequence of being thus enabled to indulge their natural propensity for the acquisition of knowledge, on easy terms: nay, I could almost be vain enough to assert, that I have thereby been highly instrumental in diffusing that general desire for READING, now so prevalent among the inferior orders of society; which most certainly, though it may not prove equally instructive to all, keeps them from employing their time and money, if not to *bad*, at least to *less rational* purposes."[73]

Other haunts of the less-well-to-do reader in London were the stalls and barrows of the secondhand booksellers, who probably were quite numerous, though they have little place in the records of the trade. The German traveler Carl Philip Moritz, visiting London in 1782, wrote that from these "antiquarians" one could buy odd volumes of Shakespeare for as low as a penny or a halfpenny; he himself bought from one such dealer the two volumes of *The Vicar of Wakefield* for 6d.[74] The bookishly inclined resorted to these tiny oases of literature no more to buy than to read on the spot, standing up, at no expense to themselves but frequently to the annoyance of the vendor. Stall-readers probably haunted Westminster in Caxton's time; and according to Macaulay, they crowded St. Paul's Churchyard, day after day, toward the end of the seventeenth century.[75]

It was these impecunious booklovers who were in some degree responsible for the development of the circulating library, the principal means by which the eighteenth-century reader circumvented the high purchase price of books. As early as 1661 the bookseller Francis Kirkman advertised that his books were "to be sold, or read for reasonable considerations."[76] Not until after the first quarter of the eighteenth century, however, did a systematic scheme of book-lending appear. The first real circulating library in Britain seems to have been that of Allan Ramsay, the poet and ex-wigmaker of Edinburgh, who began to rent books from his shop in 1725. Within a very few years circulating libraries appeared at

[73] *Memoirs*, pp. 231–32.

[74] *Travels in England*, p. 44.

[75] *History of England*, ed. Charles H. Firth (1913), I, 384.

[76] Quoted in Taylor, *Early Opposition to the English Novel*, p. 24.

some of the spas, where books were ideal to relieve the boredom of taking the waters.

There was none in London in 1725, when Benjamin Franklin, lodging in Little Britain, arranged with a neighboring bookseller to be allowed to borrow from the shop's stock upon the payment of a certain fee.[77] The circulating library did not arrive in the capital until the early 1740's. At that time Rev. Samuel Fancourt conducted one for the special use of the learned professions, particularly the nonconformist clergy; a fact which, in the light of the later clerical attitude toward circulating libraries, is not without its humor. A more popular brand of reading matter seems to have been dispensed in the two other libraries of which a hint survives from about 1741, Thomas Wright's and Samuel Bathoe's, both in the neighborhood of the Strand.[78]

From these beginnings, the practice of lending books on a subscription basis developed into two quite separate kinds of libraries during the remainder of the century. Fancourt's library, for the serious student, was imitated—at least so far as the nature of books offered was concerned—by the non-profit proprietary libraries. These were either separate institutions or collections attached to the "literary and philosophical societies" that sprang up in the larger towns during the second half of the century, and they were important agencies for the extension of learning among the better-educated portion of the middle and upper classes. A typical proprietary library was the one founded at Liverpool in 1758 by the members of two reading clubs that met at the Merchant's Coffee House and the Talbot Inn. The collection grew to over 8,000 volumes by 1801, and eighty years later it had between 70,000 and 80,000 volumes. A similar library at Leeds boasted 4,500 volumes in 1790; a third at Birmingham had 3,400 at the same period. The minor place "light reading" occupied in these collections is suggested by the 1785 catalogue of the Leeds Library, in which such works occupy only four and a half pages out of ninety.

[77] Benjamin Franklin, *Autobiography*, ed. Max Farrand (Berkeley, Calif., 1949), pp. 53–54.

[78] Many articles have been written on the early history of the circulating library. The present account relies on the two latest and fullest scholarly studies, McKillop, "English Circulating Libraries, 1725–50," and Hamlyn, "Eighteenth-Century Circulating Libraries in England," both of which are based on contemporary documents.

The social exclusiveness of these libraries, enforced by the fees they charged, prevented their ever being of use to the wider reading audience. At Liverpool the entrance fee, which was a guinea and a half in 1770, was increased to five guineas in 1784; at Leeds, it was a guinea in 1768, three guineas in 1786, and twenty in 1822. In addition, members had to pay annual subscriptions, which in the eighteenth century were only a few shillings but which grew to as much as a guinea early in the nineteenth century.[79]

But as interest in serious reading spread to the lower-middle class, they adapted the proprietary-library principle to their own needs. Book clubs were numerous in the last decades of the century. In some, the members clubbed together to buy certain books which, after they had been read by all who cared to, were then sold and a new assortment bought with the proceeds. In others, the idea was to build up a permanent rather than a rotating collection. In Lewes, Sussex, for example, a group of some sixty subscribers managed to amass a library of about 1,000 volumes between 1786 and 1794.[80]

These little societies flourished for at least the next half-century, especially in the country and in Scotland. Burns was connected with the "Monkland Friendly Society" at Ellisland, which was established by the tenants and farmer neighbors of his friend Captain Riddell. The entrance fee was 5s., and at every monthly meeting 6d. was levied from each member. In Burns's time the collection amounted to 150 volumes.[81]

But far more important to the growth of the mass reading audience were the commercial libraries that dispensed fiction and other "light literature." While it may have been only a coincidence that a few obscure book and pamphlet vendors were experimenting with the lending of their wares at the very time of the *Pamela* craze, the circulating library was destined shortly to complete the triangle whose other legs were the expanded middle-class audience and the new fascination of the novel. As the fiction-reading habit spread, circulating libraries sprang up in London, the watering

---

[79] Beckwith, "The Eighteenth-Century Proprietary Library in England," *passim;* Peter Cowell, "The Origin and History of Some Liverpool Libraries," *Transactions and Proceedings of the Library Association* (1886 for 1883), pp. 32–33.

[80] *Gentleman's Magazine*, LXIV (1794), 47.

[81] Franklyn B. Snyder, *Life of Robert Burns* (New York, 1932), pp. 324–25.

places, the provincial towns, and even in small villages. By 1791 William Lane, whose Minerva Press was a byword for sensational and violently sentimental novels, was advertising "complete CIRCULATING LIBRARIES, . . . from One Hundred to Ten Thousand Volumes" for sale to grocers, tobacconists, picture-framers, haberdashers, and hatters eager for a profitable side line. Lane's own Minerva Library, begun in 1770, was as famous and prosperous in its sphere as Lackington's Temple of the Muses was in another. In 1790 it offered 10,000 volumes for loan: "Works" (as a prospectus issued eight years later put it) "of Genius and Taste, both ancient and modern, whether History, Biography, Philosophy, Voyages, Travels, Poetry, &c., &c. . . . Also [and actually most important] for Pleasure and Amusement, every Novel, Romance, Tale, and Adventure in the English Language, together with all Dramatic Publications."[82]

Lane's annual subscription fee of a guinea in 1798 was the highest rate of the century, the result no doubt of the increased price of books. In the 1740's the subscription in London libraries had ranged from 15s. to a guinea; later it had fallen to 10s.6d. or 12s. and then risen again to 16s. and above. In Bath, where there seems to have been a price-fixing agreement, the fee was 10s.6d. down to 1789, when it was raised to 15s. Non-subscribers could borrow a library's books at a flat fee per volume, depending in some cases upon its format—a shilling for a folio, 6d. for a quarto, and so on.[83]

Though these fees were by no means low, considering the purchasing power of the shilling during the period, at least the renting of books was less expensive than outright purchase. Thus the libraries made books available to a much wider audience. From how far down in the social scale they drew their customers, it is difficult to say. If we are to believe the constant burden of contemporary satire, domestic servants attended in great numbers on their own account, not merely to exchange books for their mistresses; but it is possible that they were singled out for blame because the effects of novel-reading were most irritating when errands went unfulfilled, a roast burned on the spit, or an imperiously pulled bell rope went unanswered.

It was the circulating libraries' chief stock in trade, the ordinary

[82] Blakey, *The Minerva Press*, p. 114.
[83] *Ibid.*, p. 116; Hamlyn, pp. 209-12.

novel, that, more than any other form of literature, helped democratize reading in the eighteenth century. The common reader has always relished a good story, and nowhere has the taste been more pronounced than on the very fringes of the literate public, to which no other form of reading has an equal appeal. Small shopkeepers, artisans, and domestic servants—people who had gone to school for only two or three years—at the beginning of the century had devoured *Robinson Crusoe* and the narratives that imitated it, notably *The Adventures of Philip Quarll*. But the *Crusoe-Quarll* sort of fiction was far from satisfying the appetite of this audience, and not until the full development of the popular novel in the wake of Richardson and Fielding did the relatively uncultivated reader have an abundant supply of books to his taste. Then, when the writing and sale of fiction became the occupation of hacks and booksellers who cultivated a shrewd awareness of the special interests and limitations of their semi-educated audience, the novel became the favorite fare of the common reader, a distinction it has had ever since.

When novels became easily available through circulating libraries, their popularity (and, by association, that of the libraries themselves) touched off the first widespread discussion of the social effects of a democratized reading audience. The tone had been well anticipated by the abuse heaped upon the first circulating library on record. When Allan Ramsay began to lend books in Edinburgh, a writer raged: ". . . this profannes is come to a great hight, all the villanous profane and obscene books and playes . . . are gote doun from London by Allen Ramsay, and lent out, for an easy price, to young boyes, servant weemin of the better sort, and gentlemen, and vice and obscenity dreadfully propagated. Ramsay has a book in his shope wherein all the names of those that borrou his playes and books, for two pence a night, or some such rate, are sett doun; and by these, wickedness of all kinds are dreadfully propagat among the youth of all sorts."[84] The rush to the libraries after mid-century provoked a great quantity of antifiction, antilibrary diatribe, which differed from this early blast only in the

[84] Robert Wodrow, *Analecta* (Edinburgh, 1842–43), III, 515–16. The authorities winked at this alleged propagation of "all abominations, and profaness, and leudness" until they inspected Ramsay's book of borrowers, whereupon they determined to raid his shop. But "he had nottice an hour before, and had withdrauen a great many of the worst [books], and nothing was done to purpose."

number of variations played upon a single theme.[85] All who opposed the spread of literacy among the common people found their
worst fears realized. Here, they said, was proof enough of what
happened when people who had no business reading—women and
domestic servants in particular—turned to books: they cultivated
habits of idleness and lost themselves in unwholesome, overheated
dreams. Sir Anthony Absolute summed up conservative opinion
when he fumed: "A circulating library in a town is as an evergreen tree of diabolical knowledge! It blossoms through the year!
—and depend on it, Mrs. Malaprop, that they who are so fond of
handling the leaves, will long for the fruit at last."[86]

In the latter half of the century the appearance of hundreds of
trashy novels every year and the establishment of ever more libraries to distribute their "poison" among the populace greatly
strengthened opposition to the spread of education. From the
prevalent climate of social opinion sprang the fatalistic conviction
that the inferior orders, simply because they *were* inferior, intellectually as well as socially, would never be capable or desirous of
reading anything but the hair-raising, scandalous, or lachrymose
tales upon which they then battened. Every new reader would
automatically and irreparably become a victim of circulating-library fiction. So it was futile, indeed dangerous, to promote the
extension of literacy.

Some groups, it is true, did not go that far. The Methodists
and Evangelicals, while yielding to no one in their detestation of
current fiction, felt that the intelligent course was not to deprive
people of literacy but to make sure that they used their gift for
the right purposes. In more than one of the chapters that follow
we shall observe the ambiguous effects of their campaign to endow
the masses with a strictly moral brand of literacy.

Among pessimists and optimists alike sprang up a rigid, ineffaceable association of the mass reading public with low-grade
fiction. This was to have far-reaching consequences during the
nineteenth century, for out of it grew the whole vexatious "fiction
question." The eighteenth-century moralists who pressed the issue

---

[85] Taylor, *Early Opposition to the English Novel*, chap. ii, collects thirty pages of excerpts
from contemporary attacks. See also W. F. Gallaway, Jr., "The Conservative Attitude
toward Fiction, 1770–1830," *PMLA*, LV (1940), 1041–59.

[86] Sheridan, *The Rivals*, Act I.

were on fairly secure ground so long as their opposition stemmed from a sincere disapproval of current circulating-library fare, which was at best innocuous but oftener frivolous and even licentious. But what happened, more often than not, was that opposition to fiction on religious and moral principles became a convenient stalking-horse for other motives which it was becoming less politic to avow. This tendency was already marked in the eighteenth century; people who, for social or economic reasons, opposed the expansion of the reading public found it handy to conceal their true purposes by harping on the common reader's notorious preference for the novel. The popular reading audience owed its birth in large part to the novel, but, as things turned out, it could hardly have been unluckier in its parentage.[87]

And now to cast a quick glance backward over the century. What progress, taking all in all, had the taste for reading made? The low state of elementary education had prevented all but a few members of the common laboring class from joining the audience for printed matter. The class of tradesmen and artisans formed the dividing line, in this period, between the reading and the non-reading public. And it was in the region above them, the commercial middle class, that reading made its greatest gains. Reading was still concentrated in the cities and towns, where only a minority of the total English population lived; in the country the literacy rate was lower than in the city, and reading matter was much more scarce.

The popularity of circulating libraries and coffeehouses during the century was a sign that more reading was being done than the bare sales figures for books and periodicals would suggest. Most reading matter was too expensive to buy outright; the ordinary booklover could build his own collection only slowly, by shrewd dealings with secondhand vendors. But the coming of cheap reprint series toward the end of the century, along with Lackington's impetus to the cheap remainder trade, seemed to promise better days ahead.

Most important of all was the emergence of the reading public

---

[87] After this book was completed, the author was enabled, through the courtesy of Professor Ian Watt, to read the proofs of his *The Rise of the Novel* (1957), chap. ii of which, an excellent survey of the expansion of the eighteenth-century reading public, provides welcome substantiation of many of the points made in the present chapter.

as a social problem. The long-standing opposition to the spread of literacy was strengthened by the discovery that, when the common man and woman wanted something to read, they gravitated toward the circulating library. Until the 1790's, the growth of the reading public was viewed with an alarm originating largely in concern for the individual reader's personal morality and his ability, faced with the luxurious temptations of print, to give an honest day's work for a modest day's wage. But in the last decade of the century, as we shall now see, the figure of the common reader suddenly became a lowering threat to the nation's very security.

CHAPTER 3

The Time of Crisis
1791–1800

In 1780 Robert Raikes, the proprietor of the *Gloucester Journal*, was annoyed by the screams of urchins breaking the Sabbath beneath his window as he prepared the next day's edition. Suddenly the idea came to him of killing two birds with one stone. By starting Sunday schools for these ignorant children, he would guarantee the town's peace and at the same time give them a socially useful occupation on the one day when they were not at work.[1]

Sunday schools were not Raikes's invention. There had been a few scattered ones in England for at least ten years before. But Raikes, a man who swaggered through the streets of Gloucester with an unmistakable air of proprietorship, made them a national institution. Both through his own paper and through the *Gentleman's Magazine*, whose editor, John Nichols, allotted much space to the subject, Raikes energetically propagandized for Sunday schools. Five years later (1785), the national Sunday School Society was formed. Within two years 201 schools, having an enrolment of 10,232 children, were affiliated with it, and by 1797 there were 1,086 schools and 69,000 pupils.[2]

The atmosphere of the earliest Sunday schools smacked more of the correctional than of the educational institution. Interviewed in 1863, a Gloucester ancient recalled that "some turrible bad chaps went to school when I first went. . . . I know the parents of one or two of them used to walk them to school with 14-lb. weights tied to their legs . . . to keep them from running away. Sometimes

[1] The most recent biography of Raikes is Guy Kendall, *Robert Raikes: A Critical Study* (1939).

[2] Jones, *The Charity School Movement*, p. 153. Raikes's own boast that there were 250,000 Sunday scholars as early as 1787 (*ibid.*) may be dismissed as the hyperbole of a typical projector.

boys would be sent to school with logs of wood tied to their ankles, just as though they were wild jackasses, which I suppose they were, only worse." Another old man said that he "heard stories about the boys being 'strapped' all the way to school by their parents."[3] The interesting aspect of this is not the young ragamuffins' quite understandable reluctance to spend six or seven hours of their only free day learning the catechism and the lessons of diligence, sobriety, and humility, but the attitude of their parents. The popular hunger for education had revived since the days of the S.P.C.K. charity schools. The new conditions of industrial labor, as well as a faint sifting down to the working class of the age's reverence for intellectual enlightenment, put a premium on literacy. The Sunday-school movement would not have prospered as it did had there not been some enthusiasm for it on the part of the parents, who, after all, did not have to enter the classrooms themselves.

We must not overestimate the number of literates whom the Sunday schools produced; it is ingenuous to assume, as is often done, that since they were set up to teach poor children to read, they therefore did so. Even supposing that most of the pupils were abrim with eagerness (which was certainly not the case), no high degree of literacy can be imparted in once-a-week classes. Nevertheless, the Sunday schools did swell the total of the nation's literates, both directly and by sharpening popular interest in reading, so that there was considerable home study on the part of adults. Children who acquired some rudimentary skill in the art often shared it with their elders.

Many people, however, looked upon the Sunday-school movement with deep apprehension. The conservative opposition to education for the poor had lost none of its vigor. When Hannah More, converted from successful London dramatist to pious Evangelical, set up her little Sunday schools in the Mendip hills, she faced bitter antagonism from the local farmers. Unimpressed by her plea that by spreading literacy she meant simply to extend an appreciation

---

[3] J. Henry Harris, *Robert Raikes: The Man and His Work* (1895?), pp. 38, 40. This book contains vivid evidence of the unacademic atmosphere that pervaded the early Sunday schools. Much additional material can be found in the various reports of parliamentary inquiries into popular education, especially that of 1834; in Jones, *The Charity School Movement*, pp. 142–54, and Mathews, *Methodism and the Education of the People*, chap. ii.

of true Christian principles, above all an abiding sense of the divine intention that lay behind social rank, her neighbors observed sourly that the region "had never prospered since religion had been brought into it by the monks of Glastonbury."[4] Religion apart, to create a literate and therefore discontented peasantry was an act of national disservice. Hannah undoubtedly wrote from her own experience when, in her story "The Sunday School," Farmer Hoskins raged that "of all the foolish inventions, and new-fangled devices to ruin the country, that of teaching the poor to read is the very worst."[5]

Just as the Sunday-school movement became national in scope, the French Revolution broke out, and the reaction in England was immediate and feverish. The social and political discontent that had hung in uneasy suspension among certain reformist elements of the commercial and artisan classes since the days of Wilkes suddenly was crystallized. Some Englishmen had long cherished libertarian, equalitarian notions, but on the whole they had spent their energies in harmless talk. Now the French were taking violent action, and English radicals, watching the bloody spectacle unfold, applauded and awaited the day—it could not now be long put off—when the English people too should strike off their shackles.

On November 1, 1790, appeared Edmund Burke's *Reflections on the Revolution in France*, an eloquent statement of the conservatives' horror at what was happening in France and concern over what might well occur in England. It sold 30,000 copies and called forth at least thirty-eight replies from men representing every shade of liberal opinion, from the moderate constitutional reformer to the fire-eating republican.[6] Among these replies by all odds the most influential was Tom Paine's *The Rights of Man*. Part One of this masterpiece of radical propaganda was published on March 13, 1791, at 3s.—the same price charged for Burke's pamphlet and high enough, the onlooking Tories thought, to keep it out of the hands of people who had no business reading it. With-

[4] William Roberts, *Memoirs of the Life and Correspondence of Mrs. Hannah More* (2d ed., 1834), II, 206.

[5] More, *Works* (1853), I, 190.

[6] James Prior, *Memoir of the Life and Character of the Right Hon. Edmund Burke* (1824), pp. 364, 373.

in a few weeks, powerfully aided by the London Constitutional Society, which distributed it among "the lower orders," it had sold 50,000 copies.[7] Interest in what Paine had to say extended far beyond the confines of the class which could afford 3s. for a pamphlet. *The Rights of Man* was quoted at every meeting of the "corresponding" and "constitutional" societies that sprang up in every English town, and urgent appeals flowed in to Paine to make it available in cheaper form.[8]

Consequently, when Paine published the second part of *The Rights of Man*, in the spring of 1792, he issued it not only in the expensive form already adopted but in a 6d. edition as well; and he accompanied this with a similarly inexpensive reprint of the first part. In a month's time, over 32,000 copies of this edition were sold.[9] By the following year (1793), it was alleged that a total of 200,000 copies of *The Rights of Man* were in circulation.[10] In 1802 Paine wrote that "the number of copies circulated in England, Scotland and Ireland, besides translations into foreign languages, was between four and five hundred thousand," and at the time of his death seven years later, the total circulation of Part Two alone is said to have been nearly 1,500,000 copies.[11]

To gauge the impact of Paine's writings upon the English reading public one does not have to accept such figures as being even approximately accurate. In 1801 the total population of England, Scotland, and Wales was 10.5 million, and that of Ireland, where Paine had an immense following, was estimated four years later as being around 5.4 million. If the figure of 1,500,000 were true, it would mean that in the space of seventeen years there was roughly one copy of *The Rights of Man*, Part Two, for every ten people in the United Kingdom, men, women, and children.[12] But this is almost incredible. The figure of 200,000 for sales in the first two years is itself hard to believe. No single piece of nonce literature,

[7] Paine, *Complete Writings*, ed. Philip S. Foner (New York, 1945), I, xxviii.

[8] *Ibid.*, II, 486.   [9] *Ibid.*, II, 481.

[10] Moncure D. Conway, *Life of Thomas Paine* (New York, 1892), I, 346.

[11] Paine, I, 345; II, 910.

[12] Paine's earlier, American, best-seller, *Common Sense*, had sold one copy for every twenty-five people in the colonies. "Not since its time," says a recent historian of American popular reading, "has any book had such a quick or widespread sale relative to the population" (James D. Hart, *The Popular Book: A History of America's Literary Taste* [New York, 1950], p. 45).

so far as the few available records indicate, had ever approached such a circulation. At the beginning of the eighteenth century, Defoe's *True-Born Englishman*, a political verse-satire, had gone through nine regular editions in four years and had had a dozen pirated editions totaling 80,000 copies.[13] A few years later three different pamphlets associated with the Sacheverell controversy had sold between 40,000 and 60,000 apiece; and in 1776 Price's *Observations on the Nature of Civil Liberty* is said to have sold 60,000.[14] While such sales may have been equaled during other outbursts of public agitation during the century, it is not likely that they were greatly surpassed.

Yet, even if we make the most generous allowance for exaggeration, the circulation figures of *The Rights of Man* are impressive. And we are encouraged toward the suspension of disbelief by the abundant non-statistical records of how Paine's message made its way through a section of the public whose literacy, until now an almost unused talent, suddenly had been called into play. The "Jacobin" societies, composed of enthusiasts from the middle class and the ranks of the skilled workmen who sympathized with the ideals of the French Revolution, sent scores of thousands of copies broadcast through the nation. Some provincial groups arranged for editions by local printers. Radical bookshops, and barrows like the one the former Newcastle schoolmaster, Thomas Spence, set up at the head of Chancery Lane, attracted many workingmen. The prosecution of Paine for seditious libel, following the appearance of the second part of *The Rights of Man*, intensified popular enthusiasm for his work. A bookseller in Scotland, having sold one copy in a week, a fortnight later disposed of 750 copies.[15]

It is impossible to tell to what extent the circulation of *The Rights of Man* and the host of propaganda pieces that followed it permanently broadened the reading audience. Some men, certainly, retained the reading habit they had suddenly acquired. Francis Place, the radical tailor, recorded that the artisans who belonged

[13] James Sutherland, *Defoe* (1937), p. 68.

[14] Beljame, *Men of Letters and the English Public*, p. 309; Collins, *The Profession of Letters*, p. 21.

[15] Philip A. Brown, *The French Revolution in English History* (1918), pp. 71, 84. This volume gives a good account of the propaganda war led by Paine and its reverberations in the country. See also Walter F. Hall, *British Radicalism, 1791–97* (New York, 1912), and Webb, *The British Working Class Reader*, pp. 36–45.

to the inner circle of the London Corresponding Society did so. Their political activity, he wrote, "compelled them to think more correctly than they had been accustomed to do; it induced them to become readers of books, and the consequence . . . was that every one of them became a master, and permanently bettered his condition in life."[16] But these men belonged to the aristocracy of workers, and those who were less prosperous are not as likely to have kept on reading after the Jacobin fervor wore off. The day of cheap books and periodicals was still in the future, and when radical propaganda was swept from the bookstalls by government decree, little—apart from unexciting religious tracts—was left for the ordinary workman to read. He had become a reader for an occasion, and, when the occasion ceased, his interest in print died with it.

The major result of the surge of popular interest in reading during the 1790's, therefore, was not so much any permanent expansion of the reading audience as the reaction of the ruling class. Suddenly, in the supercharged atmosphere of a nation plunged, unprepared and bewildered, into a general war, the potentialities inherent in the press spread alarm among the people who prized above all the settled stability of the nation. The widespread belief that printed exhortations to "sedition" and "atheism" found their way into every calloused hand in the kingdom was nothing short of a nightmare. Compared with the threat of internal subversion, that of military invasion was small.

The obvious course for the government was to try to silence the press that spread the inflammatory alien doctrine of "natural rights." Hence the Royal Proclamation of May 21, 1792, just after the cheap edition of *The Rights of Man* appeared, against "divers wicked and seditious writings"; the frequent arrest and fining or jailing of radical booksellers; and the State Trials in 1794 of Hardy, Tooke, and Thelwall, three doughty disseminators of Jacobin literature.

But these were at best negative measures, and they had the disadvantage, among others, of advertising the very literature they were designed to wipe out. The heart of the crisis lay not in the circulation of radical propaganda, which could be, and was, effectively suppressed, but in the existence of crowds of readers, who

[16] Graham Wallas, *Life of Francis Place* (3d ed.; New York, 1919), p. 22 n.

after all could be deprived of their literacy by no device short of extermination.

To the horror of the well-intentioned people who had started thousands of Sunday schools, and to the sardonic satisfaction of those who had warned against such foolhardiness, the chickens hatched in the schools had come to roost wearing liberty caps. Whether or not the alumni of Sunday schools were especially numerous among Paine's followers, the blame was laid on Raikes's establishments simply because, apart from dame schools, they were at the time the best-known and most plentiful agencies of working-class education. Their teaching of reading, it seemed, had been disastrously successful; but the moral and social lessons that accompanied it had been wasted. Indeed, some Anglicans suspected that the dissenters, with whom they had been associated in the Sunday-school movement, did not preach the truth as wholeheartedly as they might, with the result that Sunday schools under non-Anglican control were looked upon as hotbeds of Jacobinism.[17] Nor did the epidemic suspicion of the period end there. Even Hannah More, the Evangelical, was condemned for her innocent attempts to instruct the poor; in her own words, she stood charged with "sedition, disaffection, and a general aim to corrupt the principles of the community"—surely one of history's most irresponsible accusations.[18]

It was too late, however, to turn back. And so the Evangelicals sought somehow to repair the damage they and others had inadvertently done by their failure to foresee the coming of Tom Paine. The ability to read having now turned out to be a two-edged weapon, it remained for the Evangelicals to restore it to the use they had originally had in mind. "When it was impossible to prevent our reading something," wrote Hazlitt twenty years later, "the fear of the progress of knowledge and a *Reading Public* . . . made the Church and State . . . anxious to provide us with that sort of food for our stomachs, which they thought best."[19]

At the urging of her Evangelical friends, Hannah More proposed

---

[17] Jones, *The Charity School Movement*, pp. 153–54.

[18] Roberts, III, 124. See also Jones, *Hannah More*, chap. viii, on the "Blagdon Controversy"—a pamphlet war which demonstrated the power and vehemence of the anti-Evangelical, anti-educational party.

[19] "What Is the People?" *Works*, ed. Howe, VII, 273.

to take over the whole of English popular literature for the greater
glory of God and the security of the nation. Belatedly, she and her
class became acutely alarmed by the fact that there was—and had
been for many years—a brisk traffic in unseemly reading matter
for the masses. Chapbooks, broadsides, and ballads, many of them
heartily vulgar if not actually licentious, had ridden in peddlers'
packs to country fairs and markets, and through the mired lanes
to the cottages of peasants and handicraftsmen. As the eighteenth
century wore on, more and more hole-in-the-wall printers had
sprung up in the country towns to supply these hawkers. So long
as only popular tales and songs had been in demand, the governing
class had not stirred itself. But when the same obscure printers
began to issue cheap editions of Paine's blasphemy, which the
peddlers carried cheek-by-jowl with the *Seven Champions of Chris-
tendom*, it was time to take notice. "Vulgar and indecent penny
books were always common," wrote Hannah, "but speculative
infidelity, brought down to the pockets and capacities of the poor,
forms a new æra in our history."[20]

As her early biographer explains in language that should be pre-
served: "The friends of insurrection, infidelity and vice, carried
their exertions so far as to load asses with their pernicious pamphlets and to get them dropped, not only in cottages, and in highways, but into mines and coal-pits. . . . When she considered the
multitudes whose sole reading was limited to these vicious performances; and that the temptation was obtruded upon them in
the streets, or invitingly hung out upon the wall, or from the window, she thought that the evil she wished to oppose was so exceedingly diffused, as to justify her in employing such remedial methods as were likely to become effectual, both by their simplicity and
brevity. . . . As the school of Paine had been labouring to undermine, not only religious establishments, but good government, by
the alluring vehicles of novels, stories, and songs, *she thought it
right to encounter them with their own weapons;* and having observed
that to bring dignities into contempt, and to render the clerical
character odious, was a favourite object with the enemy, her constant aim was to oppose it in the way she thought most likely to
produce effect."[21]

[20] Roberts, II, 458.   [21] *Ibid.*, II, 424–25 (italics supplied).

Hence the Cheap Repository Tracts, a long series of moral tales and ballads, over fifty of them from Hannah's own pen, which were designed frankly to drive "seditious" and "anti-Christian" literature from the face of England. With a shrewdness that was not uniformly evident in their operations, she and her co-workers designed the tracts to look like the pamphlets they were intended to supersede. "Decked out with rakish titles and woodcuts," they were "sent out, like sheep in wolves' clothing, to be sold by hawkers in competition with their 'old trash.' "[22] On March 3, 1795, three years after the cheap edition of *The Rights of Man* had appeared, the first batch of tracts and broadsides was made available to the hawkers, old professionals who already had a large and confiding clientele.

Thanks to contributions from members of the Clapham Sect and other well-wishers, it was possible to keep the price of the Cheap Repository Tracts down to the level already established for hawkers' wares. The retail price was $\frac{1}{2}d.$, $1d.$, or $1\frac{1}{2}d.$, and the chapmen could buy quantities at the discount to which they were accustomed— about twenty-five for $10d.$ Members of the gentry who enlisted as amateur chapmen also could buy job lots, though they got a smaller discount.[23]

There had never been anything like it in the history of English books. In the first six weeks (March 3–April 18, 1795) 300,000 copies of the various tracts were sold at wholesale; by July of the same year, the number had more than doubled; and by March, 1796, the total number sold reached the staggering figure of 2,000,000.[24] Two printing houses, Samuel Hazard's at Bath and John Marshall's in London, were kept working at capacity to supply the English demand alone. In response to suggestions from the gentry, who were themselves captivated by Hannah's mixture of entertainment and sound principles, a second printing, on good paper, was arranged for, to give to their own children and bind up for preservation.[25] Thus the tracts were found not only in the

---

[22] Spinney, "Cheap Repository Tracts," p. 295. Spinney's is the most detailed history of the whole venture. Hannah More's part in it may be traced through her letters printed in Roberts' *Memoirs*. See also the excellent account in Jones, *Hannah More*, pp. 132–50.

[23] Spinney, p. 303.

[24] *Ibid.*, pp. 301–302. The figure is given in the *Gentleman's Magazine*, LXVI (1796), 505, and in Hannah More's diary, September 22, 1798 (Roberts, *Memoirs*, III, 61).

[25] Spinney, p. 303.

chapman's pack but in regular bookshops; not only in cottages but in the houses of the wealthy.

The series closed officially in September, 1798. Those three and a half years had been momentous ones in the history of the English reading public. The astounding circulation figures for the tracts, along with those for the writings of Paine, had enabled the ruling class of England for the first time to grasp in concrete terms the size of the existing public. Every new reader in the lower ranks of society meant another potential victim of radical contagion. The immediate danger, to be sure, had receded. The common Englishman's revulsion at the slaughter in the French streets and his patriotic response to the Napoleonic peril probably would have smothered the fires of Jacobinism even if Pitt's agents and Hannah More's tract-bearers had never lifted a finger. But the specter of insurrection could not easily be forgotten. Jacobinism, though temporarily defeated, could rise again. Thus the problem remained: How could the people's reading be made safe? It was a question which was to occupy some of the best minds of England for the next half-century.

Their experience with the Cheap Repository Tracts encouraged the Evangelicals to believe they had found the right formula. If correct morality and sound religious and political doctrine were embedded in wholesomely entertaining tales and songs, humble readers would accept those principles, and the nation would be secure. Thus emerged the rationale, half religious, half political, which was to govern the vast program of tract distribution for a long time to come.

Equally important, it was through the publication of the Cheap Repository Tracts that influential middle-class Englishmen got their first experience in the mass production and distribution of reading matter. The Methodists had shown how it could be done on a smaller scale fifty years earlier, but, since they were dismissed as vulgar fanatics, their example had been wasted. The radical clubs, in turn, had borrowed leaves from the Methodists' book of procedure, and it was their success which had stirred the Evangelicals into action. The Evangelicals, careless of the ancestry of their methods so long as they worked, now felt they were equipped to initiate and carry through, in the years to come, mass publishing ventures as ambitious as that of the Repository Tracts. They had learned the technique of organization—how to form auxiliary societies all over Britain to raise funds and help distribute their tidings of social inequality. They had learned how to deal with outside agencies, with printers and booksellers and itinerant hawkers, and how to dress up their wares so as to compete with more worldly literature for the favor of the people.

Such lessons were to prove valuable for several decades, not only among religious denominations but among secular propagandist groups, notably the Society for the Diffusion of Useful Knowledge. Until the belated advent of commercial cheap publishing, these purposeful societies were to be the chief purveyors of reading matter to the masses: they, and the new generation of radical propagandists whose success challenged them to still greater activity.

Thus, in the turbulence of the 1790's, the emergence of a reading public among the humble brought England face to face with a major social problem, a problem destined to be shadowed for several decades by the threat, real or imaginary, of a revived Jacobinism. Tom Paine and Hannah More between them had opened the book to the common English reader. But was it merely a book— or a Pandora's box of infinite trouble?

THE NINETEENTH CENTURY

CHAPTER 4 { *The Social Background*

I. The mass reading public developed in nine-teenth-century England against a background of profound social change. From 1760 to 1801 the population of England and Wales had increased from roughly seven million to almost nine million; but this was only a moderate growth compared with what was to come.[1] In the first half of the nineteenth century the population doubled (from 8.9 million to 17.9 million), and by 1901 it was more than three and a half times as great (32.5 million) as it had been a hundred years earlier. In no decade was the rate of increase less than 11.7 per cent, and in one (1811–21) it was over 18 per cent. Meanwhile the population of Scotland, which formed an important market for English books and periodicals, grew from 2.09 million in 1821 to 4.5 million in 1901.[2]

The reservoir from which the reading public was drawn there-fore became larger and larger.[3] At the same time, the class struc-ture and the occupational and geographical distribution of the people underwent alterations which affected the availability of reading matter, educational opportunities, the conditions under which reading could be done, and the popular attitude toward print. The development of the mass reading public, in fact, was completely dependent upon the progress of the social revolution.

At once, therefore, we must acquire a general notion of the

[1] Basil Williams, *The Whig Supremacy* (Oxford, 1939), p. 119.

[2] Porter, *The Progress of the Nation* (1912 ed., used throughout unless otherwise noted), pp. 3–4.

[3] Gross population figures are not, of course, an accurate indication of the size of either the practicing or the potential reading audience. From the totals must be deducted over a third who were under fifteen years of age and who therefore would not ordinarily have been interested in adult reading matter. In addition, there is the all-important factor of literacy, which will be dealt with in chapter 7.

social structure. Unfortunately no uniform system of nomenclature or of census classification prevailed throughout the century, so that a consistent statistical summary is not possible. The greatest disagreement was on the difference between the lower-middle and the lower classes, and especially on the social level to which skilled artisans belonged. As the economist Leone Levi pointed out in 1884, mechanics and skilled artisans were "as far removed from common labourers and miners as clerks and curates are from those who have reached the highest places in the liberal professions or wealthy merchants and bankers, all of whom pass under the category of the middle classes."[4] Some authorities ranked them in the lower class; others gave them the relative dignity of place at the bottom of the middle class. In any case, the rule of thumb favored during most of the century was that the "working class," taking the lower-middle and lower classes together, constituted at least three-quarters of the total population. In 1814 Patrick Colquhoun estimated that out of about 17 million people in the United Kingdom (hence including Ireland), 1.5 million belonged to the upper and "respectable" middle classes, while 2.8 million were of the shopkeeper–small farmer class, and 11.9 million were mechanics, artisans, menial servants, paupers, and vagrants. (In that period, just before Waterloo, slightly less than a million additional men and their dependents were credited to "Army and Navy.")[5] In 1867 the economist Dudley Baxter, classifying 9.8 million actual recipients of income in England and Wales (and omitting, therefore, some 11 million dependents), numbered the upper and middle classes at 200,000, the lower-middle class at 1.85 million, and the working class (including 1.1 million skilled laborers) at 7.78 million.[6]

Whatever classification was used, one fact was undeniable. There was a great increase in the amorphous stratum between the old-established middle class (merchants and bankers, large employers of labor, superior members of professions) and the working class proper—the ranks of unskilled labor. This increase, brought

[4] Levi, *Wages and Earnings of the Working Classes*, p. 25.

[5] Patrick Colquhoun, *A Treatise on the Wealth, Power, and Resources of the British Empire* (1814), pp. 106–107. For two different detailed charts based on Colquhoun's estimates, attributed to 1801 and 1814, respectively, see Cole and Postgate, *The Common People*, 1938 ed., p. 70, and 1947 ed., p. 63.

[6] Cole and Postgate (1938 ed., used hereafter unless otherwise noted), p. 347.

about by the changing economic basis of English life, has special significance in the history of the reading public. It was principally from among skilled workers, small shopkeepers, clerks, and the better grade of domestic servants that the new mass audience for printed matter was recruited during the first half of the century. These were the people who chiefly benefited from the spread of elementary education and whose occupations required not only that they be literate but that they keep their reading faculty in repair. And because these people shared more in the century's prosperity than did the unskilled laborers, they were in a somewhat better position to buy cheap books and periodicals as these became available.

The growth of two occupational groups is particularly noteworthy. By 1861 the total of domestic servants of both sexes was more than a million—a few thousands more than the total employed in the textile industry.[7] Whatever newspapers and other periodicals a household took in would, in the normal course of events, filter down to the servants' quarters. In estimating the number of hands through which a given copy of a middle-class paper, or even a cheap book, might pass, one must not forget that the Victorian household contained not only a sizable family but also one or more servants with whom the paper wound up its travels.

The segment of the middle class proper which grew with unusual speed was that of physicians, teachers, civil servants, and other professional or white-collar workers. In 1851, the census placed 357,000 persons in that class; ten years later there were 482,000, and in 1881 the total was 647,000—an increase of 80 per cent in only thirty years.[8] These people, because of the special requirements of their daily work as well as the general cultural tradition of the professional class, constituted an important audience for reading matter.

As the century began, most of the English people, despite the spread of the enclosure system and the growth of factory industry, still were engaged in farming or in cottage crafts. But the peasant, the yeoman, and the handicraftsman steadily were being trans-

[7] Porter, pp. 31, 42.

[8] Robert Giffen, "Further Notes on the Progress of the Working Classes in the Last Half Century," *Journal of the Statistical Society*, XLIX (1886), 90.

formed into the factory-hand, and the process gathered momentum with the years. Of the total employed population of England and Wales in 1841 (6.7 million), 39.05 per cent were engaged in commerce, trade, and manufacture, and less than half as many— 18.80 per cent—in agriculture. Fifty years later, the percentages in commerce and industry and in agriculture were 68 and 10, respectively.[9]

The industrial revolution caused a vast migration of the people, from village and farm to the sprawling new factory towns of the Midlands and the North. Manchester and Salford more than quadrupled their joint population between 1801 and 1861; Leeds grew from 53,000 to 172,000 in the same period; and Bradford from 13,000 to 104,000.[10] By the 1880's, approximately two-thirds of the English were town-dwellers.[11] The occupational and geographical relocation of the people—the total disruption of their old way of life; their conversion into machine-slaves, living a hand-to-mouth existence at the mercy of their employers and of uncertain economic circumstances; their concentration in cities totally unprepared to accommodate them, not least in respect to education; the resultant moral and physical degradation—these, as we shall see, had significant consequences in the history of the reading public.

In the first half of the century English society was shaken as it had not been since the end of the Middle Ages. The ancient class structure, which generally, in past centuries, had well served the cause of domestic peace, began to crumble. The working class, losing its old sense of place under the stress of hunger, bewilderment, and the exhortations of radical politicians, began to demand social, economic, and political rights unthought of only a generation or two earlier. The widening of economic opportunity afforded by the development of industrial capitalism permitted many thousands to climb in the social scale. They quickly acquired the social prejudices characteristic of the class in which they found themselves, among which was a powerful desire to protect their substance and privileges against the encroachments of the class they had lately left. Those above them, in turn, felt all the more

[9] Porter, p. 38; Lynd, *England in the Eighteen-Eighties*, p. 28.

[10] Cole and Postgate, p. 300.

[11] Clapham, *Economic History of Modern Britain*, II, 489.

strongly the need for defending their own position against the newly arrived.

Hence the nineteenth century witnessed on every hand a sharpening of class consciousness. To the upper class and especially the older portion of the middle class, everything depended upon preserving the hallowed structure, though cautiously modified here and there to suit new conditions; to the lower class, or at least its more sensitive part, the supreme need was for sweeping social reconstruction in the direction of democracy. These conflicting aims inevitably bred social tensions which deeply affected the fortunes of the mass reading audience. For, as literacy and interest in reading spread, the "superior orders of society"—a term much in favor in the period—reacted to the phenomenon in terms of their special interests. Once they conceded it was impossible to prevent the lower ranks from reading, they embarked on a long campaign to insure that through the press the masses of people would be induced to help preserve the status quo and bulwark the security and prosperity of the particular sort of national life that they, its upper- and middle-class rulers, cherished. This campaign took many forms. Its battles and skirmishes, its victories and defeats are the subject of several of the chapters to follow.

II. What, now, of the conditions of life that encouraged the spread of reading, or, on the other hand, inhibited it?

Obviously, one cannot read without some leisure in which to do so. Leisure has never been equitably distributed in any civilized society, but in nineteenth-century England it was allotted with particular unevenness. In the middle class, even to some extent in its lower reaches, growing prosperity and the cheapness of labor enabled men and women to hire others for tasks they had hitherto done for themselves. The greater availability of cheap manufactured and processed goods—soap and candles, for instance, and food—gradually led people to give up producing such commodities for their own use, a practice that in any event was impossible for city-dwellers. Households in which repair work had formerly been done by father and sons now called in carpenters and masons. And most important of all, the menial chores which were traditionally the lot of wife and daughters could be transferred, at small expense, to domestic servants, one of whose regular duties, as often as not, was to exchange books at the circulating library or buy the new issue of *Eliza Cook's Journal* from the corner news agent. Hence to scores of thousands of families touched by the prosperity of the new age, relief from household duties provided a degree of leisure undreamed of in earlier generations.

But while leisure increased in the middle class, the ways it could be used were drastically limited, since this was the class most affected by the spread of evangelical principles. "For multitudes of the respectable population, outside entertainments, such as the theatre or the music-hall provided, were practically non-existent. Dancing was a snare of the devil. Even concerts, though Catalani might be singing and Paganini playing, were not encouraged by the unworldly; and it was not till the undeniable 'goodness' of Jenny Lind conquered the prejudice, that anything but oratorio was considered safe.[12] Nonconformists and Claphamites, there-fore, on evenings not set aside for missionary meetings, shunned outside dangers, and spent the time in 'profitable' instruction and 'harmless' entertainment. Cards, of course, were forbidden, and, while a game of bagatelle might be allowed, billiards, even in the home, were never mentioned."[13] In so scrupulous an atmosphere, the reading habit flourished. The place of the evening reading circle in Victorian middle-class family life is so well known that it need be merely mentioned here. How widespread the institution was, and how deeply it influenced the tastes of the children who grew up in such homes, is attested in countless memoirs.

However, only the relatively well-to-do minority of the middle class, the merchants, bankers, professional men, manufacturers, and so on, could spend full evenings with their families and their books. In the lower levels of that class, most men spent long days at their work, small employers and overseers keeping as long hours as their workmen.[14] Retail tradespeople, a million and a quarter of them by the 1880's, were in their shops from seven or eight in

---

[12] And there were plenty of people, among them George Eliot during her brief but fervent flirtation with Evangelical principles, who regarded even oratorio as dangerously sensuous.

[13] Kellett, "The Press," p. 49.

[14] The ensuing discussion of working hours is based on Sidney Webb and Harold Cox, *The Eight Hours Day* (1891), *passim;* Gregg, *Social and Economic History of Britain*, pp. 134–36. On the "Early Closing" movement, see E. S. Turner, *Roads to Ruin* (1950), chap. iii.

the morning until ten at night, and on Saturdays until midnight. For skilled and unskilled laborers, the working day was so long during the first half of the century as to be a national scandal. Hundreds of thousands of miners and factory- and mill-hands crept to their employment before dawn and emerged after sunset. The fourteen-hour day was commonplace, and the sixteen-hour day was not rare. Only gradually were the hours reduced. London handicraft workers won a ten-hour day before the 1830's, and in 1847 a bitterly fought act of Parliament introduced it into the textile industry. Actually, however, the working day was longer than the bare figure suggests, for artisans and handicraftsmen frequently worked overtime, and in textile mills "ten hours" really meant 6:00 A.M. to 6:00 P.M. By the seventies, London artisans, after long agitation, achieved a fifty-four-hour week, while the textile trades worked two and a half hours longer. In the nineties the average workweek for such trades as shipbuilding, iron founding, cooperage, and building ranged from fifty to sixty hours, depending on the locality and, in outdoor trades, the season of the year. In the warehouses of the so-called "Manchester trade" the fourteen-hour day was still common.

On weekdays, therefore, few workers had time to read. Those in even the most favored trades came home no earlier than six or seven o'clock, and after the evening meal only an hour or two remained until fatigue and the prospect of rising before dawn the next day drove them to bed. Not until the sixties was the Saturday half-holiday generally introduced; and this involved only a modest curtailment of the working day—in the case of London building artisans, for instance, from eleven to seven hours. For shop assistants there was no relief at all. Saturday remained their longest day, a matter of sixteen hours behind the counter. Under such circumstances it was only natural that the workman confined most of his reading to Sundays. Hence the great popularity of the Sunday newspaper, and, beginning in the late forties, the weekly miscellany-*cum*-sensational-fiction paper which was issued on Saturday.

During the decades which witnessed the worst oppression of the wage-earning masses, the townsman with time to kill on Saturday night and Sunday had little choice of diversion. He could get drunk at a public house, or, to the accompaniment of song, at a concert room or a dancing saloon; he could visit a brothel, he could get

into a fist fight or attend a bear-baiting, he could loaf in the streets
—and not much else. The teeming cities had virtually no provision
for decent public recreation: few theaters or music halls, no parks
for strolling and picnicking, no museums or art galleries, no free
libraries. In 1844 Preston was the only town in all of Lancashire
with a public park. But shortly thereafter, local authorities were
for the first time allowed to use public funds for recreational facilities, and parks and other places of resort appeared in most cities.[15]
There remained, however, the somber pall of the English Sunday.
While the working class as a whole was indifferent to Sabbatarianism, it nevertheless shared the consequences of the ban on Sunday
recreation. In 1856 proposals to open the British Museum and the
National Gallery after church services on Sunday and to hold
Sunday band concerts in the London parks were shouted down
from the pulpit, and not until forty more years had elapsed were
London museums and art galleries opened on Sunday afternoons.
Only in the seventies did the Midland workman have access to
such institutions on his one day of relaxation.[16] Until well past mid-
century, therefore, the man who was not content with aimless
loafing or with grosser amusements had little alternative but to
spend his Sunday leisure with a book or paper.

When the workweek was shortened and strict Sabbatarianism
began to fade, the English worker found many ways of passing his
leisure apart from reading. Railways ran special cheap trains to
the country and the seaside; theaters and music halls multiplied;
cricket, football, and other spectator sports became increasingly
popular. Among the middle class, the partial emancipation of
women encouraged the whole family to move outdoors for its
pleasure, so that the domestic reading circle declined as an institution. The new fashion for participant sports—cycling, rowing,
tennis, walking, croquet—offered powerful competition to the
reading habit. Thus the spread of leisure both favored and discouraged the development of the reading public. There was more
time to read, but eventually there were also many more things to
do with one's spare time.

One major innovation, at least, resulted in an unquestionable

---

[15] Hammond, *The Age of the Chartists*, pp. 29–30. The Hammonds' two chapters on
"The Loss of Playgrounds" are a good summary of this topic.

[16] Gregg, p. 349.

increase in reading: the coming of railway travel. Cheap, swift, and more or less comfortable transportation was available to the ever greater number of men whose business required travel, as well as to those who wished to visit relatives or have a holiday in the Cotswolds or by the sea. A railway trip meant an hour or a day of enforced leisure; and to escape the boredom of staring out the window or listening to one's chance companions, one read. It was by no means accidental that from the 1850's onward a whole class of cheap books was known as "railway literature," and that a large portion of the retail book and periodical trade of England was conducted at railway terminals. Every passenger train of the hundreds that roared down the rails in the course of a single day carried a cargo of readers, their eyes fixed on *Lady Audley's Secret* or the *Times*. Perhaps no other single element in the evolving pattern of Victorian life was so responsible for the spread of reading. The effect was increased still further when, with the rise of dormitory suburbs around the great cities, commuting between home and business became a daily occupation of many thousands.

In the country, meanwhile, conditions of life among the masses offered little incentive or opportunity for reading. Education was hard to come by, and most children, if they went to school at all, did so for only a year or two and then were put to work in the fields, at crow-scaring if they were not yet strong enough for manual labor. Working hours for all laborers were long. Paul Tregarva, the studious gamekeeper in Kingsley's *Yeast*, observed: "As for reading, sir, it's all very well for me, who have been a keeper and dawdled about like a gentleman with a gun over my arm; but did you ever do a good day's farm-work in your life? If you had, man or boy, you wouldn't have been game for much reading when you got home; you'd do just what these poor fellows do,—tumble into bed at eight o'clock, hardly waiting to take your clothes off, knowing that you must turn up again at five o'clock the next morning to get a breakfast of bread, and, perhaps, a dab of the squire's dripping, and then back to work again; and so on, day after day, sir, week after week, year after year. . . ."[17]

While printed matter became more easily accessible in the towns and cities, with their coffeehouses and news vendors and free libraries, the humble countryman met few books or papers in

[17] *Yeast*, chap. xiii.

his way through life. Hawkers came to his door occasionally with broadsides, tracts, and number-publications; but, with agricultural wages consistently the lowest in the nation, there was little money to buy them. In a certain Kentish farming parish in the 1830's, only four out of fifty-one families possessed any books besides the Bible, Testament, and prayer and hymn books, and only seven parents "ever opened a book after the labours of the day were closed."[18] Nor was this parish unusual. Again and again in the records of the time we find evidence of how little printed matter—perhaps no more than a copy or two of a cheap magazine —regularly came to a country village. Not until the cheap periodical press made efficient use of railway transportation and local distributors, and rural education received much-needed aid under the Forster Act of 1870, did the majority of country-dwellers acquire much interest in reading.

III. Victorian writers and speakers never tired of reminding their audiences that the taste for reading has an almost unique advantage in that it can be indulged at any time and in any place. One must go from home to satisfy a love of nature or sports or the fine arts, and he must do so at certain hours or seasons; but one can read any time at one's own fireside—a great point in an age that venerated domesticity. Such a notion was not, however, very realistic. The typical nineteenth-century home was not a place where a man could read quietly and uninterruptedly during whatever free hours he had. For every household in which it was possible there were a hundred where it was out of the question.

This is not the place to rehearse the appalling story of housing conditions in the new industrial England, or, for that matter, in the countryside, where the sentimentally celebrated English cottage was, oftener than not, a ruinous hovel. It is enough to recall that town workers lived in bestial squalor, packed together in dark, stinking warrens in which privacy, quiet, and the most rudimentary comforts were alike unknown. To such people, as to the gamekeeper Tregarva, praise of books as a means of contenting one's self during a peaceful evening or a Sunday must have seemed a bitter jest. How, with a distraught, sickly wife complaining and

[18] *Central Society of Education Publications*, III (1839), 108.

a brood of ill-fed squalling children filling the room, and drunken neighbors brawling next door, could a reader, no matter how earnest, concentrate upon a book? It was even worse if, as was true of many working-class dwellings, some sort of handicraft was carried on on the premises. In 1849 a missionary to the hand-weavers of Spitalfields—once aristocrats of labor, with neat gardens beside their homes, and mutual-improvement societies—told a committee of Parliament, "I frequently find as many as seven or eight persons living all in one room; in that room, perhaps, there will be two looms at work, so that the noise and discomfort render it almost impossible that a working man, if he were ever so well inclined to read, could sit down and read quietly."[19] John Passmore Edwards, the son of a Cornish carpenter, recalled how as a child he read by the light of a single candle in the midst of a talkative and active family. "Hundreds and hundreds of times I pressed my thumbs firmly on my ears until they ached, in order to read with as little distraction as possible."[20]

To try to read in the midst of the domestic hurly-burly meant, too, that one would be subject to the ridicule, or at best the well-meant disapproval, of those who failed to share one's inclination. Thomas Burt, the future trade-union leader and M.P., grew up in a cottage that was virtually a neighborhood crossroads. "At it again, Thomas!" a constant visitor, who was a Methodist coal miner, would exclaim. "What can thoo be aiming at? Thou won't join the church; thou won't preach or address temperance meetings. What's the meaning of all this poring over books, this plodding search for knowledge that thou won't use? Thou'll destroy thy health, and nobody will be the better for thy labours."[21] This was not the least of the difficulties which the pursuer of knowledge had to face.

It was not to be marveled at, then, that most workingmen, no matter how much they may have wished to read, sought relaxation outside the home. The street, the public house, the cheap theater if one was nearby, and later the park and the sports field were to

[19] Public Libraries Committee, Q. 2751.

[20] *A Few Footprints* (1905), p. 6. It was Edwards' recollection of this maddening experience which led him, as the millionaire proprietor of the London *Echo*, to found free libraries where people could read in comparative tranquillity.

[21] Burt, *Autobiography*, pp. 122–23.

be preferred to a fireside which was anything but peaceful. Nor was overcrowding confined to working-class tenements and cottages. It was found, to a scarcely smaller degree, in the homes of the lower-middle class. At no time in the century did residential building keep pace with the growth of the population, and in any case incomes were insufficient to rent quarters that were adequate according to the most modest standards of our own day. Taking the nation as a whole, the average number of persons to a living unit fell in the course of the century only from 5.67 to 5.2, and as late as the 1880's one-fifth of the entire population of London lived more than two to a room.[22]

Nor was this all. In the ordinary home, decent lighting was not to be found until late in the century. In the period 1808–23 the window tax, a relic dating from 1696, reached its highest level. Houses with six windows or less were taxed 6s.6d. to 8s. annually; seven-window houses, a pound; nine-window houses, two guineas, and so on up. Even an aperture only a foot square was considered a window. Although in 1823 the tax was halved, and in 1825 houses with less than eight windows were exempted, builders still were discouraged from putting any more openings in a house than were absolutely necessary, with the result that only one-seventh of all the houses in Britain fell under the tax.[23] Not without reason did Dickens remark that the window tax (abolished, finally, in 1851) was an even more formidable obstacle to the people's reading than the so-called "taxes on knowledge"—the duties on newspapers, advertisements, and paper.[24]

The average early nineteenth-century home was dark enough during the day; at night it was no brighter. In most houses at the beginning of the century tallow dips (rush lights) or candles were the only sources of illumination apart from the fireplace. During the thirties and forties colza-oil and whale-oil lamps were introduced into the households of the well-to-do, followed by paraffin lamps in the fifties and eventually by gas. It may well be that these improvements were hastened as much by the increased amount of reading being done in such homes as by the contrast between the brilliancy of gas lighting in streets and public places and the

[22] Clapham, II, 490; Porter, p. 91.

[23] Hammond, pp. 84–85 n.; Cole and Postgate, p. 300.

[24] Dickens, *Letters* (Nonesuch ed.), II, 205.

feeble illumination afforded by candles. In the dwellings of the working class, however, candles and rush lights remained the usual sources of light. They were not cheap. In the first half of the century a pound of candles (two dozen) cost about 7*d*. and in humble homes was made to last a week or longer. Each candle provided from two to three hours' light. When only one or two were used at a time, continuous reading was a trying experience. Rush lights, being cheaper, were used in the poorest households, but they gave an even feebler light. To the devoted reader, however, even they were precious; Kingsley's Alton Locke, for instance, recorded how, after putting out his candle for the night, he continued his studies by the glimmer of a rush light he had earned by bringing bits of work home from the tailor's sweatshop.[25]

Reading in such light could not help taxing the eyes. This was a powerful deterrent to the spread of the reading habit, especially in an age when print was villainously small (largely because the high paper duties requiring crowding as much as possible on a page). The eyestrain involved in many manufacturing operations, such as loom-tending, was great, and mills and factories were often wretchedly lighted. Furthermore, since the diet of the masses was not only scanty but ill balanced, poor nutrition must have affected the sight of countless thousands.

Spectacles were used, of course, but by no means everybody who needed them had them; in the country and slums especially they were something of a luxury. It was a remarkable event in the life of young Carlyle when he was able to send presents of two pairs of glasses to his parents from Edinburgh in 1821.[26] Not until the middle of the twentieth century, indeed, were spectacles freely available to all Englishmen. Without them, during the nineteenth century, a multitude of would-be readers, their eyes weakened by faulty diet or taxing occupation or simply by age, were barred irrevocably from the pleasures of print.

There was, finally, the element of sheer fatigue. A man's eyes might be perfect, but after working all day at some monotonous or strenuous task he was so tired that unless his will to read was

[25] This material on household illumination is derived from Porter (1851 ed.), p. 582; Marjorie and C. H. B. Quennell, *A History of Everyday Things in England, 1733–1851* (1933), p. 181; *Early Victorian England*, ed. G. M. Young (1934), I, 81, 127, 129; Kingsley, *Alton Locke*, chap. iii.

[26] *Early Letters of Thomas Carlyle*, ed. C. E. Norton (1886), II, 2–4.

very strong he was likely to fall asleep over his book or paper. Far preferable in his state of exhaustion was a refreshing visit to a public house (where, to be sure, he could glance over a paper if he were so disposed) or simply an hour or two spent loafing before his door. It would take a type of literature especially suited to men and women with dulled minds and tired bodies to turn manual workers into habitual readers.

IV. It is hard, perhaps impossible, to recreate the spirit of so large and inarticulate a community as the English working classes in the nineteenth century. If we attempt to do so by examining only the immense body of sociological data assembled by parliamentary committees and statistical societies, we must believe that men and women were so brutalized out of any semblance to normal mortals that they were physical organisms and economic units alone, without any of the emotional life and the intellectual and spiritual aspirations which mark the man from the animal. But this is an incomplete view, springing from the limited nature of the age's humanitarianism. Reformers like Chadwick, Kay-Shuttleworth, and Shaftesbury were concerned simply with ameliorating the common man's physical existence, and parliamentary inquiries never showed the slightest curiosity, except where it was a question of religious observance or ordinary morality, about the inner lives of the workers—a subject which in any case hardly lends itself to investigative treatment.

One-sided though it is, the impression we receive of the worker and his family from the classic sources of early nineteenth-century social history is not wholly false. If there was ever a time when the English masses approached a state of downright bestiality, it was then. The great migration from village to city produced a crisis in popular culture. Though they were already deteriorating, there had still survived in the eighteenth century the rural institutions of holiday-making, pageantry, and fairs. There was still the lore of the countryside and the songs and stories that had been handed down in the cottage from generation to generation. Illiterate though the common countryman may have been, his participation in the popular cultural tradition saved him from being a stolid brute.

When the villager was transformed into the slum-dwelling factory laborer, however, this tradition was lost to him. In addition, whatever contact he had earlier had with printed matter became more tenuous. Many cottages had had their little shelf of worn and precious books, family possessions passed down through a century or more—the Bible, *Robinson Crusoe*, *Pilgrim's Progress*, ballads, and chapbooks bought at a fair long ago or from a peddler at the door. But when the children moved to the cities, the books were left behind or soon were lost in the course of their owners' restless migration from one tenement to another, and there was little chance to replace them. The custom of reading by the fireside vanished, along with other homely habits, and books no longer were prized as symbols of a family's continuity.

Tragically, it was at this very time that the worker most needed the spiritual and emotional strength which reading might provide. He desperately needed some relief from the deadly monotony of factory work, which was, Friedrich Engels observed, "properly speaking, not work, but tedium, the most deadening, wearing process conceivable. The operative is condemned to let his physical and mental powers decay in this utter monotony, it is his mission to be bored every day and all day long from his eighth year."[27] It was no cause for surprise, as Engels went on to say, that drunkenness and sexual promiscuity—the only two solaces the worker had regularly available—reached such alarming proportions in the manufacturing towns.

Even more dreadful was the loss of personal individuality. Workers' lives were regulated by the ringing of the factory bell and regimented by a system of rules and penalties. They had no personal pride in their work, for the product of their labor was not theirs alone but that of many other workers. They had no sense of personal destiny, for their lives were totally at the mercy of conditions beyond their control, the fluctuations of trade, the whim of the employer, the invention of new labor-saving machinery.

And perhaps worst of all was the overwhelming loneliness the individual man and woman felt in the midst of the crowd. "The sons of farmers and agricultural laborers who congregated in newly created slums were natives of all four corners of England and Wales. They were foreign to each other, they even spoke different dialects and they were completely lost in that human flotsam and

[27] *Condition of the Working Class in 1844*, p. 177.

jetsam. The new rows of tenements had no parish church, no local vicar with his school, no cultural background or local tradition. In their native villages they were human personalities, although sub-ordinate; here they became ciphers, an economic commodity which was bought and sold according to the market price of labour."[28] The only strong bond that held the victims of the industrial revo-lution together was a common misery of body and soul.

Torn away from the old cultural tradition, battered and adrift in a feelingless world, the millions of common people needed decent recreation more urgently than any generation before them. As Sir John Herschel, who was gifted with rare insight in this matter, observed in 1833, "The pleasant field-walk and the village-green are becoming rarer and rarer every year. Music and dancing (the more's the pity) have become so closely associated with ideas of riot and debauchery, among the less cultivated classes, that a taste for them for their own sakes can hardly be said to exist. . . . While hardly a foot of ground is left uncultivated, and unappro-priated, there is positively not space left for many of the cheerful amusements of rural life. . . . It is physically impossible that the amusements of a condensed population should continue to be those of a scattered one."

Books, said Herschel, were the answer to the pressing problem of the workingman's amusement. Reading "calls for no bodily exertion, of which he has had enough, or too much. It relieves his home of its dulness and sameness, which, in nine cases out of ten, is what drives him out to the ale-house, to his own ruin and his family's. It transports him into a livelier, and gayer, and more diversified and interesting scene, and while he enjoys himself there, he may forget the evils of the present moment, fully as much as if he were ever so drunk." And most important of all, Herschel re-marked, "Nothing unites people like companionship in intellectual enjoyment." With books, the dreary clouds of despair and loneli-ness could be driven away.[29]

With a few noteworthy exceptions like Herschel and Dickens, contemporary social critics and reformers failed to understand, or at least to sympathize with, this imperative need for escape on the

[28] Nicholas Hans, *New Trends in English Education in the Eighteenth Century* (1951), p. 211.

[29] "Address," pp. 8–10.

part of the physically and spiritually imprisoned. The great majority of the missionaries of reading, who came bearing social soporifics put up by the church or by Brougham's Society for the Diffusion of Useful Knowledge, simply could not countenance this motive. The result was that their zeal to spread the taste for reading was seriously, almost fatally, misapplied. They preached true doctrine—the rewards that lie in the printed page—but for the wrong reasons. Had they recognized the deep-seated desire for imaginative and emotional release which disposes ordinary people to read, and not insisted upon their own well-meant but unrealistic program, their efforts would have borne far healthier fruit. Any man, observed Wilkie Collins, "can preach to them [the common people], lecture to them, and form them into classes; but where is the man who can get them to amuse themselves? Anybody may cram their poor heads; but who will lighten their grave faces?"[30]

The obstacles in the way of the spread of reading among the masses were varied and numerous, as the following chapters will show. But while the impediments were great, the need was greater. The hunger for diversion was only one of the incentives that sooner or later drew men to the printed page. Others were almost as powerful: the desire to keep up with the events of the fast-changing world; the spirit of self-improvement which permeated down to the masses from the prevalent individualistic philosophy of the age; and the seething social unrest which found expression and focus in the radical propaganda of the period from 1815 to 1850. The size of the audience that devoured the writings of Cobbett and the Chartists is perhaps the best proof that the working class had not been reduced to a completely bestial condition. "The very vileness of the life in the herded towns and the very misery and discontent," says A. S. Collins, "became creative forces. . . . For the harsh discipline of the factories and the ugly wretchedness of the houses that were often no better than hovels, led men naturally to a sphere where they might find some self-expression, and to dreams and theories which might feed hope in their starved spirits. . . . Those gloomy tenements were the forcing houses of intellectual discontent, and from them shot up a new class of uneducated readers."[31]

[30] *A Rogue's Life*, chap. vi.
[31] *The Profession of Letters*, pp. 42–43.

Whatever they read—escapist fiction, or recipes for improving their economic position through increased knowledge and application to their trade, or virulent diatribes against political and social injustice—the English common people of the nineteenth century were, like human beings in all ages, dreamers of dreams. However drab, weary, and monotonous their lives, somewhere in their oppressed souls persisted an unquenchable desire for a happier gift from life than unremitting toil and poverty. Of these millions of Englishmen, H. G. Wells's late Victorian Mr. Polly is as good a symbol as any. Deep in his being, despite the deadening influence of the elementary school and life as a draper's assistant, "deep in that darkness, like a creature which has been beaten about the head and left for dead but still lives, crawled a persuasion that over and above the things that are jolly and 'bits of all right,' there was beauty, there was delight, that somewhere—magically inaccessible perhaps, but still somewhere, were pure and easy and joyous states of body and mind."[32]

There were uncounted numbers of Mr. Pollys in nineteenth-century England. Few read as widely or as constantly as he did; but a great many found in the printed word at least something of the same excitement and imaginative release. Among them, whose forebears had lived on the outermost fringes of the literary tradition, if, indeed, they had touched it at all, the frustration produced by the birth-throes of a new society bred a wholly novel veneration for the printed word.

[32] *Mr. Polly*, chap. i.

CHAPTER 5 } *Religion*

I. The two most potent influences upon the social and cultural tone of nineteenth-century England were evangelical religion[1] and utilitarianism. As more than one historian has noted, evangelicalism and utilitarianism had numerous bonds of affinity; Élie Halévy observed that "the fundamental paradox of English society" in the nineteenth century "is precisely the partial junction and combination of these two forces theoretically so hostile."[2] Not the least of their similarities was a curiously ambivalent attitude toward reading. At one and the same time, the evangelicals on the religious side and the utilitarians on the secular did much to popularize reading (for certain purposes) and equally much to discourage it.

Like their Puritan forebears, the evangelicals, believing as they did in the supreme importance of Scripture, stressed the act of reading as part of the program of the truly enlightened life. They believed that the grace of God could, and did, descend to the individual man and woman through the printed page. The cultivation of the reading habit was therefore as indispensable as a daily program of prayer and observance of a strict moral code. With the Bible always at the center, there grew up a huge literature of admonition, guidance, and assurance.

So insistently did the evangelicals emphasize the spiritual necessity of reading that the old seventeenth-century bibliolatry revived. Wherever their influence reached, Bible-reading was prac-

[1] For the sake of conciseness, the term "evangelical"—uncapitalized—will be used to designate the range of nineteenth-century English Protestantism from the Low Church through Methodism to the older dissenting sects like the Baptists—omitting, therefore, the so-called "High and Dry" Anglicanism. When the narrower meaning of the word is intended, the "Evangelical" party within the Anglican church, it will be capitalized.

[2] *History of the English People in 1815*, p. 509.

ticed less as a conscious exercise of the intellect than as a ritual which was an end in itself. Actual comprehension was not necessary; enough if the reader were able to pronounce, in a fashion, most of the words he looked upon. Hence the evangelicals, in their charitable educational activities, contented themselves with spreading the barest rudiments of reading among the humble. One who knew his letters, regardless of any further education, was sufficiently equipped to perform the sacred rite which lay at the very heart of religion.

Since the printed word was the chosen weapon of aggressive, proselytizing religion, the distribution of Bibles and didactic literature became a large industry. Three major religious agencies were active in the field throughout the century. The first was the interdenominational Religious Tract Society (founded 1799). This organization, dedicated to carrying on the work begun by the Cheap Repository Tracts, became the century's greatest single distributor of Bibles, Testaments, tracts, and, later, improving works of all sorts. The British and Foreign Bible Society (1804), also sponsored jointly by Evangelicals and nonconformists, distributed the Scriptures in an immense variety of editions and translations. The third of these organizations was the venerable Society for Promoting Christian Knowledge, which had been in the book business long before Hannah More was born. It had, however, shared in the general lethargy that had overcome the Anglican church in the course of the eighteenth century, and only after the success of the bustling Religious Tract Society did it rouse itself to do for the High Church what the Tract Society was accomplishing in behalf of the Evangelicals.

In addition, religious literature poured from the headquarters of innumerable independent agencies, including those of the various nonconformist denominations. There was, for example, Drummond's Tract Depository at Stirling, in Scotland, from which, it is said, "hundreds of millions" of tracts were circulated.[3] The long-established Wesleyan Book Room in London in 1841 alone issued 1,326,000 copies of tracts.[4] Even the Roman Catholics, according to Coleridge, borrowed the Cheap Repository Tracts technique and smuggled their own tracts into farmhouses and cottages

[3] L. E. Elliott-Binns, *Religion in the Victorian Era* (2d ed., 1946), p. 349.
[4] Mathews, *Methodism and the Education of the People*, p. 172.

through traveling peddlers, "at a price less than their prime cost, and doubtless, thrown in occasionally as the make-weight in a bargain of pins and stay-tape."[5] Certain tract-writers, though now almost wholly forgotten, were as famous in their time as Hannah More had been. Three homely little tales by an early secretary of the Religious Tract Society, Rev. Legh Richmond—*The Dairyman's Daughter*, *The Young Cottagers*, and *The Negro Servant*—together circulated 1,354,000 copies in less than half a century.[6] The Maidstone bookseller John Vine Hall won himself a place in the *Dictionary of National Biography* by writing *The Sinner's Friend* (1821), which went through 290 editions, totaling over a million copies, in thirty-four years.[7] Another well-known writer was John Charles Ryle, Bishop of Liverpool, over twelve million copies of whose tracts are said to have been issued.[8]

It would be futile even to try to estimate how many copies of religious and moral works of all sorts were distributed in Britain in the nineteenth century. Since the figures announced by at least some societies include great quantities intended for territories not yet reconciled to evangelical Christianity, they are not an accurate indication of the home market. But even when the most liberal allowance is made for export, the size of the output is staggering. Between 1804 and 1819 the British and Foreign Bible Society issued over two and a half million copies of Bibles and Testaments, nearly all of which were for domestic use, the foreign missionary activities of the society having barely begun at the time.[9] In its first half-century of existence (1804–54) it distributed about sixteen million English Bibles and Testaments.[10] In 1804 the Religious Tract Society printed 314,000 copies of tracts; by 1861 its annual output was in the neighborhood of twenty million tracts, in addition to thirteen million copies of periodicals.[11] The S.P.C.K.,

[5] *The Friend, Works* (New York, 1853), II, 58.

[6] William Jones, *The Jubilee Memorial of the Religious Tract Society* (1850), cited in Quinlan, *Victorian Prelude*, p. 124.

[7] John Vine Hall, *Hope for the Hopeless: An Autobiography* (New York, n.d.), p. 211. This figure includes translations into twenty-three languages, not all of which, obviously, had wide circulation in England itself. In his autobiography Hall gives many interesting details of the methods by which he circulated his work.

[8] Elliott-Binns, p. 348.

[9] Browne, *History of the British and Foreign Bible Society*, I, 84.

[10] *Ibid.*, II, 543.

[11] Quinlan, p. 124; Mayhew, *London Labour and the London Poor*, IV, xxiii.

meanwhile, raised its yearly production from 1,500,000 in 1827 to over eight million in 1867.[12] In 1897 the Religious Tract Society sent out from the "home depot" alone over 38,720,000 pieces of literature, of which 18,320,000—less than half—were tracts, the rest being books (especially but not exclusively children's) and periodicals, such as *Sunday at Home, Leisure Hour, The Boy's Own Paper, The Girl's Own Paper*, and *Cottager and Artisan*.[13] In the same year the S.P.C.K. issued a total of 12,500,000 pieces, of which only about a fourth were tracts.[14]

Pages of such statistics could be copied from the annual reports and centenary histories of the various societies, but the effect would be more numbing than illuminating. What the statistics never show, of course, is how many copies fell upon stony ground. One of Henry Mayhew's informants may have been exaggerating when he said that of forty London costermongers who received tracts from the hands of passing benefactors, scarcely one could read;[15] but an immense number of the tracts must have been wasted because their recipients were either unable or unwilling to read them. The distributors were aware of this, but they seem always to have preferred saturation coverage to selective distribution, and a large element of waste was therefore unavoidable.

The distribution machinery improved in efficiency as the years went by. The system of local auxiliary societies which originated at the time of the Cheap Repository Tracts steadily expanded. In the year of Waterloo the Religious Tract Society had 124 local groups at work, whose volunteers, taking up the burden for which the old-time professional hawkers had never been too keen, canvassed from house to house.[16] In 1854 the British and Foreign Bible Society's network of volunteer agencies had far exceeded this mark. In Great Britain alone it had 460 "auxiliaries," 373 "branches," and 2,482 "associations"—a total of over 3,300 sepa-

[12] Allen and McClure, *Two Hundred Years*, p. 198.

[13] *Publishers' Circular*, March 26, 1898, p. 356.

[14] Allen and McClure, p. 198. The variety of publications sent forth by the various religious publishing houses—which included, in addition to those already mentioned, such other prolific agencies as the Sunday School Union, the Wesleyan Conference Office, and the Roman Catholic firm of R. Washbourne—may be studied in their catalogues, which were bound up in the successive editions of the *Reference Catalogue* from 1874 onward.

[15] Mayhew, I, 23.

[16] Quinlan, p. 125.

rate groups, of which "the far greater part," it was said, "are conducted by Ladies."[17]

The ladies were assisted in some regions by hawkers hired for the express purpose of selling religious literature through the countryside. This device had been introduced in Scotland as early as 1793, when an eccentric tradesman called Johnny Campbell founded the Religious Tract and Book Society of Scotland, more familiarly known as the Scottish Colportage Society. By 1874 this agency employed 228 colporteurs, who sold, in that year, 55,000 copies of Scripture, 120,000 copies of "various works of a religious and morally-elevating character," 840,000 periodicals for adults, 400,000 for the young, and 300,000 cheap hymnbooks.[18] In 1845 the British and Foreign Bible Society adopted the same system in order to intensify its campaign in areas where the incidence of Scripture-reading was unusually low. One of its first hawkers, whom a contemporary account describes, credibly enough, as "an indefatigable young man," made 18,727 calls in a single year, and sold 3,795 books. The next year, possibly because he was footsore, his total calls dropped some four thousand; but, his sales technique having greatly improved, he nevertheless sold almost twice as many Bibles.[19]

Religious literature, therefore, was everywhere in nineteenth-century England. Tracts were flung from carriage windows; they were passed out at railway stations; they turned up in army camps and in naval vessels anchored in the roads, and in jails and lodging-houses and hospitals and workhouses; they were distributed in huge quantities at Sunday and day schools, as rewards for punctuality, diligence, decorum, and deloused heads.[20] They were a ubiquitous part of the social landscape.

Simply by making the printed word more available, the religious literature societies stimulated the spread of literacy. If one had nothing to read, there was no particular point in becoming literate; but when Manchester hovels and Hampshire cottages began to

[17] Browne, II, 541.

[18] William Alexander, "Literature of the People," p. 95. See also the abstract of a paper by William Boyd, "Colportage in Scotland," *Transactions of the National Association for the Promotion of Social Science* (1863), pp. 381–82.

[19] Browne, I, 208–209, 226–27.

[20] On reward books, see the article by P. E. Morgan in *Notes and Queries*, CLXXXV (1943), 70–74.

have a few stray tracts or pious songs on the premises, there was a psychological incentive to do so. Some people were content to have the words spelled out to them by the scholar of the family, but many more wanted to be able to read on their own account. In addition, tracts offered a means by which the reading faculty, once learned, could be exercised and improved. Until the development of cheap secular periodicals the productions of the Religious Tract Society, the S.P.C.K., and their sister agencies kept literacy alive among large numbers of the poor who otherwise had little contact with the printed word.

But the flood of tracts had other effects which were far less conducive to the spread of interest in reading. The most serious mistake made by Hannah More and her generations of disciples was to underestimate the independence and intelligence of the humbly born Englishman. Their assumption was that he was a dull beast who, if he were treated with some kindness, could be relied upon to follow the bidding of his superiors. They did not reckon on the possibility that he had a mind of his own, a stubborn will, and a strong sense of his own dignity even in the midst of degradation. Because of this, tracts and the bearers of tracts often rubbed him the wrong way.

The tract people made it plain that they were out to substitute good reading matter for bad. They conducted an endless war against "dangerous" publications which the common reader not only considered harmless but, more important, truly enjoyed. Hannah More rejoiced that one of her co-workers, Lady Howard, had succeeded in ending the sale of impious literature at six shops where the Cheap Repository Tracts were being sold. "This is doing the thing effectually," she wrote, "for though it is easy to furnish shops with our tracts, it requires great influence to expel the poison of the old sort."[21] But the reader often resented this high-handed attempt to interfere with his freedom of choice, especially when the new product seemed in many ways less exciting than the old. He accepted narrative tracts and read them, if nothing better was to be had; but as often as not, when the choice could be made, his penny went for old-fashioned chapbooks and, a little later, instalments of sensational tales.

Again, as Charles Knight observed, "the besetting weakness of

[21] William Roberts, *Memoirs of Hannah More* (2d ed., 1834), II, 457.

the learned and aristocratic, from the very first moment that they began to prattle about bestowing the blessings of education," was that they "insisted upon maintaining the habit of talking to thinking beings, and for the most part to very acute thinking beings, in the language of the nursery."[22] The language of the tracts may have been adapted well enough to the capacities of their semi-literate readers, but there were plenty who knew they were being talked down to, and reacted accordingly.

Sir John Herschel, who shared his townsman Charles Knight's shrewdness in this matter, defined the case against the tract very well when he remarked in 1833, "The story told, or the lively or friendly style assumed, is *manifestly* and *palpably* only a cloak for the instruction intended to be conveyed—a sort of gilding of what they cannot well help fancying must be a pill, when they see so much and such obvious pains taken to wrap it up."[23] For this air of condescension in religious literature went deeper than mere language; it was inseparable from the social message the tracts embodied. "Beautiful is the order of Society," wrote Hannah More, "when each, according to his place—pays willing honour to his superiors—when servants are prompt to obey their masters, and masters deal kindly with their servants;—when high, low, rich and poor—when landlord and tenant, master and workman, minister and people, . . . sit down each satisfied with his own place."[24]

This attitude—the sociology of a Dr. Isaac Watts—may have been appropriate at some other juncture in history, but it was grievously unsuited to a period of intensifying democratic ferment. The common people, especially those who came under the influence of radical journalists after 1815, were quick to realize that the sugar-coating of religious and moral counsel concealed a massive dose of social sedation. This was true particularly of the popular literature emanating from the Anglican church, which was increasingly looked upon as the religious arm of the hated Tory government. It is probably significant that when Hannah More, "the old Bishop in petticoats," as Cobbett called her, was induced to return to the battle of the books in 1817, to combat a new home-

[22] *Passages of a Working Life*, I, 242–43.

[23] "Address," p. 14.

[24] Quoted in Hodgen, *Workers' Education*, p. 30.

grown Jacobinism in the person of that same Cobbett, she did not sign her name to her productions.[25] It had become a liability to the cause.

The personal advice offered in many tracts was scarcely better calculated to win the assent of humble readers. Injunctions to ceaseless diligence had a bitterly ironic ring when there was no work to be had; recommendations of frugality were irrelevant when there was no money to save; admonitions to leave one's fate in the hands of an all-wise ruling class were ill timed when desperate workingmen were being mowed down by the rifles of the soldiery or sentenced to transportation for forming trade unions. The contrast between the writers' bland assurance that all would be well and the actual state of affairs as social tensions mounted was too blatant to be ignored.

Nor was it only the contents of the tracts and their characteristic tone which aroused the enmity of many people. The very methods the societies employed, their indifference to human feelings, often defeated their own purposes. When a depression struck Paisley in 1837, throwing thousands of children and adults out of work, Bibles were rushed to the relief of the starving. The British and Foreign Bible Society prided itself on distributing its Bibles and Testaments to the poor in the city slums "in anticipation of the visitation of cholera."[26] The absence of sound epidemiological knowledge at the time spared the recipients the bitterness of reflecting that it was their water supply, more than their souls, that needed disinfecting; but even so, the provision of pious reading matter must have struck many as a feeble substitute for some sort of drastic practical action to put down the disease.

While the Mrs. Jellybys and Pardiggles whom Dickens acidly caricatured may not have been entirely typical of their class, they were not exceptional. The Bible Society had a scheme whereby thousands of eager ladies, pencils and subscription pads in hand, invaded the homes of the poor, trying to persuade them to pay a penny a week toward the purchase of a family Bible. Not until the full sum was paid was the book delivered. Thus, the theory went, the poor could be taught thrift as well as piety. The Religious Tract Society's volunteer workers made their rounds at weekly or

[25] Roberts, IV, 11.
[26] Browne, I, 136, 179.

fortnightly intervals, picking up one tract at each house and leaving another—and at the same time collecting a small fee for the loan.[27] The recurrent appearance of these amateur missionaries in the midst of squalid wretchedness, armed with a fresh tract, inquiring about the spiritual as well as the physical welfare of the household, and offering wholesome admonitions, aroused widespread resentment. Well might the St. Albans slum-dweller, in *Bleak House*, berate Mrs. Pardiggle: "Is my daughter a-washin? Yes, she *is* a-washin. Look at the water. Smell it! That's wot we drinks. How do you like it, and what do you think of gin, instead! An't my place dirty? Yes, it is dirty—it's nat'rally dirty, and it's nat'rally onwholesome; and we've had five dirty and onwholesome children, as is all dead infants, and so much the better for them, and for us besides. Have I read the little book wot you left? No, I an't read the little book wot you left. There an't nobody here as knows how to read it; and if there wos, it wouldn't be suitable to me. It's a book fit for a babby, and I'm not a babby. If you was to leave me a doll, I shouldn't nuss it."[28]

Inevitably the whole idea of reading was associated in many poor people's minds with the tract-distributors, and as a result the printed word became a symbol of their class's degradation. Tracts were inseparable from charity, and charity, as practiced in Victorian times, involved the rubbing in of class distinctions. Working people thought of reading matter in terms of the sort that came with the kettles of free soup in bad times, or the Bibles for which canvassers importuned them to spend a penny a week when their children were too ragged to go to school. The tract-bearers' motives were too obvious to be mistaken. Beneath the veneer of altruism could be seen all too plainly the image of class interest. Tracts were supposed to keep one from thinking wicked Chartist thoughts, to make one content with his empty stomach and stench-filled hovel. A young London pickpocket whom Henry Mayhew interviewed at mid-century said, "They bring tracts to the lodging-houses—pipes are lighted with them;[29] tracts won't

[27] Quinlan, pp. 125, 130.

[28] Dickens, *Bleak House*, chap. viii.

[29] Cobbett hinted, plausibly enough, at another practical use to which the common people put the Religious Tract Society's printed messages; a use which, in his own words, it "would be hardly decent to describe" (*Political Register*, July 21, 1821, p. 62).

fill your belly. Tracts is no good, except to a person that has a home; at the lodging-houses they're laughed at."[30]

The intended audience for religious literature was not, of course, limited to the hungry; the well fed were equally affected by the century-long torrent of print. From the time that a special printing of the Cheap Repository Tracts was ordered for distribution among the children of Evangelical families, the middle class, where evangelicalism was most at home, formed an insatiable market for the edifying tales and the serious didactic and inspirational works that flowed from pious pens.[31] Few are the nineteenth-century autobiographies which fail to contain, among the lists of their authors' early reading, a substantial proportion of religious works, biographical, historical, homiletical, exegetical, reflective. Religious literature formed the largest single category of books published in Britain. Charles Knight, analyzing the *London Catalogue of Books* for the period 1816–51, found that of 45,260 titles published in those years, 10,300, or more than a fifth, were "works on divinity," as against 3,500 works of fiction, 3,400 of drama and poetry, and 2,450 of science.[32] As late as the 1880's, in the annual classification of new books prepared by the *Publishers' Circular*, works of "theology, sermons, biblical, etc." were more numerous than any other class. In 1880, 975 such works were published, as compared with 580 novels, 187 books of poetry and drama, 479 in arts and science, and 363 in history and biography.[33] These figures refer to what are known today as "tradebooks," and do not include reprints and pamphlets (such as individual sermons and tracts), or material published by firms which did not contribute their lists to current book-trade bibliography.

II. Along with the evangelicals' deep faith in the efficacy of print, however, went an equally profound distrust. Rightly used, books could make men wiser, purer, and more de-

---

[30] Mayhew, I, 458.

[31] A good description of the place of religious literature in Victorian middle-class life is found in Cruse, *The Victorians and Their Reading*, chap. ii. One should add that the particular methods used to proselytize the lower classes through print were not necessarily successful when applied to the middle class. In Wilkie Collins' *The Moonstone*, for example, Miss Drusilla Clack made an intolerable nuisance of herself by leaving a trail of religious pamphlets behind her in the substantial households she frequented.

[32] *The Old Printer and the Modern Press*, pp. 260–62.

[33] Cited in *Journal of the Statistical Society*, XLIV (1881), 96.

vout; but misapplied, they could prove a snare of the devil. For the evangelical denominations had a passionate suspicion of imaginative literature: a suspicion which fatefully determined the reading experience of millions of people during the whole century. This neo-Puritan proscription of literature which did not directly enrich its reader's Christian character had so far-reaching an effect upon English culture that it deserves thorough treatment in a separate book. Here it will be possible only to suggest the general tendency of evangelical thinking.[34]

One of the most extended and influential statements of evangelical views on literature was that of the Baptist minister John Foster in his *Essays in a Series of Letters to a Friend* (1805). His proposition was that "far the greatest part of what is termed polite literature . . . is hostile to the religion of Christ; partly, by introducing insensibly a certain order of opinions unconsonant, or at least not identical, with the principles of that religion; and still more, by training the feelings to a habit alien from its spirit."

After a forty-page condemnation of ancient literature as anti-Christian, Foster turned to the "elegant literature" of England itself, which he found unacceptable on several counts. Most such literature, he declared, excluded the basic principles of Christian doctrine. For example, the virtuous people in literature are not sufficiently Christian: "the good man of our polite literature never talks with affectionate devotion of Christ, as the great High Priest of his profession." Again, since much polite literature was moral in intention, and thus was devoted to the subject of happiness, Foster was distressed to find happiness defined and recommended in non-Christian terms, especially in terms of this life alone, whereas "Christian testimony" insisted that the reader should not be "allowed to contemplate any of the interests of life in a view which detaches them from the grand object and conditions of life itself"—namely, the prospect of heavenly bliss. The student of polite literature should be, but seldom was, "impressively reminded of futurity." When adversity, old age, and death were treated in literature, the authors, instead of infusing their reflections with strong Christian sentiment, inclined toward stoical resignation, a sense of inevitability and release.

[34] Among recent treatments of the evangelical antipathy to imaginative literature should be mentioned Quinlan, *Victorian Prelude*, especially chaps. viii and x, and Mineka, *The Dissidence of Dissent*, pp. 55–58, 69–70.

Hence, said Foster, "an approving reader of the generality of our ingenious authors will entertain an opinion of the moral condition of our species very different from the divine declarations." What, for instance, of the motives of action which English authors stressed? They were in direct conflict with the ideals of evangelical Christianity; witness the unseemly celebration, in many literary classics, of the love of earthly glory as an incentive to heroic conduct.

Having canvassed in 250 pages what he conceived to be the eternal conflict between the teachings of Christianity and those of polite literature, Foster nevertheless admitted that "polite literature will necessarily continue to be the grand school of intellectual and moral cultivation." Man could not be prohibited from reading it; but the reader of taste had "the very serious duty of continually recalling to his mind . . . the real character of the religion of the New Testament, and the reasons which command an inviolable adherence to it."[35]

This conclusion, as reluctant as it was realistic, did not commend itself to many other strict evangelical thinkers. They considered it too dangerous for good Christians to expose themselves to the blandishments of imaginative literature. The human will was too frail to be so powerfully tempted, and the only safe course was to avoid reading matter which could in any way imperil the soul. This was the argument underlying the extended discussion in the *Christian Observer* in 1815–17. Here the attack was concentrated upon the most dangerous of all literary forms, the novel. The contribution of someone signing himself "A.A.," a long, intemperate denunciation of fiction, is fairly characteristic of the whole symposium. The most sinister danger residing in the novel, he found, was "the continual feeding of the imagination . . . which, once deceived, becomes itself the deceiver; and instead of embellishing life, as it is falsely represented to do, it heightens only imaginary and unattainable enjoyments, and transforms life itself into a dream, the realities of which are all made painful and disgusting, from our false expectations and erroneous notions of happiness." The constant exercise of the imagination unfitted the

[35] "On Some of the Causes by Which Evangelical Religion Has Been Rendered Unacceptable to Persons of Cultivated Taste," *Essays in a Series of Letters to a Friend* (3d ed., 1806), Vol. II.

reader to meet the harsh realities of life: it divested "the future of all those pangs which yet we must endure when we pass through this future." Furthermore, despite the claims of moralists and aestheticians, we cannot indulge the imagination as mere dispassionate observers. "We cannot . . . read continually a display of human passions and feelings, and remain wholly exempt from their contagion: no; we cannot view the war of passion with the cold and critic eye of an artist, who views the dying agonies of his fallen men only to imitate them on canvas with nicer skill. Let not the analyser of human passions and vices imagine that he can rise uncontaminated from the contemplation." He ended, in a manner hallowed by immemorial usage and still serviceable today, by pointing to the deplorable state of contemporary society. "The last age in France was characterized by the number of profligate novels, and behold the consequences in the total corruption of the present. . . . [And in England] behold their [the novels'] effects in the dissipation, the low tone of public morals, and I will add, the numerous and disgraceful divorces of the day."[36]

Another contributor, "Excubitor," got down to cases. Fielding, Smollett, and Sterne, he said, were "registered in the *index expurgatorius* even of accommodating moralists, and [are] found, I presume, in no decent family." The "romances in rhyme" of Scott and Byron were doubly dangerous, because they were smuggled into the house in musical settings, thus adding deception to other vices. "How unconscious of the evil veiled beneath its decorated surface are those young persons . . . whose voice and speech are suffered to add to their master's compositions a new and living potency!" "Excubitor" admitted that "there is an indulgence, and almost a plenary indulgence, at this day allowed in many religious families, both in retirement and in town life, with regard to secular literature." But he made amply clear that such families were playing with fire.[37]

"Excubitor's" alarm over the rising generation's infatuation with Scott and Byron reflects two more grave counts against imaginative literature: the moral degradation of contemporary writing and the unwholesome appeal which works of the imagination in general had for susceptible youth. Henry Kirke White

[36] *Christian Observer*, XIV (1815), 512–17.
[37] *Ibid.*, XVI (1817), 298–301, 371–75, 425–28.

couched the first charge in these somewhat overelegant sentences: ". . . Literature has, of late years, been prostituted to all the purposes of the bagnio. Poetry, in particular, arrayed in her most bewitching colours, has been taught to exercise the arts of the *Leno*, and to charm only that she may destroy. The Muse, who once dipped her hardy wing in the chastest dews of Castalia, and spoke nothing but what had a tendency to confirm and invigorate the manly ardour of a virtuous mind, now breathes only the voluptuous languishings of the harlot, and, like the brood of Circe, touches her charmed chord with a grace, that, while it ravishes the ear, deludes and beguiles the sense."[38]

The evangelicals were morbidly afraid of overexciting the sensibilities of the young. In its review of Bowdler's purified Shakespeare, the *Christian Observer* began, as was quite customary in the period, with the assumption that adolescence is a period of virtual psychosis, and then went on to maintain that by reading Shakespeare "the mind is enervated and deranged at a time when it ought to be braced and organized. . . . It is scarcely possible for a young person of fervid genius to read Shakespeare without a dangerous elevation of fancy." If only Shakespeare had confined himself to presenting "elves, fairies, and other denizens of their ideal world"! But he presents real life so powerfully that the reader imagines himself to be a king, a warrior, a lover—and thereby loses touch with sober reality, a terrible calamity at a stage in life when the mind should be achieving a permanent insight into things as they are. After going on to show how the same dangers reside in fiction, the reviewer concluded by warning parents to select for their children's reading "such works, and if possible such only, as arrest the attention without alluring it to unsafe objects."[39]

These admonitions were harrowingly documented from personal experience. Charlotte Elizabeth Browne, the daughter of a Norwich clergyman, was seven years old when she innocently came across a copy of *The Merchant of Venice*. "I drank a cup of intoxication under which my brain reeled for many a year," she averred in her reminiscences (1841). "I revelled in the terrible excitement that it gave rise to; page after page was stereotyped upon a most retentive memory, without an effort, and during a sleepless night

[38] *Remains of Henry Kirke White* (10th ed., 1823), I, 218–19.
[39] *Christian Observer*, VII (1808), 326–34.

I feasted on the pernicious sweets thus hoarded in my brain. . . .
Reality became insipid, almost hateful to me; conversation, except
that of literary men, . . . a burden; I imbibed a thorough contempt for women, children, and household affairs, entrenching
myself behind invisible barriers that few, very few, could pass. Oh,
how many wasted hours, how much of unprofitable labour, what
wrong to my fellow-creatures, must I refer to this ensnaring book!
My mind became unnerved, my judgment perverted, my estimate
of people and things wholly falsified, and my soul enwrapped in
the vain solace of unsubstantial enjoyments during years of after
sorrow, when but for this I might have early sought the consola-
tions of the gospel. Parents know not what they do, when from
vanity, thoughtlessness, or over-indulgence, they foster in a young
girl what is called a poetical taste. Those things highly esteemed
among men, are held in abomination with God; they thrust Him
from his creatures' thoughts, and enshrine a host of polluting idols
in his place. . . . My mind was so abundantly stored with the
glittering tinsel of unsanctified genius, as it shone forth in the
pages of my beloved poets, that no room was left for a craving
after better studies."

Having gone through purgatory on account of her indulgence
in books of the imagination, Charlotte Elizabeth, following her
redemption, cherished strict notions on how the reading of the
young should be safeguarded. "I have known many parents and
teachers argue that it is better to bring the young acquainted with
our standard poets and prose authors, of a worldly cast, while they
are yet under careful superintendence, so as to neutralize what
may be unprofitable by judicious remark, and to avert the dangers
attendant on such fascinating introductions at a riper age when
the restraints of authority are removed. Against this, two reasons
have prevailed with me to exclude from my book-shelves all the
furniture of a worldly library, and to watch against its introduction from other quarters": first, since death may strike at any
moment, no time is to be lost in having the child read books of
sacred import—precious hours may not be wasted upon worldly
literature; and second, "the flesh and the devil will assuredly do
their parts without help from me."[40]

[40] Charlotte Elizabeth Browne Phelan Tonna, *Personal Recollections* (New York, 1845),
passim. One may sensibly infer from her whole curious book, as well as from her career

It was easy to amass a list of evils that fiction and the drama achieved; impossible, in the strict evangelical view, to think of any benefits. "Ask the man," urged a writer in the *Methodist Magazine*, "who with a smiling but vacant countenance, rises from reading *Tom Jones, Don Quixote*, etc. if his judgment is better informed; if his mind is more expanded; his stock of ideas increased; or if he is better prepared for performing the duties of his station?" The answer was obvious: reading fiction was a waste of time, "that precious boon of heaven." The same writer argued that God specifically forbade the reading of novels, and he offered citations from Scripture to prove it.[41]

Little wonder, then, considering this imposing variety of objections to imaginative literature, that the "Spiritual Barometer" of the evangelicals should have allotted it a low place in the moral scale of human activity. This barometer, published in the *Evangelical Magazine*[42] for 1800, began with plus 70 ("Glory; dismission from the body"), descended to zero ("indifference"), and reached down to minus 70 ("death, perdition"). On this interesting scale, "love of novels, etc.; scepticism; private prayer totally neglected; deistical company prized" were lumped tog ther at minus 40—ten degrees lower than "the theatre; Vauxha. Ranelagh, etc." and but ten degrees higher than "parties of pleas . on the Lord's day; masquerades; drunkenness; adultery; profan ness; lewd songs."[43]

Why the contriver of the barometer was slightly more tolerant of theater-going than of novel-reading we cannot tell, for the evangelicals were as firmly opposed to the drama as to fiction. The Methodists especially were active in suppressing the theater wherever their influence was felt in municipal affairs.[44] In a great many families affected by the religious revival there was a stern prohibition upon attendance at any sort of dramatic entertainment, no matter how innocent. This fact has its own direct bearing

---

as a prolific ultra-Protestant writer, that she was more than a little inclined to hysteria. It is a relief therefore to have her assurance that, despite her woeful childhood, she had "grown up to be one of the healthiest of human beings, and with an inexhaustible flow of ever mirthful spirits."

[41] *Methodist Magazine*, XLII (1819), 606–609.

[42] An organ of the nonconformists, not, as its title might suggest, of the Low Church Anglicans.

[43] Quinlan, p. 115.   [44] Hammond, *The Age of the Chartists*, p. 258.

on the history of the reading public, for, by boycotting the play-house, the evangelicals effectively removed one source of competition to books. For want of anything else to do in the evenings, they had to stay home and pass their leisure hours in reading.

       III. So far, our evidence has confirmed the familiar view of the early nineteenth-century evangelical reader as a person of inflexible seriousness, shuddering at the thought of worldly amusement. Such a stereotype has much truth in it. Yet every generalization concerning evangelical attitudes toward books and reading must immediately be qualified. Theory is not identical with practice, and practice itself varied from denomination to denomination, from decade to decade, from household to household, and, indeed, from book to book.

       Though Zachary Macaulay, one of the leading lay Evangelicals of the time, was opposed to novels on principle, he was too indulgent a parent to forbid his children to read fiction, and he lived, as his grandson, G. O. Trevelyan, said, to see himself "the head of a family in which novels were more read, and better remembered, than in any household of the United Kingdom."[45] It was his sixteen-year-old son, Thomas Babington Macaulay, who shattered the unanimity of the *Christian Observer*'s discussion of fiction, already mentioned, with a warm defense of the novel. Writing as "Candidus," he argued that though the imagination could be abused, still it was "both useful and delightful, when confined to its proper province. Then it awakens the sympathies and softens the heart, excites the strongest veneration for all that is great, elevated, or virtuous, and the utmost detestation and disgust for the meanness and misery of vice."[46] While "Candidus" may have intended a prank, his arguments were quite cogent, and they set forth a position which numerous moderate evangelicals shared.[47]

       The Ruskin household is commonly thought of as a domain of strait-laced, humorless puritanism. But that is only because Mrs.

[45] G. O. Trevelyan, *Life and Letters of Macaulay*, in his edition of Macaulay's *Works* (1908), IX, 61.

[46] *Christian Observer*, XV (1816), 784–86.

[47] Other contributors to the symposium supported Macaulay's view: see *ibid.*, XVI (1817), 227–31.

Ruskin's insistence on reading the Bible straight through with her son once a year, from Genesis to Revelation, and the confinement of his Sunday reading to *Pilgrim's Progress*, Foxe's *Book of Martyrs*, Quarles's *Emblems*, and the improving tales of Mrs. Sherwood, are better remembered than the more genial side of the story. Ruskin's father was a devotee of Scott, and as a child Ruskin himself knew the Waverley novels and Pope's *Iliad* better than any other book except the Bible. After tea, it was the father's custom to read aloud to his wife and son, and the choice of authors in these sessions was as broad as one could find in any cultured early nineteenth-century household: Shakespeare's comedies and histories, *Don Quixote*, Spenser, Pope, Goldsmith, Addison, Johnson. By the time he was fifteen Ruskin was thoroughly acquainted with Byron, a poet who according to orthodox evangelical canons was as wholesome, say, as Aretino. And though Mrs. Ruskin was opposed to the playhouse, she did not object seriously to her husband's taking the boy there; when it was a matter of seeing the dancer Taglioni, she went along too.[48]

But even more startling is the revelation that Mr. and Mrs. Ruskin, according to their son, "enjoyed their *Humphry Clinker* extremely." This is not the sort of taste one would expect to find openly avowed in an evangelical household, even one with a pronounced Scots flavor, but it well illustrates the charming illogicality of evangelical practice in respect to the great eighteenth-century novelists. William Wilberforce, a man of extremely strict principles, specifically exempted Richardson from his general censure, and in this he was followed by many evangelicals who regarded Richardson as a paragon of morality.[49] Young "Candidus" Macaulay, in his *Christian Observer* article, wrote a spirited defense of Fielding: "The man who rises unaffected and unimproved from the picture of the fidelity, simplicity, and virtue of Joseph Andrews and his Fanny, and the parental solicitude of Parson Adams, must possess a head and a heart of stone."[50]

[48] Ruskin, *Praeterita, passim.*

[49] Frederic T. Blanchard, *Fielding the Novelist: A Study in Historical Criticism* (New Haven, 1926), p. 266.

[50] *Christian Observer*, XV (1816), 785. The spread of evangelical literary prejudices could be measured by systematically studying the declining popularity of the classic eighteenth-century novelists. In the first third of the nineteenth century these novelists were still popular enough to warrant their being made the backbone of reprint series de-

Generally the Evangelicals proper (the Porteus-More-Wilber-force-Macaulay sect) were more liberal than the dissenters. While their principal organ, the *Christian Observer*, gave prominent space to reviews of *The Lady of the Lake*, Crabbe's *Borough*, and the first cantos of *Childe Harold*, dissenting periodicals, such as the *Eclectic Review*, paid little or no attention to current secular literature, except by way of condemnation. During the first decades of the century, the Methodists severely contracted the limits of their toleration, placing out of bounds large areas of literature which their founder had encouraged his followers to read. Only gradually, long after Victoria's reign had begun, did the *Wesleyan Methodist Magazine* (as it was called after 1821) begin to review secular books.[51]

Yet even among the Methodists we find the same evidence of varying practice. One of the innumerable charges of heterodoxy brought against the Primitive Methodist preacher, Joseph Barker, was that his superintendent, ransacking his room one day, found books of "an objectionable character," among them the works of Byron and Shakespeare. Barker recorded, however, that he was not the only preacher who valued the cheerier side of life and let-ters. He knew another who descended from his pulpit to revel in *Don Quixote*, Boswell, and Johnson's *Lives of the Poets*. "One hour he would be preaching with all the horror and solemnity imaginable about the eternal and infinite torments of the damned, and then in an hour or two he would be laughing at a ridiculous story, as if his sides could hardly hold him together."[52]

The autobiography of Benjamin Gregory, another minister, who became editor of the *Wesleyan Methodist Magazine* in 1876,

---

signed for the middle-class audience. But then, as evangelical attitudes (or what we call, more generally, "Victorian prudery") affected more and more readers, and as Dickens' generation of fiction-writers took over, the eighteenth-century novel lost ground. In 1866 Alexander Macmillan considered bringing out a "Globe Series" of novels. "The difficulty," he wrote his friend James MacLehose, "is the selection. You begin with Richardson, Fielding, Smollett, Sterne. But what are you to do with their dirt? Modern taste won't stand it. I don't particularly think they *ought* to stand it. Still less would they stand cas-tration" (Charles L. Graves, *Life and Letters of Alexander Macmillan* [1910], p. 249). The project was dropped; and in the multiplying classic-reprint series down to the end of the Victorian era the great novelists Macmillan mentions seldom appeared.

[51] Mathews, *Methodism and the Education of the People*, p. 173; *Wesleyan Methodist Magazine*, LXXVIII (1855), 12–13.

[52] Barker, *Life*, pp. 110–11, 116.

gives us what is possibly the most detailed account of a young Wesleyan's reading, in this case between 1825 and 1840. Showing as it does how relatively broad a selection of reading matter was available in a Methodist household and school, and how poignantly a youth could be torn between attitudes received from the church and his own literary inclinations, it is a useful corrective to facile generalizations concerning the place of reading in nonconformist life.

Gregory's father, a Methodist circuit-rider in northern Yorkshire, shared with his wife a strong appetite for reading. In addition to the works of Maria Edgeworth and Hannah More, the child's earliest books included Mrs. Sherwood's *The Fairchild Family*, which, looking back after many years, he praised for its "unforced humour, and its wholesome tenderness." In this household the great event of the month was the arrival of a package from "City Road," the London headquarters of Wesleyanism, containing the *Youth's Instructor* and the *Methodist Magazine*. From both periodicals, Gregory's mother and sister immediately read all the poetry aloud and memorized it: Wordsworth, Scott, Byron, and many other contemporary figures—Bernard Barton, Felicia Hemans, Bishop Heber, Milman, Croly, Bowring, the Howitts—most of it extracted from the then popular annuals. The child's imagination also was constantly stirred (with no ill effects that he could later remember) by the denominational magazines' tales of travel and lives of missionaries. Even in bleak Yorkshire there was no lack of exotic atmosphere and adventuresome narratives so long as Methodist periodicals kept arriving from City Road.

The Gregorys' successive homes during their years of itineracy were well supplied with books. When a circulating library was nearby, the mother would subscribe, "for elegant and entertaining literature seemed to her, and became to some of her children, as one of the necessaries of life." At one time, too, the Methodist Book Room being in difficulties, many ministers and laymen contracted to buy five pounds' worth of books each. The books the Gregorys acquired by this means included Coke's *History of the West Indies*, Gambold's *Poems*, and Clarke's *Wesley Family* (a particular favorite, which "supplied the preacher's family with delightful reading for many 'evenings at home' "). By a friend's bequest the household also obtained a set of the *Lady's Magazine*, which, "though morally unexceptionable, and, indeed, in most respects, high-toned, improving, and refined, . . . was spiritually and practically unhelpful and unhealthful, having about it the feverish flush of a sort of subtropical sentimentalism. Thus was generated a taste for a kind of literary confectionery which could not nourish a robust fibre either of the mind or heart." Even worse were two novels published in instalments, which Gregory's sisters persuaded their mother to buy from vendors who came to the door—*Fatherless Fanny* and *The Mysterious Marriage*. "The new-fangled novels were like the deceitful bakemeats of some huxtering heathen, smuggled into a Levite's tent."

When he was eight years old, Gregory—who at the time had been busily reading the Apocrypha, *The Arabian Nights*, Jane Porter's *The Scottish Chiefs*, and Mrs. Barbauld's *Evenings at Home*—was sent to a Methodist school, Woodhouse Grove, near Leeds. The library there, he says, "was not an ill-assorted collection, although to a great extent a stud of 'gift-horses.' " Fiction was excluded (note the difference, in this respect, between the policy of a Methodist school and that of a Methodist preacher in his own household), but the works of non-fiction "contained a vast amount of literary pemmican, well-pounded and well-packed, not dried to hardness, and sufficiently seasoned to be palatable, and not destitute of 'officinal properties.' " Among the books Gregory delighted in were Mavor's *Universal History*, Cook's *Voyages*, Robertson's histories of Scotland and America, Bryant's *Analysis of Ancient Mythology*, and Hill's *Miniature Portraits; or, Brief Biography*. Standard English literature was represented by the *Spectator* and Hume's *History of England;* among books of travel, Bruce's *Abyssinia* and Mungo Park's *Interior of Africa* were noteworthy; among biographies, the lives of Colonel Gardiner and Colonel Blackader. *Rasselas*, however, Gregory found a dull book, "with its stilted style, its soporific cadences, and its tedious moralising," and Fénelon's *Telemachus* he decided was "very tiresome."

Gregory had the opportunity also to read books borrowed from his schoolmates, and the variety of these books, especially when we remember that they came chiefly from the family libraries of Methodist ministers, is remarkable: narratives of the *Bounty* and of Arctic expeditions; Anson's *Voyages;* Buffon's *Natural History;*

Pope's *Homer;* translations of *Orlando Furioso* and *The Lusiads;*
"an exquisite selection of most graceful classic poetry, which well
sustained its title of *Calliope*"; *Hudibras;* Dryden's translations
of Virgil and Ovid; Ossian; and "some volumes of Elegant
Extracts."

Inescapably, young Gregory's life witnessed an agonizing conflict between Christ and Apollo. "The literary fever did eat into the
heart of my spiritual constitution. I became vain in my 'imaginations,' and 'my foolish heart was darkened.' Surely I 'walked in a
vain show' of heathenish and worldly phantasy." Between his
eighth and twelfth years he had been seduced by three tempters,
the classics ("my fancy . . . became completely hellenised and
therefore heathenised"), romanticism—the lyrics of Goldsmith,
Prior, Pope, and the romantic narratives of Ariosto and Spenser—
and contemporary hack fiction, which he had discovered in circulating libraries during his school vacations—*The Farmer's Daughter of Essex, The Gipsy Countess*, and *The Cottage on the Cliff.* "The
effect which all this had upon my spiritual life is but too easily
described," he says. "I gradually lost all interest in 'the things that
are not seen' but 'eternal.' " He sacrificed his Bible-reading to poring over more worldly books. In such a condition, he was ripe for
the spiritual crisis and the eventual conversion he underwent in
early adolescence. For the first nine months of his "new-born life,"
he kept "aloof from the over-mastering fascinations of secular literature. . . . 'The primrose-path of dalliance' with the Graces and
the Muses was Bye-path Meadow to my as yet unsteady feet."
Accordingly, he read nothing but the Bible and exegetical works.

But after the crisis was past and Gregory was firmly in command
of his Christian character, he had no hard feelings toward the literary companions of his childhood. Seductive though they had
been in some ways, in others he is frank to admit they were good
for him. From the sentimental stuff he read he had acquired "a not
ignoble sensibility," and from the Greek and Roman writers "an
intense admiration and eager emulation of . . . *the public and social
virtues:* such as patriotism and fidelity in friendship." Now that he
was sure of his ground, he felt strong enough to return to secular
reading. In his nineteenth year, just before he became a candidate
for the ministry, he devoted himself to Shakespeare and Wordsworth. At the same time he read *The Spirit of the Age*, and "the

spell of Hazlitt's eloquence conjured up within me the old poetic passion." A year or two later, he discovered the poetry of Bryant and Willis, "which acted on my mind like a balmy breath from the transatlantic shores," and Channing's essay on Milton, which made a deep impression on an extraordinary number of contemporary readers.

Then his health broke down, and, forbidden to do any serious reading, this earnest probationer for the ministry turned to *The Vicar of Wakefield*, Scott's novels, the then popular tales of Samuel Warren, and *Blackwood's, Fraser's*, and the *Quarterly Review*. The next year, his health regained, he spent his holidays at his father's cottage reading Heber's life of Jeremy Taylor, Beattie's *Minstrel*, Mason's *Life of Gray* ("a most delectable book"), and the poetry of Byron and Shelley, despite "the flippant irreligion and the cynic immorality of the former, and the rabid and blaspheming God-hate of the latter": because, says Gregory, "I could not but acknowledge both as masters of the English tongue."[53]

This case history of a future minister's reading down to his twenty-first year is not, perhaps, typical; but on the other hand it cannot be unique. It indicates that there resided in at least certain areas of nineteenth-century evangelical religion, with all its anxieties about overindulgence in worldly literature, a greater tolerance and respect for letters than is ordinarily credited to it.

Gregory's remarks on the contents of the *Methodist Magazine* and the volumes sent from the Book Room remind us, furthermore, that the reading matter produced under religious auspices in the early nineteenth century was not quite as arid and heavy as we are prone to imagine. There was, to be sure, far too much piety and moral didacticism. Even the researcher, occupationally inured to bone-dry, dreary reading, soon abandons his foray into the desolate wastes of evangelical print. But what is desert to him was a land flowing with milk and honey to those who were barred from great areas of secular literature. In it, they found at least some of the basic satisfactions that any reader desires.

For the disapproval of fiction never extended to narratives specially written to convey some useful moral or religious lesson. The Cheap Repository Tracts and the shoal of leaflets that followed in their wake, the little stories in children's magazines and Sunday-

---

[53] Gregory, *Autobiographical Recollections, passim.*

school reward books, and the tales of such unimpeachably orthodox writers as Mrs. Sherwood and Miss Edgeworth all depended
for their appeal upon a story element, no matter how far this was
subordinated to their message.

The contents of the popular religious periodicals reflected their
editors' awareness of the human craving for wonder and romance.
Long before fiction itself was admitted to their pages, "true fact"
material offered a substitute of a sort. For instance, in a single
volume (1812) of the *Methodist Magazine*, under the heading "The
Works of God Displayed" (an important section of the magazine
for many years), appeared pieces on Jonah and the whale, on the
unicorn, and on the "hippopotamus amphibia, or river horse"—
disquisitions with obvious didactic purpose but capable nevertheless of removing the mind many leagues from the grime of Birmingham or London. In another regular section of the magazine,
"The Providence of God Asserted," were printed short "factual"
narratives: "Dreadful Death of a Profane Man in the County of
Bucks," "Preservation of the Moravian Brethren in North America from a General Massacre," "A Singular Dream, and Its Consequences," "Conversion and Preservation of a Poor Woman," "Aw-
ful Death of a Profane Man at Dublin." If the pious reader were
prevented from reading sensational fiction or historical romance,
his craving for the emotions of pity, horror, and fear was to some
extent met by such accounts. And if it was the music and imagery
of poetry he desired, these too were supplied by the generous extracts the *Methodist Magazine* printed from approved poets like
Heber and Montgomery, Wordsworth and Bernard Barton.

The same rewards were found in thousands of the books that
circulated among the various evangelical denominations. A modern writer, E. E. Kellett, has observed that "instead of novels, our
grandfathers had a large and fascinating literature of their own,
which, if this generation would consent to read it, might drive out
the detective novel." The countless religious biographies were not
merely interesting, they often were out-and-out thrillers. "If you
wanted a touch of the antique, you read the *Tracts* of John Eliot,
the Apostle of the Red Indians, or George Fox's *Journals;* if you
were martially inclined, there was Doddridge's *Colonel Gardiner*,
or Catherine Marsh's *Captain Hedley Vicars*."[54] It will not do,

[54] *As I Remember*, pp. 117–18.

therefore, to think of the evangelical reader as suffering emotional and imaginative deprivation in direct proportion to his abstinence from secular literature. Like his Puritan ancestor, he found intense excitement in much of his reading, though it was an excitement bred for the most part by substance rather than by style.

IV. "What then," exclaimed Southey in 1810, "must be the effect of a confederated and indefatigable priesthood, who barely tolerate literature, and actually hate it, upon all those classes over whom literature has any influence!"[55]

The effect was immense, and, as the preceding pages have suggested, it was felt most strongly in the realm of secular fiction. The hostility to novels which had been building up for several decades reached its peak in the early nineteenth century. The primary target was the circulating-library novel, compact of sensationalism, sentimentality, and (in the evangelical view) salaciousness. It was this very kind of book, however, which was best adapted to the taste of the reader whose limited education equipped him to relish little else. "If put to the vote of all the milliners' girls in London," Hazlitt remarked, "*Old Mortality*, or even *Heart of Midlothian*, would not carry the day (or, at least, not very triumphantly) over a common Minerva-press novel."[56]

To most critics of popular reading habits, the Minerva Press novel was synonymous with fiction in general, and the great fear was that, left to its own devices, the semiliterate audience would read nothing else. And so, in pulpit, periodical, pamphlet, and book, the religious parties warned against the evils of "light literature," and in every scheme for public enlightenment and moral correction in which they had a part, one of their supreme motives was to kill the addiction in the germ, or, if the time had passed for that, to cut off its means of nourishment.[57] In the long run they

---

[55] *Quarterly Review*, IV (1810), 506–507.

[56] "Outlines of Taste," *Works*, ed. Howe, XX, 386.

[57] Another book as large as this could be made by collecting the contemporary utterances on the subject, but one sample must suffice. It is especially noteworthy because of its date, 1845. At that time the evangelical campaign against circulating-library fiction was more than half a century old. The crusaders' fund of invective had held out well, but their target had proved indestructible. "[The circulating library system] secured . . . the certain flow and overflow of the worst and most perverting and corrupting nonsense throughout the country, and poured it in torrents on the heads of those in whom it was likely to produce the most ruinous and calamitous effects. . . . To what an extent of corrupted views, im-

failed; eventually the mass audience got all the fiction it wanted. But the long crusade against fiction undoubtedly slowed the spread of reading among the common people. By barring from cheap religious reading matter the qualities most attractive to the novice reader; by denying him any acquaintance with pleasurable reading in elementary schools, village libraries, and other educational agencies under their control; and by spreading the notion that "the very name of a labourer has something about it with which amusement seems out of character,"[58] the religious parties severely limited both the range and the attractiveness of the literary experience available to the working class.

Among the middle class the evangelical campaign was so successful that after the first third of the century the prevailing attitude toward fiction gradually softened. This was not so much a retreat from the extreme position of earlier years as a sign that the novelists themselves had bowed to religious pressure, which was manifested in the changed climate of taste. To find a market in the purified society of Victorian days they had to conform to rigid moral specifications. Once they had learned to do so, and once the scrupulous Mr. Mudie had been confirmed in his police power over newly published novels, the way was open for the "respectable" reading public to enjoy fiction with a clear conscience. Writing in 1876, Trollope commented on the great change that had occurred in fifty years: "The families in which an unrestricted permission was given for the reading of novels were [then] very few, and from many they were altogether banished. The high poetic genius and

---

practicable notions, impossible wishes, and miserable regrets and disappointments in life; of seduction, of lazy and unsettled habits, of dishonesty, robbery, and even murder, the habit of reading the ever-pouring stream of high-flown and sentimental fiction from the circulating library has been the origin—especially amongst females of the lower orders— it would be difficult to calculate; but it is awfully great. Those who have made it a Samaritan duty to visit the obscure dwellings of the poor, must often have detected in the miserable mother of better days, now surrounded by squalor and wretched children, the desolating effects of the spirituous dram, and the fascination of circulating-library reading" ("New and Cheap Forms of Popular Literature," *Eclectic Review*, LXXXII [1845], 76). For a good collection of antifiction opinion before 1830, see Taylor, *Early Opposition to the English Novel*, chap. v, as well as the article by Gallaway (cited in n. 85 to chapter 2) and Winfield H. Rogers, "The Reaction against Melodramatic Sentimentality in the English Novel, 1796–1830," *PMLA*, XLIX (1934), 98–122. On the place of fiction in early Victorian literary thought, see George H. Ford, *Dickens and His Readers* (Princeton, 1955), pp. 24–34.

[58] Herschel, "Address," pp. 9–10.

correct morality of Walter Scott had not altogether succeeded in making men and women understand that lessons which were good in poetry could not be bad in prose. . . . There is . . . no such embargo now. . . . Novels are read right and left, above stairs and below, in town houses and in country parsonages, by young countesses and by farmers' daughters, by old lawyers and by young students. It has not only come to pass that a special provision of them has to be made for the godly, but that the provision so made must now include books which a few years since the godly would have thought to be profane."[59]

Trollope was thinking of an episode in his own career. In 1863 Dr. Norman Macleod, one of the queen's chaplains and editor of the family periodical *Good Words*, had asked Trollope to write a novel for his pages.[60] Although Macleod declined the resulting book, *Rachel Ray*, as not quite suitable, the episode exemplifies the changed situation in the mid-Victorian era. Religious papers had been printing fiction for some time, but it was didactic fiction from the pens of clergymen and pious females. Here, however, was an editor who sought a novel by a professional writer belonging to the secular press. To Macleod, according to his son, "the gulf which separated the so-called religious and the secular press was . . . caused by the narrowness and literary weakness of even the best religious magazines. He could see no good reason for leaving the wholesome power of fiction, the discussion of questions in physical and social science, together with all the humour and fun of life, to serials which excluded Christianity from their pages."[61]

Macleod did not have clear sailing, for the old prejudices were still alive in some quarters. The *Record*, an extreme evangelical paper, spoke out vituperatively against *Good Words*, and attempts were made to have the periodical blacklisted by the tract societies and the Society for the Diffusion of Pure Literature among the People, an organization headed by the Earl of Shaftesbury which sought to elevate the reading tastes of the masses by promoting the sale of cheap family periodicals that met its strict evangelical requirements and by preventing the sale of those that did not.[62] The

[59] *Autobiography*, ed. B. A. Booth (Berkeley, Calif., 1947), pp. 182–83. [60] *Ibid.*, p. 156.

[61] Donald Macleod, *Memoir of Norman Macleod* (New York, 1876), II, 97.

[62] *Good Words* was denounced not only because it printed fiction. Macleod's critics worried lest "young persons" would be tempted to read "secular" articles on Sunday. He re-

squabble agitated the religious and literary worlds, but the outcome was certain. From the sixties onward, religious publishing houses issued novels in ever greater profusion, and the pages of denominational periodicals were open to short stories and serial fiction supplied from the literary marketplace. Romance, once the outlaw of nineteenth-century popular literature, had become domesticated.

Throughout the century, the concern for wholesomeness in literature resulted in the production of the "extract," a strained broth concocted from the original work. It was recognized that many books of earlier times could not be read in their complete form without peril to the soul; yet those same classics undeniably had sound qualities which should not be withheld from the virtuous. Hence the old eighteenth-century practice of printing "beauties" of various individual authors and "elegant extracts" from the whole range of polite literature now became a favorite device of censorship. This was particularly handy in connection with Shakespeare, who, though admittedly a national ornament, had had the ill grace to associate himself with the playhouse. As a popular Methodist preacher observed in 1806, "Barefaced obscenities, low vulgarity, and nauseous vice so frequently figure and pollute his pages that we cannot but lament the luckless hour in which he became a writer for the stage."[63] Some sixty years later, a speaker at a meeting of the extremist sect to which Edmund Gosse's father belonged declared, "At this very moment there is proceeding, unreproved, a blasphemous celebration of the birth of Shakespeare, a lost soul now suffering for his sins in hell."[64] And even later, when the secretary of a literary guild in a Methodist church proposed to conduct "An Evening with Shakespeare's Contem-

torted: "If any members of a Christian family are compelled to endure such severe and dry exercises on the Sunday as would make them long for even the scientific articles in *Good Words* . . . why not lock up *Good Words?*" Another objection was that the contributors were drawn from various schools of theology and literature, Trollope, Kingsley, and Dr. Stanley rubbing shoulders with strong Evangelicals. Macleod defended this eclecticism but gave his solemn promise that "no infidel, no immoral man or woman, no one whom I could not receive, in so far as character is concerned, into my family, will ever be permitted to write in the pages of *Good Words*"—a revealing sidelight on Victorian editorial policy (*ibid.*, II, 135–43).

[63] Quoted in Quinlan, p. 226.

[64] Edmund Gosse, *Father and Son* (New York, 1907), p. 306.

poraries," the minister changed it to "An Evening with Long-fellow."[65]

Since it was almost universally acknowledged that Shakespeare was the supreme poetic philosopher, he could hardly be ignored completely. The less rigorous moralists encouraged the use of heavily expurgated versions of the plays; Thomas Bowdler and James Plumptre, the two most energetic wielders of the blue pencil early in the century, were succeeded by numerous editors who enabled the "March of Modesty," in Southey's sardonic phrase, to keep pace with the March of Intellect.[66] But to many others a play was a play, however pruned, and this school relied instead upon collections of the master's wise observations, wrenched completely from their dramatic matrix. Down through the century "Proverbs from Shakespeare" and "Select Beauties of Shakespeare" were fixtures in middle-class libraries, and alongside them were similar nosegays from other authors whose works it was deemed imprudent to read in their original form.

There remains, in this cluster of evangelical influences upon reading, the matter of Sabbatarianism. Even in households which otherwise were little touched by the religious revival, Sunday was a day upon which only books of serious significance might be opened. They might be secular works, such as histories or travels, or in the case of the boy Ruskin (in deference, as he wryly remarked, to the hardness of his heart) a book of natural history.[67] Preferably, however, they had a religious flavor. For that reason countless children acquired an intimate knowledge of *Paradise Lost* and *Pilgrim's Progress*—books which they might never have known but for an English Sunday. Faced with the alternative of a volume of sermons or *Paradise Lost*, they chose the less dull; and in such a fortuitous manner they got to know, and in many cases to admire, a great monument of English literature. As Mrs. Leavis has observed, "The difference that the disappearance of the Sunday book a generation ago has made, its effect on the outlook and mental capacity of the people, would repay investigation."[68] Certainly the audience for the great serious writers of the time was

[65] Edwards, *Methodism and England*, pp. 225–26.

[66] *The Doctor*, ed. M. H. Fitzgerald (1930), p. 327.

[67] *Praeterita*, chap. iv.

[68] *Fiction and the Reading Public*, p. 117.

increased by the discipline to which readers' minds had been subjected, from earliest childhood, on the Sabbath. To such people the
"prose of ideas"—Carlyle, Mill, Newman, Ruskin, Spencer, for
example—offered little of the difficulty it presents to readers today, who devote their Sundays, if they read at all, to newspapers
and magazines.

Another major influence of Sabbatarianism upon reading habits
was mentioned in the preceding chapter. By limiting the ways in
which time could be passed on Sunday, it forced many people to
read who would otherwise have played games, attended concerts or
plays, or wandered through parks or museums. Since the English
Sunday affected saint and sinner alike, even those who did not
share evangelical prejudices were driven to books, unless they were
content to spend the heavy hours staring vacantly into space. How
many children and adults discovered the pleasure of reading by
being immobilized on Sunday? On the other hand, how many potential readers acquired a lifelong distaste for books by the somber
association between reading and Sunday discipline? We cannot
tell. But the fact that Sabbatarianism cut both ways is one final
illustration of the complex and contradictory effect that nineteenth-century religious mores had upon the spread of the taste for
reading.

CHAPTER 6 } *The Utilitarian Spirit*

I. Utilitarianism, the philosophy begotten by eighteenth-century French rationalism upon eighteenth-century English materialism, is associated most immediately with the coterie dominated by Jeremy Bentham and James Mill. But just as the spirit of evangelicalism permeated English society far beyond the denominational boundaries, so utilitarianism spread out from its originating group until it was part of the atmosphere every nineteenth-century Englishman breathed. Like evangelicalism, utilitarianism became not so much a set of formal tenets as a state of mind. All sorts of people embraced one cluster or another of the characteristic utilitarian assumptions and prejudices.[1] These notions operated deviously or directly as the case may be, potently, and often with opposite effect, upon the development of a mass reading audience.

As we observed at the opening of the last chapter, evangelicalism and utilitarianism sometimes worked with unexpected harmony toward identical ends. The two movements, the one religious, the other not only secular but in its pure state anti-Christian, were jointly responsible for the early nineteenth century's veneration of the printing press.

"Until printing was very generally spread," wrote the mathe-

---

[1] Hence it should be kept in mind that throughout this book, the terms "utilitarianism" and "Benthamism" will be used as broadly as "evangelicalism." Some of the material in this chapter refers specifically to the ideas of Bentham and his immediate followers, and to those of the "philosophical radicals" led by John Stuart Mill, who were unable to swallow strict Benthamism whole. But it is also generally applicable to that "wider Benthamism" which, as D. C. Somervell says, became "the spirit of the new age": the spirit of middle-class Victorian liberalism at large, hard-headed, sanguine, bustling, and intolerant of romantic idealism (*English Thought in the Nineteenth Century* [New York, 1936], p. 49). The semantic difficulty could be overcome if the word "Broughamism" were current in the vocabulary of history, for Henry Brougham and his disciples best typify this broadly defined utilitarianism.

matician Charles Babbage, "civilization scarcely advanced by slow and languid steps; since that art has become cheap, its advances have been unparalleled, and its rate of progress vastly accelerated."[2] No sentiment was more frequently or grandiloquently repeated in the first half of the century. Ebenezer Elliott, the Corn-Law Rhymer, put it into panegyric verse:

> Mind, mind alone,
> Is light, and hope, and life, and power!
> Earth's deepest night, from this bless'd hour,
>   The night of minds, is gone!
> "The Press!" all lands shall sing;
>   The Press, the Press we bring,
>   All lands to bless:
> Oh, pallid want! oh, labor stark!
> Behold, we bring the second ark!
> The Press! The Press! The Press![3]

And in phrases indistinguishable from those of the Benthamites themselves, Richard Carlile, the free-thinking republican, asserted: "The Printing-press may be strictly denominated a Multiplication Table as applicable to the mind of man. The art of Printing is a multiplication of mind, and since the art is discovered, the next important thing is to make it applicable to the means of acquirement possessed by the humblest individual among mankind, or him whose means are most scanty. Thus it is evident that a compression of sound moral truths within pamphlets, as the smallest and cheapest forms of giving effect to this multiplication of mind, is most conducive to the general good, and the future welfare, of mankind."[4]

Radical or conservative, laissez faire liberal or Owenite, evangelical or skeptic, everyone seemed to share this faith in a machine that could usher in the social millennium just as surely as the power of steam was transforming the outward face of English life. Each party, naturally, had its special brand of Truth to disseminate through print. The utilitarians' own goal was "the diffusion of useful knowledge." To them, useful knowledge was of two kinds. In the first place, it embraced whatever sort of information was

[2] Quoted in Timperley, *Encyclopaedia of Literary and Typographical Anecdote*, p. 808.

[3] "The Press," *Poetical Works* (1844), I, 122.

[4] Quoted from Carlile's *Republican*, March 1, 1822, in Wickwar, *The Struggle for the Freedom of the Press*, pp. 214–15.

necessary to multiply and spread the blessings of machinery. Useful knowledge was the good, solid, employable facts of mechanics and chemistry, metallurgy and hydraulics—facts that could be applied in the workshop and on the railway line, to produce goods more cheaply and efficiently, to communicate and transport more swiftly. In addition, "useful knowledge" was a set of economic and political principles. Possessing an almost religious faith in the supposedly immutable economic and social laws formulated by Adam Smith, Ricardo, Malthus, Bentham, Mill, and the other Jeromes and Augustines of industrial-age thought, the utilitarians were convinced that only by safeguarding the free operation of those laws could the nation be spared future social anarchy and economic catastrophe. Once he saw the reasonableness of classical economics, every man would wholeheartedly support laissez faire and all that went with it, and dangerous heresies—socialism, republicanism, Cobbettism, Chartism—would be extinguished. That was why Brougham's Society for the Diffusion of Useful Knowledge was dedicated as much to justifying the ways of God to economic man as it was to explaining the mysteries of calico-printing and iron-founding. The "scientific" doctrines behind political liberalism were as useful as any body of technological information.

Even more important than books and pamphlets in the utilitarian program of enlightenment were newspapers, which appealed to a public that shrank from exploring more extensive tracts of print. "Here," wrote Brougham, ". . . is a channel through which, alongside with political intelligence and the occurrences of the day, the friends of human improvement, the judicious promoters of general education, may diffuse the best information, and may easily allure all classes, even the humblest, into the paths of general knowledge."[5] Superficially, such a statement would suggest that the utilitarians aided the battle for a cheap press out of entirely disinterested motives. But when we recall how loaded such terms as "information," "knowledge," and "education" can be, it is plain that they regarded the newspaper press as an adjunct to their other propaganda agencies—their cheap libraries of "useful" and "entertaining" knowledge, the *Penny Magazine*, and the mechanics' institutes. Their participation in the campaign to abolish the burdensome taxes on newspapers rested on the assumption

[5] *Edinburgh Review*, LXI (1835), 184.

that the press, once freed, would fall into the hands of responsible interests who could be relied upon to disseminate correct ideas. They admitted the possibility that the floodgates would also be opened for the worst sort of demagoguery, but, adopting for the occasion the eighteenth century's trust in the power of reason, they were confident that the common man would discriminate between the false dogma of the Cobbetts and O'Connors and the truths of middle-class liberalism.

Hence the evangelicals and the utilitarians together worked to widen the reading audience, the religious parties to point the way to the kingdom of God, the utilitarians to insure the greater glory of the workshop of the world. Behind this joint effort lay an essential compatibility of temperament, for both parties (and they often overlapped, the Sunday evangelical being the weekday utilitarian) were distinguished by their deep seriousness. Though the evangelical lifted his eyes to the heavenly ledger while the utilitarian fixed his on the state of his bank balance, neither had much time for frivolity, for relaxation, for self-indulgence. Profoundly aware that each passing moment was precious and that life had to be lived with the utmost methodicalness, they deplored what they called the habit of "desultory" reading. If one were to read at all, it should be with a fixed end in mind, not a random flitting from one subject to another. This was implicit in the whole gospel of self-improvement that sprang from the union of evangelicalism and Benthamism. The ambitious artisan was to share in the diffusion of useful knowledge, not by following his own inclinations but by systematically reading what he had to learn in order to become a better workman. Reading for the mere sake of reading—finding amusement in one book, instruction in a second, a bit of inspiration in a third—could not be too severely condemned.

To this deep-seated prejudice against random reading may be traced much of the opposition to free libraries and cheap periodicals in the second half of the century. The aimless reader had a perpetual field day in the library, idly wandering through hundreds of novels, with perhaps side excursions into biography or poetry or travel narratives, but with never any tangible profit to his mind or his soul. It is true that the first mass-circulation periodicals were highly miscellaneous, but they escaped censure because their tone was impeccably earnest; and in addition, the rewards of more systematic reading were constantly pointed out in their pages. But later, the cheap weeklies retained their precursors' variety but largely abandoned any pretense of seriousness. This was the great objection to scissors-and-paste sheets like *Tit-Bits* and *Answers* at the end of the century.

In effect, this denial of the ordinary reader's right to browse at will was one manifestation of the utilitarians' prejudice against the use of books for what they considered frivolous purposes. None of Jeremy Bentham's crotchets is better remembered than his exclusion of poetry, in fact all imaginative literature, from his ideal republic. Whenever his pleasure-pain calculating machine ground out the quotient of utility for any form of art, the result was the same: a round, infinitely reproachable zero. In Bentham's craggy terminology, the arts proved to be "anergastic (no-work-producing) or say aplopathoscopic (mere-sensation-regarding)."[6] In short, literature, like the other arts, had no practical utility.

This verdict was supported by several allegations, which together took in most of the territory covered by the utilitarian ethical system. Here again it is striking how frequently the utilitarian and the evangelical spoke with a single voice.[7]

The first charge was the ancient one that had called forth Sidney's defensive eloquence over two centuries before: the charge, so dear to the Puritan heart in the reigns of both Elizabeth I and Victoria, that imaginative literature is compact of lies. This, in an epoch when all blessedness seemed to spring from a steadfast regard for practical truth, was a grave count. "Whatever may be the subject of which the poet treats," William Ellis, a disciple of the Mills, wrote, "his principal object, as it appears to me, is to excite intense feeling, to interest his reader warmly; and to produce this effect, there is no degree of exaggeration that poets will not sometimes practice. Exaggeration, let it be ever so much disguised, is disregard of truth, and a disregard of truth is always mischievous."[8] The Benthamites desired to see life with the calm eye of the empiricist, not sweeping from earth to heaven in the manner of the poet. In the geometrical pattern of life there was no room for

[6] Quoted in Alba H. Warren, Jr., *English Poetic Theory, 1825–1865* (Princeton, 1950), p. 66.

[7] The following passage is much indebted to Nesbitt, *Benthamite Reviewing*, especially chaps. iv and v.

[8] *Conversations upon Knowledge, Happiness and Education between a Mechanic and a Patron of the London Mechanics' Institution,* quoted in Edmund K. Blyth, *Life of William Ellis* (2d ed., 1892), pp. 45–46.

disorderly fancy. This was the doctrine of the school inspector in
Hard Times: "You are not to have," he tells Sissy Jupe, "in any
object of use or ornament, what would be a contradiction in fact.
You don't walk upon flowers in fact; you cannot be allowed to
walk upon flowers in carpets. You don't find that foreign birds and
butterflies come and perch upon your crockery; you cannot be permitted to paint foreign birds and butterflies upon your crockery.
You never met with quadrupeds going up and down walls; you
must not have quadrupeds represented upon walls. You must use
. . . for all these purposes, combinations and modifications (in primary colours) of mathematical figures which are susceptible of
proof and demonstration. This is the new discovery. This is fact.
This is taste."[9]

Poetry, the utilitarian asserted, had its place in the world when,
as Macaulay put it, the Platonic philosophers lovingly and futilely
cultivated the flowers of philosophy. But with the ascendancy of
inductive reason, which converted those flowers into edible Baco-
nian fruits, poetry became *démodé.* "A poet in our times," wrote
Thomas Love Peacock in an essay so faithful to the Benthamite
point of view that its ironical intention is sometimes overlooked,
"is a semi-barbarian in a civilized community. He lives in the days
that are past. His ideas, thoughts, feelings, associations, are all
with barbarous manners, obsolete customs, and exploded supersti-
tions. The march of his intellect is like that of a crab, backward.
The brighter the light diffused around him by the progress of reason, the thicker is the darkness of antiquated barbarism, in which
he buries himself like a mole, to throw up the barren hillocks of his
Cimmerian labours." Poets and their readers delude themselves,
Peacock said, that the art is "still what it was in the Homeric age,
the all-in-all of intellectual progression, and as if there were no
such things in existence as mathematicians, astronomers, chemists, moralists, metaphysicians, historians, politicians, and political
economists, who have built into the upper air of intelligence a
pyramid, from the summit of which they see the modern Parnassus
far beneath them. . . ."[10]

[9] Dickens, *Hard Times,* Book I, chap. ii.

[10] "The Four Ages of Poetry," *Works,* ed. H. F. B. Brett-Smith and C. E. Jones (1934),
VIII, 20–25. For a non-satirical statement to the same effect, see Leslie Stephen, *The
English Utilitarians* (1900), II, 363.

In an age of rationalism, the deliberate excitation of the feelings, through literature or any other means, was to be deplored. Man's primary duty to himself was to discover the truth by which he could live a happy life, and to stir up the emotions, thus clouding the pure light of reason, was foolhardy. John Stuart Mill found even Hume at fault in this respect.[11]

Reading literature was a form of dilettantism and an especially deplorable one; for it was not by literature, the Benthamites asserted, but by "the sciences of politics, of law, of public economy, of commerce, of mathematics; by astronomy, by chemistry, by mechanics, by natural history," that the nation had risen to the heights she now occupied. "Literature . . . is a cant word of the age; and, to be literary, to be a *littérateur*, . . . a bel esprit, or a blue stocking, is the disease of the age. . . . But ledgers do not keep well in rhyme, nor are three-deckers [warships, not fashionable novels] built by songs, as towns were of yore. . . . Literature is a seducer; we had almost said a harlot. She may do to trifle with; but woe be to the state whose statesmen write verses, and whose lawyers read more in Tom Moore than in Bracton."[12]

"She may do to trifle with"—a grudging concession that the reading of imaginative literature might be used to occupy such small leisure as one might have after a busy day's work. But the utilitarians immediately added that, since leisure should be used for the further development of one's faculties, many other branches of learning could contribute more to that object than polite letters. The general reader, therefore, could not flatter himself that by reading fiction or poetry in his spare time he was measurably adding to his permanent happiness or his usefulness to society. Such a practice might afford amusement, but it would not, as Froude said many years later, help a man to stand on his feet and walk alone.[13]

Finally, there was the matter of style. In 1826 John Stuart Mill decried the English author's love for ornamentation. Frenchmen, on the other hand, he asserted, "write as if they were conscious that the reader expects something more valuable from them than mere amusement. Though many of them are highly gifted with the

[11] *Westminster Review*, II (1824), 346.

[12] *Ibid.*, IV (1825), 151, 165–66.

[13] James Anthony Froude, *Short Studies on Great Subjects*, Ser. 2 (New York, 1872), p. 332.

beauties of style, they never seem desirous of shewing off their own eloquence; they seem to write because they have something to say, and not because they desire to say something."[14] In other words, literature could be useful only if it were stripped of its decoration and made into a strictly functional vehicle for the expression of ideas.

II. This, then, was the utilitarian doctrine as it was set forth in the first third of the nineteenth century and as it permeated the Victorian climate of opinion for decades to come. But just as the evangelicals' rigor eventually relaxed, so did the Benthamites' leathery antipathy to imaginative literature. As early as 1830 they discovered that poetry was not really, or at least not always, a seducer; for did not all great poets unite, in a single mind, the imaginative *and* the logical faculties? "Produce who can," they challenged, "the name of any first-rate poet who was not a sound reasoner."[15] Reviewing Tennyson's *Poems* the following year, John Bowring said forthrightly that poets "can influence the associations of unnumbered minds; they can command the sympathies of unnumbered hearts; they can disseminate principles; . . . they can excite in a good cause the sustained enthusiasm that is sure to conquer; they can blast the laurels of the tyrants, and hallow the memories of the martyrs of patriotism; they can act with a force, the extent of which it is difficult to estimate, upon national feelings and character, and consequently upon national happiness."[16] Poetry, it appeared, had utility after all.

In coming to this conclusion, the utilitarians were merely adopting the position held by non-Benthamite criticism generally in the early part of the century. Literature, and poetry in particular, was judged above all in terms of its didactic power, its moral usefulness; "the instruction of the understanding and the improvement of the moral fiber was about the highest purpose a poet could serve."[17] Other values, such as the pleasure arising from the music of the verse or striking images or felicity of phrase, were always

[14] *Westminster Review*, VI (1826), 63.

[15] *Ibid.*, XII (1830), 1.

[16] *Ibid.*, XIV (1831), 224.

[17] William S. Ward, "Some Aspects of the Conservative Attitude toward Poetry in English Criticism, 1798–1820," *PMLA*, LX (1945), 394.

subordinate to this, if indeed they were recognized at all. The function of literature as sheer entertainment was seldom conceded in critical discussion.

But theory and practice were no more closely reconciled in this period than in any other, and regardless of critics' views, the middle-class readers who patronized the Minerva Library and devoured the poems of Byron and the romances of Scott were looking for diversion more than anything else. While evangelicals and Benthamites alike raged against this time-wasting, frivolous, and morally injurious habit, it flourished with the passage of years, and nothing could be done about it. But the new lower-class readers were largely at the mercy of religious and utilitarian educational and publishing agencies, who enforced the supremely serious view of reading that has just been described. Those who forthrightly opposed the Gradgrind philosophy of reading as applied to the "inferior orders" were more than a little heretical. Sir John Herschel, for example, decried the "want of amusement" among the wage-earning class. "Equally with any other principle of our nature," he said in 1833, "it calls for its natural indulgence, and cannot be permanently debarred from it, without souring the temper, and spoiling the character. Like the indulgence of all other appetites, it only requires to be kept within due bounds, and turned upon innocent or beneficial objects, to become a spring of happiness; but gratified to a certain moderate extent it must be, in the case of every man, if we desire him to be either a useful, active, or contented member of society."[18]

Herschel therefore urged that entertaining books be supplied in abundance to the workers. Adherence to such a view, in the decades that followed, was the sign of a certain type of humanitarian reformer. Dickens never ceased attacking the assumption that "the very name of a labourer has something about it with which amusement seems out of character. Labour is work, amusement is play."[19] In his *American Notes* (1842), Dickens wrote with admiration of the Lowell, Massachusetts, factory girls, who had "joint-stock" pianos in their boarding houses, subscribed to circulating libraries, and put out a periodical called the *Lowell Offering*. The

[18] "Address," p. 7.

[19] *Ibid.*, pp. 8–9. Although the words are Herschel's, he refused to subscribe to the idea.

average Englishman's reaction, said Dickens, would be "How very preposterous!" "Perhaps," he went on, "it is above their station to indulge in such amusements, on any terms. Are we quite sure that we in England have not formed our ideas of the 'station' of working people, from accustoming ourselves to the contemplation of that class as they are, and not as they might be? I think that if we examine our own feelings, we shall find that the pianos, and the circulating libraries, and even *The Lowell Offering*, startle us by their novelty, and not by their bearing upon any abstract question of right or wrong."[20]

These were strong words, but they fell for a long time upon deaf ears. The Chadbands and Gradgrinds clung to their control of the machinery which provided the masses with "suitable" reading matter. But slowly, and with the utmost caution, middle-class Victorians came to liberalize their notions of the role books have in life, even the life of wage-earners. Gradually they accepted as desirable results of the reading experience not only the exercise of the emotions, the temperate indulgence of the fancy, and the cultivation of wise spiritual insights, but even—finally—simple, pleasurable relaxation. The icecap of evangelical seriousness and utilitarian distrust of the feelings was melted by the attitudes we associate with the "romantic" temper. It was symptomatic of the times, not merely of Dickens' own opinion on the subject, that, when *Household Words* was being planned in 1849, poetry was to be included in every number if possible, "but in any case something of romantic fancy. This was to be a cardinal point. There was to be no mere utilitarian spirit; with all familiar things, but especially those repellent on the surface, something was to be connected that should be fanciful or kindly; and the hardest workers were to be taught that their lot is not necessarily excluded from the sympathies and graces of imagination."[21] The success of *Household Words* and other papers with a similar policy demonstrates how great was the need for liberation from the utilitarians, "those Blights and Blasts of all that is Human in man and child."[22]

[20] *American Notes*, chap. iv.

[21] John Forster, *Life of Charles Dickens* (1874), II, 422.

[22] The phrase suggests Dickens, but it was in fact uttered by Charles Lamb, execrating Mrs. Barbauld and the other early nineteenth-century writers who were out to transform juvenile literature from a treasure house of fancy into a repository of useful knowledge (*Letters*, ed. Lucas [New Haven, 1935], I, 326).

Meanwhile, another tendency helped temper the utilitarian attitude toward books: the emotionalizing of the very idea of literature. With men like Lamb and Leigh Hunt, books (especially old ones) aroused emotions almost as fervent as those with which Wordsworth regarded nature. To them, the book was a sacred object, not so much because it contained religious or practical wisdom as because it was the key by which the feelings could be unlocked and the imagination given the freedom it demanded. Another side of this same secular bibliolatry was the development of the book-collecting passion, as indulged in and celebrated by men like Dibdin and the elder Disraeli. Thus, either because of their joy-bringing contents or because of some extrinsic appeal—rarity, physical beauty, the sentimental associations of certain copies—books, as objects, came to have a magical glamour about them. At first this attitude had little currency beyond a small, select circle. But in the long course of time, popular writers and speakers, having acquired it from their reading of the essays of Lamb, Hunt, and Hazlitt, passed it on to their audiences, and the whole notion of books and literature came to be surrounded with a sentimental aura that contrasted strangely with the orthodox Benthamite view.

These developments can be traced in the great body of popularized commentary on books that appeared in the wake of Leigh Hunt. Like Addison, Hunt was a missionary of literary culture to a class that still largely lacked it, and as such he started a new journalistic fashion. The cheap family periodicals that sprang up after 1832 in imitation of *Chambers's Journal* and the *Penny Magazine* constantly urged the advantages of cultivating the bookish habit. Literally thousands of chatty homilies were printed, with such titles as "The Blessedness of Books," "The Personality of Books," "Uses and Abuses of Books," "Little Books with Large Aims," "Good Habits in Reading," "Reading as a Means of Culture," "Books That Have Helped Me," "What a Single Book May Do for a Youth."[23] No less voluble on this theme were the orators who spread the same doctrine in speeches at the opening of mechanics' institute libraries and, later, of public libraries. From Brougham, Peel, and Herschel in the early Victorian period down to Lord

[23] See the long (but by no means exhaustive) lists of such articles, under "Books" and "Reading," in *Poole's Index to Periodical Literature*.

Avebury and Gladstone at the century's end, every public figure discoursed on the topic.[24]

To the modern reader, these disquisitions on the uses of reading seem hardly more than patchworks of platitudes, and so they are; but the history of platitudes is an invaluable index to changing opinion, and these thousands of journalistic pieces and occasional speeches would repay close study. The tune became sweeter with the passage of years, and the variations on it more abundant; the basic pattern of notes, however, remained the same. Despite the eventual recognition of amusement as a valid motive for reading, the evangelical-utilitarian temper of the age insisted that books were, first of all, a means of self-improvement.

This assumption lay behind the long, dogged attempt to divert the mass reading habit away from its natural course—a course required by the innate preferences of poorly educated human beings caught in the toils of industrial society. The following chapters will reveal how the governing middle class sought to withhold from the newly literate multitude the sort of reading that Herschel and Dickens insisted they needed above all—reading that would give them simple pleasure after a hard day's work. At no time did the campaign to dictate popular reading preferences wholly succeed, since the human yearning for entertainment is far stronger than any combination of forces that can be mustered against it. But a formidable set of devices was used to prevent the humble from discovering what kind of reading they would most enjoy, or, if that failed, from getting hold of it in quantity. The very diversity of these stratagems, beginning with the bleak pedagogy of the elementary schoolroom, is testimony to the pervasiveness of the utilitarian outlook in Victorian society.

[24] Abundant quotations from such speeches toward the end of the century are found in the various professional library journals, especially the *Library*. Many were printed *in toto* in general periodicals.

CHAPTER 7 { *Elementary Education* *and Literacy*

I. In the wake of the Jacobin panic of the 1790's, England felt a renewed concern to provide elementary education for the working class. The first impetus came from the religious denominations, particularly the Anglicans, whose interest in conducting charity schools, dormant for many decades, had suddenly been revived by alarm over the Methodists' activity in the field. In Parliament and the Whig press the necessity for schools for the poor was strongly urged by Henry Brougham and others more or less Benthamite in their thinking, who, however, insisted that national education be non-denominational and supported by the government.

Although from the outset the religious parties disagreed sharply with the Brougham faction on many educational issues (and the chasm between them widened as time went on), they at least agreed that the first aim of popular schooling was to wet down the smoldering embers of discontent. Adam Smith had observed more than a generation earlier that the laboring classes of a highly industrialized society, in which every man works at a narrowly specialized task all day long, tend to lose their mental flexibility and powers of discrimination, and thus to become easy marks for the demagogue.[1] Smith's theory seemed amply proved by the common man's response to Tom Paine; and the machinery-smashing Luddite riots of 1811–16 and the ominous disturbances at the time of the "Peterloo" massacre (1819) gave it additional credibility. If, however, the millions could be herded into classrooms, if only for a brief time, they could be permanently immunized against Jacobinism, radicalism, subversion, blasphemy, atheism, and every other ill to which they were exposed by the east wind of social change.

[1] *The Wealth of Nations* (1910), II, 263–64, 269.

141

Their native reason, however crude and untutored, could be depended upon to accept the truths of religion and society as laid before them by the superior classes, and the storms that were roiling the waters of English life would end.

Not only would a little schooling safeguard men's minds against thoughts of rebellion; it would improve their morals and manners and eliminate the frightening threat of a rabble's replacing the well-behaved, dependable "lower orders" of sturdy English tradition. "An instructed and intelligent people," Adam Smith had written, ". . . are always more decent and orderly than an ignorant and stupid one."[2] All backers of education for the masses were convinced that ignorance and illiteracy were responsible for most crimes. Strong drink, it was admitted, was a contributory factor, but drunkenness, so prevalent among the masses at the beginning of the century, was a result of ignorance; the rational man never took too much. Such notions could be bulwarked with statistics: one of the favorite occupations of the newly founded London Statistical Society in the 1840's was to demonstrate, in elaborate charts, the relationship between ignorance and the crime rate.[3] The more schools in a locality, the fewer felons. When enough schools were built, most of the prisons in England could be closed. This was not a rhetorical flourish; it was the sober conviction of the friends of mass education, as their writings show.[4]

In addition, popular education was felt to be indispensable in an age of commerce and industry. A reasonable bit of elementary schooling made better workers: it increased production, reduced

[2] *Ibid.*, II, 269.

[3] See the earlier volumes of the *Journal of the Statistical Society, passim.*

[4] The old refrain was a long time dying. In 1897, T. H. S. Escott, one of the leading exponents of late Victorian smugness, pointed out that since the Education Act of 1870 "no new prison has been built; while several buildings which were prisons have been changed into public libraries" (*Social Transformations of the Victorian Age*, p. 367). In contrast to the visionary pronouncements earlier in the century, this at least had the advantage of stating an accomplished fact. The liberals' faith in education as a deterrent of crime was not universally shared, however. As Peacock's Dr. Folliott said (*Crotchet Castle*, chap. xvii), "Robbery perhaps comes of poverty, but scientific principles of robbery come of education." Some critics of the "education craze" early in the century seriously maintained that with the spread of the ability to write, the masses would turn into a race of forgers; for a single instance of this view, see John Weyland, *A Letter to a Country Gentleman on the Education of the Lower Orders* (1808), p. 52. This apprehension was found among the humble themselves. As late as the 1870's, a workman, told that he must send his boy to the board school, replied, "What, educate that kid? Not if I know it. Why, there's one forger in the family now" (Rogers, *Labour, Life, and Literature*, pp. 52–53).

waste, assured more intelligent handling of machinery, even increased the possibility of a workman's hitting upon some money-saving short cut. This was a frequent allegation before parliamentary committees of inquiry. In a certain factory, for instance, there had been a controlled experiment in which twelve "educated" women and twelve "ordinary" (i.e., illiterate) ones had been set to do the same task; the educated twelve turned out 30 per cent more work than the others.[5]

These goals had no relation whatsoever to the possible cultural improvement of the nation at large or the inner satisfaction of the individual. In the age's educational theory, as in its theory of humanitarianism generally, a man or woman of the masses was regarded solely as an atom of society, not as a person. The function of reform was to strengthen the English social structure, not to enrich people's intellectual or emotional lives. It was an exceptional man indeed who ventured to suggest that popular education might, for example, encourage a taste for reading for private satisfaction, entirely apart from its social benefits. Such an idealist would have been a liability to the cause, for the advocates of popular education had a hard enough task soothing conservative fears. Fund-raising appeals were always cautious and defensive, and they not infrequently echoed the social attitude of Soame Jenyns. Witness, for example, this invitation to subscribe to a school for the poor in Westminster: "It is not . . . proposed . . . that the children of the poor should be educated in a manner to elevate their minds above the rank they are destined to fill in society. . . . Utopian schemes for an extensive diffusion of knowledge would be injurious and absurd. A right bias to their minds, and a sufficient education to enable them to preserve, and to estimate properly, the religious and moral instruction they receive, is all that is, or ought ever to be, in contemplation. To go beyond this point would be to confound the ranks of society upon which the general happiness of the lower orders, no less than those that are more elevated, depends; since by indiscriminate education those destined for laborious occupations would become discontented and unhappy in an inferior situation of life, which, however, when fortified by virtue, and stimulated by industry, is not less happy than what is experienced by those who move in a higher sphere, of

[5] *Hansard*, Ser. 3, CIX (1850), col. 849.

whose cares they are ignorant, and with many of whose anxieties
and distresses they are never assailed."[6]

The most disputed feature of popular education was the teaching of reading, which many conservatives continued to regard as
pure Jacobinism. The school people fully realized, even without
the solemn reminders of their opponents, that they were playing
with fire. The events of the 1790's had proved that a pair of opened
eyes could read "seditious" and "atheistic" propaganda quite as
easily as Scripture, and in many cases much more eagerly. Furthermore, those same eyes, susceptible to the attractions of a highly
spiced romance, could seduce a reader into habits of luxurious idleness and thence to jail or the workhouse—transforming him, in
either case, from a productive member of society into a parasite.
Thus there were impressive reasons, political, religious, and economic, why the masses should not be made literate at all. But the
educationists still believed it possible to draw a line between literacy for the sole purpose of learning one's religious duties and or-
dained place in life, and literacy for undesirable ends. If the poor
were taught to read only the Bible and related religious material,
and if great care were taken not to encourage a taste for entertaining books, there would be no trouble; the nation would enjoy all
the benefits of a literate populace and none of the dangers.[7]

By the time of the first Reform Bill (1832) the principle of popular education, thus restricted, was accepted by most people, the
chief exception being the "agricultural interests" who were anxious
to preserve their supply of cheap field labor. But now it was the
friends of education who became also education's worst enemies.
The prickly personalities of the two leading practitioners of mass
education, Andrew Bell and Joseph Lancaster, to say nothing of
the scarcely more equable temperaments of some of their followers,

[6] Patrick Colquhoun, *A New and Appropriate System of Education for the Labouring People* (1806), pp. 12–13.

[7] "The humblest and least educated of our countrymen must have wilfully neglected the inestimable privileges secured to all alike, if he has not himself found, if he has not from his own personal experience discovered, the sufficiency of the Scriptures in all knowledge requisite for a right performance of his duty as a man and a Christian. Of the laboring classes . . . more than this is not demanded, more than this is not perhaps generally desirable. They are *not sought for in public counsel*, nor need they be found where politic sentences are spoken. It is enough if every one is wise in the working of his own craft: so best *will they maintain the state of the world*" (Coleridge [1816], in *The Statesman's Manual, Works* [New York, 1853], I, 422–23). Italics in the original.

had led to the movement's being divided into two irreconcilable camps. From the initial, completely futile quarrel over who had first conceived (actually, reinvented) the monitorial plan, the difference developed into a much more fundamental one: namely, which party, Church or dissent, was to control the education of the country's poor and thus determine whether or not particular religious doctrines were to be taught. Springing up at the very beginning of the century, the controversy between the British and Foreign School Society (non-sectarian and Benthamite) and the National Society for the Education of the Poor in the Principles of the Established Church in England and Wales (Anglican) was destined to rage for the next hundred years. As Brougham observed in the House of Lords in 1843, "The Church was anxious to educate the people, but the Church was still more anxious to get the better of the sects; the sects were anxious to have popular education, but the sects were still more anxious than this to overturn the Church."[8] The upshot of this acrimonious debate was that the educationists devoted themselves less to improving the quality of their schools than to safeguarding their respective parties' interests. "Wesleyan and Catholic, Puseyite and Dissenter, Baptist and Churchman, Evangelical and Tractarian, denouncing one another, treated St. Paul's famous letter on charity and the needs of the English child with equal indifference."[9]

Not until 1833 were any public funds allotted for education, and for almost four decades thereafter the amount of governmental support was severely limited, the result partly of bickering among the religious factions and partly of opposition to governmental encroachment in a realm traditionally sacred to private, or at least clerical, enterprise. Hence during most of the century popular education was wretchedly short of funds. Private benevolence alone could not possibly establish and support the thousands of schools required by the concentration of workers in the new industrial cities.

Expenditures for buildings, equipment, and teachers' salaries had to be as low as possible. From the contemporary standpoint this was not as regrettable as it might seem, because "cheapness"

[8] *Hansard*, Ser. 3, LXVIII (1843), col. 1247.

[9] Hammond, *The Age of the Chartists*, p. 215. The Hammonds' whole long chapter (xi) on working-class education in the early Victorian era is an excellent discussion of the topic.

meant "multiplication of utility"—making money go farther than it had ever gone before, just as machinery was multiplying human productivity. The writer of the Westminster school prospectus already quoted was a shrewd judge of his audience when he disavowed any intention "that an expense should be incurred beyond the lowest rate ever paid for instruction."[10] To educate a single child for a year at Lancaster's Borough Road School cost 16s.8d., and in the Sunday schools the average annual expense per child was but 2s.6d.[11]

Its cheapness was the principal (though not the only) reason why the monitorial system was so prized in early nineteenth-century educational circles. A job was to be done—the teaching of reading, writing, ciphering, much religion and morality, sometimes an elementary craft or two; and the monitorial system was believed to accomplish it with factory-like efficiency and economy. Coleridge called the system, without irony, "this incomparable machine, this vast moral steam-engine";[12] as Sir Thomas Bernard wrote in 1809, "The principle in schools and manufactories is the same. The grand principle of Dr. Bell's System is the division of labour applied to intellectual purposes."[13] The teacher, once he had hastily indoctrinated a corps of pre-adolescent monitors, became simply a foreman. All the teaching (so called) thenceforth was done by the boys, who passed on to their inferiors, with what grotesque inadequacy we can readily imagine, the tricks and miscellaneous scraps of information acquired in those preliminary briefing sessions. Thus several hundred children could be exposed to the benefits of education at the cost of but one teacher. In the monitorial schoolroom there actually came true the nightmare, supposedly unique in our own century, of automatons turning out new regiments of automatons on a mass-production line.

What has been said so far of the aims and methods in vogue in the first half of the century is true particularly of the thousands of schools run by the two great voluntary organizations, the British and Foreign and the National School Societies. But the same ob-

[10] Colquhoun, p. 12.

[11] Hill, *National Education*, I, 91, 113.

[12] *The Statesman's Manual*, p. 444.

[13] Quoted in Jones, *The Charity School Movement*, p. 337.

servations hold good, in the main, for the other working-class schools which, though they left little trace in the official records of the time, were no less influential in molding the mass reading public. Dame schools still were common all over the country. Conducted by women or by men whose fortunes, if they had ever bloomed, were now in the last stages of decay, they were for the most part as deplorable as the religious schools, though here and there a superior mistress or master did lay a foundation for future culture. Situated in basements or lofts, they were overcrowded, ill ventilated, heated by a single stove, almost totally unequipped; and their educational value was further reduced by the mistress' frequently leaving the room to tend the shop she also kept or to quiet her babies, or by the master's having to turn his wife's mangle. The instruction offered in these squalid establishments was dear at the 4*d*. or 6*d*. a week that parents paid.

On a somewhat higher social level were the private schools designed especially for the children of master artisans and tradesmen who scraped together the required fees in order to avoid the stigma of relying on charity. These, wrote an indignant student of education in 1837, were "very frequently mere ergastula, to which boys are sent out of the way to be boarded and birched at £20 a year," or more cheaply if, as day scholars, they were merely birched. "The acquirements of the scholars," he added, "even in the rudiments of learning, would disgrace any Lancasterian school"— which is saying a good deal. In them "every abuse of omission and commission is allowed to flourish, almost without the competition of a superior system."[14] Upon leaving, at the age of thirteen or fourteen, the boy could look back without fondness on wasted years. These self-styled "middle-class" schools persisted in great numbers through most of the century. In 1851 England and Wales together had some 30,000 private day schools (including all types, from the tiniest dame school to the expensive academy) and in them were enrolled 700,000 children, or a third of the whole number of children at school.[15] Rudimentary education in the three R's was also provided in endowed schools, of which there were about 2,200 in 1842. Most of these were elementary schools by the terms

[14] *Central Society of Education Publications*, I (1837), 59–61 n.

[15] *Education: England and Wales* (Parliamentary Accounts and Papers, Session 1852–53, Vol. XC), p. cxxii.

of their foundation, but some were grammar schools which had fallen upon evil days.[16]

Some of these schools were as committed to the monitorial system as were their humbler "voluntary" counterparts, thanks both to its obvious economy—a great boon to a profit-seeking or indolent schoolmaster—and to the prestige the method enjoyed from Bentham's advocating it in his educational treatise, *Chrestomathia*. As a group (there were of course exceptions), the best that can be said of the private elementary schools is that since they were not bound by the religious and social restrictions under which the voluntary schools labored, they could be less sparing in the degree of literacy they imparted. But it is doubtful whether they added many more readers to the population, in proportion to the numbers they enrolled, than did the voluntary establishments.

In addition to regular day schools, some instruction in reading was also available in Sunday schools, which were attended by hundreds of thousands of children who toiled in shops, mills, factories, and mines the other six days of the week. These schools were certainly no more attractive or efficient than the day schools, and to teach reading to dead-tired and sullen children in an hour or two a week was a demanding task. The Factory Act of 1833, the first such act whose educational provisions were anything more than a dead letter from the outset, resulted in the setting up of school facilities in many factories, to which children of a certain age were required to repair two hours a day. But since the "schoolrooms" were often coal holes, and the "teachers" were firemen or equally unqualified persons, the children could hardly have received much more benefit than a change of occupation and an opportunity to sit down. By the 1850's, however, government inspectors noted a general improvement in conditions and it was felt that some real good had been achieved by this early attempt to combine work with schooling.[17]

For adults, finally, there were evening schools, some of them, like Bartle Massey's in *Adam Bede*, conducted by private individuals, and others by philanthropic bodies. Beginning at Bristol in 1812, there was a concerted movement, fostered especially by the

[16] Adamson, *English Education*, p. 259.

[17] Gertrude Ward, "The Education of Factory Child Workers, 1833–1850," *Economic History*, III (1935), 110–24.

Quakers, to provide such schools for adults who had never been taught to read. From the south and west it spread to London, where the Prince Regent and other eminent persons took it up as the newest fashion in charities, and thence into the Midlands. How many recruits these schools added to the reading public is problematical. Of 12,400 men and women attending about a hundred schools in 1832, only 3,148 were accounted able to read as a result of their schooling.[18] In the thirties and forties, enthusiasm cooled, because of the patronizing attitude of the sponsors in many localities and the worsening economic situation, which brought more desperate concerns to the pupils. In Leicester in 1842, for instance, the Chartist Thomas Cooper was forced to close the school he had been conducting for workers. "What the hell do we care about reading," the men grumbled, "if we can get nought to eat?"[19] Evening elementary schools languished from this time on to near the end of the century, when, absorbed into the national educational system, they enrolled tens of thousands of adolescents who had left day schools before mastering the fundamentals.

II. But to return to the day schools: Just what place had reading in their actual practice during the first half of the century?

If a child is to be started on the road to being a regular reader, one who will employ his literacy for ends more ambitious than deciphering handbills and legends in shop windows, a number of elements must be present in his early education. For one thing, to acquire a liking for reading, as for any other subject, he must associate it with a context of enjoyment. There are few records of a

[18] Hudson, *Adult Education*, pp. 3–14. Contemporary advocates of adult schools found it easier to dwell upon the reformation in manners and morals that the institutions accomplished. A man who had lived with a woman for twenty years, suddenly becoming "convinced of the sinfulness of his conduct," married her. Another man, eighty-eight years old, who had learned to spell words of two syllables, was reported to be "much improved in his moral character" since he had gone in for education—though one doubts that a man of his age was capable of vice on any really impressive scale. A shoemaker who for many years had found recreation in stabbing his wife with the knives of his trade renounced not only this practice but profanity and drunkenness as well. He became so honest, according to his happy, healing wife, that "he will not let any one carry out his shoes for sale, fearing they should ask for them more than they are really worth" (Thomas Pole, *A History of the Origin and Progress of Adult Schools* [New York, 1815], pp. 77, 87–88; this little book, originally printed at Bristol in 1814, is a firsthand source on the aims and practices of the adult education movement in that town).

[19] Cooper, *Life*, p. 172.

child's having had a pleasurable time in a nineteenth-century English school for the laboring or the lower-middle class. The physical accommodations were incredibly bad. In monitorial schools, the children were crowded into a single barnlike room, in which there was the constant hubbub of a score or more of monitors with their respective classes. Heating and ventilating arrangements were such as to breed headaches and slumber at best, and epidemics at worst. The smell of several hundred unwashed bodies and all too frequently filthy clothing was overpowering. The military discipline and stern punishments customary in the schools, though often rendered unnecessarily brutal by the sadism of master or monitors, were to a great extent required by the riotous conduct of the children, many of whom seem to have been infant desperadoes. The means taken to keep order and encourage the learning process—birching at the slightest provocation or just on general principles, the ridiculing of dunces, the hoisting of especially offensive trouble-makers in cages suspended from the classroom ceiling—did not enhance any pupil's happiness while at school. "A dull boy," commented the poet John Clare, "never turns with pleasure to his schooldays, when he has often been beat 4 times for bad reading in 5 verses of Scripture."[20]

The typical day-school teacher represented the acme of incompetence, and if his was a monitorial school, the mischief he did was compounded by the ignorance of the monitors. Teachers were, in Macaulay's words, the "refuse of other callings—discarded servants, or ruined tradesmen; who cannot do a sum of three; who would not be able to write a common letter; who do not know whether the earth is a cube or a sphere, and cannot tell whether Jerusalem is in Asia or America: whom no gentleman would trust with the key of his cellar, and no tradesman would send of [sic] a message."[21] Until the 1830's there were no teacher-training institutions. And even when normal schools were set up, they attracted some of the least ambitious and least gifted members of the working class, many of them former monitors who, having failed in other occupations, drifted back to teaching in preference to starving. None had had more than a primary education.

These were the teachers to whom England intrusted the nurture

[20] *Sketches in the Life of John Clare*, ed. Blunden (1931), p. 51.

[21] *Hansard*, Ser. 3, XCI (1847), cols. 1016–17.

of the future mass reading public. But the nation's requirements in this respect were modest enough. The art of reading was to be taught as a totally mechanical exercise, a pedantic discipline of the young mind. The goal was to enable the child to translate printed symbols into their spoken equivalents. In the earlier decades, if he were able to recite from a tattered book, he was deemed a reader, and the extent to which he understood what he read was not inquired into. As time went on, some attempt was made to have the child grasp the meaning of the individual words before him, but the way in which it was done discouraged far more incipient readers than it inspired. Upon being asked "In what way do you endeavour to improve the general frame and capacity of their minds?" a witness before the Select Committee on Education (1834) said, "By requiring the meaning of every word they read, and of every word they write, and of every thing they do. We never allow them to do any thing without asking how they do it, and why they do it. We avail ourselves very fully of the principle of interrogation."[22]

From one dreadful extreme to the other! All we know of the fanatical use of the "principle of interrogation" in nineteenth-century schools forces us to believe that its use in the teaching of reading must have bred a deep distaste for the printed word in countless pupils. The child was seldom urged to reflect on the total meaning of a sentence or a paragraph, let alone allowed to take any pleasure in what he read. Instead, there was the constant, nagging necessity of parsing, explaining derivations, searching a desperate memory for the fixed definition of this word and that, a definition modified at the pupil's peril. It was little wonder, then, that more than one government inspector discovered that the children were "as utterly unacquainted with the subject-matter of their [the Scriptures'] simplest narrative portions as with their fundamental doctrines."[23]

No provision was made for silent reading. Lessons were introduced and practiced aloud, and the pupil eventually was tested aloud. Most pupils therefore never learned that the primary use-

[22] *Select Committee on the State of Education*, Q. 273.

[23] Kay, *Education of the Poor*, p. 305. Inspection began in 1839, six years after the government instituted grants-in-aid. It extended, of course, only to schools that received such aid—those conducted by the religious societies—and never touched the private establishments.

fulness of a book resides in its ability to bring writer and reader together without the peevish intervention of schoolmaster or monitor. As a matter of fact, many children who went to the typical common school in the earlier nineteenth century never even touched a book. One of the money-saving devices in Lancaster's system of education was, as a chapter heading in his treatise phrased it, "A Method of teaching to spell and read, whereby one Book will serve instead of Six Hundred Books."[24] The reference is to flash cards, which are still favored in the modern classroom before children turn to books. But in monitorial classrooms flash cards often represented not merely the beginning but the end of the process of learning to read.

This was especially true when, as was usual, a child went to school for only a year or two. One who remained longer had a slightly better chance of getting a book into his own hands, but the books used in the schools were hardly calculated to advertise the lifelong pleasures of reading. In the religious societies' schools until about 1840 reading lessons were limited to Scripture, catechism, and works of a directly related nature. In the British and Foreign Society's schools the Bible was for over thirty years the *only* book used for reading lessons, partly because it was the cheapest book available.

In a halfhearted effort to atone for this lack of books in the classroom, many voluntary schools had little lending-libraries attached to them. Most of the books had "a bearing towards the works of God or the word of God." The laborious treatises of the Society for the Diffusion of Useful Knowledge, which sometimes appeared on the library shelves, presumably belonged to the first category. In the early thirties, great satisfaction was expressed over the popularity of these libraries. "Admission to or exclusion from the privilege of having a book from the library," it was said, "almost supersedes the necessity of any other reward or punishment." The books most in request were histories, biographies, voyages and travels: a significant indication of the ordinary child's thirst for narrative of any sort, whether it be a memoir of an intrepid missionary or the story of the Reformation in Germany.[25]

[24] Joseph Lancaster, *Improvements in Education as It Respects the Industrious Classes of the Community* (1805), p. 55.

[25] *Select Committee on the State of Education,* Qq. 525, 1252, 2259, 2339. For additional material on school lending-libraries see the Index to this report.

Deprived of contact with secular fiction, the child seized upon any other book, however moralized or ponderous, that promised a story. But the attractiveness and influence of these libraries was greatly exaggerated by those eager to put the best possible face upon the societies' activities. There is considerable difference between drawing books from a library and actually reading them. In 1845 an inspector of schools noted that it was "a rare occurrence to find a child in any degree acquainted with the subject-matter of the book which has been for some weeks probably in its possession."[26]

In private-venture schools, whose proprietors were free to use whatever reading material they could obtain, practice varied widely. In the humblest—the dame schools and the so-called common day schools—the Bible, spelling book, and primer were supplemented only by whatever stray printed matter the children themselves brought in. In the town of Salford, in 1837, only five of the sixty-five dame schools surveyed by the Manchester Statistical Society were "tolerably well provided" with reading material.[27] Although the various educational societies offered penny leaflets, dames and masters refused to adopt them because of the strong aversion the pupils' parents had to any contact with charity.[28]

Elementary schools for middle-class children in the first third of the century used reading collections of the "elegant extracts" type. As a Scottish educator told the Select Committee on Education in 1834, these were "the worst that can be imagined" for the purpose they were intended to serve. "They consist of extracts from all our best authors, selected because they are fine specimens of style, and upon subjects generally beyond the conception of children, and it is that in a great measure, which has led to the fact of the children so often reading without comprehending. A dissertation on virtue, or beauty, or taste, a speech of Cicero, Demosthenes or Lord Chatham, a passage from Milton, Shakespeare, or Young, are things beyond the comprehension of children of eight or ten years old."[29]

[26] Kay, p. 306.

[27] *Central Society of Education Publications*, I (1837), 296.

[28] *Journal of the Statistical Society*, I (1838), 195, 457–58. This volume of the *Journal* contains a mass of valuable information on the various kinds of schools in Westminster: the books used, the side-occupations of the teachers, the physical accommodations, etc.

[29] *Select Committee on the State of Education*, Q. 525.

The same witness praised the "Kildare Place" reader produced
by the Irish educational authorities, which, "without pretending
to give very choice specimens of composition, presents amusing
stories in plain language, and all of a good moral tendency, and
curious facts in natural history."[30] This reader, one of an eventually large series of Irish schoolbooks, was widely adopted in
English voluntary schools once the ban on non-scriptural reading
lessons was relaxed, and many imitators appeared. All were "calculated to improve the minds and characters of young persons, to
promote the cultivation of a humble, contented, and domestic
spirit, and to lead to the more intelligent perusal of the sacred
Scriptures." In the interests of this ambitious program, each lesson
in the first reading book adopted by the British and Foreign
School Society normally included a text from Scripture, "a brief
poetical extract adapted to improve the taste and excite the affections," and "a portion of useful knowledge."[31] The cheapness of
these readers and their superiority to the old "elegant extracts"
insured their popularity. But by the sixties their shortcomings
troubled many inspectors, who complained bitterly of their failure
to appeal to the child's imagination and emotions.[32]

Not only must the material a child reads be suited to his years
and natural tastes, but, even more important, his schooling in general must include sufficient information to give meaning to what he
reads. Even on the elementary level, he must be enabled to recognize common allusions. This is obviously impossible when information is conveyed, as it was in the nineteenth-century school, in
frozen blocks, and through the dreary catechetical method; and
when it is limited to personages and events in the Bible, the
geography of the Holy Land, and certain rudimentary aspects of
natural science.[33] Not until after mid-century were materials relat-

[30] *Ibid.*

[31] Binns, *A Century of Education*, pp. 160–61.

[32] Adamson, *English Education*, p. 215.

[33] A typical question in arithmetic was: "Of Jacob's four wives, Leah had six sons,
Rachel had two, Billah had two, and Zillah had also two. How many sons had Jacob?"
(*Central Society of Education Publications*, II [1838], 358). In 1835, Brougham shared with
the House of Lords his amazement at the accomplishments of the pupils in the (Lancasterian) Borough Road School. They dispatched in their heads such problems as "What
is the interest of £535 7s.4d. for fifteen seconds?" and drew from memory outline maps
of Palestine and Syria, marking all the bays, harbors, and creeks, and adding both their
modern and ancient names. "Now all this," said Brougham without a trace of irony,

ing to the broader world—great legends, characters of mythology, basic facts of geography and history, facts, even, that would assist in reading the newspaper—introduced to the attention of lower- and lower-middle-class children. Until then, their intellectual horizons were rigidly confined by religious and utilitarian prejudices. A little education was all that the common pupil should have, and it was so circumscribed and penurious that only the unusual child, upon emerging from the valley of the shadow of education, would have much taste for reading.

III. During the high tide of Victorian optimism in the fifties and sixties, glorifiers of British progress pointed to the gains for which education was responsible: the decline in brutality, coarseness, and drunkenness among the masses; the increase in church attendance; the disappearance of the workers' accustomed surliness and rebelliousness and instead the development of good humor and loyalty to their masters. Whether or not the schools really could be credited with the change, the social ends for which they had been founded had largely been achieved. Not only had popular manners and morals improved; British productivity had never been higher, and, best of all, the Chartist fiasco of 1848 had marked the virtual end of the revolutionary threat.

The passage of the Reform Bill of 1867, which more than doubled the electorate, gave a fresh urgency to schools for the masses. "We must educate our masters," asserted a famous epigram whose substance (though not the actual words) derived from a remark of Robert Lowe, vice-president of the Committee of Council on Education. Now that the workers held the balance of political power, it was time to re-examine completely both the aims and the practices of popular education. In a paper read before the Social Science Congress in 1867, the educational reformer W. B. Hodgson questioned

---

"is real, substantial, useful knowledge, fitted alike to exercise and to unfold the faculties of the mind, and to lay up a store of learning at once the solace of the vacant moments, and the helpmate of the working hours in after years. . . . When those children leave the school they will be governed by such worthy principles, and stimulated by such generous appetites, as will make their pursuits honest and their recreations rational, and effectually guard them from the perils of improvidence, dissipation, and vice" (*Hansard*, Ser. 3, XXVII [1835], cols. 1322–23). Quite plainly Brougham and his confreres considered mental arithmetic and reconstruction of Palestinian geography to be at least as good means of occupying leisure as reading books—and probably much better.

the assumptions upon which popular education had operated since the century began. Was teaching the masses to read and write a good in itself? Was it true, as the familiar axiom had it, that "ignorance of reading and writing is productive of, or accompanied by, a great amount of crime," and that therefore the ability to read and write would diminish crime? And now that so many more people had the vote, would literacy guarantee that they would perform their duty as citizens honestly and intelligently? Hodgson thought not. The great question, he submitted, was what the children were taught to do with their literacy once they had it. Reading and writing were instrumentalities only, and it was up to the nation, and the nation's educators, to review the ends they might serve.[34]

But Hodgson's refreshingly skeptical remarks went unheeded. The current preoccupation was not with the quality of popular education, nor with a new evaluation of the purposes of mass literacy, but with quantity. Recurrent surveys showed that hundreds of thousands of English school-age children were totally uncared for. To provide facilities for them was the first order of business, one that was to require many years of work. Meanwhile, the nature of elementary schooling was little changed. What appeared to be a new departure, the "payment by results" plan, merely gave the schools' most hallowed defects a new lease on life.

"Payment by results" was the scheme, instituted in the Revised Code of 1862, whereby inflexible, nation-wide standards of accomplishment were set up for all elementary schools receiving governmental subsidy. It was the invention of Robert Lowe, who was execrated in his own time as bitterly as utilitarian schoolmen like Brougham had been denounced by Wordsworth and Coleridge. Lowe was, indeed, a reincarnation of the early nineteenth-century educationist. His ideal of popular instruction was this: "The lower classes ought to be educated to discharge the duties cast upon them. They should also be educated that they may appreciate and defer to a higher cultivation when they meet it, and the higher classes ought to be educated in a very different manner, in order that they may exhibit it to the lower classes that higher education to which, if it were shown to them, they would bow down and

[34] W. B. Hodgson, "Exaggerated Estimates of Reading and Writing," *Transactions of the National Association for the Promotion of Social Science* (1867), pp. 393–405.

defer."[35] The curious reasoning is Lowe's own; the spirit is Hannah More's, or Joseph Lancaster's.

The immediate occasion of the Revised Code was the clamor for economy. In 1861 Palmerston's government budgeted approximately £26,000,000 for the army and navy, £813,441 for education. Educational grants had, therefore, to be cut to the bone.[36] No money could be wasted on ineffective education. The proof of the pudding henceforth was to be in the tasting; each school would have to show it had used its yearly budget to maximum advantage before it could expect any more money. "Hitherto," said Lowe, "we have been living under a system of bounties and protection; now we propose to have a little free trade."[37]

And so bureaucracy, which then controlled the education of about two-thirds of all the children who were in school, prescribed the subjects each child was to take during a given year, the lesson books he was to study, and, most important of all, the nature of the examination to which he was to be subjected at the excruciating annual day of judgment, when every failure, per pupil, per subject, lost the school 2s.8d. from the next year's grant. The result was that a new premium was put upon rote memory, for throughout the year every effort was bent toward grinding into the child the sentences or the facts that the inspector might demand of him. The best child (assuming he was not struck mute on examination day) was the one who had memorized the whole book.

The atmosphere produced in the schoolroom by the eternal necessity of working for the next year's government allowance was such as to breed lifelong antipathy to education. "Children hated their schooldays, left them behind as soon as possible, soon forgot what they had learnt, and when they became the parents of the next generation . . . in all too many cases could neither contribute culture to their own children in the home nor readily modify the attitude which they had learnt towards their teachers in their own

[35] Quoted (imperfectly?) in Curtis, *History of Education*, p. 148, from Lowe's pamphlet, *Primary and Classical Education* (1867), which has not been available. For a concise summary of Lowe's part in formulating educational policy, see Asa Briggs, *Victorian People* (Chicago, 1955), pp. 254–58.

[36] They were. By 1865 the new system enabled the government to reduce its aid to schools to £636,000 (Porter, *The Progress of the Nation*, pp. 134, 648, 658–59).

[37] Quoted in Curtis, pp. 149–50.

schooldays."[38] By inescapable association, this antipathy extended
to the printed word, the source of so much misery in school.[39]

The standards required for reading proficiency were these:

I. Narrative monosyllables

II. One of the narratives next in order after monosyllables in an elementary
reading book used in the school

III. A short paragraph from an elementary reading book used in the school

IV. A short paragraph from a more advanced reading book used in the school

V. A few lines of poetry from a reading book used in the first class of the
school

VI. A short ordinary paragraph in a newspaper, or other modern narrative

VII. (Added in 1882.) A passage from Shakespeare or Milton or some other
standard author, or from a history of England[40]

Only in the sixth and seventh standards, it will be noticed, could
material be used which possibly had not been in the possession of
the child during the whole preceding year. That in itself was
enough to insure that for the younger children the reading lesson,
day after day and week after week, would consist of nothing but
drill, drill, and still more drill upon a single book—the book appointed for the examination. It is a tribute to the grim patience of
the teachers (and witness to how much they dreaded the loss of every
2s.8d.) that about 90 per cent of the children passed the reading
tests—the greatest success enjoyed in any subject. But the inspectors were not deceived. They "repeatedly pointed out that if
fluency of uttering the printed words increased, understanding
steadily declined." The value of the reading test, they said, was
"altogether insufficient and almost illusory. It does not convey the
idea that the reader is interested in his book, or hold out the hope
that he will voluntarily take to it when he is his own master in
life."[41] With reading in the classroom confined to preparation for

[38] Lowndes, *The Silent Social Revolution*, p. 14.

[39] In reviewing so misguided a system of education, one strives to find some redeeming
circumstance, however small. Perhaps it may be the fact that, in order to earn as much
money as possible for the school, teachers spent more time than they would otherwise
have done with the sluggish pupils; the bright ones could be depended on to perform credita-
bly at the examination with relatively little coaching. The result was that the schools produced a greater proportion of literates than earlier, when the failure of pupils to learn
their letters did not have such immediate financial repercussions. This probably contributed
as much to the decline of illiteracy as the steady increase of school population.

[40] Curtis, p. 151; Adamson, *English Education*, p. 372.

[41] Smith, *History of English Elementary Education*, p. 268. Smith's chap. viii is a devas-
tating account of the "payment by results" system.

the inspector's visit, it was scarcely to be expected that many children would acquire bookish habits. Indeed, as a recent historian has said, "The child who ever opened a book at home shone at H.M.I.'s visits like a good deed in a naughty world."[42]

We have seen that by 1840 voluntary schools were beginning to use small readers along with the Bible. The Bible, however, remained the chief book from which reading was taught to elementary pupils. Only when its difficulties were overcome were children allowed to practice upon relatively easy reading matter. A critic remarked in 1867, "It is as if we were to begin the teaching of our children with Milton's *Paradise Lost*, and then advance them into *Robinson Crusoe*, or Miss Edgeworth's *Tales*. . . . I have heard of a boy so taught who, having been asked by his mother to read a passage in a newspaper, was suddenly roused from his monotonous chaunt by a box on the ear, accompanied by these words— 'How dare ye, ye scoundrel, read the newspaper with the Bible twang?' "[43]

The quality of the school reading books aroused Matthew Arnold's ire in his school-inspector's report for 1860. If the book was "a jejune encyclopaedia of positive information, the result is that he [the pupil] has, except his Bible, no literature, no *humanizing* instruction at all." If, on the other hand, the book was made up of "literary selections," it was in all probability laden with "the writing of second or third-rate authors, feeble, incorrect, and colourless." "Dry scientific disquisitions," Arnold wrote, "and literary compositions of an inferior order, are indeed the worst possible instruments for teaching children to read well. But besides the fault of not fulfilling this, their essential function, the ill-compiled reading-books I speak of have, I say, for the poor scholar, the graver fault of actually doing what they can to spoil his taste, when they are nearly his only means for forming it. I have seen school-books belonging to the cheapest, and therefore the most popular series in use in our primary schools, in which far more than half of the poetical extracts were the composition either of the anonymous compilers themselves, or of American writers of the second and third order; and these books were to be some poor child's Anthology of a literature so varied and so powerful as the English!" Arnold there-

[42] Lowndes, p. 34.

[43] Hodgson (cited in n. 34 above), pp. 400–401.

fore urged the creation of a new set of reading books containing well-chosen and interesting selections. "Such lessons," he was confident, "would be far better adapted than a treatise on the atmosphere, the steam-engine, or the pump, to attain the proper end of a reading-book, that of teaching scholars to read well; they would also afford the best chance of inspiring quick scholars with a real love for reading and literature in the only way in which such a love is ever really inspired, by animating and moving them; and if they succeeded in doing this, they would have this further advantage, that the literature for which they inspired a taste would be a good, a sound, and a truly refining literature; not a literature such as that of most of the few attractive pieces in our current reading-books, a literature over which no cultivated person would dream of wasting his time."[44]

Arnold's later reports give no sign that his specifications were met. In 1867 and again in 1871 he reminded his superiors that since the reading book was in most cases the only book of secular literature the child owned, special care should be taken that it have a good influence on his taste. Yet "the whole use that the Government . . . makes of the mighty engine of literature in the education of the working classes, amounts to little more, even when most successful, than the giving them the power to read the newspapers."[45]

There was at least this improvement, that under Mundella's code of 1883 inspectors were empowered to hear the children in Standards V, VI, and VII read from books of extracts from standard authors, or from "such works as *Robinson Crusoe*, Voyages and Travels, or Biographies of eminent men." In Standards VI and VII a play of Shakespeare, a single book from one of Milton's longer poems, or a selection of extracts of equivalent length from the works of either poet was also acceptable. Textbook publishers quickly produced sets of books "specially adapted for the new code." Macmillan offered Cowper's *Task* and *John Gilpin*, Lamb's *Tales from Shakespeare*, Scott's *Lay of the Last Minstrel* and *Lady of the Lake*, *The Vicar of Wakefield*, a selection by Coventry Patmore called *The Children's Garland from the Best Poets*, and Charlotte Yonge's *Book of Golden Deeds*. Ward, Lock and Company advertised in their "Geikie's School Series" such items as *Marmion*

[44] Arnold, *Reports on Elementary Schools*, pp. 87–89.

[45] *Ibid.*, pp. 129, 157.

(2d. per canto), Byron's *Prophecy of Dante* (same price), and Thomson's *Seasons* ("Spring" only: 2d.). At the same time and at the same modest price Chambers' were selling *Paradise Lost* (Book I), Wordsworth's *Brothers*, and selections from Macaulay, Mrs. Hemans, Thomas Campbell, and other "standard authors."[46]

Some of these books were useful in connection not only with the reading exercise required in every standard but also with a new subject introduced in 1871, "English literature." This called for the memorizing of a passage of poetry—one hundred lines the first year, two hundred the second, three hundred the third, a different passage each year—and a "knowledge of meaning and allusions."[47] Whether or not Matthew Arnold was at least partly responsible for instituting this exercise, it met with his hearty approval.[48] By 1880 "English literature" had become the most popular subject in the schools. What now concerned Arnold most was the choice of poets to be memorized. There is no better measure of the gulf that divided the school inspector from the Oxford professor of poetry than his praise of Mrs. Hemans' poems, "The Graves of a Household" and "The Homes of England," on the ground that they "have real merits of expression and sentiment, the merits are such as the children can feel, and the center of interest, these pieces being so short, necessarily occurs within the limits of what is learnt."[49]

The Victorian mania for graduated examinations and rote-memory work extended, not unnaturally, to the preparation of teachers. Having successfully memorized and parsed the hundreds of lines of verse set for the highest standards of the elementary school, prospective masters and mistresses became pupil-teachers, and then,

[46] Advertisements in *Publishers' Circular*, August 15, 1883, p. 710; January 18, 1884, pp. 55, 73. By the 1870's and 1880's hundreds of reading books were on the market; of miscellaneous "poetical selections" alone there were some eighty in 1876, a hundred in 1887. The ten authors most favored for classroom dissection were—to take the number of separate school editions in print in 1887—Shakespeare (upward of 80 editions), Milton (39), Scott (25), Goldsmith (23), Cowper (14), Bacon (12), Pope, Byron, Lamb (10 each), and Gray (9). These books were used not only in higher standards of the elementary schools but in preparation for the various "external examinations" to be described in the next chapter ([Walter Low, ed.], *A Classified Catalogue of . . . Educational Works* [1887]; this volume and the two previous editions [1871, 1876] are the best guides to late Victorian schoolbooks).

[47] Birchenough, *History of Elementary Education*, pp. 370, 372.

[48] See Arnold, pp. 210–11.

[49] *Ibid.*, p. 228.

if they survived entrance examinations,[50] went on to a normal college, whose course of studies also pointed undeviatingly toward that event to which, after 1862, the whole of Victorian education moved—the certificate examinations. "It was inevitable," says the historian of English teacher-training in a classic understatement, "that commonly the memory should be developed at the expense of the intelligence."[51]

By the middle of the century occasional lip-service was given to the idea that it was the teacher's duty not only to impart "the mechanical power to read" but to establish a link with the "pleasurable emotion derivable from it."[52] Kay-Shuttleworth, the founder of the teacher-training school at Battersea, wrote that "the teacher should be inspired with a discriminating but earnest admiration for those gifts of great minds to English literature which are alike the property of the peasant and the peer; national treasures which are among the most legitimate sources of national feelings."[53] Nevertheless, the course in "English literature" remained confined to rote material the student teachers parroted back to their instructors, just as later on they would require their own pupils to parrot it to them.

It was the same story to the very end of the century: the institutions that fed teachers into the expanding elementary-school system were pedant-factories, whose machinery efficiently removed whatever traces of interest in humane culture the scholars had somehow picked up earlier in their careers. "Répétez sans cesse," it was said, was the tutor's motto, and the policy bred anecdotes which would be funnier if it were not so easy to believe them. As

[50] Applicants for admission to the Church of England Training Schools for Schoolmasters in 1851, in addition to demonstrating their knowledge of grammar, had to paraphrase and parse a passage from Young, Milton's *Areopagitica*, or Wordsworth's *Excursion*, and to answer such questions as: "What other languages have united with the Anglo-Saxon to form the English language; and under what circumstances?" "Who were the troubadours? To what country did they belong?" "Give some account of Geoffrey Chaucer. What great foreign writers belong to the same age?" "Give some account of the great writers of the Commonwealth, and of the reigns of Charles II and James II" (Kay-Shuttleworth, *Public Education* [1853], pp. 437–38). Aspiring teachers obviously formed a good market for the capsule histories, outlines, sketches, conspectuses, and manuals of literature that were published in increasing numbers at this time.

[51] Rich, *The Training of Teachers*, p. 141.

[52] Kay, *Education of the Poor*, p. 306.

[53] Kay-Shuttleworth, *Four Periods of Public Education*, p. 339. (Not to be confused with the book cited in n. 50.)

one class in a teacher-training college worked its way drearily through a textbook of dates, student after student recited from memory the events that occurred in successive years. "The book wound up with its final date something like this: '1870. May 1st. Outbreak of Franco-German War.' The man who had successfully recited this very last date upon this very last page had barely sat down when up sprang his next neighbour quite mechanically with 'Printed and published for C. J. Curtis, B.A., by Smith and Son, Stamford Street, S.E.' "[54]

Matthew Arnold, it is true, repeatedly praised the inclusion of poetry recitation in the program of studies for pupil-teachers. But there is more than a hint of resignation in his tone. The general cultural level of the apprentice teachers was abysmally low; "how difficult it seems to do anything for their taste and culture," Arnold sighed in 1863. "How much easier it seems to get entrance to their minds and to awaken them by means of music or of physical science than by means of literature; still if it can be done by literature at all, it has the best chance of being done by the way now proposed."[55] Committing to memory choice extracts from great poets might possibly evoke some humane response from these cowlike adolescents. Certainly it was worth trying. The meagerness of their elementary-school preparation, the time and energy required to memorize great chunks of information, and the authorities' indifference to the possibility that other qualities besides a capacious memory might be valuable to the teacher, prevented the future masters of the future masters of the English nation from learning the place of reading in a well-rounded life.

The intellectual atmosphere during the second half of the century was as hostile to such an ideal as it had been during the first. In educational thought Benthamism was re-costumed as "intellectual liberalism," which held that schooling in the natural sciences was the gateway to the brave new world. In his influential book, *Education* (1860), Herbert Spencer preached a gospel which

---

[54] Rich, p. 195. Rich's book gives a well-documented and thoroughly depressing account of the training of teachers in Victorian times. Cf. Dickens' comments on Mr. M'Choakumchild's preparation for his task (*Hard Times*, Book I, chap. ii) and James Runciman, *Schools and Scholars* (1887), a collection of sketches and short stories, some obviously autobiographical, dealing with life in a teachers' college and the early board schools. Runciman's chapter on "The Crammer" is a bitter indictment of the Revised Code's effect on well-intentioned teachers.

[55] Arnold, p. 106.

utilitarian England welcomed as an up-to-date version of the old orthodoxy—the gospel that "accomplishments, the fine arts, *belles-lettres*, and all those things which . . . constitute the efflorescence of civilization, should be wholly subordinate to that knowledge and discipline in which civilization rests. *As they occupy the leisure part of life, so should they occupy the leisure part of education.*"[56] But in Spencer's scheme, the student's absorption in the sciences that gave the key to successful living left scant leisure for dabbling in the frills. There is no reason to suppose, despite his polite nod in the direction of "aesthetic culture," that Spencer would have deplored its total neglect.

Like the older utilitarianism, the new scientism opposed the verbal emphasis of traditional education.[57] Scientific discipline—close observation, shrewd empiricism—was infinitely preferable to mere acquaintance with words. Spencer echoed Robert Owen and a host of other educational innovators: "Parents thrust primers into the hands of their little ones years too soon, to their great injury. Not recognizing the truth that the function of books is supplementary—that they form an indirect means to knowledge when direct means fail—a means of seeing through other men what you cannot see for yourself; they are eager to give second-hand facts in place of first-hand facts."[58]

Even Charles Kingsley, who knew better, joined in the intensified hue and cry after bookishness. "They say knowledge is power," he told a student audience in 1863, "and so it is. But only the knowledge which you get by observation. Many a man is very learned in books, and has read for years and years, and yet he is useless. He knows *about* all sorts of things, but he can't *do* them. When you set him to do work, he makes a mess of it. He is what is called a pedant: because he has not used his eyes and ears. He has

---

[56] Herbert Spencer, *Education: Intellectual, Moral, and Physical* (New York, 1883), pp. 74–75. Italics in the original.

[57] The great preponderance of nineteenth-century educational thought, to be sure, was opposed to verbalism. Rousseau's and Pestalozzi's cries of "things, not words" and "doing rather than reading" were taken up by such influential theorists as the Edgeworths, Robert Owen, Bentham, and the pioneer teacher-trainer, David Stow. But never was theory more at odds with practice. The characteristic textbooks of the early part of the century were modeled after the Edgeworths', and in them children read about the way in which other children learned by direct observation and experience. Hence, ironically, the antiverbalism of the period was manifested in books.

[58] Spencer, p. 60.

lived in books. He knows nothing of the world about him, or of men and their ways, and therefore he is left behind in the race of life by many a shrewd fellow who is not half as book-learned as he: but who is a shrewd fellow—who keeps his eyes open—who is always picking up new facts, and turning them to some particular use."[59]

Among those who came under the spell of Spencer, the habit of general reading, especially in polite literature, fell into as great disrepute as it had been among the most dedicated Benthamites. And, since it was now less fashionable to deny or depreciate the place of the imagination in life, the news began to spread that the scientific discipline held some of the very satisfactions which the advocates of humanistic education had always maintained could be discovered only in the arts. "It is not true," Spencer insisted, "that the facts of science are unpoetical; or that the cultivation of science is necessarily unfriendly to the exercise of imagination or the love of the beautiful. On the contrary science opens up realms of poetry where to the unscientific all is a blank. . . . The truth is, that those who have never entered upon scientific pursuits know not a tithe of the poetry by which they are surrounded."[60]

Thus the potential usefulness of the elementary school as a starting-bed for the reading habit was as little regarded as ever. Admittedly, the late-Victorian child now had to read and construe excerpts from the "standard classics," and memorize lengths of poetry. But this was only a reluctant concession to the prevalent idea that a little smattering of culture does no harm, though it should never occupy a child's time to the exclusion of more practical subjects. The assumption probably did much more to discourage children's interest in reading than to encourage it.

So it is probably not a matter for regret, everything considered, that the term of education was as brief as it was for the great majority of nineteenth-century children. One state inspector, shortly after the middle of the century, declared that "at certain schools he could tell pretty accurately by the pupils' faces how long they had been at school. The longer the period, the more stupid, vacant, and expressionless the face."[61] During the first half of the century

---

[59] *Charles Kingsley: His Letters and Memories of His Life* (1894), II, 146–47

[60] Spencer, pp. 82–83.

[61] Joseph Payne, *Lectures on the Science and Art of Education* (Boston, 1883), p. 284.

most children from the working class left school after two or three years, and toward the end of the century the maximum period of attendance was only six or seven years. Throughout the era the usual leaving age for lower-middle-class pupils was thirteen or fourteen. But if they had remained longer they would merely have undergone further stretching of their powers of memory; no attempt would have been made to arouse their critical or creative intelligence. What little the customary pattern of popular education accomplished, it accomplished in the first short years. And from our point of view, that achievement resided in their learning, some of them, how to read.

IV. This chapter has been unique among all treatments of nineteenth-century popular education in that its pages seldom have been sullied by statistics. Not that figures are not available; many volumes were devoted to tabulations amassed by governmental and private agencies in the course of the century. But as Carlyle remarked, "Tables are abstractions, and the object a most concrete one, so difficult to read the essence of. There are innumerable circumstances; and one circumstance left out may be the vital one on which all turned."[62] In this case, the vital omitted circumstance on which all turns is the quality of the schooling. And that quality, we have seen, was fearfully low.

Hence the only real usefulness the copious statistics of English education would have for our purposes would be to show what percentage of the total population went to school at all—that is, how many were exposed to whatever training in reading was provided. Unfortunately, the available figures cannot settle the question. The closest the successive investigations and census returns come to doing so is in their estimate of the number of school-age children who were in school at a given time. Brougham estimated that in 1818 one out of every three children in England between the ages of seven and thirteen was unaccounted for on the school rolls.[63] In 1835, he estimated that some 300,000 children in that age-range were not at school.[64] Horace Mann concluded from the census reports of 1851 that of the five million children in England

[62] *Chartism*, chap. ii.

[63] *Hansard*, Ser. 2, II (1820), col. 61.

[64] *Ibid.*, Ser. 3, XXVII (1835), col. 1303.

and Wales between the ages of three and fifteen, almost three million were not in school.[65]

These figures are based on the assumption that all children of a certain age, say three to fifteen, should be in some sort of school. But since on the average the masses of children spent no more than two or three years in school, in reality a larger proportion of the total population went to school *at some time or other* than is reflected by such figures. On the other hand, the figures are often grossly inflated, reporting the number of children formally enrolled rather than the considerably smaller number of those actually in attendance. The Lancasterian school which once submitted a total of 1,000 pupils, whereas its capacity was but 594, was hardly unique.[66]

The only firm generalization possible is that during the first half of the century, scores and even hundreds of thousands of children never went to school at all. The situation was worst in the swollen factory cities and in London, where the inexorable increase of population defied every effort to keep pace with it.[67] But it was bad, too, in the agricultural districts, where the demand for child labor was hardly less acute than in the factories. A substantial segment of the population therefore was doomed to illiteracy unless the art of reading could somehow be acquired informally. We must not underestimate the number who learned to read outside the schoolroom, for plenty of boys and girls learned their three R's from a parent or some other older person, or taught themselves.

But what of the children who attended school: how many of them actually learned to read? All we know about the condition of popular elementary education—the gross incompetence of most teachers, the brevity and irregularity of attendance, the fact that large numbers of children went to school only on Sunday—warns us against too roseate a view.[68] The few scattered figures relating

[65] *Education: England and Wales* (Parliamentary Accounts and Papers, Session 1852-53, Vol. XC), p. xxx.

[66] Smith, *History of English Elementary Education*, p. 115.

[67] In Manchester in 1833, one-third of all children between five and fifteen were receiving no instruction, not even in Sunday school; and in Liverpool, more than half of the children of that age went to no school at all (*Central Society of Education Publications*, I [1837], 293-94).

[68] Until near the middle of the century, almost the only information available on the literacy rate was that gathered in certain small areas by statistical groups or flourished by

to children's literacy that come down to us from before 1850 are depressing. In 1836, of 2,000 thirteen- and fourteen-year-old children in Manchester Sunday schools, 53 per cent could not read.[69] In an artisan-class district of Christ-Church, Marylebone, about the same time, 747 children could at least spell, while 823 could not even do that (of their parents, 777 could read, 267 could not); and in eight rural parishes of Kent, 111 out of 262 children above fourteen could not read.[70] In 1845, a school inspector reporting on 176 schools in his Midland district (which were overwhelmingly monitorial, and where the average period of attendance was a year and a half) said that 75 per cent of the children who left those schools annually were, for all practical purposes, illiterate.[71]

Assuming that such figures are reasonably accurate, it must be remembered that a great many former pupils, who once could read in a fashion, lost the ability either through disuse or through imperfect learning in the first place. When a committee of the Manchester Statistical Society examined the state of education in the township of Pendleton in 1838, it reported: "A considerable number of persons stated that they were once able to read in the Bible, but had now forgotten it. This takes place, according to some, because they have 'so mitch else to think about;' others consider that hard work drives it out of their heads; and one woman attributed her loss of learning to having had 'such a big family.' A hand-loom weaver, speaking in reference to his ability to read formerly, said, 'I could say th' catechis fro' end to end, and ne'er look at book [a dubious indication of literacy in the first place], but I cannot read now; I can only spell out words i' th' Testament, but cannot *expenale* [*sic*] them, or summut o' that.' . . . A crofter said he was

---

the various educational agencies as testimony to their accomplishments. The latter are open to suspicion, since, as a contemporary put it, "without intending it, societies are from their constitution braggarts, and the committees are generally too anxious, as advocates, to make the best of their statements, to be very rigid in examining the details upon which they are founded. Reports are drawn up as advertisements; failures are judiciously passed over, and by that very circumstance the good accomplished is given in an exaggerated and therefore an untrue form" (Walter F. Hook, *On the Means of Rendering More Efficient the Education of the People* [10th ed., 1846], p. 7).

[69] Mathews, *Methodism and the Education of the People*, p. 53.

[70] *Central Society of Education Publications*, I (1837), 340–44.

[71] Kay, *Education of the Poor*, p. 309.

at least three years at a day school, and could read the Bible, but has 'quite forgotten how it's done now.' "[72]

At the same time, investigators for the Central Society of Education were collecting case histories of boys between thirteen and seventeen years of age who, despite their sojourn in a voluntary school, were either totally unable to read or were able only to spell out "penny books about Jack the Giant Killer, and . . . Robinson Crusoe."[73] In 1851 a self-styled "old educationist" told a parliamentary committee of inquiry, "I have often observed that boys at the National [and] British schools, and others, are taught apparently to read, and after a few years appear to have forgotten almost the whole of what they were taught, so as not to be able to read." The reason, he said, was that they had learned only how to spell their way through a chapter of the New Testament, and "nothing was afterwards put into their hands that had sufficient novelty to induce them to keep up the habit of reading till they had overcome the mechanical difficulty, and found a pleasure in the art."[74] This observation later was expanded, in a speech in the House of Commons, to the statement that "of adults who were unable to read more than one-half were in that condition, not from never having been to school, but because, after leaving school, they had met with nothing to tempt them to the exercise of the faculty they had acquired, and that faculty had died from pure inanition."[75]

The criteria then employed to test literacy are of little help in trying to estimate the extent of the public that was able to read. In the schools, a pupil was judged literate if he were able to stammer his way through a few verses of Scripture or a few questions and answers in the catechism. For census purposes, the test was ability to sign the marriage register. It is generally assumed, and justly so, that the ability to write was less common than that of reading, that the former presupposes the latter, and that literacy percentages thus obtained must be substantially increased if abil-

---

[72] *Journal of the Statistical Society*, II (1839), 68 n.

[73] *Central Society of Education Publications*, II (1838), 365–67, 388–97.

[74] Newspaper Stamp Committee, Q. 3240.

[75] *Hansard*, Ser. 3, CXXXVII (1855), col. 1144.

ity to read alone is in question. On the other hand, numbers of men and women who could sign their names, and therefore were enrolled among the literate, probably could write nothing else. Whether or not they could read, there is no way of telling.[76]

Hence the Victorian literacy figures that come down to us are, for one reason or another, very unsatisfactory evidence of how many people were able to read. The first nation-wide report, made in 1840 and based on ability to sign the marriage register, was that 67 per cent of the males and 51 per cent of the females were literate.[77] Generalizing from a variety of local tabulations made in the thirties and forties, a recent student has concluded that between two-thirds and three-quarters of the working class were literate.[78] The census of 1851 placed the rate for the whole nation at 69.3 per cent for males and 54.8 per cent for females. But even if these figures happen to be a reasonably accurate reflection of the number able to *read*, they tell us nothing of the quality of literacy. There was a large fringe area of the population which, though technically literate, could barely spell out the simplest kind of writing.

The revelations of the 1851 census did much to intensify the campaign for wider educational opportunity, and surveys made in connection with that campaign during the next two decades proved that England still was plagued with widespread illiteracy. In 1867, a house-to-house canvass of a working-class district in Manchester revealed that barely more than half of the adults could read, and in another district of the same city a quarter of the "youthful population" were similarly illiterate. The rate of school attendance was still low—35 per cent of the children in one area of Manchester had never been to any sort of day school—and Sunday-school attendance had decreased.[79] In the nation at large, it

---

[76] Victorians who were disturbed by what they considered the unrealistically low literacy rate obtained by this method took refuge in the supposition that some brides and grooms, though fully able to sign their names, were so nervous that they preferred to scrawl a cross instead; or that when a literate man took an illiterate bride, he chivalrously wrote his *X* instead of his name to save her embarrassment—a gesture that doubtless augured well for a blissful married existence (W. L. Sargant, "On the Progress of Elementary Education," *Journal of the Statistical Society,* XXX [1867], 86–87).

[77] *Second Annual Report of the Registrar-General* (1840), p. 5. The report covers the year ending June 30, 1839.

[78] Webb, "Working Class Readers in Early Victorian England," p. 349. Webb's article collects a wealth of source material on literacy in this period.

[79] Ashton, *Economic and Social Investigations in Manchester,* pp. 65–66.

was estimated that between 250,000 and two million children of school age were not in the classroom.[80]

The climax of the agitation for a national system of schools came with the passage in 1870 of W. E. Forster's education bill. The Forster Act is usually spoken of as a great landmark in the history of the reading public, because, by establishing governmental responsibility for education wherever voluntary effort was insufficient, it made schooling easier to obtain (and less easy to avoid) than ever before in England's history. Yet the act's importance can easily be exaggerated.[81] This is clearly shown by the decennial figures for literacy in England and Wales:[82]

	MALES		FEMALES	
	Percentage of Literates	Percentage Gain	Percentage of Literates	Percentage Gain
1841........	67.3	...	51.1	....
1851........	69.3	2.0	54.8	3.7
1861........	75.4	6.1	65.3	10.5
1871........	80.6	5.2	73.2	7.9
1881........	86.5	5.9	82.3	9.1
1891........	93.6	7.1	92.7	10.4
1900........	97.2	3.6	96.8	4.1

In the two decades before the Forster Act, the literacy rate for males had increased by 11.3 percentage points and that for females by 18.4 points. In the next two decades (the census of 1891 was the first to reflect fully the results of broader educational opportunity) the increase was 13.0 and 19.5, respectively. Hence the Forster Act did not significantly hasten the spread of literacy. What it did do was to insure that the rate at which literacy had increased in

[80] Adamson, p. 347. "The truth was," says Adamson, "that nobody knew."

[81] Even so good a historian as G. M. Trevelyan is misleading on the subject. Compulsory education, he says, "has produced a vast population able to read but unable to distinguish what is worth reading, an easy prey to sensations and cheap appeals. Consequently both literature and journalism have been to a large extent debased since 1870, because they now cater for millions of half-educated and quarter-educated people, whose forbears, not being able to read at all, were not the patrons of newspapers or of books" (*English Social History* [Toronto, 1944], p. 582). The truth is that, far from "producing" a semiliterate audience, the Forster Act and its successors merely enlarged it; and the "debasement" of literature and journalism began long before 1870. Trevelyan's use of statistics also is inaccurate. "Between 1870 and 1890," he writes, "the average school attendance rose from one and a quarter million to four and a half millions." But these figures refer only to *state-aided* schools. When private, non-inspected schools are taken into account, the totals are much higher. In 1858, more than a decade before the Forster Act, over 2.5 million children were enrolled in public and private schools together (Newcastle Commission, I, 573).

[82] From the registrar-general's returns, in Porter, *The Progress of the Nation*, p. 147.

1851–71 would be maintained. Had the state not intervened at this point, it is likely that the progress of literacy would have considerably slowed in the last quarter of the century, simply because illiteracy was by that time concentrated in those classes and regions that were hardest to provide for under the voluntary system of education. In short, the Forster Act was responsible for the mopping-up operation by which the very poor children, living in slums or in remote country regions, were taught to read.[83]

In the light of the circumstances reviewed in this chapter, it is surprising that literacy made the headway it did, especially during the first half of the century. But the deficiencies of formal education were somewhat atoned for by certain elements in the social scene. The political turmoil, stirred and directed by popular journalists; the way in which even menial jobs in commerce and industry now required some ability to read; the gradual cheapening of printed matter attractive to the common reader; and (never to be underestimated) the introduction of the penny post in 1840, which gave an immense impetus to personal written communication—these together were responsible for the growth of a literate population outside the schoolroom.

[83] The fact that in 1900 the literacy rate was approximately 97 per cent must not be misinterpreted to mean that in that year the nation as a whole was approaching total literacy. It means simply that 97 per cent of those who married in that year, most of whom were between the ages of sixteen and twenty-five, could sign the marriage register. But these constituted only a fraction of the total population, and side by side with them lived the older men and women who had been entered in the "illiterate" column at the time of their own marriages and whose status presumably had not changed in the interval.

CHAPTER 8 *Secondary Education*

Not until the middle of the twentieth century was secondary education to be recognized as the free right of all English classes. Throughout the nineteenth century only children of the upper and middle classes were to be found in the private or proprietary academies and "colleges" and the endowed grammar schools which provided education beyond the rudiments. How long a youth remained in school was determined largely by his prospects in life, and these in turn were regulated by his social position. As a rule, those destined to become tenant farmers, tradesmen, and superior artisans quit the schoolroom at fourteen or fifteen. Those who were going into the army, the professions, or the civil service left at sixteen or seventeen. Only the tiny minority who were heading for the universities remained at school until they were eighteen or nineteen.

With these groups, literacy may be taken for granted. But how far did the schooling they received beyond the elementary level feed their taste for reading? To seek the answer, as we shall do, only in terms of their exposure to the classics of English literature, admittedly is not the way to the whole truth, for any good general education, regardless of specific branches, may contribute to the love of books. A young boy enthralled by history, for instance, may become as voracious and wide-ranging an adult reader as one whose taste is nourished initially by poetry or fiction. Still, by measuring the place literature had in the education of the middle-class Englishman, we can obtain a fair idea of the role that reading was expected to play in his mature life.

In 1828 Charles Knight, writing in the *London Magazine*, attacked the inadequacies of both elementary and secondary education. How little progress was made in the next third of a century is suggested by the fact that in his autobiography, published in 1864–65, he quoted these criticisms to point out their continued validity. After decrying the lack of decent schooling for workers' children, Knight went on: "And how much better off, in point of real knowledge, are the sons of the middle classes, who at fifteen are placed in attorney's offices, or behind the counters of the draper or the druggist? They have been taught to write and read; they have fagged at arithmetic for seven years, under the wretched old boarding-school system, without having attained the remotest conception of its philosophy; . . . their literature is confined to a few corrupting novels, the bequest of the Minerva press to the circulating library of the last age."[1]

Knight felt that during the first half of the century the schools catering to the commercial and professional class had done nothing whatsoever toward inculcating literary taste. This possibly is an overstatement, but not by much. For the studies in the private boarding and day schools to which children of this class were sent were dictated by the utilitarian spirit, and those in the endowed grammar schools by a desiccated classicism. In neither type was the love of books for their own sake cultivated to any great extent.

Most private schools derived their philosophy and curriculum from the dissenting academies of the previous century. But whereas the academies generally had kept alive the classical curriculum side by side with "modern," or commercially useful, subjects, under the influence of Benthamism the balance dipped heavily in favor of the latter. Some small obeisance still was made to the ideals of literary culture, for even the utilitarian conceded that reading was an unobjectionable pastime, provided that it did not interfere with the more important concerns of life.

The most liberal contemporary attitude toward the study of belles-lettres was that exemplified by Vicesimus Knox, the Tunbridge schoolmaster who in the 1790's had taken issue with those of "austere wisdom" who said flatly that reading imaginative literature was a waste of time. On the contrary, said Knox, it had substantial usefulness. "Many young persons of natural genius would have given very little attention to learning of any kind, if they had been introduced to it by books appealing only to their reason and judgement, and not to their fancy. Through the pleasant paths of

[1] *London Magazine*, Ser. 3, I (1828), 7; quoted in *Passages of a Working Life*, II, 68.

Poetry they have been gradually led to the heights of science: they have been allured, on first setting out, by the beauty of the scene presented to them, into a delightful land, flowing with milk and honey; where, after having been nourished like the infant at the mother's breast, they have gradually acquired strength enough to relish and digest the solidest food of philosophy." Furthermore, a taste for polite letters prevented "that narrowness which is too often the consequence of a life attached, from the earliest age, to the pursuits of lucre. . . . Young minds, indeed, have commonly a taste for Verse. Unseduced by the love of money, and unhacknied in the ways of vice, they are, it is true, pleased with simple nature and real fact, though unembellished."[2]

This defense of literary culture against the growing Benthamite emphasis on materialism, empiricism, "practicality" was timid enough, but even it, in the view of many schoolmasters, went too far. The dictum of Locke, to the effect that one seldom discovered mines of gold or silver in Parnassus,[3] found ready assent among middle-class fathers who had never heard of Bentham. "Why," they asked, echoing Maria Edgeworth, "should the mind be filled with fantastic visions instead of useful knowledge?"[4] Only incorrigible romanticists like Wordsworth, Lamb, Coleridge, and Dickens, all of them enemies of utilitarianism in education and everywhere else, had an answer, and the age was deaf to them. The Gradgrinds told the M'Choakumchilds, "Teach these boys and girls nothing but Facts. Facts alone are wanted in life. Plant nothing else, and root out everything else. You can only form the minds of reasoning animals upon Facts; nothing else will ever be of any service to them."[5]

For the most part, therefore, the role of books in utilitarian middle-class education was only to purvey factual knowledge. The most advanced schoolmasters took care that reading should never be a slothful substitute for actual experience and observation. That indeed was the danger of books: they encouraged the mind to luxuriate instead of strengthening itself, to wander aimlessly off rather than hewing to its business. Rowland Hill omitted literature

[2] Knox, *Elegant Extracts* (1801), pp. [iii]–v.

[3] John Locke, *Educational Writings*, ed. J. W. Adamson (Cambridge, 1922), p. 141.

[4] Quoted in Adamson, *English Education*, p. 98.

[5] Dickens, *Hard Times*, Book I, chap. i.

for this reason from the curriculum of his famous Hazelwood School, which was all the rage among Benthamites. "Dryden says of Shakespeare," wrote his brother in a description of the school, "that 'he did not see men through the spectacles of books.'—This pithy expression of the merits of our great bard will not be lost on the reflecting teacher. We have no hesitation in declaring our firm conviction that many a fine mind has been lost by an exclusive attention to books. Reading may degenerate into a very idle method of spending time; the more dangerous, as it has the appearance of something better. We could wish all our pupils, whenever they are not occupied in something really beneficial, to be engaged in no employment which might lull the feelings of self-disapprobation."[6]

If polite literature entered the schoolroom at all, it was in the form represented by Vicesimus Knox's *Elegant Extracts: or, Useful and Entertaining Pieces of Poetry, Selected for the Improvement of Young Persons*, which was for generations a standard schoolbook. Although it turned up sometimes even in elementary schools, its intended place was in the hands of middle-class adolescents, and in the classroom it was used according to Knox's directions, "just as the Latin and Greek authors are read at the *grammar-schools*, by explaining every thing grammatically, historically, metrically, and critically, and then giving a portion to be learned by memory"[7]—a procedure sacred to educational practice since the Renaissance. This drudgery scarcely recommended the study of literature to many boys. But "spouting pieces," as contemporary slang called them, were the closest the typical middle-class school came to encouraging a taste for general reading. And this was a most incidental aim; far more important, it was thought, was the mental discipline that supposedly resulted from parsing, glossing, and memorizing.

Elegant extracts were much favored, and far less apologetically, in female seminaries. In these schools, at least, was no sour breath

---

[6] [Matthew Davenport Hill], *Public Education: Plans for the Government and Liberal Instruction of Boys in Large Numbers* (2d ed., 1825), p. 319. Note that after praising Shakespeare, Hill proceeds to a position which makes it impossible for one to read Shakespeare.

[7] Knox, p. vii. It is only fair to Knox to add that he hoped his book would be "particularly agreeable and useful *in the private studies* of the amiable young student, whose first love is the love of the Muse, and who courts her in his summer's walk, and in the solitude of his winter retreat, or at the social domestic fire-side."

of utilitarianism, and there alone, among the various sorts of schools patronized by the English during the first half of the century, could the ideal of reading as a pastime be candidly advanced. Girls of the middle class had no vocational future to prepare for; virtually the only aim of their education was to prepare them to relieve boredom and be ornamental. A taste for literature was deemed as harmless as singing at the piano or sketching. But there were serious obstacles in the way of developing that taste. Since, as F. D. Maurice sarcastically observed, "the imagination is a terrible object of the dread, the hatred, and hostility of the mistresses of establishments and the governesses of young ladies,"[8] books were tested for traces of unhealthy warmth before being placed in the girls' hands. In addition, many parents objected to spending much for books of any sort, with the result that the girls' official reading (overlooking the romances they smuggled in from the circulating library, and the Byrons they hid under their pillows) was usually confined to cheap anthologies and compendiums of knowledge.[9]

One of the few outspoken critics of the elegant-extracts mode of encouraging interest in literature was Charles Kingsley, who told an audience at Queen's College in 1848: "The young have been taught to admire the laurels of Parnassus, but only after they have been clipped and pollarded like a Dutch shrubbery. The roots which connect them with mythic antiquity, and the fresh leaves and flowers of the growing present, have been generally cut off with care, and the middle part only has been allowed to be used— too often, of course, a sufficiently tough and dry stem. . . . By having the so-called standard works thrust upon them too early, and then only in a fragmentary form, not fresh and whole, but cut up into the very driest hay, the young too often neglect in afterlife the very books which then might become the guides of their taste. . . . 'Extracts' and 'Select Beauties' are about as practical as the worthy in the old story, who, wishing to sell his house, brought one of the bricks to market as a specimen."[10]

[8] Quoted in Archer, *Secondary Education in the Nineteenth Century*, p. 232.

[9] Anne Jemima Clough, "Hints on the Organization of Girls' Schools," *Macmillan's Magazine*, XIV (1866), 435.

[10] "On English Literature," *Literary and General Lectures and Essays* (2d ed., 1890), pp. 246–57.

This attitude is especially striking when contrasted with Matthew Arnold's acceptance of the anthology as the appropriate means of developing taste among children in elementary schools. Equally radical was Kingsley's plea for some attention to the works of contemporary authors. "I cannot see," he said, "why we are to teach the young about the past and not about the present."[11] But he was far in advance of his time. For decades to come, middle-class literary education was to concentrate exclusively upon the works of dead-and-gone authors. If nineteenth-century pupils acquired any knowledge of the books written in their own age, they did so far from the classroom.

In the endowed grammar schools, even elegant extracts had no formal place. Here the trouble was not the utilitarianism of the nineteenth century but the classicism of the sixteenth, or, more accurately, its withered husks. With the accumulated inertia of centuries, few masters saw any reason to give their boys an education more appropriate to the reign of Victoria than to that of Elizabeth I. Until 1840 they were forbidden to do so, in any case, by the schools' charters, which required the teaching of the venerable classical curriculum. In a few instances, notably that of the Leeds Grammar School in 1805, attempts were made to legalize the introduction of modern subjects, such as English, but Lord Eldon held that schools were obliged to remain faithful to the letter of their foundation instruments down to the crack of doom; in the vocabulary of law, "grammar" meant the same thing in the industrial age that it had meant in Tudor times. This and subsequent decisions discouraged further attempts to liberalize the curriculum. Only a few schools were energetic enough to circumvent the Eldon ruling by obtaining special acts of Parliament enabling them to introduce modern subjects. Even after the Grammar Schools Act of 1840 permitted courts to interpret foundation statutes in the light of changed conditions, the lethargy of the grammar schools was one of the most remarkable educational phenomena of the age.[12]

Hence during most of the century the grammar-school curriculum clung to the line laid down by the Renaissance humanists. But the cultural relevance and vitality it had once possessed had

[11] *Ibid.*, p. 254.

[12] Curtis, *History of Education*, pp. 59–61; Adamson, *English Education*, pp. 43–49.

almost completely evaporated. Whatever the shortcomings of their own formula for education, the utilitarians had a strong case against the sort of schooling they ceaselessly denounced. They did not object to the teaching of Greek and Latin per se, but they could not countenance the overwhelming emphasis upon "dead languages"—and least of all could they condone the method of teaching, which was gerund-grinding pure and simple.[13]

The endowed grammar schools at least were no more petrified than the great public schools and the universities. Indeed, the ultimate fault lay at the top, for the universities were to remain officially unaware of English literature until the very close of the century. As the universities stood, so stood the public schools which prepared students for them, and so in turn stood the ordinary grammar schools which could do no better than imitate the public schools.

Although some historians of nineteenth-century education allude to the informal teaching of English literature in the public schools, there is little real evidence of it. The notoriously riotous, anarchic atmosphere of the schools in the first part of the century was not conducive to quiet reading.[14] Boys who did manage to be studious, in the midst of frequent disorder sometimes culminating in mass insurrections, devoted their energies to the age-old classical grind. The testimony of Bulwer-Lytton's hero, Pelham, is characteristic: "I was in the head class when I left Eton. . . . I could make fifty Latin verses in half an hour; I could construe, *without* an English translation, all the easy Latin authors, and many of the difficult ones *with it;* I could *read* Greek fluently, and even translate it through the medium of the Latin version technically called a crib. . . . As I was never taught a syllable of English during this period; as, when I once attempted to read Pope's poems out of school hours, I was laughed at, and called 'a sap;' and as, . . . whatever schoolmasters may think to the contrary, one learns nothing nowadays by inspiration;—so of everything which relates to English literature, English laws, and English history (with the excep-

---

[13] See, for example, Southwood Smith in *Westminster Review*, I (1824), 46. The whole article (pp. 43–79), a review of Bentham's *Chrestomathia*, sets forth the utilitarian views on middle-class education.

[14] The most extensive scholarly treatment of the nineteenth-century public schools, especially as they were affected by contemporary ideas, is Mack, *Public Schools and British Opinion*.

tion of . . . Queen Elizabeth and Lord Essex) . . . I was, at the age of eighteen, when I left Eton, in the profoundest ignorance."[15]

On the other side there is the testimony of Rev. Edward Coleridge, for thirty-two years an assistant and lower master at Eton. He told the Clarendon Commission, which investigated the condition of the great public schools in 1864, that during the earlier part of his career "any average boy of ordinary taste at Eton on leaving school had read much of the English poets, and a great deal of English history, as well as other literature. I know very well that the boys used greedily to devour every poem of Sir Walter Scott, Lord Byron, Southey, and other modern poets, as fast as they came out. I recollect that there was a perfect rush to get the first copies of 'The Corsair.' The boys used to spend a great deal of their pocket money in buying English books."[16] Masters and pupils always have given strikingly different versions of what went on in school, but the weight of evidence seems to favor Bulwer-Lytton.

Coleridge may have glorified the past in order to emphasize the sorry state of literary culture at Eton in the sixties: "The old English dramatists, a great deal of Dryden, a great deal of Pope, and an immense deal of other English poetry were then [*ca.* 1830] read at Eton, besides most of the modern poems, but now I doubt whether you would find many boys out of the whole eight hundred that Eton contains who have read ten plays of Shakespeare."[17] This gloomy estimate was supported by Oscar Browning, then assistant classical master at Eton, and by a former student, who agreed that present-day Etonians did "very little" private reading and used the school library "very little indeed." The masters, said the latter witness, were indifferent to what the boys read, and even if they had not been, "I do not think the boys would care much for what the masters said about their reading." Most boys, he continued, "read nothing at all except novels and books of that sort"—Bulwer and Lever more than Thackeray.[18]

Such evidence led Lord Clarendon to comment: "A great

---

[15] Bulwer-Lytton, *Pelham*, chap. ii.

[16] Clarendon Commission, III, 123.

[17] *Ibid.*

[18] *Ibid.*, III, 178, 248–49. Another old Etonian attempted to salvage the good name of his school by remarking, profoundly, that "all those of literary tastes would read a good deal." But even he had to admit that "a very small proportion" had read Shakespeare, and only "a few, no doubt" read Milton (*ibid.*, III, 278).

change, and not for the better, has certainly taken place in the taste of the boys at Eton for English literature."[19] Though the other public schools came off somewhat better, it was distressingly plain that they did nothing formally to cultivate literary taste, and little, if anything, informally. Some boys read a fair amount, but the impulse came from within. English literature entered the stated curriculum of the schools only as a handy source of material for translation—at Harrow, for instance, the sixth form was required to translate into Latin "fourteen copies of not less than twenty-five lines from Cowper, Campbell, Keats, Wordsworth, Arnold, Dryden, Hood, Byron"—or as an occasional, rather dubious alternative to a certain Latin exercise. At Shrewsbury, fourth-formers who were excused from studying Ovid's *Fasti* were expected to memorize about twelve hundred lines from Milton.[20]

Other witnesses before the Clarendon Commission gave illuminating evidence of the reading tastes and habits of public-school boys in the fifties and early sixties. An old Harrovian said that there was little private reading of books apart from assigned exercises.[21] A witness from the Merchant Taylors' School felt that "a fair average amount" of private reading was done in the boarding houses at night. The school library was accessible only to the head form and not much used even by them, "because the monitors and prompters had collections of books of their own."[22] A young man who had left Shrewsbury in 1858 testified that there was "a great deal" of private reading in the sixth form, mostly of novels; but he had never heard of a boy reading Gibbon or anything similar. Shrewsbury boys had three hours a day which they could use for private reading if they wished, though the witness confessed that he himself usually went fishing.[23]

The examination of H. L. Warner, a student at Rugby from 1854 to 1860, was especially revealing:

"Was there much private reading of modern literature?"

"I do not think there is very much."

"Did boys read much poetry?"

"Yes, a good deal of poetry, and Carlyle."

"Do you suppose many of the boys had read Shakespeare?"

[19] *Ibid.*, III, 123.

[20] *Ibid.*, II, 429, 454.   [22] *Ibid.*, IV, 144.

[21] *Ibid.*, IV, 230.   [23] *Ibid.*, IV, 356.

"Yes, a great many read Shakespeare, and whilst we were there we occasionally read Shakespeare together."

"Carlyle you mentioned; was Carlyle a favorite author?"

"Yes."

"What other modern authors should you say were favorites?"

"I think they generally were novels."

"Was any poet particularly favored—Tennyson?"

"Yes, they always took out Tennyson; I do not know how much they read it."

"Wordsworth?"

"I do not think much Wordsworth."

"Living authors, I suppose, more than others?"

"Yes."

"Did they read Macaulay?"

"Yes."

"Were they obliged to read any of what is called classical poetry, such as Dryden and Pope?"

"No, I do not think they took that out, except in reading Homer and Virgil."

"I suppose Shakespeare?"

"Yes."

"A boy might leave Rugby without having read a line of Dryden?"

"Yes."

"What sort of novels were they, Sir Walter Scott's?"

"Sir Walter Scott and Kingsley were very popular; Dickens, of course."

"Thackeray, perhaps?"

"Thackeray was not a favorite so much."[24]

The Clarendon Commission and, a few years later, the Taunton Commission, which inquired into the state of all endowed grammar schools except the ancient public schools, were more concerned about the place of reading in the lives of English schoolboys than any previous investigating body had been. Witness after witness before the Taunton Commission pleaded that the study of English be substituted for, or at least made coequal with, the traditional Latin curriculum. "The beauty of English literature," the commissioners wrote in their summary report; "its power to culti-

---

[24] *Ibid.*, IV, 294-95.

vate and refine the learners; the fact that French and German children were carefully instructed in their respective languages; the example of the classic nations themselves, who certainly studied their own great writers; these and other similar arguments were urged upon us with great force. . . . Assuredly it would be a most valuable result if anything like a real interest in English literature could be made general in England.

"The true purpose of teaching English literature," the commissioners went on, was "not . . . to find material with which to teach English grammar, but to kindle a living interest in the learner's mind, to make him feel the force and beauty of which the language is capable, to refine and elevate his taste. If it could be so taught, . . . the man would probably return to it when the days of boyhood were over, and many who would never look again at Horace or Virgil, would be very likely to continue to read Shakespeare and Milton throughout their lives."[25]

More and more it was realized that the lack of literary culture in the middle-class environment from which the typical secondary-school boy came had to be remedied in the schools. "In his own home, perhaps," wrote J. R. Seeley, a leading educationist and historian, "he sees no books at all, or feeds only on monstrous romances, or becomes prematurely wise and rancorous and cynical by perpetual reading of newspapers. I am pleading for a class which have no intellectual atmosphere around them; in the conversation to which they listen there is no light or air for the soul's growth; it is a uniform gloomy element of joyless labour, bewildering detail, broken with scarcely a gleam of purpose or principle."[26]

Already a subject called "English literature" had been included in the competitive examinations that were instituted for the Indian civil service in 1855 and for the home civil service somewhat later. In the Indian examinations (1871) a satisfactory knowledge of English literature counted 500 points (as against 1,250 for mathematics and 1,000 for natural science).[27] G. W. Dasent, the

[25] Taunton Commission, I, 25–26.

[26] "English in Schools," *Lectures and Essays* (1870), p. 237. Sir Walter Besant said that when he was a child, in the 1840's, "Very few middle-class people . . . had any books to speak of, except a few shelves filled with dreary divinity or old Greek and Latin Classics" (*Autobiography* [New York, 1902], p. 37).

[27] For the subjects included in the civil service examinations, and the points assigned to each, see *Transactions of the National Association for the Promotion of Social Science* (1860), p. 319, and (1877), pp. 335–36, 372.

examiner in this subject for the Indian civil service and for the
Royal Military Academy at Woolwich, told the Taunton Com-
mission what he expected of his candidates: "I should take forty or
fifty passages, selected from what I call fair authors—Shakespeare,
Milton, Pope, and some of the later writers, Sir Walter Scott and
Tennyson. I have set this question over and over again. 'Here is a
passage. State where it comes from, explain any peculiarities of
English in it, and state the context as far as you are able to do so.'
If you set fifty passages, if the candidates are at all instructed, you
will find that they answer it in various degrees. I remember an
Irishman answering forty-five out of fifty right. I am sure I do not
know how he did it." However, he added, "if six or ten are answered it would be quite enough to show considerable acquaintance with English literature." The members of the Commission
rightly were concerned about the importance of cramming in preparing for such an examination. Dasent replied that overt evidence
of cramming, for instance the fact that every boy recited verbatim
from the same manual an account of the character of Richard III,
would mean loss of marks. But he added that in his opinion cramming was not to be deplored; "I would rather," he said, "have a
boy who is able to learn something by cram, than a boy who is not
able to be taught anything by any process at all."[28]

The limited usefulness of such an examination in testing, let
alone promoting, a genuine interest in literature hardly needs to be
pointed out. But the age had an almost superstitious reverence for
such tests, and by 1875 boys leaving secondary schools could
choose from seventeen different examinations, depending on
whether they wished to enter the civil service, the armed forces,
the professions, or the universities.[29] In nearly all these examinations "English literature" was a set subject, and everywhere the
practice was the same—to test the candidate's memory of certain
facts and his ability to parse and gloss.

Despite the growing importance of these examinations, by the
mid-sixties little attention was yet given to literature as a classroom subject. The Taunton Commission found that very few
schools gave lessons in English literature. In Staffordshire and

[28] Taunton Commission, Qq. 13,973–76.

[29] Barclay Phillips in *Transactions of the Society for the Promotion of Social Science*
(1875), p. 460.

Warwickshire, for example, only one or two schools did so, and in Norfolk and Northumberland it was said that "English literature is hardly taught at all."[30] In preparing for the examinations, therefore, students relied almost exclusively on the short manuals, outlines, and annotated texts published in ever larger quantities for the cram market. G. L. Craik's *Compendious History of English Literature* and its abridgment, *A Manual of English Literature;* T. B. Shaw's *Student's Manual of English Literature* and the same author's *Students' Specimens of English Literature;* Robert Chambers' *History of the English Language and Literature;* Joseph Payne's *Studies in English Poetry;* and Austin Dobson's *Civil Service Handbook of English Literature* were but a few of the examination helps to crowd the field. Henry Morley's *First Sketch of English Literature* sold between 30,000 and 40,000 copies in the years 1873–98.[31] Between 1871 and 1887 the number of such books in the publishers' lists grew from about fifteen to forty-four.[32] Editions of English classics, containing all the exegetical material the pupil was likely to be examined upon, were published by the hundreds. In 1887 *Low's Educational Catalogue* listed some 280 school editions, exclusive of Shakespeare's plays, which were the most favored of all for examination purposes.

After the Taunton Commission had exposed the schools' negligence, literature quickly became an almost universal class subject. The practical reason of course was the pressure of the so-called "external" examinations; but the theoretical justification was that the study of literature was indispensable to an understanding of the English language. One witness before the Taunton Commission, the Right Honorable Earl of Harrowby, K.G., described with admiration the way in which students at a Liverpool school "took passages from Milton, read them backwards and forwards, and put them into other order, and they were obliged to parse them and explain them. The same faculties were exercised there in construing Milton as in construing Latin, only there was an interest in the one and there was no interest in the other." The noble lord urged that "English reading of the highest order ought to enter into every part of every English education" for the rather mys-

[30] Taunton Commission, I, 135–37.

[31] Henry S. Solly, *Life of Henry Morley* (1898), p. 305.

[32] See *Low's Educational Catalogue* for 1871 and 1887.

terious reason that "the English language contains the highest
morals of any language."[33] J. R. Seeley, another witness, after
hammering away at his favorite theme that the study of English
literature could redeem middle-class youths from boredom and "a
constant temptation to coarse and even vicious amusements," told
exactly how this aim could be achieved: "The classical English
writers should be read in class, sentences analyzed, synonyms distinguished; a great deal of poetry should be committed to memory,
and compositions written in imitation of particular writers. All
this should be closely connected with the teaching of elocution."[34]

This was the philosophy that carried the day; indeed, it was almost unquestioned. Not until the eighties, at the earliest, was its
soundness publicly challenged. In 1887 John Churton Collins, the
great crusader for university recognition of English literature as a
humane study, complained: "To all appearance . . . there is no
branch of [secondary] education in a more flourishing condition or
more full of promise for the future. But, unhappily, this is very far
from being the case. In spite of its great vogue, and in spite of the
time and energy lavished in teaching it, no fact is more certain
than that from an educational point of view it is, and from the
very first has been, an utter failure. Teachers perceive with per-
plexity that it attains none of the ends which a subject in itself so
full of attraction and interest might be expected to attain. It fails,
they complain, to fertilise; it fails to inform; it fails even to awaken
curiosity."[35]

The reason was as plain to Collins as it is to us, more than half a
century later: English literature "has been taught wherever it has
been seriously taught on the same principle as the classics. It has
been regarded not as the expression of art and genius, but as mere
material for the study of words, as mere pabulum for philology.
All that constitutes its intrinsic value has been ignored. All that
constitutes its value as a liberal study has been ignored. Its masterpieces have been resolved into exercises in grammar, syntax,
and etymology."[36] As the century drew to a close, few educators
had yet heeded Carlyle's remark, uttered in 1831, that mind does

[33] Taunton Commission, Qq. 14,056 and 14,072.

[34] *Ibid.*, Q. 16,616.

[35] "Can English Literature Be Taught?" *Nineteenth Century*, XXII (1887), 642.

[36] *Ibid.*, p. 644.

not grow like a vegetable, "by having its roots littered with etymological compost."[37]

In addition to the regrettably mistaken method of teaching literature, other elements in later Victorian education worked against the inculcation of the reading habit. One was the anti-intellectualism of the public schools, which inevitably affected the tone of the other secondary institutions—the unhappy result of Thomas Arnold's reforms as popularized through the fiction of Thomas Hughes. Although Arnold himself was no enemy of book-learning (he did much to re-emphasize the humane aspects of classical literature as against grammatical dissection), his general educational philosophy, as it worked out in practice, was to encourage in the schools a transcendence of the athletic body over the meditative mind, a devotion to stiff moral uprightness rather than a cultivation of intellect or imagination. The muscular Christian who was the ideal secondary-school product of the later nineteenth century was not typically a booklover. Writing in 1885, Henry Salt observed flatly that the Etonians of the day were "irretrievably unintellectual. They know little; they hate books."[38] The same might have been said, though less sweepingly, of the boys at most of the other schools.

Finally, the most characteristic educational innovation of the late Victorian period was the technical secondary school, whose birth and growth were due to a combination of circumstances—the influence of Spencer's educational theories, the pressing need for technologists to help Britain regain the ground she had lately lost in her race with America and Continental nations, the slow acceptance of the idea that a few selected children of modest station should have the benefit of additional schooling. In these new technical schools, which grew in number and influence toward the end of the century, little time was allowed for such impractical subjects as literature. It took some courage for a witness before the Bryce Commission in 1894 to plead that two or three hours a week be set aside for the study of literature which, as he put it, "goes a very long way to make childhood happy, if nothing more, and which gives breadth of view, and a certain amount of culture in after-life."[39]

[37] *Sartor Resartus*, Book II, chap. iii.

[38] "Confessions of an Eton Master," *Nineteenth Century*, XVII (1885), 179.

[39] *Royal Commission on Secondary Education* ["Bryce Commission"], Qq. 2819–26.

CHAPTER 9

The Mechanics' Institutes and After

I. The mechanics' institutes represented the adult's share of the educational program that Brougham and his colleagues laid out for the English masses. Their uneasy history offers a fascinating microcosm of the forces and counterforces, the tortuous eddies and currents, in early Victorian social life. Ideally, they could have been potent instruments for enlarging the reading public, and in some ways they actually were. But the contribution they made was directly proportional to the degree to which they abandoned their original purposes. They were a typical product of the utilitarian social philosophy, and only as the utilitarian motive was diluted and, eventually, expunged did they swell the number of general readers.[1]

Their basic purpose was to impart the elements of scientific knowledge to workingmen through classes, lectures, and libraries.[2] If these men knew more about chemistry, physics, astronomy, and

---

[1] Despite the importance of the subject and the abundance of source material, no modern book on the mechanics' institute movement exists. The major sources on which the present chapter is based are indicated in the following notes. Hudson's is by all odds the fullest contemporary treatment, but it may profitably be supplemented from Hole (*Essay on . . . Mechanics' Institutions*), Baker (*Central Society of Education Publications*, I [1837], 214–55), and Hill (*National Education*, II, 186–229). Hammond, *The Age of the Chartists*, pp. 322–33, provides a good summary. For several contemporary articles examining the successes and shortcomings of the movement, see the Bibliography in the present volume, under "Mechanics' Institutes." On the history of the British adult education movement generally, see Adamson, *English Education*; Hodgen, *Workers' Education*; Dobbs, *Education and Social Movements*; Martin, *The Adult School Movement*; Rowntree and Binns, *History of the Adult School Movement*.

[2] Considerable confusion has arisen from the use of the term "mechanic" in respect to the movement. Brougham and his friends intended their new institutions for skilled artisans rather than for common laborers. "Mechanics" who joined the pilot organization in London paid a guinea for a year's subscription, which is proof enough that they belonged to the aristocracy of labor. As the movement spread, however, "mechanics" was commonly used more loosely, to include ordinary machine-tenders and other semiskilled or even unskilled laborers. It was these who stayed away in the largest numbers.

other branches of science, they would make better workers. The more ingenious among them might even prove to be new Arkwrights and Stephensons, who would apply their new knowledge to making revolutionary labor-saving, wealth-producing inventions. But the benefits expected from mechanics' institutes went far beyond this. A knowledge of science, Brougham insisted, "would strengthen [the mechanic's] religious belief, it would make him a better and a happier, as well as a wiser man, if he soared a little into those regions of purer science where happily neither doubt can cloud, nor passion ruffle our serene path."[3] Mechanics' institutes would therefore be still another bulwark against irreligion. Equally would they combat the spread of objectionable political notions; "by means of lectures and popular discussions, those narrow conceptions, superstitious notions, and vain fears, which so generally prevail among the lower classes of society, might be gradually removed, and a variety of useful hints and rational views suggested, promotive of domestic convenience and comfort." And, of course, the institutes would help police the nation. "A taste for rational enjoyments," lectures and books rather than gin parlors and bear pits, would be cultivated among the common run of men; "habits of order, punctuality, and politeness, would be engendered."[4]

"The spectacle of hundreds of industrious individuals, who have finished the labours of the day, congregating together in a spacious apartment, listening with mute admiration to the sublime truths of philosophy, is truly worthy of a great and enlightened people."[5] So wrote one of Brougham's fellow pamphleteers in 1825. The vision in the minds of the mechanics' institute promoters was lofty and, according to their lights, disinterested. Granting their utilitarian assumptions, they were idealists working for a happier society.

The movement was inspired by the work of Dr. George Birkbeck, who at the very beginning of the century had organized and taught classes in applied science for Glasgow artisans. After Birk-

[3] "Address to the Members of the Manchester Mechanics' Institution," *Speeches* (Edinburgh, 1838), III, 164. (The whole speech [pp. 155–78] is a good place to study the motives behind the mechanics' institute movement.) This faith in useful knowledge as a pathway to religious belief and moral perfection, expressed by Peel, led to Newman's eloquent counterblast in his "Tamworth Reading Room."

[4] Hudson, *Adult Education*, p. 55.

[5] James Scott Walker, *An Essay on the Education of the People* (1825), p. 45.

beck moved to London in 1804, his work was continued by others, in both Glasgow and Edinburgh. In 1823, J. C. Robertson, editor of the *Mechanics' Magazine*, and Thomas Hodgskin, the socialist, proposed to found a London Mechanics' Institution for similar purposes. Immediately Brougham and his disciples, scenting a rich opportunity, moved in, and Dr. Birkbeck, one of the circle, was installed as first president. With some 1,500 subscribers, the institution got under way in March, 1824.[6] The first lecture was the talk of the London season. Francis Place, writing to Sir Francis Burdett, expressed his satisfaction at the spectacle of "800 to 900 clean, respectable-looking mechanics paying most marked attention" to a lecture on chemistry.[7] Four months later Brougham reported that "scarcely three days ever elapse without my receiving a communication of the establishment of some new mechanics' institution."[8] In the October *Edinburgh Review* he published an article explaining, with his customary brisk optimism, the enormous potentialities of the new movement.[9] An expanded version, issued in pamphlet form as *Practical Observations upon the Education of the People*, quickly ran through many editions and carried the message to all of cultivated Britain. Soon the mechanics' institute was as familiar a part of the social and cultural landscape as the National school. By 1850 there were 702 such organizations in the United Kingdom, of which 610, with a membership of 102,000, were in England alone.[10] But by that time most of them had lost all but a superficial resemblance to the institutes envisaged by Brougham.

At first, the mechanics came willingly, even eagerly. This was a novelty; it was well advertised; it promised to equip them to earn better wages; and above all it appealed to the sense widespread among them that, in this age of the March of Mind, ignorance was not only a handicap but a stigma. From the beginning, however,

---

[6] Among numerous narratives of the antecedents of the movement (to 1824) are those in Hammond, *The Age of the Chartists*, pp. 322–23, Hudson, pp. 26–53, and an article in *Chambers's Papers for the People* (Philadelphia, 1851), III, 197–201 (cited hereafter as "*Papers for the People*").

[7] Graham Wallas, *Life of Francis Place* (New York, 1919), pp. 112–13.

[8] Quoted in *Papers for the People*, p. 201.

[9] "Scientific Education of the People," *Edinburgh Review*, XLI (1824), 96–122.

[10] Hudson, p. vi.

potent forces worked against the success of the institutes as originally conceived.

The name of Brougham, and therefore of his Society for the Diffusion of Useful Knowledge, which propagandized for the institutes, was anathema to the Tory party and its spiritual arm, the Church of England. Rick-burnings, riots, and seditious meetings were too common to allow conservatives to view with equanimity the deliberate encouragement of large working-class gatherings, no matter how laudable their announced purpose. Once people were brought together, mischievous ideas were bound to be generated and to spread with irresistible speed. And it was well known what effect the application of reason—a term indelibly associated with Jacobinism—had on the common man's allegiance to Christian principles. Despite Brougham's protestations that a thinking workman would be a devout workman, the portion of the Church which had earlier opposed even the teaching of reading and writing to poor children believed otherwise. Hence in many localities the parson had the power of life and death over the institute; he held the keys to the village schoolroom, which was often the only suitable place for the institute, and his opposition was enough to discourage his parishioners from attending.[11]

The movement was no more popular with working-class leaders, who never wasted any love on Brougham and his party. Cobbett, for example, though he had contributed £5 to the fund for the London institute when Hodgskin and Robertson were its sponsors, took alarm as soon as Brougham, Place, and Birkbeck appeared on the scene. He accurately foresaw that with the advent of these formidable philanthropists, control of the institute would be wrested from the mechanics, and in the *Political Register* he waxed sarcastic over the Broughamites' "brilliant enterprise to make us '*a*' enlightened' and to fill us with '*antellect*, brought, ready bottled up, from the north of the Tweed.' "[12]

What happened in the London institute within the next few years happened sooner or later in the great majority of institutes: the mechanics departed, or were pushed out, and in their place came business and professional men and their families. As early as 1840, only sixteen years after the movement began, the Yorkshire Union

[11] See *ibid.*, pp. 201–202, and Hole, pp. 92–93.

[12] Cole, *Life of Cobbett,* pp. 264–65.

of Mechanics' Institutes reported that no more than one member out of twenty was a true workingman; all the rest were "connected with the higher branches of handicraft trades, or are clerks in offices, and, in many instances, young men connected with liberal professions."[13] In the early fifties it was said that of thirty-two flourishing mechanics' institutes in Lancashire and Cheshire, only four, all in small villages, were attended by workingmen.[14] The mechanics' exodus seems to have been most pronounced in the larger institutions. Some of the smaller ones kept their original character and were important influences in local workers' lives.

The reasons why mechanics were not served by the establishments erected for their use throw much light on the difficulties that beset workers' education in the early Victorian era. These were, with one or two exceptions, the same obstacles that prevented a more rapid expansion of the mass audience for books.

However eager he may have been for intellectual improvement, the workman was in no condition, after a long, hard day's work, to profit from the instruction the institute offered. Weary in mind and body, he was expected to sit on a hard chair, in an ill-ventilated room, while a lecturer droned on and on about the chemistry of textile dyeing or the principle of the steam engine. The sleep that overcame him, though not provided for in the Broughamites' roseate calculations, was an inescapable fact of nature.

Again, the general atmosphere, unless the institute was one of the few conducted by the workers themselves, was not attractive. The managers' benevolent smiles as the workingman entered did not wholly conceal a critical examination of his clothes, personal cleanliness, and sobriety. And no matter how tactful the management may have tried to be, inevitably there was a certain amount of condescension which the workingman, with his ineffaceable natural dignity, resented. As a mechanic once observed, "You must remember we have masters all day long, and we don't want 'em at

[13] Hole, p. 21. In 1859, however, a spokesman for Yorkshire insisted that in his county most institutes "not only supply the educational wants of workingmen, but are mainly supported, and, in many instances, managed by them" (Barnett Blake, "The Mechanics' Institutes of Yorkshire," *Transactions of the National Association for the Promotion of Social Science* [1859], p. 335).

[14] *Papers for the People*, p. 204. For further data on the social and occupational distribution of membership in the mechanics' institutes, see Hudson, pp. 61, 87, 131; E. Renals, "On Mechanics' Institutions and the Elementary Education Bill," *Journal of the Statistical Society*, XXXIII (1870), 452–55; and Munford, *Penny Rate*, pp. 138–41.

night"[15]—particularly, he might have added, when his employers by day turned up as patrons of the institute by night. The presence of local employers and other middle-class dignitaries on the subscription rolls, to say nothing of the movement's connection with Brougham and his circle, fed the ordinary man's suspicion that, if simple ignorance had been the opiate recommended for the poor of the eighteenth century, the new prescription was a scientific education. For this was the very time when the laboring class's distrust of middle-class motives was steadily growing; after 1832 it was sharpened by the discovery that the Reform Bill for which the masses had entertained such high hopes was an instrument to solidify middle-class control of the nation. In these decades politics, not physics, engaged the common man's attention. "Take at random any score of working-men," wrote a contributor to *Chambers's Papers for the People*, "and it will almost invariably be found that they would sooner attend a political meeting, to demand what they consider their 'rights,' than a scientific lecture; that they would rather read a party newspaper than a calm historical narrative; and that they would sooner invest money in a benefit club or building society than in a mechanics' institute."[16]

Furthermore, the institutes were founded on the assumption that education could begin at the age of twenty, or thirty, or forty. The truth was that most of the men for whom they were intended were totally unequipped to deal with the topics of the classes and lectures. Men who had barely learned the rules of arithmetic were in no position to grapple with problems in hydrostatics. Most institutes, to be sure, had adult classes in elementary subjects; but by the time the pupils got to the point where they could more or less understand formal scientific lectures, they had reached the limit of their interest and endurance. In any case, the workman who was willing to become again as a little child, and to learn to read and do sums just as his own children were doing at the local school, existed mostly in the reformers' imagination. It took a burning passion for self-improvement to lead bearded men to the school bench, and though many may have desired education, they could not face the embarrassment of starting with the three R's.

[15] Henry Solly, "*These Eighty Years*" (1893), II, 250.

[16] *Papers for the People*, p. 205.

Many of these handicaps might still have been overcome had the art of popularization been understood. Its necessity was recognized, but few lecturers yet had the knack of it. Lectures were generally presented on the academy or even the university level, and if many of the audience fell sound asleep, it was not only because of muscular fatigue.

What working people wanted after twelve or more hours in factory or mill was diversion. "After working at wheels all day," one lecturer is quoted as saying, "they ought not to be made to study wheels at night."[17] Yet that was precisely what they were expected to do. Their lives were to be devoted to their occupations even in their precious after-hours. For what other recreation but the study of wheels had the same social usefulness and at the same time was as safe? Though there were a great many other topics in the world besides the natural sciences and their application to English industry, they were deemed inappropriate for study by men destined to be lifelong hewers of wood and drawers of water.

In 1825 a clergyman flatly warned the members of the newly formed Aberdeen Mechanics' Institution that "Belles Lettres, Political Economy, and even History, were dangerous studies."[18] Although the proponents of the institutes wished to encourage discussion of political and economic matters, so that under proper guidance the honest workingmen would be persuaded of the truth of middle-class doctrines, the conservative opposition was so strong that in many places there was an absolute ban on "controversial" topics. The study of polite literature was forbidden for obvious reasons. To divert workingmen with poetry, drama, and above all novels not only would put a quietus to the cause of scientific instruction but would encourage the very habits of idleness and extravagant dreaming that the institutes were designed to wipe out.[19]

[17] Newspaper Stamp Committee, Q. 1073.

[18] Quoted in Hudson, p. 59.

[19] Another serious obstacle in the way of the common workman's participation in the mechanics' institutes was the subscription fee, which ranged from 5*s.* to 20*s.* a year. In some institutes there were different grades of membership; for example, 2*s.* per quarter for admission to classes, 3*s.* for admission to lectures and the use of the library, and 4*s.* for classes, lectures, and library privileges together. In a period when wages were low and unemployment frequent and protracted, such fees were out of the question for those below the master-artisan class (Hudson, pp. 222–36; Hole, p. 86).

II. So far as the interests of the present study are concerned, the chief significance of these restrictions is their effect upon the choice of books in institute libraries. The libraries gave more trouble than all the other institute activities put together. Since they were to be used principally, if not exclusively, by the working class, they could contain only books that were proper for mechanics to read, and neither works of "controversy" nor of fiction should be admitted to the shelves.

Here and there were realists who saw that a library thus limited would never recommend itself to the common reader. A forerunner of the mechanics' institute libraries, the Edinburgh Mechanics' Subscription Library, had had no such limitations. When it was founded in 1825, it received large gifts of books from publishers like Constable and Adam Black, who explicitly desired that "it should not be restricted to works of science, but embrace *every department of literature*." But this was a library run by the mechanics themselves—1,200 of them at the peak of its prosperity, who paid a 5s. entrance fee and a quarterly subscription of 1s.6d.— and it was thus free of control from above.[20] On the other hand, when the Leeds Mechanics' Institute was being formed at the same time, its middle-class sponsors as a group maintained that "it was desirable to confine the attention of the artizans to the study of science, which would not be done if books of a more interesting kind were placed within their reach: . . . such books would dissipate their attention." The liberal-minded Edward Baines, one of the founders, nevertheless was in favor of giving the readers "works of general literature." But to have forced the issue would have risked alienating the prospective financial backers, so Baines let the matter drop.[21] Within ten years, as he might have predicted, a dissident group formed the Leeds Literary Institution, whose library was to include "all works of value and interest in the English language." Eventually the original institute was forced to let down the bars against non-scientific works.[22]

Some sponsors argued that no principle would be sacrificed by using a few selected works of fiction as bait to get book-shy work-

[20] Hudson, pp. 200–201. Italics supplied.

[21] Edward Baines [Jr.], *Life of Edward Baines* (2d ed., 1859), pp. 105–106.

[22] Hudson, p. 90.

men inside the library. Once they were there, their native intellectual ambition would cause them to take up more serious reading matter.[23] But this was not the ordinary view. Mechanics' institute backers had a curiously mixed notion of their intended clients, whom they thought of as being eager for scientific knowledge and at the same time flabbily susceptible to the wiles of the novelist. In this divided being, temptation would always triumph over will power, and the ordinary man would linger indefinitely over the appetizer rather than go on to the main course. The only thing to do, therefore, was to serve him good tough scientific meat to begin with.

Had this policy prevailed unmodified after the first decade or so, mechanics' institute libraries would have played little part in extending the reading habit. Even so, it lasted long enough to help drive away the workingmen, who, having come for bread, were given a hard utilitarian stone. But the irony is that once their places began to be filled with representatives of a higher social class—warehousemen, clerks, small businessmen, and their families—the libraries began to admit the very types of books which had hitherto been forbidden. The spirit of the new membership was that of the versifier who sang,

> When science turns with dreary look
> The leaves of her ungainly book,
> I say the dotard fool would dream
>   Who'd turn the leaves with thee—
> The bard who sang by Avon's stream
> Has brighter charms for me.[24]

Faced with this demand for general literature, the promoters had either to sacrifice their principles or see the establishments collapse for lack of interest. To the extent that they chose the former course and relaxed the ban upon non-utilitarian books, they contributed significantly to the spread of reading among the middle class.

The people who ran the institute libraries never yielded an inch without a struggle that rocked the whole community. Often their intransigence in the face of a strong cry for a more liberal policy caused outright secessions, and when the fallen angels formed their own libraries they showed their true colors by immediately buying

[23] See, for example, Walker, *Essay on the Education of the People*, pp. 44–47.

[24] Quoted in *Papers for the People*, p. 214.

works like Howitt's violently anti-Anglican *History of Priestcraft.*[25] It is an open question which sort of books, imaginative literature or controversial works on religion, politics, and social organization, stirred up more trouble. Shelley's *Queen Mab,* which falls into both categories, nearly disrupted the Brighton Workingmen's Institute soon after it was founded by Rev. F. W. Robertson. At its opening in 1848, the institute seemed to face a bright future, because Robertson was not averse to allowing fiction in the library. But two years later a few of the members, still not satisfied, agitated to have *Queen Mab* put on the shelves. Robertson then called the membership together and administered a severe rebuke, saying that while he yielded to no man in his veneration of the spirit of free inquiry, he could not countenance the inclusion of atheistical works in the library. The result was a thorough reorganization of the institute, in the course of which the atheistically inclined seem to have been purged.[26]

Elsewhere, though the original policy was unaltered, its application was remarkably inconsistent. At the inception in 1823 of the Sheffield Mechanics' and Apprentices' Library (which, though not itself an appendage of a mechanics' institute, was quite characteristic of those that were), "novels, plays, and works subversive of the Christian religion" were forbidden—and they continued to be forbidden a quarter-century later. But, as a testy contemporary writer observed, "successive committees held that there is a real distinction between the tales of Miss Martineau, illustrating some principle of political economy, and Sir Walter Scott's novels. . . . The tragedies of Lord Byron and the translations of the plays of Sophocles and Euripides find a place on the shelves from whence the works of Shakspeare, presented by virtue of a legacy, were cast out and sold by auction. The novels of Bulwer, Washington Irving, Thackeray, and Warren are admitted; but the writings of Scott, Galt, James, Marryat, and D'Israeli are contraband. Howitt's *Priestcraft* and Cobbett's *Legacy to Parsons* are admissible in the opinion of those who refuse to purchase a copy of the *Vicar of Wakefield;* no doubt upon the same principle which induces a committee of a Mechanics' Institution on the east coast of

[25] Public Libraries Committee, Q. 1229.

[26] F. W. Robertson, *Lectures and Addresses on Literary and Social Topics* (Boston, 1859), pp. 52–92.

Yorkshire to refuse even donations of novels, yet re-purchases
Jack Sheppard as often as it is worn out, because it is to be found in
the pages of a monthly periodical."[27]

As evangelical hostility to fiction wore off and the utilitarians
began to concede that the reading of imaginative literature in
moderation could contribute to the health of English society, the
advocates of a more liberal policy in the institute libraries gained
ground. Some at least of the newer generation of clergymen and
public men, prodded by writers like Dickens and Wilkie Collins,
announced their conviction that men and women in an industrial
society must somehow indulge their fancy and feelings or their
souls would shrivel up. Poetry, F. W. Robertson told the members
of his institute, can "enable the man of labour to rise sometimes
out of his dull, dry, hard toil, and dreary routine of daily life, into
forgetfulness of his state, to breathe a higher and serener, and
purer atmosphere."[28] But this new broad-mindedness was far from
universal. As the next chapter will show, when attention shifted
after mid-century from mechanics' institute libraries to the new
rate-supported libraries, the question of "light literature" went
with it, to feed the fires of tiresome controversy for fifty more
years.

The importance of mechanics' institute libraries in the spread of
book-reading among the middle class is suggested by the fact that
in 1850 the 610 English institutes owned almost 700,000 volumes
and circulated 1,820,000 a year.[29] The largest libraries were in
Liverpool (15,300 volumes) and Manchester (13,000), but the
typical library in a fair-sized city contained anywhere from 8,000
volumes (Newcastle) to 2,000 (Reading, Plymouth, Durham,
Norwich).[30] In the seventy-nine establishments belonging to the
Yorkshire Union of Mechanics' Institutes, the average collection
included 900 books.[31] But by no means all the books appealed to
the ordinary reader. George Dawson, a prominent figure in the
institute movement, asserted in 1849 that "many of the books are

[27] Hudson, pp. 159–60.

[28] Robertson, p. 103. Quoted from one of two lectures Robertson delivered to his mechanics' institute on "The Influence of Poetry on the Working Classes."

[29] Hudson, pp. vi–vii.

[30] *Ibid.*, pp. 222–36.

[31] Public Libraries Committee, Q. 1959. The witness was Samuel Smiles.

gift books, turned out of people's shelves, and are never used, and old magazines of different kinds, so that, out of 1,000 volumes, perhaps there may be only 400 or 500 useful ones. The rest are, many of them, only annual registers and old religious magazines that are never taken down from the shelves."[32] Even when the books were supplied fresh from the booksellers, their inappropriateness was sometimes appalling. In 1846 a wealthy lady, having decided to donate sets of books to a number of English and Scottish institute libraries, asked Bishop Whately what titles might be suitable. He responded with a list of books that were as weighty as his own theological and philosophical works (some of which he included), and she passed it on to the Edinburgh bookseller George Wilson. "Hurrah!" wrote Wilson to his English correspondent, Daniel Macmillan. "Take your share of happiness in the business, my good friend. Who knows what service they may render to the unwashed immortals."[33] However profitable the business was to Wilson and Macmillan, we may well wonder how great the service rendered really was. But when the libraries were so largely dependent upon philanthropy for their books, they had to take what they could get.

Hence, while the middle-class reader in village and town had more books available to him than ever before, the selection was far from adequate. The greater part of a typical institute library slumbered undisturbed on the dusty shelves, while the minority of truly popular books were read to tatters. There was little money for additional purchases, and when purchases were made, although the clients' tastes were consulted more freely now that the "respectable" part of the population had taken over the institutes, strong prejudices remained against the acquisition and circulation of certain types of books. Mudie's standards were quite easygoing by comparison. Thus the mechanics' institute libraries, all except the very largest, did more to whet the common reader's appetite than to satisfy it.[34]

This was, of course, a great gain, for as the demand grew, other ways of meeting it appeared. Frequently, in the recollections of men who belonged to the institutes, we encounter warm praise of

[32] *Ibid.*, Q. 1212.

[33] Thomas Hughes, *Memoir of Daniel Macmillan* (1882), p. 169.

[34] Public Libraries Committee, Qq. 1952–56.

the libraries' stimulating influence upon their taste for reading. This is especially true of the very small establishments, which remained genuinely dedicated to the needs of the working-class reader. We hear, for instance, of Daniel Hudson, a cottage lace-weaver at Ilkeston in South Derbyshire, who made sure, first, that the local institute ordered the best new books, and second, that he had quick access to them, to prop before his loom as he worked.[35] And we read of the little Edwinstowe Artisans' Library in Nottinghamshire, which enrolled members at a shilling each, with a weekly subscription of a penny. This income being grievously inadequate, the members held an annual New Year's Eve celebration which, despite some villagers' outrage "that ever good books should be bought with wicked dancing money," replenished the coffers for the next several months. In 1846, when it was eight years old, the library boasted five hundred volumes, including Knight's *Pictorial Shakespeare*, his *Pictorial History of England*, the *Penny Cyclopaedia*, and the works of Byron, Cowper, Scott, and Goldsmith, as well as such current periodicals as *Tait's Magazine*, the *People's Journal*, and *Howitt's Journal*.[36] For a third example, Thomas Burt, the future labor leader, delighted in the library of the Blyth Mechanics' Institute in the sixties, discovering all manner of books new to him—the novels of George Eliot, for instance, and the social gospel of Ruskin.[37] Burt and the uncounted thousands like him, who got to know the joys of reading through a mechanics' institute library, might well have joined in the cry of Christopher Thomson, the autobiographical house-painter of Edwinstowe: "Who, then, shall say that our time has been misspent?"[38]

III. Libraries were not the only means by which the mechanics' institutes aided the growth of the reading public. When the institutes first sprang up, their most formidable competitors—indeed, the resorts from which they were designed to entice patrons—were the coffeehouses, public houses, and radical newsrooms where newspapers were freely available, and where

[35] Gregory, *Autobiographical Recollections*, p. 272.

[36] Thomson, *Autobiography of an Artisan*, pp. 336–40.

[37] Burt, *Autobiography*, pp. 188–90.

[38] Thomson, p. 342.

political discussion was always going on. When workmen proved reluctant to desert newspaper reading for scientific lectures, the institutes set up newsrooms of their own. Despite solemn promises that only papers with a "healthy" political tone would be taken in, every proposal to open a newsroom in an institute was bitterly fought.

Once a newsroom was started, it further diverted attention from the original purpose of the institute. A writer in 1837, deploring this attempt to give mechanics' institutes "a popular character," admitted that "an accession of members has been obtained, but these members have been of a different *caste* to those for whom such institutions are intended. Where newspapers have been received, it has been found that the objects connected with mental and scientific cultivation have been disregarded, the taste for sound acquirements has to a greater or less extent disappeared; and on this account we cannot but deprecate their introduction."[39] Although by the fifties most institutes had newsrooms, they never attracted many workmen. A few institutes pathetically bid for more readers by serving coffee along with the papers. But what the readers really wanted was a relaxing pint, a pipe, a selection of papers with working-class sympathies—and a place to air their opinions. These luxuries continued to be available only in their customary haunts. The institute newsrooms were patronized only by the highly skilled artisan, the tradesman, and the clerk.

A third contribution of the mechanics' institutes to the reading audience was popular lectures. These, in conspicuous contrast to the formal scientific discourses envisaged by the founders, were concerned less with "useful arts" than with history, travel, biography, music, and literature. This was the most far-reaching revolution brought about by the domination of the middle-class clientele: the institutes, as a contemporary sighed, were forced to place Apollo in the seat of Minerva.[40] In doing so, they were more or less aping the august "literary and philosophical institutions" which had long been rallying places of the cultural aristocracy.[41] But whereas the audiences that listened to the lectures of men like Coleridge and Hazlitt at the Surrey Institution and elsewhere had

[39] *Central Society of Education Publications*, I (1837), 248.
[40] *Papers for the People*, p. 202.
[41] See Halévy, *History of the English People in 1815*, pp. 491–93.

come with serious intellectual purpose, the men and women who attended the mechanics' institutes as a rule were bent on achieving the illusion of being instructed when in reality they sought, and obtained, mere amusement.

Dr. J. W. Hudson, a leading figure in the movement at mid-century, spoke of the change with acid disapproval: "Those Institutions which have adhered to their original scheme, rejecting novels from the library and newspapers from the reading-room, have, for the most part, become extinct . . . while their officers declaim at the apathy of the working classes. Others have been led into unhealthy excitement by weekly lectures, frequent concerts, ventriloquism, and Shaksperian readings, directing their chief energies into a wrong channel. . . . The plain and easily understood discourses on the elements of the sciences, and their application to the useful arts, illustrated by numerous experiments, have been abandoned; and the preference shown for light literature, criticism, music, and the drama, has given just occasion for the statement, that even the elder Metropolitan [London] Mechanics' Institution, since its establishment, has given more attention to *the Drama* than to the entire range of physical science."[42]

The trend away from scientific lectures to platform ramblings on "literary" topics is recorded in many statistical summaries. In the first half of the period 1835–49, for instance, the balance at the Manchester Athenaeum was 173 lectures on "physical and mental science" as against 179 on all other topics; in the second half, the total of scientific discourses dwindled to 81, while the categories of literature, "education," and the fine arts accounted for 313.[43] In 1851 an analysis of a thousand lectures recently delivered at forty-three institutes revealed that "more than half (572) were on literary subjects; about one-third (340) on scientific; and 88 on musical, exclusive of concerts."[44]

[42] Hudson, pp. xii–xiii, 57–58.   [43] *Ibid.*, p. 118.

[44] *Papers for the People*, p. 212. "Nothing too much" was the motto of the latter-day mechanics' institutes: a little of this, a little of that. Witness the variety of lectures and other entertainments scheduled for the 1857 season at the London Mechanics' Institution: The Atlantic Ocean Telegraph; A Gossiping Concert; Christmas Books of Charles Dickens; A Second Peep at Scotland; A Broad Stare at Ireland; Characters in Imaginative Literature; The Romance of Biography; Concert by the Vocal Music Class; On the Apparent Contradictions of Chemistry; Gems of Scottish Song; On Explosive Compounds; Entertainment by the Elocution Class (C. Delisle Burns, *A Short History of Birkbeck College* [1924], pp. 74–75).

The term "literary" had, of course, a comprehensive meaning; it embraced all that was not scientific or musical. Thus "literary" lectures touched on such diverse topics as the funeral rites of various nations, the habits and customs of the Eskimos, the life, death, and burial of Mary, Queen of Scots, the games of Greece, the theosophy of India, the sons of Noah, and an inquiry into the esoteric riddle, "Are the Inhabitants of Persia, India, and China of Japhetic or Shemitic Origin?"[45]

In this mélange, however, literature in the narrower, more modern sense was especially prominent. The italicized report that came from Birmingham as early as 1836, "*Popular lectures on Poetry and the Drama have been most of all attractive,*"[46] echoes throughout the remaining history of the mechanics' institute movement. Among the thousand lectures mentioned above, twenty-three dealt specifically with Shakespeare, who was, the analyst observed, "an inexhaustible quarry out of which materials for lectures and essays innumerable have been dug."[47]

As time went on, "lectures" tended more and more to become programs of excerpts from favorite authors, sometimes interlarded with appreciative comments. The most popular professional lecturers were elocutionists who offered "A Night with Swift [or Defoe, Dr. Johnson, Thomas Hood, Sydney Smith, Spenser, Carlyle, Burns, etc.]." Platform artists who read plays aloud were in particular demand. As there was a world of difference between watching a play in the theater, which was still out of bounds to many Englishmen, and hearing it read by a respectable gentleman in the decorous precincts of the mechanics' institute, countless middle-class men and women now enjoyed a form of literature from which, a generation earlier, religious scruples had completely barred them.

Mechanics' institute lectures and readings brought the middle class into contact with literature in another way. Because lecturing was fairly lucrative (the fee for a single appearance ranged from three to twelve guineas, and a popular lecturer could make from £500 to £1,000 a year),[48] it attracted numerous early- and mid-

[45] *Papers for the People*, p. 212.

[46] Hill, *National Education*, II, 192.

[47] *Papers for the People*, p. 212.   [48] Public Libraries Committee, Q. 2434.

Victorian men of letters, from giants down to hacks. Provincial audiences thus had the chance to behold authors in the flesh, and it is only reasonable to assume that the experience stimulated interest in their books. Dickens' famous career as a dramatic reader began with a series given for the benefit of the Birmingham and Midland Institute in 1853; but for some years earlier he had been a speaker and prize distributor at the soirées and *conversaziones* of large Midland and Scottish institutes.[49] Between November, 1847, and February, 1848, Emerson gave sixty-four lectures in twenty-five towns, leaving behind him a trail of controversy because in a number of towns severe exception was taken to the institute's having sponsored an address by a man of distinctly unorthodox religious views.[50] Charles Cowden Clarke, Keats's schoolmaster, the friend of Lamb and Hunt, and the modernizer of Chaucer, went the rounds for twenty-one consecutive seasons with his lectures on the English humorists, the dramatists, Shakespeare's minor characters, and a host of other literary subjects.[51]

How great an effect the mechanics' institute lectures had upon the growth of the reading public is debatable. Many Victorian men and women attended them as a painless substitute for reading; at little or no expenditure of intellectual energy, and in the pleasant excitement of a social gathering, they could acquire a smattering of literary culture sufficient at least to sustain them in polite conversation. Having spent an hour or two listening to a spellbinder discussing the beauties of Milton's poetry or delivering droll extracts from Douglas Jerrold, they felt under no compulsion to pursue their education further, book in hand. Nevertheless, in every lecturer's audience there were at least a few who went forth to read on their own. In 1849 it was asserted that the greatest single benefit of the lectures was that they stimulated the use of the institute libraries.[52] Were it possible at the distance of a century, it would be most interesting to examine the effects of lectures upon the incidence of reading in a given community; upon not only the use of the libraries, but the sale of books and periodicals as well.

[49] For Dickens' speeches on these occasions, see his *Collected Papers* (Nonesuch ed.), Vol. II.

[50] Hudson, p. 84.

[51] Richard D. Altick, *The Cowden Clarkes* (1948), pp. 109–15.

[52] Public Libraries Committee, Q. 2444.

IV. Although by the fifties there was widespread pessimism over the future of mechanics' institutes, in some localities the movement survived to the 1890's. In 1891 the Yorkshire Union of Mechanics' Institutes boasted 280 affiliates, with a membership of over 60,000, and there were five other such regional groups.[53] In general, however, the institutes now devoted themselves to social rather than cultural pursuits; chess, billiards, excursions, and theatricals took the place of lectures. In many places the book collections passed to the new rate-supported libraries. Elsewhere the institute became the nucleus of a "polytechnic" or even, in one or two instances, of a local university.

But what, meanwhile, of the men in fustian jackets who had discovered that whenever they ventured into an institute reading room, the men in broadcloth pushed their chairs away? During the years when the institutes were proving inadequate as educational agencies for the working class, the pervasive admiration for learning and the electric political atmosphere had stimulated popular hunger for education. This was manifested in the number of little mutual-improvement clubs that sprang up, many of them composed of members of institutes who had been alienated by the absence of democratic management and the rigid censorship of discussion and reading.

We know little about those mutual-improvement clubs. No statistical society ever collected information about them—an impossible task, of course, since they were deliberately kept informal—and we cannot tell how numerous they were. But from the many allusions found in memoirs of working-class men, it appears that hardly a village was without at least one such group, and usually there were several; for they had various purposes. Some went in for theology, some for radical politics, some simply for general literature. In some the emphasis was on reading and discussion, in others it was on the writing of essays and verse, which were passed among the members for criticism. In a book published in 1867 we read of a little club in Sunderland made up of six workmen—a cork-cutter, two woodcarvers in the shipyards, a watchmaker, an engine-fitter, and a painter of photographs—who specialized in collecting old ballads. Their ambition was to subscribe to the publications of the Early English Text Society "so soon as work gets

[53] Greenwood, *Public Libraries*, pp. 489–90.

better."[54] Most of these groups gathered little libraries of books which they read and then sold off to buy new ones. Their funds were limited, but their thirst for knowledge was immense.[55]

To his membership in one such group, "The Liberals," who met in Newport Market, London, William Lovett attributed the awakening of his intellectual interest. The workingmen who composed it "met together . . . on two evenings in the week, on one of which occasions they had generally some question for discussion, either literary, political, or metaphysical. . . . My mind seemed to be awakened to a new mental existence; new feelings, hopes, and aspirations sprang up within me, and every spare moment was devoted to the acquisition of some kind of useful knowledge." Later Lovett joined several other such organizations, with the result that for years he had a book of some sort before him at every meal.[56]

To his early experience in mutual-improvement societies, also, can be traced Lovett's advocacy of universal education. Hitherto the goals of the working-class movement had been almost exclusively political and economic—steady employment, cheap bread, the right to organize, protection of civil rights, a voice in government. Lovett and his group, the "moral-force" Chartists, were the first influential English working-class leaders to take up the cry that education was one of the natural rights of man. The object of education, they maintained, was "the equal and judicious development of all . . . faculties, and not the mere cultivation of the intellect."[57] Such an education would make liberal provision for the use of books through which men would become "wiser, better, and happier members of the community."[58] Lovett insisted that children's education should be financed, but not controlled, by the

[54] Ludlow and Jones, *Progress of the Working Class*, p. 180.

[55] Better remembered than most is the Leeds Mutual Improvement Society, founded in 1844 by a group of "young operatives" who first met in a garden house among rakes, hoes, and broken flowerpots. Soon they moved to a disused cholera hospital. By 1850 the group boasted eighty members, among them machine-makers, silk dressers, joiners, coach-makers, and shopkeepers, whose average age was twenty-three. Each member paid between $\frac{1}{2}d$. and $2d$. a week to the general fund (Hudson, pp. 94–95; Samuel Smiles, *Autobiography* [New York, 1905], p. 131).

[56] Lovett, *Life and Struggles*, pp. 35–36.

[57] *Ibid.*, p. 147.

[58] William Lovett and John Collins, *Chartism: A New Organization of the People* (1840), p. 50.

state, and that it should be completely divorced from religion. By a natural extension, he felt that the education of adult workers should be placed in their own hands, without the oppressive supervision and censorship from above that rendered the atmosphere of the mechanics' institutes so uncongenial to them. In small local organizations, such as the ones in which he himself had participated, lay the best hope for spreading culture among adult workers.[59]

Among the moral-force Chartists could be found a remarkably strong element of literary culture. The leaders, Lovett and Thomas Cooper in particular, were self-educated and widely read men, and the prominence they achieved at the head of the movement helped advertise the idea of self-improvement through reading. Chartist meetings were unusual in the history of English political agitation in that, when no immediate political topic required discussion, Cooper lectured on Milton, Shakespeare, and Burns, and recited sections of *Paradise Lost, Hamlet*, and "Tam o' Shanter."[60] At least one Chartist publication, W. J. Linton's *The National: A Library for the People* (1839), printed selections from great English authors, among them Wordsworth, Shelley, Keats, Spenser, Coleridge, Herrick, Leigh Hunt, Sidney, Dr. Johnson, and Tennyson. Whenever possible, excerpts were chosen which would illustrate some Chartist doctrine, but it is obvious from the list of authors that many were selected simply for their literary merit. In the movement, too, there was a strong feeling that the common people should produce their own literature. Cooper and Thomas Prince were practicing poets, and a frequent note in Chartist propaganda is "Go ye and write likewise." *Cooper's Journal* reminded its readers that in the midst of their studies they should "all join hands and heads to create a library of your own. Your own prose and your own poetry: you ought to be resolved to create these."[61]

These ideals, however, were not characteristic of the whole Chartist movement that agitated the country in the late thirties and forties. Only a minority of Chartists adopted education as

[59] On Chartism and education generally, see Lovett, *Life and Struggles*, and R. H. Tawney's introduction to the edition of 1920, pp. xxiii–xxvi; Hodgen, *Workers' Education*, pp. 85–96.

[60] Cooper, *Life*, p. 169.

[61] Quoted in Helen D. Lockwood, *Tools and the Man* (New York, 1927), p. 72.

their primary long-term means of fashioning a new social order. The "physical-force" Chartists, led by Feargus O'Connor, were chiefly proletarians of the North and Wales whose first and only concern was to achieve immediate political reform, if necessary through revolution. The hundreds of thousands of hard-pressed laborers who followed the banners in those tumultuous years would have scoffed at the idea of risking imprisonment or death merely to crusade for educational opportunity and access to good books.

Despite their sweeping generalizations, Lovett and his followers actually were expressing the feelings not of the rank and file of laborers but of the workers' intellectual aristocracy and of their middle-class sympathizers. The awakening they did so much to advertise and advance—the growing desire for knowledge of all sorts, political, economic, scientific, literary—was not a true proletarian phenomenon. It had, nevertheless, great importance, since it foreshadowed the end of the old religious-utilitarian monopoly upon adult education and asserted the common man's right to share in a culture that did not end with a knowledge of the principles of the steam engine and the Christian theory of social subordination. As Kingsley's Alton Locke apostrophized the governing class: "We are not all by nature dolts and idiots; . . . there are differences of brain among us, just as great as there is between you; and . . . there are those among us whose education ought not to end, and will not end, with the putting off of the parish cap and breeches; whom it is cruelty, as well as folly, to toss back into the hell of mere manual drudgery, as soon as you have—if, indeed, you have been even so bountiful as that—excited in them a new thirst of the intellect and imagination."[62]

What the moral-force Chartists proposed, certain middle-class humanitarians, after 1848, tried to achieve. The campaign to educate the adult worker, vitalized by the writings and other labors of Kingsley and his fellow Christian Socialists, set off in new directions: toward workingmen's clubs, workingmen's colleges, university extension. The history of such ventures reveals that the glowing, Lovett-inspired faith in the ordinary worker's readiness for further education was still premature.

In the sixties the reformer Henry Solly, troubled by the failure

[62] *Alton Locke*, chap. vii.

of mechanics' institutes to appeal to the workman, started the workingmen's club movement. Backed by F. D. Maurice and a little later by philanthropic forces headed by Lord Lyttelton, he was instrumental in providing numerous meeting places where the tired workman might relax and participate in informal discussion groups. The movement flourished for a few years, then withered away for lack of beer. Few men, it appeared, however bent upon self-improvement, could be happy in the teetotal workingmen's club when their mates were enjoying themselves in the smoky public house. In some clubs, once philanthropic support of the venture had ceased, malt beverages were admitted; but the result was hardly happier.[63] A man who sometimes discussed Shakespeare with such groups on Sunday mornings recorded that he had to pause midway in his talk to allow a waiter from the adjoining public house to go round with the beer.[64]

The educational aims of these clubs were extremely modest, but even they failed of realization. Those of another venture participated in by F. D. Maurice were far more ambitious. Ever since 1842, the People's College of Sheffield had been attracting attention as a practical fulfilment of Chartist educational ideals. Controlled entirely by a committee of students and supported only by the small fees it charged (9d. per student), it provided workmen with courses in non-utilitarian subjects like language and literature.[65] In 1848 Maurice, aided by several of his colleagues at King's College and some young university graduates, started night classes on a similar model in Little Ormond Yard, London. Six years later, upon losing his professorial chair for entertaining unacceptable views on the nature of hell, Maurice began a full-fledged Working Men's College. The purpose behind the new college was a measure of the change that had occurred since Brougham's day. The workingman was conceived to be "a person, not a thing, a citizen and not a slave or even a wage-earning animal." Hence less stress was laid upon science and other utilitarian branches than upon the humane disciplines. In the curriculum some attention was paid to literature, but chiefly as the handmaiden of history and ethics. Maurice seems to have felt that the primary function of lit-

[63] Solly, *"These Eighty Years,"* II, 50–51, 160–63, 256.

[64] Rogers, *Labour, Life, and Literature,* p. 96.

[65] Adamson, *English Education,* pp. 163–64.

erature in the classroom was to illustrate other subjects, rather than to whet an appetite for reading for its own sake. During the first season, for example, he lectured on "Political terms illustrated by English literature" and on Shakespeare's *King John* as an aid in understanding English history. Outside the lecture room, however, literary interests were more directly encouraged. In the social gatherings that were a prominent feature of life at the college, there was much reading of poetry; in the early days a "Shakespearian Reading Club" was formed; and the institution's library grew to include 5,000 books by 1867.[66]

The fact remained, however, that the working class was so completely unprepared for higher education that all but the most indomitable spirits soon lost hope. In Maurice's college the old story of the mechanics' institutes repeated itself: though at the outset an even balance existed between "operatives" and white-collar workers, the latter soon far outnumbered the true working-men.[67] This was just as true of the university extension program which began timidly in 1873, in response to the feeling that the universities should do their share in the general expansion of national education. With Cambridge taking the lead, "extension centers" were set up in a number of populous towns. University lecturers offered courses of weekly or fortnightly lectures, followed by classes for the more serious students, on a variety of subjects taught in the universities themselves. While the classes were, in general, well attended, in the daytime by ladies and other persons of leisure and in the evening by men of the middle class, artisans were conspicuous by their absence. Despite occasional aid from trade unions, university extension courses became more and more the possession of women and business and professional men. In a course given by R. G. Moulton on "Greek Tragedy for English Audiences," of the ninety-three students who were admitted at a reduced rate (the rest—two-thirds of the whole number—being "persons in easy circumstances"), forty-four were teachers, twenty-three private governesses, eleven pupils in schools, ten business employees, four artisans, and one a domestic servant. A noteworthy exception to the general rule occurred in Northumberland,

[66] *Ibid.*, pp. 164–68; Hodgen, pp. 103–104; J. Llewellyn Davies, *The Working Men's College, 1854–1904* (1904), *passim.*

[67] Adamson, p. 168.

where 1,300 miners attended a course of lectures on political economy and, in subsequent seasons, patronized series on a wide variety of other topics, from physiology to English literature.

University extension progressed slowly. One reason seems to
have been that the later history of the mechanics' institutes had
given currency to the idea that adult education was, almost by
definition, a large coating of amusement encasing a small grain of
instruction; an hour's excursion to ancient Greece one week, a dip
into Thomas Hood the next, the season concluding with a gala
soirée to raise funds for the library. It was an unpleasant shock,
therefore, to be subjected to the serious discourses of university
teachers, who week after week doggedly pursued the same topic,
armed with a syllabus containing bibliography, statistics, quotations, and suggestions for thinking. Popularization was desperately
needed, but few of the men sent forth by the universities had had
occasion to acquire the skill. Accustomed as they were to lecturing
to university audiences, it was not easy for them to accommodate
their methods to the limited capacities and educational back-
grounds of their extension students.[68]

While the university extension courses turned out to be of benefit principally to the middle class, in the later decades of the century the need for further education among the workers was served
in other ways. The flourishing co-operative movement and the
trade unions formed study groups, in which numbers of workers
inquired into the arcana of economics and allied fields. As a new
era of industrial enlightenment began, employers encouraged their
workers to form various sorts of recreational organizations, among
which often were reading circles. Churches and settlement houses,
too, had their groups of men and women who sought instruction
and entertainment in books.

Finally, in the 1890's the National Home Reading Union dedicated itself to encouraging reading among the isolated and the imperfectly educated. Modeled somewhat upon the American Chau-
tauqua and sponsored by such men as Max Müller, James Bryce,
Archdeacon Farrar, Churton Collins, and Frederic Harrison, the

[68] H. J. Mackinder and M. E. Sadler, *University Extension, Past, Present, and Future*
(1891), pp. 27–62; R. D. Roberts, *Eighteen Years of University Extension* (Cambridge,
1891), pp. 12–43; William H. Draper, *University Extension . . . 1873–1923* (Cambridge,
1923), pp. 19–45. A firsthand account of the experiences of an early extension lecturer is
found in James Stuart, *Reminiscences* (1911), pp. 157–76.

Union issued reading lists and monthly magazines with articles on literary subjects. Members in a given locality formed circles to discuss the books they had been reading, and in the summer they had national assemblies, at which they were addressed by scholars from the universities.[69]

What, then, in retrospect, had the nineteenth-century adult educational movements accomplished by way of cultivating a taste for reading? The record is spotty, and often discouraging. Most workingmen and their families, though the volume of reading they accomplished was markedly greater by 1900 than it had been even a half-century earlier, had been largely untouched by any organized adult education scheme, and their tastes remained crude and uninformed. But in the populous class just above, whose members had their roots among the artisans and their aspirations among the solid middle class, the gain had been great. These were the people who profited by mechanics' institutes, and, in the latter half of the century, by public libraries; the people who bought cheap books and periodicals in great quantities.

Hampered at every turn by difficulties—social prejudices, utilitarian narrowness, the inadequacy of elementary schooling, the lack of widespread cultural interest among the masses—the century's experiments in adult education had fallen far short of their ambitious goals. But their very existence, and the public discussion they constantly stirred up, helped spread the spirit of self-improvement and the desire for reading to large sections of the population. By the end of the century the slow but steady growth of democratic attitudes in education and the appearance of good cheap literature in many forms made the ideals of men like Lovett and Kingsley no longer seem visionary.

[69] *Publishers' Circular*, August 1, 1889, p. 878; M. E. Sadler (ed.), *Continuation Schools in England and Elsewhere* (2d ed.; Manchester, 1908), pp. 82–84.

CHAPTER 10 } *Public Libraries*

I. As early as the fifteenth century, posthumous benevolence in England sometimes took the form of library endowment. Here and there, instead of leaving part of one's fortune to found and maintain a grammar school, or to relieve future generations of the worthy poor, a decedent provided for the establishment of a library which he usually directed was to be freely open to the public. In Bristol one such library (endowed by various members of the Kalendars guild) was begun in 1464, and a second in 1613. In Manchester the merchant and cloth-manufacturer Humphrey Chetham, who died in 1653, left a fund to establish a library bearing his name. In London in 1685, Rev. Thomas Tenison, then rector of St. Martin's-in-the-Fields and later Archbishop of Canterbury, varied the pattern by performing the same worthy act during his lifetime. When some thirty or forty young clergymen in his parish told him they repaired to taverns and coffeehouses only because they had no books to read, he forthwith built a library for them. It was in London, too, in 1716, that Dr. Daniel Williams, a Presbyterian divine, bequeathed his extensive library to the use of the public.[1]

The existence of these foundation libraries was habitually celebrated by eighteenth- and early nineteenth-century writers on the current state of English culture. Contemporary guidebooks, local histories, and travelers' accounts are speckled with references to the better-known collections, which proved England to be an enlightened nation indeed, since thousands upon thousands of weighty volumes were available to the studious. This was, how-

---

[1] On these early libraries, see Minto, *History of the Public Library Movement;* Predeek, *History of Libraries in Great Britain and North America;* Public Libraries Committee; and John Taylor, "The Earliest English Free Libraries," *Library Chronicle,* III (1886), 155–63. On Tenison's library, see John Evelyn's *Diary* (Everyman ed.), II, 198–99.

ever, the emptiest of boasts. None of these libraries was of service
to the general reading audience. Seldom had their founders provided for maintaining their buildings or for adding to the collections. As was true also of endowed schools, the stipulation in the
libraries' foundation instruments that they be freely open to the
public was interpreted in contemporary, not modern, terms: the
words "free" and "public" have undergone considerable semantic
liberalization in the age of democracy. And regardless of how the
provisions were interpreted, in practice they were freely violated.
But even if the libraries had been open without question or qualifi-
cation to ordinary men and women, they still would have lacked
visitors, for virtually all of them were collections of theological or
other heavily learned works alone, of value to relatively few
readers, and as they acquired few recent works even in this limited
field, the collections came more and more to possess merely antiquarian interest.[2]

The true measure of the old foundation libraries' uselessness was
exposed when their curators were summoned from their dusty
leisure in 1849 to testify before the Public Libraries Committee of
the House of Commons. The Chetham librarian was subjected to a
particularly searching examination, because his library unquestionably was required to be open to all comers, and because, unlike
most, it had money to increase its holdings. His testimony did not
noticeably gratify the committee. Of the 19,500 volumes in the
library, he said, most were folios; "the managers have always
given the preference to old books, and there are but few libraries of
the same extent in the kingdom which have so large a number of
works of the 16th century." There were, he continued, twenty-five
readers a day; but since the managers did not regard the library as
a facility for "the poor," they never considered buying books use-

[2] The same objections applied to the parochial libraries founded by Dr. Thomas Bray
and his Scottish coadjutor, Rev. James Kirkwood, early in the eighteenth century. These
collections were very numerous; Bray himself and "The Associates of Dr. Bray," an
organization formed to carry on his work after his death in 1730, founded at least 140,
and Kirkwood's zeal was responsible for at least 77. But as they were all small and confined to works of divinity, only the local clergy and amateur theologians benefited from
them. By the middle of the nineteenth century nearly all had "fallen into desuetude,"
neglected, destroyed, or dispersed into private hands or secondhand bookshops. In addition
to the above sources, especially Edward Edwards' testimony before the Public Libraries
Committee, Qq. 3326–40, see T. W. Shore, "Old Parochial Libraries of England and
Wales," *Transactions of the Library Association* (1879 for 1878), pp. 51–53 and Appendix.

ful to that class. He complained that even despite this studied re-
buff, frivolous readers did demand admittance: "there are too
many people who come merely to amuse themselves; they ask for
the *Edinburgh Review,* the *Quarterly Review,* or the *Gentleman's
Magazine.*" In his view the proper function of his library was "for
the purposes of students and persons pursuing some kind of literature as a pursuit [*sic*]."[3]

Tenison's Library, the 1849 committee discovered, was of even
less service to the general public. It had been taken over by the
members of the St. Martin's Subscription Reading Society, who
gathered there to read newspapers and modern "popular literature" and to play chess. The old books were in deplorable condition; the dust of more than a century was heavy on them, and heat
from the gas lighting had ruined their bindings. Little wonder that
only one "studious person" had applied in the past eighteen
months to come regularly to read Tenison's books, and that after
three or four days he "left in despair."[4]

There was, of course, the British Museum—the "national" library. But for various reasons ordinary citizens of London knew
the Museum (if they were acquainted with it at all) as an exhibition hall rather than as a library. While foreigners were still impressed, as the German traveler Moritz had been in the eighteenth
century, by the representatives of "the very lowest classes of the
people"[5] who wandered among the Museum's exhibits by way of
asserting their rights as free Englishmen, the reading room was
anything but "public." Admission was difficult; one had to be introduced by a peer, member of Parliament, alderman, judge,
rector, or some other eminent man. The hours of opening were
short, and on dark days the reading room closed entirely. Until the
middle of the nineteenth century, when the energetic librarian
Antonio Panizzi began to enforce the provision in the copyright
law that required copies of all new publications to be deposited in
the Museum, relatively little current literature was received. Even
despite these handicaps, the reading room attracted more and
more clients; "for every reader in 1799 there were nearly a hundred

[3] Public Libraries Committee, Qq. 1060–1176.

[4] *Ibid.,* Qq. 875–924.

[5] Carl P. Moritz, *Travels in England* (1924), p. 68.

in 1835." But the resultant overcrowding acted as a further discouragement to would-be readers.[6]

It was with good reason, then, that the writer of a slashing article in the *Westminster Review* in 1827 deplored the failure of all the supposedly "public" libraries to serve the common reader's needs. "We cannot believe," he wrote, "that any nation under the canopy of heaven can equal, much less surpass us in locking readers out of libraries; we are unrivalled in all exclusions."[7] Carlyle, in 1840, took up the cry. At a meeting of London men of letters he fulminated, "London has more men and intellect waiting to be developed than any place in the world ever had assembled. Yet there is no place on the civilized earth so ill supplied with materials for reading, for those who are not rich. (*Cheers.*) I have read an account of a Public Library in Iceland, which the King of Denmark founded there. There is not a peasant in Iceland that cannot bring home books to his hut better than men can in London. Positively it is a kind of disgrace to us"—and much more in the same Carlylean vein.[8]

Carlyle and his auditors solved their own problem by founding the London Library, which began in 1841 with 500 subscribers and a collection of 3,000 books and grew in the next century to an institution with 4,000 members and 470,000 books.[9] But while the resources of the London Library permitted Carlyle to read for his *Life of Cromwell* undisturbed by the unsavory atmosphere and distractions of the British Museum reading room—among them an alleged lunatic who blew his nose punctually every half-hour[10]—it was never intended to be a popular library. Nor were the fairly numerous proprietary libraries in the provinces, of which a brief account has been given in chapter 2. During the first half of the nineteenth century these libraries were still playing an important role in the cultural life of certain leading towns. But their social exclusiveness prevented their having any usefulness to the general reading public.

[6] The best books on the British Museum Library in the nineteenth century are G. F. Barwick, *The Reading Room of the British Museum* (1929) and Arundell Esdaile, *The British Museum Library* (1946).

[7] "Public Libraries," *Westminster Review*, VIII (1827), 106.

[8] *New Letters of Thomas Carlyle*, ed. Alexander Carlyle (1904), I, 199 n.

[9] E. M. Forster in *New Statesman and Nation*, May 10, 1941, p. 481.

[10] See Barwick, pp. 94-95.

Meanwhile the commercial circulating library was growing in importance. The heavy tax burden, imposed to carry on the war against Napoleon, and the increased prices of new books had converted many middle- and upper-class families from buying to borrowing. Hence establishments like the famous Minerva Library, Hookham's in Old Bond Street, and Booth's in Duke Street did a great business lending books to town and country customers. Early in the century there were at least twenty such libraries in the City.[11] Their subscription fees, however, confined their clientele to the well-to-do. In 1814, the Minerva, for instance, charged two guineas a year for an ordinary subscription and five guineas for one that entitled a patron to borrow twenty-four volumes at a time if he lived in London, thirty-six if he lived in the country.[12]

To be sure, the circulating libraries for the upper crust of society had their humbler counterparts, which, as the fashion of reading spread, were very numerous. Usually charging a rental of a penny a volume, they were conducted in both London and the provincial towns as side lines to the barbering, confectionery, news-vending, stationery, and tobacco trades. In 1838, for example, there were thirty-eight such libraries in the three Westminster parishes of St. George, St. James, and St. Anne. The London Statistical Society's tabulation of the contents of a selected ten of these libraries is interesting both for its report of what the humble urban reader had available to him and for its reflection of the investigators' literary criteria:[13]

	Volumes
Novels by Walter Scott, and Novels in imitation of him; Galt, etc.	166
Novels by Theodore Hook, Lytton Bulwer, etc.	41
Novels by Captain Marryat, Cooper, Washington Irving, etc.	115
Voyages, Travels, History, and Biography	136
Novels by Miss Edgeworth, and Moral and Religious Novels	49
Works of a Good Character, Dr. Johnson, Goldsmith, etc.	27

[11] *Publishers' Circular*, August 8, 1896, p. 123, where a list of these libraries is given.

[12] Blakey, *The Minerva Press*, p. 116.

[13] "Moral Statistics of Parishes in Westminster," *Journal of the Statistical Society*, I (1838), 485.

	Volumes
Romances, Castle of Otranto, etc.	76
Fashionable Novels, well known	439
Novels of the lowest character, being chiefly imitations of Fashionable Novels, containing no good, although probably nothing decidedly bad	1008
Miscellaneous Old Books, Newgate Calendar, etc.	86
Lord Byron's Works, Smollett's do., Fielding's do., Gil Blas, etc.	39
Books decidedly bad	10

In his autobiography Thomas Cooper, the son of a dyer, who was to become the "Chartist poet" and the prototype of Kingsley's Alton Locke, recalled with warm affection the books he had borrowed from the circulating library conducted in his town of Gainsborough by Mrs. Trevor, a stationer. "From her shelves I drew the enchanting *Arabian Nights,* and odd plays of Shakespeare, Dryden, and Otway, and Cook's *Voyages,* and the *Old English Baron;* and the *Castle of Otranto,* and *Guiscard;* and the *Bravo of Venice;* and *Hardenbras and Haverill;* and *Valentine's Eve;* and the *Castles of Athlin and Dunbayne;* and the *Scottish Chiefs*—and a heap of other romances and novels that would require pages even to name." Later Mrs. Trevor began a "book society" for the local gentry, supplying them with the latest books and periodicals for two guineas a year. This fee was far beyond young Cooper's reach, but for him she reduced the rate to ten shillings with the understanding that he would exchange his books only near closing time, when the two-guinea patrons were not likely to be present.[14]

Mrs. Trevor's term "book society" was merely a euphemism for "high-class circulating library."[15] As commonly used, however, "book society" or "book club" referred to a quite different arrangement—a more or less informal organization of middle-class families in a given neighborhood for the buying and exchange of books. In the *Monthly Magazine* in 1821, a correspondent averred that there were "not less than 6,500 of these useful institutions of various degrees, and for various purposes, in the United King-

---

[14] Cooper, *Life,* pp. 34–52.

[15] This is an indication of the disrepute into which the term "circulating library" had fallen in the early nineteenth century, under the shadow of the Minerva and its progeny. It was destined to be rehabilitated somewhat (but by no means completely, as a study of the contemporary usage of the term would prove) under the aegis of the Evangelical Mr. Mudie. On Mudie's library, see chapter 13.

dom," serving "above 30,000" families. Some groups maintained the books they purchased as permanent collections; others sold off their stock every two or three years and bought new volumes with the proceeds.[16]

As the hunger for education spread downward, book clubs became increasingly popular among serious-minded artisans, tradesmen, and apprentices. Sometimes they were identical with the mutual-improvement societies mentioned in the last chapter. Sometimes they sprang from the class meetings organized by the Methodists and other dissenting denominations, whose choice of reading was not limited to books on religion but extended to works on politics, social conditions, and science as well.[17]

One potent element encouraging the formation of such groups was the censorship prevailing in the other non-commercial book-circulating agencies. The earliest of these were the village libraries connected with parish churches. Influenced by the church's awakening interest in the education of the poor, certain clergymen set up little collections of books which everyone in the parish might borrow. The library conducted by Rev. Francis Wrangham at Hunmanby, Yorkshire, in 1807 was typical. Believing that the poor "delight more in concretes than in abstracts, or in other words, that sermons are less read than tales," Wrangham gave most shelf space to the Cheap Repository Tracts and religious narratives, fictional and biographical.[18] Under an arrangement decided upon in 1832, any National school might receive a five-pound grant of books selected from the publications of the S.P.C.K.'s Committee of General Literature, provided that the local sponsors of the school put up a like amount.[19] The Religious Tract Society began a system of "library grants" in the same year, and by 1849 it had distributed in Great Britain and Ireland between 5,000 and 6,000 libraries, each containing an average of a hundred volumes. These were placed in church vestries, dissenting chapels, or schoolrooms, wherever someone could be persuaded to superintend their use.[20] Undoubtedly a certain number of children

[16] *Monthly Magazine*, LI (1821), 397–98.

[17] Mathews, *Methodism and the Education of the People*, pp. 79–80.

[18] Michael Sadleir, "Archdeacon Francis Wrangham," *Things Past* (1944), pp. 221–22.

[19] Allen and McClure, *Two Hundred Years*, pp. 154–55.

[20] Public Libraries Committee, Qq. 2652–57.

and adults acquired the reading habit from having access to these little libraries. But their appeal was seriously limited, since in most cases they contained nothing but tracts, volumes of moral edification and religious instruction, and a sprinkling of dull, blameless secular works.

A Buckinghamshire clergyman, testifying before the Public Libraries Committee of 1849, gave a glimpse into the working of these village libraries. "Many of the books," he said, ". . . lie upon the shelves unread, and the consequence is, we require duplicates over and over again of such works as Bunyan's *Pilgrim's Progress*, *Robinson Crusoe*, Cook's *Voyages*, and works of that description; but what we are aiming at is to raise the standard, so as to get them to read books of practical science and books of a higher description altogether."

"Have you books of political history?" he was asked.

"We have the Life of Napoleon and other books of biography."

"The history of England?"

"Yes."

"The Waverley novels?"

"No; we have no novels."

"Have you any books of poetry?"

"Yes."

"Shakespeare?"

"Shakespeare would be lost upon them, I think; I have only spoken of the village lending library; if reference be made to the more extended circle to which the library in the district would be applicable, that would be otherwise."

"Do you think that the people could not understand the beauties of Shakespeare?"

"No." (An ambiguous answer!)

The witness went on to say that his parish library was open only one night a week. Once a fortnight lectures were given to young men on "scientific subjects and historical subjects, tending to illustrate the truth of religion," with the result that there was some demand for "the higher class of books." But he emphasized that the library was much opposed by the farmers, who, like those Hannah More had had to cope with two generations earlier, wished their farm hands to have no learning whatsoever. "I am afraid if they [the farmers] do not read themselves, they do not like to see

the laboring class becoming really and truly wiser than themselves."[21]

Meanwhile, individual initiative was responsible for another
scheme. In 1817 a book-loving merchant of Haddington, named
Samuel Brown, liquidated some balances of militia insurance for
which he could find no claimants, bought two hundred volumes
with the proceeds, and started a circulating library in East Lothian. The books were divided into four sets, each of which remained in a given village for two years, after which it was replaced
by another set and moved to a second village. Additional purchases
were financed by small contributions from private individuals and
several missionary societies, as well as by the 5s. subscription
charged to residents of the larger towns in the region, who were
given first access to new books before they went into the country.
In twenty years the library grew to include 2,380 volumes which
were in "circulatory motion" in forty-seven sets.[22]

These "itinerating libraries," as they were called, received much
advertising through Brougham and other advocates of popular
enlightenment, who held them up as examples of what might be
done on a national scale. In 1837, it was reported, Sir John Franklin was trying to start a similar arrangement in Van Diemen's
Land! Even when the libraries had entered upon evil days following Brown's death in 1839, Samuel Smiles, who as a youth in Haddington had known them at first hand, asked in *Howitt's Journal*,
"What is there to prevent this scheme from being set on foot in
every town and county in England?"[23] The answer might have
been that, while there was nothing to prevent its being set on foot,
its success was doubtful unless the criteria of book selection were
revised. For in Brown's original purchase of two hundred books,

[21] *Ibid.*, Qq. 1381-1402. A later witness, it should be added—the Solicitor-General for
Scotland—patriotically hastened to put it on record that in his country the situation was
"eminently the very reverse; the intelligent farmers of Scotland . . . would rather have a
man who spends his time in reading than anything else" (*ibid.*, Q. 1486). This comment well exemplifies the difference between the English and the Scottish attitudes
toward reading, a difference that is apparent to anyone who studies nineteenth-century
records, and that is attested to by the large representation of Scotsmen in the following
chapter on "The Self-made Reader."

[22] The firsthand source for the Brown libraries is [Samuel Brown, Jr.], *Some Account of
Itinerating Libraries and Their Founder.*

[23] Samuel Smiles, *Autobiography* (New York, 1905), pp. 29-30; *Howitt's Journal*, I
(1847), 119-20.

two-thirds were volumes of a moral and religious nature, and the
remainder were serious books on travel, agriculture, popular science, and the mechanical arts. As new purchases were made, the
emphasis upon moral and religious books grew, with the natural
result that the villagers, even the most pious of whom had a
saturation point, showed diminishing inclination to borrow.[24]

The Brown libraries never got beyond the boundaries of East
Lothian, but subsequently they were imitated by various agencies
that sought to relieve the shortage of books in rural areas. The
most notable adoption of the Brown system occurred in Yorkshire,
where the Northern Union of Mechanics' Institutes circulated
book boxes as late as the nineties. At that time two hundred remote settlements were receiving fifty-volume shipments from the
central stock of 40,000 volumes, each village paying 21s. a year for
its membership.[25] The Sunday School Union, the Working Men's
Club and Institute Union, and the National Liberal Club had similar arrangements, and in the late nineties W. T. Stead, Jr., set up
the *Review of Reviews* Circulating Library, which supplied boxes of
books on three months' loan to any community subscribing £6 a
year.[26]

The mechanics' institute libraries have been described in the
preceding chapter. They were, as has been said, an important
means of encouraging reading among the middle class, but in most
places, after the first few years, they were of little benefit to the
working class for whom they were originally meant. The book collections sometimes attached to factories and mills were perhaps
more useful to the workers, but their contents were bound to reflect the prejudices of the employers who provided them.

Down to the middle of the century, therefore, no single arrangement yet devised was without some great shortcoming. Many potential readers could not afford even the modest fees of the local
circulating library, if some small shopkeeper were enterprising
enough to maintain one. Even more serious was the limited selection of books. A borrower might find sufficient volumes to keep
him occupied for a season or two—enough to thoroughly whet his
appetite for reading along a certain line of interest. But then the

[24] Public Libraries Committee, Qq. 1769–1837; Hudson, *Adult Education*, p. 199.

[25] Frank Curzon, "Yorkshire Village Libraries," *Library*, X (1898), 29–30.

[26] "W. W.," "The Book and the Village," *Academy*, LII (1897), 329.

resources of the library gave out, and he found himself at a dead end.

The gravest of all defects, however, was the voluntary nature of the village and mechanics' institute libraries. They were at the mercy of all sorts of vicissitudes—the withdrawal of financial support, dissension among the sponsors, simple evaporation of interest. Nothing could guarantee that, once the reading habit had taken hold in a town, it would continue to be nurtured. In addition, the fact that most voluntary libraries were the pet projects of religious or other partisan groups cast over them an atmosphere of controversy, latent or overt. If they were sponsored by the Church, dissenters stayed away; if they were sponsored by Brougham's Useful Knowledge party, many workingmen avoided them. Nowhere, in short, was any considerable collection of books available to all the people, without charge and completely detached from social, political, and religious prejudices.[27]

II. As early as 1827, the writer in the *Westminster Review* whom we have already quoted urged a governmental inquiry into the whole public library situation.[28] But at this period the reformers—Brougham in his *Practical Observations* pamphlet, Charles Knight in a special twenty-four-page supplement to his paper, *The Printing Machine*[29]—were still convinced that voluntary effort was adequate to provide people's libraries. It took twenty years' experience to prove that this was not the case. Even so, nothing might have been done to prod the government to step in where private interests had failed, had it not been for the appearance of Edward Edwards.

Edwards, a deaf, reclusive, and utterly humorless supernumerary assistant in the British Museum, was a man whose tragic life knew but one passion—a passion for books, and, more especially, for libraries.[30] In 1848 a paper he read before the London Statisti-

[27] Some defects of the pre–Ewart Act libraries are stated in Hudson, *passim;* others may be inferred from the same source, though Hudson considers them virtues.

[28] *Westminster Review*, VIII (1827), 124–25.   [29] April 19, 1834.

[30] Appointed librarian of the new Manchester Public Library, he was forced by temperamental difficulties to resign in 1858. Thereafter he had no settled occupation but lived increasingly hand-to-mouth, trying desperately to complete and print a second edition of his monumental *Memoirs of Libraries*. In 1885, penniless and homeless, he was taken in by a Baptist minister on the Isle of Wight. The following winter he was found almost frozen to

cal Society, closely followed by a small book, *Remarks on the Paucity of Libraries Freely Open to the Public*, revealed the appalling lack of public library facilities in Great Britain as contrasted with those in western Europe and the United States. His crusade came to the attention of two members of Parliament, William Ewart of Dumfries and Joseph Brotherton of Salford, who promptly added public libraries to the agenda of reform.[31]

In the spring and summer of 1849 a select committee of Commons, headed by Ewart and including Disraeli and Monckton Milnes, received evidence. Eminent Continental librarians and scholars, Guizot from France, Libri from Italy, Meyer from Germany, told how in their countries members of the lower classes had access to well-stocked libraries, which were kept open in the evenings for their accommodation—a practice unknown in England outside the mechanics' institutes. Their testimony, presented on the eve of the Great Exhibition which was to celebrate Britain's supremacy in the mid-nineteenth-century world, was a sharp blow to national pride. The effect was heightened by Edwards' immense accumulation of statistics and by the testimony of the curators of the English foundation libraries who made clear that while they did not absolutely forbid readers of "respectable appearance" to enter their buildings, they certainly did not welcome them with open arms.

The committee's inquiry concluded,[32] Ewart brought in a bill to enable town councils to levy a rate of $\frac{1}{2}d.$ on the pound for the

---

death in a ruined tower on the nearby down, where he had lain in the storm for three days and nights, kept warm only by sheep that came into the tower for shelter. He died a few months later, the day after he had brusquely dismissed his doctor, who had had the ill grace to call upon him while he was dining (Thomas Greenwood, *Edward Edwards: The Chief Pioneer of Municipal Public Libraries* [1902]; Munford, *Penny Rate*, pp. 15–21).

[31] The primary sources for the history of the Ewart Act are the report of the Public Libraries Committee (1849) and other documents resulting from the same inquiry, and *Hansard*, Ser. 3, CIX–CXIII. Good recent summaries are found in Wellard, *Book Selection*, chap. i; Minto, pp. 47–95, and Ditzion, "The Anglo-American Library Scene," pp. 281–91. For the history of the public library movement in the later Victorian era, see Ditzion's article; Wellard, chap. iii; and Munford.

[32] In 1927 the Public Libraries Committee of the Board of Education said of the 1849 report, "in many instances we have only to reaffirm the recommendations which were made in that report but have never been implemented, or have been implemented only on a small scale. Notwithstanding the great changes in social feeling during the same period we find in the report hardly one expression of opinion on contemporary society which we would hesitate to endorse today" ([Board of Education], *Public Libraries Committee: Report on Public Libraries in England and Wales* [1927], p. 11).

purchase or erection of public library buildings. Although the proposed law had a precedent in the act for rate-supported public museums (1845), it met strong opposition in the House of Commons. From the moment debate began, the issue of public subsidization of reading was entangled in the far broader issues of social reform and laissez faire; and the whole subsequent history of the public library movement offers an instructive cross-section of English opinion on such matters as taxation for the general benefit, the problem of drink, poverty, and crime, and the relation of the inferior classes to the ruling one. What seems to us, in the perspective of a century, a fairly simple question—shall, or shall not, government provide the people with free reading facilities?—involved all sorts of peripheral, if not actually irrelevant, considerations.

The principal argument in favor of rate-supported libraries was that they were the cheapest insurance against a revival of the public disorders which had lately culminated in the Chartist alarm of 1848. Furthermore, Ewart and his group were convinced that hunger for solid knowledge was steadily growing among the populace; although they offered no evidence of any popular demand for free libraries, they knew that once libraries were provided they would be welcomed. The inconsistency implicit in this view of the working population as being simultaneously a touchy rabble, ready for crime and revolution, and a respectable class desiring nothing more than intellectual improvement, went unchallenged then, as it usually did in Victorian discussions of reform.

None of the bill's opponents publicly disapproved of its lofty purpose. What they objected to was the means proposed—and so the debate resolved itself into a classic Victorian pattern. Ignoring the repeated insistence of the other side that the bill was wholly permissive, they denounced it as a frightening new attempt of the state to encroach upon the liberties of the people. Dedicated as they were to the principle of voluntarism, they submitted that the provision of libraries, like that of education, was totally outside the proper sphere of government. On less theoretical grounds, they fought the bill because it would add the last straw to the load of the already groaning taxpayer. The speakers uniformly denied that they were worried about their own pocketbooks, but they were deeply concerned for the agricultural interests, who, it was somewhat cynically pointed out in rebuttal, stood to lose the most when the popular rush to the libraries cut down the consumption of malt beverages.

The debate would not have been complete without some remarks by that crusty veteran ornament of Commons, Colonel Charles DeLaet Waldo Sibthorp of Lincoln, who, like his colleagues, was ready to "contribute his mite towards providing libraries and proper recreations" for the masses; "but he thought that, however excellent food for the mind might be, food for the body was what was now most wanted for the people. He did not like reading at all, and he hated it when at Oxford."[33]

The bill proceeded to a second reading with a majority of only seventeen. Though watered down and extensively amended, to require among other things the assent of two-thirds of the ratepayers present at a meeting before the rate could be imposed in a town, it encountered further opposition, some of it palpably obstructionist. Finally, however, it passed Commons, and, going through Lords without difficulty, it received the Royal Assent on August 14, 1850.

In theory, this should have been a great landmark in the progress of the English reading public. Henceforth any book-hungry reader in town or city—for rural regions were still unprovided for[34]—could have at his free disposal, either in the library itself or to take home with him, an inexhaustible selection of the books he most wanted to read. This was the view developed by the orators who helped open the first buildings erected under the Ewart Act. At Manchester in 1852, Dickens spoke of the new library as the true "Manchester school," "a great free school, bent on carrying instruction to the poorest hearths," and another celebrated guest, Thackeray, was so overcome by "the vista of popular libraries being established all over the country, and the educational and elevating influences which would necessarily flow from the extension of the movement" that he had to sit down in the middle of his speech.[35]

[33] *Hansard*, Ser. 3, CIX (1850), col. 839.

[34] In 1897 a journalist described the typical village reading room as gloomy and uncomfortable, its stock of books consisting of "odd volumes of *Chambers's Journal*, a complete set of *Chambers's Miscellany*, two or three Waverley novels, Beeton's *Dictionary of Geography*, *Uncle Tom's Cabin*, a few Ballantynes, a volume of *Sunday at Home*, five or six volumes of *Eliza Cook's Journal*, and a score or more of books, mainly devotional" ("Village Reading-Rooms," *Academy*, LII [1897], 284–85).

[35] Ogle, *The Free Library*, p. 30; Greenwood, *Public Libraries*, p. 74.

As usual, rhetoric and reality had little in common. It is true that in the large Midland cities whose parliamentary representatives had been largely responsible for the passage of the act, the complacency and optimism voiced by the dedication orators had some basis in fact. Spurred by civic rivalry and the presence of wealthy philanthropists to supplement the scanty return from the rates, cities like Manchester and Liverpool almost immediately erected large public libraries. But in Great Britain as a whole, once the initial enthusiasm wore off, the library movement had hard going for many years. Popular apathy was overwhelming. Although 22,000 workers contributed over £800 to the Manchester library fund in 1852, the secretary of the solicitation committee regretted "the lukewarm feeling and very great coldness with which . . . many of their fellow workmen have received their addresses and even refused to contribute their mite towards the consummation of this great object."[36] In town after town, proposals to "adopt the acts" were defeated, not once but repeatedly, and by large margins. As late as 1896, only 334 districts, many of them small, had levied the library rate. Forty-six districts with populations of over 20,000, among them Bath, Bury, Hastings, Huddersfield, and Glasgow, had refused to do so.[37] Opposition was particularly strong in London. In 1887, only two parishes in all of metropolitan London had rate-supported libraries, although the impetus the Queen's Jubilee of that year gave to public improvements of all sorts subsequently added a number to the list.[38] When the peak period in the founding of British libraries came (225 libraries were established in England and Wales alone between 1897 and 1913),[39] it was due not to any sudden change of opinion regarding public support of libraries but rather to the munificence of Andrew Carnegie—a vindication, perhaps, of Colonel Sibthorp's preference for the voluntary principle.

Granting the reasonable premise that the spread of popular education, the increase of leisure, and other social factors stimulated interest in reading, why did the free-library movement have to

[36] Wellard, p. 38.

[37] Ogle, p. 66 and *passim.*

[38] Greenwood, *Public Libraries*, pp. 291–92; Charles Welch, "The Public Library Movement in London," *Library*, VII (1895), 98–101.

[39] Wellard, p. 64.

travel so rocky a road? There are numerous answers.[40] One is that the movement began at the very time that books and periodicals were becoming cheaper. While this cheapening process encouraged the reading habit, it also made the need for libraries seem less urgent than it had been only a few years before, when few persons could buy an adequate supply of reading matter for their private use. Another answer is that, since this was a new field of public enterprise, both the sponsors and the librarians themselves had no precedents to guide them; they had to learn by bitter experience. And they were desperately handicapped by the inadequacies of the enabling legislation. The fact that Ewart and his followers had had to content themselves with much less than half a loaf was bound to make trouble in the decades to come.

For example, though the original halfpenny rate was raised to a full penny in 1855, that was still not enough; and since no further increase was legalized until 1919, when the statutory limitation was removed entirely, British public libraries had far too little money at their disposal. Except where additional funds came from private sources, buildings were necessarily small, and, perhaps less necessarily, inefficient; and, in the true Victorian manner, too much of the available money was spent on ornamentation rather than on practical accommodations. Towns unable to erect buildings specifically for libraries often bought whatever edifices were available, and these sometimes were grotesquely ill adapted for library purposes. At Great Yarmouth, for instance, the public library occupied a thirteenth-century building which had been used as a council chamber and law court, and readers were frequently disturbed by sightseers descending to the ancient hold that lay beneath. The Bristol free library was housed in an early seventeenth-century building which subsequently had been much added to, with the result that it had "somewhat the character of a rabbit warren."[41]

With the purchase and maintenance of buildings requiring most of the proceeds from the rate, little money was left for books.[42]

---

[40] The following discussion is based on many sources: the files of professional librarians' journals for the period; the articles and books, already cited, by Ditzion, Minto, Munford, Ogle, Predeek, and Wellard; and Greenwood's *Public Libraries*, a mine of data and "color" relating to the free libraries of the nineties.

[41] Greenwood, *Public Libraries*, pp. 209, 223.

[42] In the original act, no provision had been made for buying books. This omission was remedied in 1855.

Here again the deficiency was made good, if at all, by private bene-factors. As had been true of the mechanics' institute libraries, which in many communities formed the nucleus of the new public libraries, the shelves were often laden with the dubious harvest of housecleaning time or the specialized collections left by local clergymen and amateur scholars. There was no means of attaining the balanced diversification and popular appeal that are indis-pensable qualities of a public library collection, let alone of repair-ing dilapidated books and buying replacements. Librarians and their assistants were underpaid, and their efficiency suffered along with their morale—with regrettable effects upon the library's popularity as a place in which to spend one's leisure.

Thus a vicious circle was set up. When the local library, once established, fell short of the bright claims made by advocates of the levy, the community often washed its hands of it. The whole no-tion of free libraries, many felt during all the rest of the Victorian era, had been ill conceived and ill executed, foisted upon an indif-ferent nation by a handful of enthusiasts. This feeling was the stronger and more lasting because libraries had behind them none of the propagandizing and organizing powers of a nation-wide movement such as the Society for the Diffusion of Useful Knowl-edge. Lacking a Brougham to speak and act for them, the friends of public libraries were content to use the arguments that had served so well in his time. Having been uttered from the platform and in the press for half a century, in support of popular elemen-tary education, mechanics' institutes, and cheap periodicals, these pleas were so trite as to be almost useless; but seemingly no better could be found.

For instance, free libraries were offered as the latest answer to the drink problem. They were to be "temples erected by Literature to attract the votaries of Bacchus."[43] No matter that every other lure the nineteenth century had yet devised had failed to stem the evening march to the public house: libraries would succeed where all the rest had failed. As late as the nineties, a leading apologist for libraries alleged that "often wives and children come for books, and make the request, 'Please pick me a nice one, sir, for if I take home an interesting book, my husband (or father, as the case may

[43] Quoted from [James Sands], "A General Defence of Modern Novels," prefaced to a novel of 1802, in Taylor, *Early Opposition to the English Novel*, p. 49.

be) will stop in during the evening and read it. . . .' "[44] But this good gray argument was worn out; it had been entered in one fight too many. It was actually harmful to the cause, because the liquor interests, whom one would expect to have been at ease after the false alarms of many decades, took it seriously, and in many communities they led the fight against the adoption of the acts.

Another major argument had worn equally thin by the eighties. This was the plea of utility, of economy. As applied to free libraries, it was put into definitive form by W. Stanley Jevons in an article in 1881, but one hears familiar echoes of Joseph Lancaster expounding the virtues of his assembly-line education: "The main *raison d'être* of Free Public Libraries, as indeed of public museums, art-galleries, parks, halls, public clocks, and many other kinds of public works, is the enormous increase of utility which is thereby acquired for the community at a trifling cost. . . . [The turnover of books in a public library] is a striking case of . . . *the principle of the multiplication of utility.* . . . One natural result of the extensive circulation of public books is the very low cost at which the people is thus supplied with literature." Even if libraries cost many times more than they did, Jevons went on, they would be worth every penny, because prisons, courts, and poorhouses inevitably cost even more. Expenditure for public library purposes, therefore, "is likely, after the lapse of years, to come back fully in the reduction of poor-rates and Government expenditure on crime. We are fully warranted in looking upon Free Libraries as an engine for operating upon the poorer portions of the population."[45]

In addition to developing a more settled, sober, law-abiding populace, free libraries, it was argued, were indispensable to the progress of the English economy. "Education is spreading her pinions, and civilisation is marching with rapid strides in the footsteps of science and mechanics through the whole globe. We must remember that other nations are progressing as well as ours, and, therefore, if we are to keep pace in the march . . . our artizans must individually be taught, because, just as the mountain is composed of atoms and the ocean of drops, so an educated people, a mass of educated mechanics, will have a much better chance in the great race of competition which is taking place, than if we suffer

[44] Greenwood, *Public Libraries*, p. 35.

[45] "The Rationale of Free Public Libraries," pp. 385 ff. Italics in the original.

them to remain in ignorance."[46] The words are those of a Liverpool alderman, declaiming over a library cornerstone in 1857, but they might just as well have been spoken by Brougham at the opening of a mechanics' institute in 1827.

What one misses in all this is any sense of the intellectual and spiritual enrichment—or the simple relaxation—that an individual man or woman, boy or girl, may derive from reading, quite apart from any benefit that may accrue to the community. The Victorians' silence on this matter in their library propaganda is quite understandable, for an institution to be supported by public funds must be justified first of all in terms of the common good. Although the principle that a community might tax itself to provide facilities for recreation had been fairly well accepted in the case of parks and museums, for example, it was still generally denied when libraries were in question. The old religious and utilitarian prejudices against reading for entertainment still persisted; if the nation were to subsidize the reading habit, it should do so only for serious purposes. Sharing this feeling as they did, the proponents of free libraries were ill equipped to face what became, if not the gravest, at least the best-publicized charge against libraries once they were established: namely, that far from encouraging habits of study and self-improvement, they catered to the popular passion for light reading—above all, for fiction.

The "fiction question" which had agitated the mechanics' institute libraries now was inherited, still generating heat, by their successors, at a time when cheap papers were diligently encouraging the masses' taste for light reading. Wherever free libraries were opened, the volume of patronage bore a direct relationship to the amount of fiction available. At Sheffield in the period 1856–67, prose fiction accounted for almost half of the combined circulation of the consulting and lending departments. At Liverpool in 1867–68, out of 565,000 books called for, 189,800 were fiction.[47] But this was nothing compared with what was to come: by the 1890's most free libraries reported that between 65 per cent and 90 per cent of the books circulated were classified as fiction.[48]

[46] Peter Cowell, *Liverpool Public Libraries* (Liverpool, 1903), pp. 58–59.

[47] Edwards, *Free Town Libraries*, pp. 122, 135.

[48] Greenwood, *Public Libraries*, pp. 548–57. This volume and Edwards' *Free Town Libraries* contain many statistics on the various classes of books issued by leading libraries,

Exposed as it was, year after year, in printed library reports and then in the newspapers, this state of affairs could not fail to attract attention. The prevalent view was summarized in the *Publishers' Circular* in 1878: "Free libraries, which should only be provided for the poor and helpless, not for those who can help themselves, should be resorted to for education and instruction, and should begin at elementary works, long antecedent to works of imaginative fiction. If the ratepayers are to provide imaginative fiction, or the luxuries of the mind, for slightly poorer classes, why should they not also provide free games, free plays, *panem et circenses*, free cakes and nuts for the boys? Is not the picture of a stalwart, well-dressed lounging youth of the middle classes reading and dreaming over Mr. Smiles' 'Self-Help' in a free library, after having spent his humble ninepence on penny ices and a cigar, somewhat of a satire?"[49] The writer, too eager for a touch of irony, dulled his point somewhat by placing *Self-Help* in the hands of the negligent youth, because it was universally agreed that what loungers read when they came to the public library was *not* the wholesome works of Dr. Smiles but sensational or sentimental fiction. The evil results of devotion to "light literature" were well established in national legend; reading extracts from the correspondence on the subject in the London *Evening Standard* in January, 1891, one feels the date line could just as well be "1791" or "1831." Whenever he entered a public library, one man wrote, "I have found, as a rule, every chair occupied—and by whom? In nine cases out of ten by loafing office boys or clerks, who were using their masters' time for devouring all the most trivial literary trash they could get. . . . Many are the crimes brought about by the disordered imagination of a reader of sensational, and often immoral, rubbish, whilst many a home is neglected and uncared for owing to the all-absorbed novel-reading wife." Another correspondent alluded to a young man he knew at Brighton, "who could not be got to work.

---

as well as lists of the titles of individual books that were most in demand. In vain did the librarians point out that under some systems of classification "fiction" included not only novels but poetry and drama as well. Although the popular assumption that "fiction" meant novels alone seriously hurt the library cause, the profession did little at the time to amend its terminology so that its annual reports would give a fairer picture of what people read.

[49] *Publishers' Circular*, January 18, 1878, p. 2. During the eighties and nineties, however, this periodical became a friend of the libraries.

He was usually to be found at the Public Library, perusing light literature, and he asserts that the library ruined him. I mentioned this to a gentleman at the library (a visitor), and he said he had long seen it, and that no greater curse existed than these libraries, and he had rather see a young man hanging about a public-house than spending his time in these places."[50] William Ewart would have been saddened to know that, in the upside-down world he did not live to see, public libraries were now occasionally replacing public houses as handy explanations for wasted lives.

The librarians, of course, were in a dilemma. Should they try to give their clients what it was judged best for them to have (the traditional view) or should they give them what they wanted? If they did the former, they would drive away the people they were supposed to serve; if the latter, they would continue to arouse the wrath of a highly vocal section of press and public. The profession itself was divided at first. One librarian told a meeting in 1879 that "schoolboys or students who took to novel reading to any great extent never made much progress in after life. They neglected real practical life for a sensually imaginative one, and suffered accordingly from the enervating influence."[51] But his paper was "much criticized" at the time, and by 1889, when the Library Association held a symposium on this wearisome problem, opinion was virtually unanimous that the library should be regarded as a place for diversion as well as study.[52] Speakers pointed out the fact which had been so long obscured in the debate—that not all fiction is light and frivolous, and that not all non-fiction is elevating.

For every instance of a youth irreparably seduced by fiction, it was further argued, another could be supplied of the opposite effect. A library leader answered the tales told of promising lives

[50] Both quotations are given in Greenwood, *Public Libraries*, p. 82.

[51] Jevons, p. 398.

[52] *Library*, I (1889), 386–90; see also Thomas Mason, "Fiction in Free Libraries," *ibid.*, II (1890), 178–81. Evidently nobody thought of quoting Dickens on the subject. Gradgrind was forever worrying over the "howling ocean of tabular statements" that indicated the tastes of those who used the Coketown library. "It was a disheartening circumstance, but a melancholy fact, that even these readers persisted in wondering. They wondered about human nature, human passions, human hopes and fears, the struggles, triumphs and defeats, the cares and joys and sorrows, the lives and deaths of common men and women! They sometimes, after fifteen hours' work, sat down to read mere fables about men and women, more or less like themselves, and about children, more or less like their own" (*Hard Times*, Book I, chap. iv).

blighted by novel-reading with one about a mission-school boy who devoured penny dreadfuls by the cartload. All efforts of his teacher to wean him from this addiction were futile until he was given a copy of *Westward Ho!* with the promise that when he finished reading it, he could keep it. "Charles Kingsley's master-piece was read chiefly by the light of shop windows, and such other light as the lad could get near, and when he had read the whole of it the verdict was that he did not know such a book had ever been written. There was no more gutter rubbish after that. . . . The book was a new revelation to the lad, and today he fills an impor-tant post in a large City printing office. His reading since then has covered Carlyle, Ruskin, and a fund of history which would place many a teacher in the shade."[53] Near the end of the century the same authority insisted that "not half enough of fiction is circu-lated by Public Libraries. . . . So far from ousting more solid liter-ature, it is being itself ousted by trade and scientific journals, mag-azines, music, technical works, and sensational theology. The re-fining, stimulating and refreshing influences of the novel are being positively swallowed in the feverish anxiety of young people to equip themselves in technical and other subjects to enable them to fight competing Germans, and it looks as if imaginative literature, whether in poetry or prose, would lose its hold in the face of urgent commercial needs."[54] This, however, was an unwarrantedly pessi-mistic view. Fiction has never ceased to hold the affections of library patrons.

Whatever the librarians' personal views, the great preponder-ance of fiction issued at public libraries provided an ever handy stick with which to beat the whole movement. It gave irrefutable statistical support to the line taken by all opponents of the exten-sion of governmental functions. In 1850 Colonel Sibthorp had warned that once the authorities took it upon themselves to supply free reading matter to the people, they would move on to issuing free quoits and footballs. In the seventies these new words were set to the familiar melody: "By providing public this and public that for the lower classes, you spoil and pauperise them. The best help is self-help. A man who drinks at a public pump, washes at a public bath, sots at a public-house, and dreams away his days with a

[53] Thomas Greenwood, *Sunday-School and Village Libraries* (1892), p. 6.

[54] *Greenwood's Library Year Book* (1897), p. 116.

popular novel borrowed from a public library, is not likely to be of use to the State. . . . We are, as a people, getting by far too much in the 'public' line."[55] And in the nineties one M. D. O'Brien contributed to a collection of extreme laissez faire essays (which bore the imprimatur of Herbert Spencer) a scorching attack upon the free library as "the socialists' continuation school," an institution as deplorable as state-aided education and the state-operated post office: "Free Libraries are perfect 'god-sends' to the town loafer, who finds himself housed and amused at the public expense, and may lounge away his time among the intellectual luxuries which his neighbours are taxed to provide for him. . . . The truth is that a Free Library favours one special section of the community—the book-readers—at the expense of all the rest. . . . If one man may have his hobby paid for by his neighbours, why not all? . . . This mendacious appeal to the numerical majority to force a demoralising and pauperising institution upon the minority, is an attempt to revive, in municipal legislation, a form of coercion we have outgrown in religious matters."[56]

To such reasoning Mr. Punch had a ready answer:

> Here is an Institution doomed to scare
> The furious devotees of Laissez Faire.
> What mental shock, indeed, could prove immenser
> To Mumbo Jumbo—or to Herbert Spencer?
> Free Books? Reading provided from the Rates?
> Oh, that means Freedom's ruin, and the State's!
> Self-help's all right,—e'en if you rob a brother—
> But human creatures must *not* help each other!
> The 'Self-made Man,' whom Samuel Smiles so praises,
> Who on his fellows' necks his footing raises,
> The systematic 'Sweater,' who sucks wealth
> From toiling crowds by cunning and by stealth,—
> *He* is all right, *he* has no maudlin twist,
> *He* does not shock the Individualist!
> But rate yourselves to give the poor free reading?
> The Pelican to warm her nestlings bleeding,
> Was no such monument of feeble folly.
> *Let folks alone,* and all will then be jolly.[57]

[55] *Publishers' Circular*, December 8, 1874, p. 902.

[56] M. D. O'Brien, "Free Libraries," in *A Plea for Liberty*, ed. Thomas Mackay (New York, 1891), pp. 329 ff. A librarian's reply to O'Brien's assault is [J. Y. W. MacAlister], "Partingtonian Sociology," *Library*, III (1891), 103–108.

[57] *Punch*, CI (1891), 193. Reproduced by permission of *Punch*.

III. Free libraries, then, were by no means universally accepted in Victorian England. In some towns, when rate-payers' meetings were called to adopt the acts—a procedure finally abandoned in 1877—local opposition was so determined that organized hooliganism broke out, sometimes going so far as actually to disrupt the meeting itself. Thus did rowdyism and outright violence greet a movement which had been warranted to pacify the common people. Some advocates of libraries said that these incidents were organized and subsidized by certain interests, particularly the publicans. In all likelihood they did not represent any spontaneous working-class opposition to the establishment of libraries. On the other hand, as has been remarked, there was no strong popular sentiment *for* libraries.

Which leads to the question: How wide an audience did the free libraries, once established, serve? The answer varies greatly from town to town and time to time. In five towns, selected at random from returns published in the nineties, it was found that the number of active borrowers in a given year constituted only from 3 per cent to 8 per cent of the population; and this range is probably typical.[58] Occupational analyses of library registry books, as well as impressionistic articles published on the subject, suggest that the greater part of the readers and borrowers came from the ever growing social stratum between the middle class proper and the "laboring population." In 1857–58 the occupations of borrowers newly registered in a six-month period at two branches of the Manchester Public Library were divided thus:[59]

	Branch A	Branch B
Artisans and mechanics	250	536
Artists, designers, draftsmen	10	5
Clergymen, surgeons, other professions	11	4
Clerks, salesmen, commercial travelers	121	123
Errand and office boys	74	54
Laborers, porters, etc.	29	79
Merchants, agents, etc.	8	9
Milliners	10	0
No calling	9	0
Policemen, tax collectors	11	26
Schoolpupils	97	18
Schoolmasters and teachers	15	16
Shopkeepers and assistants	45	130
Spinners, weavers, dyers, other factory workers	68	238
Warehousemen, packers, etc.	104	180
"Entirely undescribed" (i.e., women and children)	82	621

[58] Greenwood, *Public Libraries*, p. 550; Wellard, *Book Selection*, pp. 45–46.
[59] Edwards, pp. 88–90.

At Bristol a generation later (1891), the occupational distribution, allowing for the difference between the natures of the two cities, was roughly similar:[60]

Number of Books Issued to:	Read on Premises	Taken Home
Apprentices	576	554
Artisans	2,792	2,354
Assistants	1,108	3,567
Clerks	1,055	2,553
Employers	399	778
Errand boys	604	253
Labourers	692	210
No occupation: male	1,017	621
female	502	10,476
Professionals	409	1,183
Schoolboys	6,313	6,904
Students	1,371	1,273

In 1897 the journalist T. H. S. Escott drew a romantic picture of the studious workingman trudging to the free library on Saturday night to return the book he had read and to answer the questions and explain the allusions that had turned up during his week's reading.[61] While the libraries undoubtedly had some such borrowers, they were exceptional, as a self-styled "Working Woman" pointed out in *Chambers's Journal* three years later. "In spite of modern civilization and modern education," she wrote, "workingmen, but more especially working women, have . . . 'as much use for learning as a cow has for clogs.' " Even despite the reduction of working hours, there still was insufficient time to indulge whatever intellectual interests one might possess. True, she said, children of the lower classes did patronize the libraries; the boys read Ainsworth, Marryat, Henty, Cooper, Verne, and Mayne Reid, and the girls Mrs. Henry Wood, Miss Braddon, and E. P. Roe; but "when they should be launching out into deeper waters both boys and girls cease to be members of the free libraries, and gradually drift into other and more harmful amusements."[62] If they continued to read at all, penny papers were their choice.

Probably more of "the million" would have patronized the libraries had they been encouraged to do so. But little effort was exerted to attract them; the idea that public libraries should make strenuous efforts to increase their patronage, by publicity cam-

[60] Greenwood, *Public Libraries*, p. 224.

[61] *Social Transformations of the Victorian Age*, pp. 362–64.

[62] *Chambers's Journal*, Ser. 6, III (1900), 134–36.

paigns, readers' advisory services, booklists, informal talks, and so
on, was not yet developed. Instead, in many places, the brusque-
ness of the assistants, the stern maintenance of discipline and
decorum, and the inadequate and uncomfortable accommodations
actually drove away would-be readers.

As for persons in the "superior ranks of society," they too were
deterred from using the libraries, at least in districts where their
own social class was not overwhelmingly predominant, by their
distaste for mingling with their often unwashed inferiors. The atmosphere of many libraries was disagreeable to even the moderately fastidious. From the outset, library buildings were the chosen
haunts of "public building parasites": vagrants taking shelter from
rain and cold,[63] loafers, and eccentrics. Because they received the
latest papers, libraries were the resort of the unemployed, who
flocked to inspect the advertisements of situations vacant, and of
racing enthusiasts who not only made their daily selections from
the papers but conducted financial transactions on the premises.
To frustrate these shabby turfmen, some libraries obliterated the
racing news from each paper as it arrived.

What with the unsavory odor of the ill-ventilated rooms, the
presence of dirty, snoring casuals, and the assembling on the steps
of loafers "spitting, smoking, and discussing the merits and de-
merits of horses in language unfit for quotation,"[64] it was no wonder that many women shrank from approaching free libraries, however eager their desire for books. Most self-respecting libraries set
aside separate "ladies' rooms," or at least screened off a part of
their reading room for the exclusive use of females; and some installed ladies' entrances.

The coming of the free library had helped democratize reading
to the extent that it provided book-holding buildings open without

[63] W. H. Davies, writing from personal experience, described the vagrant's technique,
which was the constant despair of the librarians: "There he sits for hours staring at one
page, not a word of which he has read or, for that matter, intends to read. If he cannot at
once get a seat, he stands before a paper and performs that almost impossible feat of standing upright fast asleep, so as to deceive the attendants, and respectable people who are
waiting a chance to see that very paper. To be able to do this requires many unsuccessful
efforts, which fail on account of hard breathing, nodding and stumbling against the paper
stand; but success has at last been attained, and there he stands fast asleep and apparently
absorbed in a most interesting paragraph" (*Autobiography of a Super-Tramp* [New York,
1924], pp. 267–68).

[64] *Library*, V (1893), 193. On the vexatious "betting evil," see the indexes to the successive volumes of this periodical.

restriction to the public; but it had engendered some totally unanticipated and perennially vexing problems. Those who were unsympathetic to rate-supported libraries did not hesitate to make the most of such difficulties. The fact remains, however, that by the closing years of the century the annual circulation of all public libraries in the United Kingdom was estimated to be between thirty and forty million volumes.[65] The great bulk of this circulation was accounted for by the class of readers who were somewhat uncharitably termed "fiction vampires"; but one can hardly doubt that every library in Britain fed, now and again, a love for general reading, either in the adolescent schoolboy or in the graying workman or small businessman to whom circumstances had denied the pleasures of books until relatively late in life. As a symbol of what free libraries meant to thousands of persons who grew up in the later Victorian era, the experience of the historian E. L. Woodward is illuminating. A son of a middle-class London family, he had discovered English poetry through reading Scott, Gray, and Tennyson. "I might perhaps have stopped at this point," he wrote many years later, "if it had not been for the Reference Room in the Hampstead Public Library. I owe this public library a great debt; and, after so many years, I am still glad to remember that, in a small way, my own grandfather was one of the people who took part in persuading the ratepayers of Hampstead to build it. Evening after evening, I used to sit in the pleasant Reference Room, reading one book after another, and walking home along the suburban roads in a ferment and turmoil of exaltation."[66]

[65] *Greenwood's Library Year Book* (1897), p. 8.

[66] *Short Journey* (New York, 1946), p. 16.

CHAPTER 11 } *The Self-made Reader*

I. The experience of mechanics' institutes and public libraries disappointed all who felt there was a thirst for literary culture among the masses. Compared with the hordes whose reading was confined to penny shockers and sensational weekly papers, serious students in the lower-middle and lower classes were few. Still, we must not underestimate the number whose intellectual curiosity and emotional and spiritual needs were too insistent to be frustrated by the limited accessibility of good books, the lack of leisure, and the absence of systematic guidance. If millions read nothing but trash, scores of thousands, no wealthier and with no more formal schooling, devoured serious fiction, poetry, essays, history, philosophy, theology, and biography. These were the people who proved that the March of Mind, though overpublicized, was no mere slogan.

The self-educated reader, like the self-educated writer, was peculiarly a product of the age. During the preceding century, when the ideal of democratic education was in eclipse, people in the higher reaches of society were captivated by the notion of a poet springing from among the unschooled: he was a picturesque anomaly out of the pages of Rousseau. Many eighteenth-century critics dwelt on Shakespeare as a happy accident, a man of the people whose native genius somehow triumphed over the lack of Latin and Greek. And in such figures as Ann Yearsley, the Bristol milkmaid, those who were touched by the current fashionable reaction against artificiality (which sometimes was synonymous with civilization itself) found refreshing proof that the muse could invade even the cowshed. "Lactilla," as she was called in the true Augustan tradition, was really no great hand at poetry, but the fact that she turned out any verse at all, considering her low station, won both the admiration and the patronage of Hannah More and her circle.[1]

As the romantic idealization of the unspoiled, the natural, and the spontaneous developed, the self-taught bard was more and more in demand. Within two or three decades after his death in 1796, Burns had become a national legend, and not alone in Scotland. The true extent of his schooling and knowledge of literature was overlooked in the general eagerness to regard him as a plowboy who had inexplicably been visited by genius. The way thus was prepared for John Clare, the Northamptonshire peasant, and James Hogg, the Ettrick shepherd, the two most successful and best remembered of the numerous early nineteenth-century versifiers who turned up just in time to provide flesh-and-blood support for romantic theory. Another (who courted inspiration in the servants' quarters rather than in the fields) was John Jones, a country butler. Jones's modestly titled *Attempts in Verse* was published by John Murray in 1831 at the urging of Southey, who added to the volume "An Essay on Uneducated Poets." The critics made short shrift of Jones, but Southey's essay, recalling with suitable emotion the careers of such versifiers of earlier ages as Ann Yearsley, milkmaid; John Taylor, Thames waterman; James Woodhouse and John Bennet, shoemakers; Stephen Duck, farm laborer; and John Frederick Bryant, tobacco-pipe maker, has permanent interest in its reflection of the era's sentimental adulation of the low-born poet.[2]

The publicity given such lives of toil and aspiration naturally stirred literary ambitions in many humble breasts. Kingsley's hero, Alton Locke, dated his interest in books from the day he encountered a copy of *The Life and Poems of John Bethune*, the weaver poet, on a bookstall. ". . . There I stood, I know not how long, on the greasy pavement, heedless of the passers who thrust me right and left, reading by the flaring gas-light that sad history of labor, sorrow, and death.—How the Highland cotter, in spite of disease, penury, starvation itself, and the daily struggle to earn his

[1] On "Lactilla," see J. M. S. Tompkins, *The Polite Marriage* (Cambridge, 1938), chap. iii.

[2] For biographical sketches of the best-known self-educated poets, see Southey's essay; and for a good recent literary study of the peasant poets, see Rayner Unwin, *The Rural Muse* (1954).

bread by digging and ditching, educated himself—how he toiled unceasingly with his hands—how he wrote his poems in secret on dirty scraps of paper and old leaves of books—how thus he wore himself out, manful and godly. . . ."[3]

Once established in the national mythology, a symbolic figure is capable of all kinds of transformations. By one of those queer twists that help make intellectual history so fascinating, the middle-class utilitarians took over the self-taught hero from the romantic idealists and made him serve their own philosophy. Just when Southey was recounting his stories of cottage bards, the Society for the Diffusion of Useful Knowledge published George Lillie Craik's *The Pursuit of Knowledge under Difficulties,* a biographical dictionary of English and foreign scholars, artists, philosophers, scientists, engineers, and inventors who had toiled up the road of learning against great handicaps. Craik's volumes were designed to be to the early machine age what collections of saints' legends had been to the Middle Ages: a vehicle of consolation, guidance, and inspiration, though couched in secular and primarily materialistic terms.

From Craik the ideal of rising by one's own bootstraps passed into the pages of the *Penny Magazine* and *Chambers's Journal,* which, being dedicated to the needs of the earnest but poor student, printed every anecdote of fruitful self-instruction that came to hand. In the middle of the century the cause was taken up by Samuel Smiles, who kept alive and flourishing in the Victorian mind the conviction that book-learning, prudently used and always given realism by practical experience, was the key to success. Though Smiles's pantheon of modern heroes was largely devoted to canal-builders and engine-makers, a few niches were reserved for artists and writers. One of his prize exhibits was Gerald Massey, the son of a ten-shilling-a-week canal boatman, who had been sent into a silk mill at the age of eight but who nevertheless combined native poetic talent with wide reading successfully enough to tempt some contemporary critics to link him with Shakespeare, Burns, and Keats. Widely advertised by Smiles and drawn upon by George Eliot for her novel *Felix Holt,* Massey's career as a versifying propagandist for Chartism and Christian Socialism and, later, as a student of psychic phenomena, Egyptology, and the

---

[3] *Alton Locke,* chap. ii.

hidden meaning of Shakespeare's sonnets illustrates the intellectual restlessness that characterized so many self-taught scholars in the Victorian age.

The extent of serious reading among the masses after mid-century is perhaps best indicated by the great sales of the various Cassell culture-at-home publications, headed by the *Popular Educator*, and by the increase in the number of cheap reprint series devoted wholly or in part to the works of standard authors. Of the Chandos Classics alone, over 3,500,000 volumes (according to the publishers) were sold between 1868 and 1884, and in five years Kent's Miniature Library of the Poets had a sale of a quarter-million.[4] The relatively inexpensive "People's Editions" of various contemporary authors sometimes enjoyed large sales, especially if they dealt with current problems. Henry George's *Progress and Poverty* sold 60,000 in the years 1881–85, largely in a sixpenny edition, and in 1882 Carlyle's *Sartor Resartus*, hardly an easy book for the ordinary reader, but with a message still potent after fifty years, found 70,000 purchasers at 6*d.* a copy.[5] Representative of these working-class students of politics and economics was Thomas Dixon, a cutter of corks for public houses and gin palaces, whose thoughtful letters Ruskin answered in the series of discourses called *Time and Tide*.[6]

Dickens may not have been exaggerating too much when he told a dinner meeting of the Birmingham Society of Artists in 1853 that "there are in Birmingham at this moment many working men infinitely better versed in Shakespeare and in Milton than the average of fine gentlemen in the days of bought-and-sold dedications and dear books."[7] In a mill town in the late 1840's, a group of girl operatives met at five o'clock in the morning to read Shakespeare together for an hour before going to work.[8] A brass finisher at Aberdeen sent notes to Clark and Glover for use in their great

[4] *Publishers' Circular*, July 1, 1884, p. 613; September 1, 1884, p. 823.

[5] Lynd, *England in the Eighteen-Eighties*, pp. 142–43; *Correspondence of Thomas Carlyle and R. W. Emerson*, ed. C. E. Norton (Boston, 1883), I, 15 n.

[6] Dixon does not have a place in the *Dictionary of National Biography*. See Ruskin's *Works*, ed. Cook and Wedderburn, XVII, lxxvii–lxxix and elsewhere; William Bell Scott, *Autobiographical Notes* (New York, 1892), II, 265–72.

[7] *Collected Papers* (Nonesuch ed.), II, 403.

[8] Henry Solly, *"These Eighty Years"* (1893), II, 30.

Cambridge edition of Shakespeare.[9] And E. E. Kellett, in his reminiscences, tells of his encounter with a pork-butcher in a crowded railway compartment. The butcher, looking about him, observed that there was no room except on the luggage rack. "I fear you speak upon the rack," Kellett replied, "where men enforcèd do speak anything." The butcher's face lit up. "That's Portia," he said; "I read Shakespeare, or something about him, every night after business." For the next two hours the men engaged in a lively discussion, during which the butcher exhibited a wide and sound knowledge of Shakespeare's plays.[10]

Such anecdotes abound in Victorian annals. If only we had the autobiography of that pork-butcher, and of the other self-educated readers whom Kellett goes on to mention! But such readers left far fewer records, in proportion to their number, than did those of superior social station, whose printed memoirs burden the shelves of our libraries. The genuine booklover—one who did not confine himself to books of direct vocational value, but ranged widely in literature—was not likely to get ahead very fast, if at all. He had values quite different from those in common currency; he spent his leisure enriching his soul, but that he would eventually fill his purse, or otherwise be a "success," did not follow by any means. The overwhelming majority of self-educated readers never made any splash at all in the world. They lived and died in ill-paid, obscure jobs, and never was there any call for their personal recollections. With few exceptions, the only humbly born members of the nineteenth-century reading public who left behind some narrative of their experience of books were those most unusual men who finally achieved prominence as politicians or in some other capacity.[11]

The autobiographies written by this little group of self-taught

---

[9] *Publishers' Circular*, July 1, 1863, p. 322.　　[10] Kellett, *As I Remember*, p. 35.

[11] The treatment of the self-made reader in fiction is worth detailed study. For one thing, we can trace the changing concept of the purposes for which poor men read. George Eliot's Adam Bede, a carpenter, read primarily for religious consolation at the very beginning of the nineteenth century. Kingsley's Alton Locke, a tailor, read for political enlightenment in the 1840's. H. G. Wells's Mr. Polly, a product of the late Victorian board school, read simply for delight and escape from the dull routine of shopkeeping. Adam Bede and Mr. Polly lived and died in obscurity; Alton Locke was persecuted and imprisoned as a Chartist. Dinah Mulock's John Halifax, on the other hand, read his way to wealth—as befitted a hero created by the lady who later married the author of *The Pursuit of Knowledge under Difficulties*.

men are far more illuminating than pages of statistics and generalizations. They tell us where individual youths managed to find their books, what they read, and under what circumstances. And, in their frequent allusions to other readers of equally humble station, they encourage the belief that the public for solid literature was at least larger than pessimists assumed.

II. These men were self-educated in the strictest sense. Most of them had only two or three years of formal schooling, leaving the classroom at eight, nine, or ten to be apprenticed or to scare crows in cornfields at a penny or two a day. Several of the group, such as Ben Tillett, one of the founders of the Labour party, never went to a day school at all; others, like the future philologist Joseph Wright, attended only the ineffectual half-day classes provided at the mills to which they were sent at the age of seven. Later, perhaps, they went to a little night school run by a dissenting schoolmaster.[12]

That these children went to school so briefly, if at all, does not necessarily mean that their parents were indifferent to education; it is simply evidence of the hard economic circumstances in which the humble lived, and of the lack of decent free educational provision for them. In at least some of the homes from which our memoirists came, there were little shelves of books, and the child's interest in reading was encouraged by one parent or by both. Alexander Somerville's father, a Scottish quarry laborer whose family nearly starved in the years following the Napoleonic Wars, prized among his few possessions a little library of theological works. (Another possession was a window, which the family carried with them from place to place, to fit into the wall of whatever cottage they occupied.)[13] The father of Thomas Burt, like his son a miner and pioneer trade unionist, also concentrated upon sermons

[12] Ben Tillett, *Memories and Reflections* (1931), p. 77; Elizabeth M. Wright, *Life of Joseph Wright* (1932), I, 30, 36–38.

[13] Somerville, *Autobiography of a Working Man*, pp. 12, 27. Somerville won national fame in 1832 when, as a member of the Scots Greys stationed at Birmingham, he wrote a letter to the press hinting strongly that the soldiers would not be loyal to the government in the threatening Reform Bill riots. For this indiscretion he received a hundred lashes. His cause was taken up by the newspapers, and a formal court of inquiry eventually censured his commanding officer. Later he became a political journalist, serving successively in the ranks of the Chartists, the Cobdenites, and the anti-Cobdenites, personal enmities accounting as much for his shifting allegiance as principle.

and theology. A devout Methodist, he owned no light literature of
any kind, indulging his love of poetry by reading the hymns of
Charles Wesley, Watts, Toplady, and Montgomery.[14] Thomas
Carter, an asthmatic tailor who would be utterly forgotten but for
his *Memoirs of a Working Man*, which Charles Knight published in
1845, recorded that his father, a cellar man to a wine merchant,
owned two Bibles, the Book of Common Prayer, a spelling book,
Watts's *Divine and Moral Songs*, and "some tattered and odd volumes of sermons and other theological disquisitions."[15]

This strong emphasis on religious literature was characteristic of
working-class libraries throughout the first part of the century—a
proof of the persistence or resurgence of the old Puritan tradition,
whether through Calvinism, as in Scotland, or through English
nonconformism. This was especially true in the country, where religious book-distributing agencies had the field virtually to themselves. In the towns poor people might own a few more secular
books; for example, the shelf of one Samuel Broadbelt, a thirty-
shilling-a-week spinner at Hyde in the 1830's, contained a book
about London, one about Columbus' discovery of America, *Robinson Crusoe*, a pamphlet on the Reform Bill, "a small novel," and a
co-operative-movement periodical, in addition to various religious
items.[16] Although secular books and periodicals became more available as time passed, the religious element remained strong. The
French literary critic Hippolyte Taine, touring England in the sixties, recorded his impression that cottage shelves contained chiefly
religious works, books of history, biography, and travel, and practical handbooks on family health, the rearing of rabbits, hus-
bandry, and similar topics.[17] In 1904 a survey of a Lancashire community revealed that the Bible, Bunyan, religious or at least
moralized prize-books which the children had brought home from
day or Sunday school, and such popular religious fiction as *The
Lamplighter*, *The Wide, Wide World*, and *Queechy* were most often
found in working-class homes.[18]

[14] Burt, *Autobiography*, pp. 113–14.

[15] *Memoirs of a Working Man*, p. 28.

[16] *Supplementary Report of the Central Board of His Majesty's Commissioners Appointed To Collect Information in the Manufacturing Districts*, Part I (1834), D. 2, p. 204.

[17] *Notes on England*, trans. W. F. Rae (1872), pp. 156–57.

[18] Leigh, "What Do the Masses Read?" p. 170.

Here and there we find mention of a parent with somewhat broader tastes: the ex-sailor father of Frederick Rogers, for example, who as a London dock laborer "knew something of literature, loved Byron's sea descriptions, regarded Falconer's 'Shipwreck' as a great poem, and had a passionate admiration for Dibdin's sea-songs."[19] The mother of Joseph Arch, the man who in the 1870's became the much-persecuted organizer of the agricultural laborers, was the daughter of a gentleman's coachman and before her marriage a servant at Warwick Castle. Her son remembered her as "a great admirer of Shakespeare" who "used to talk about him very often, and . . . was well versed in his works. She would read bits aloud to me of an evening, and tell me tales from the plays. On Sundays she used to read the Bible to me in the same way, and tell me stories from it. Shakespeare and the Bible were the books I was brought up on, and I don't want any better."[20]

Even in the humblest station of life, therefore, one could find parents who, though poorly educated, cherished their little collection of books and started the germ of reading interest in their children. Nor was a liking for books communicated only from the older generation to the younger; it passed from wife to husband, and from man to man. Alexander Somerville's father worked with a man whose wife had taught him to read, and who "had read eighteen different authors on astronomy, besides many others on other subjects. . . . He would travel twenty miles on a Sunday, and back again, to borrow a book on astronomy." On Sunday he would take his lunch (a hollowed-out loaf filled with treacle or sugar) and lie in a cornfield, reading to his heart's content all day. Young Somerville himself discovered Burns through the talk of a fellow harvester who was given to reciting Burns's poems and telling of his life. From this true Scot he succeeded in borrowing a tattered volume of the national hero: "I had special charges to take care of it, as it was not every one that it would be lent to." Somer-

---

[19] Rogers, *Labour, Life, and Literature*, p. 269. Rogers was one of the very few self-educated Londoners to leave a memoir; he was born in Whitechapel and spent his whole life in London. After leaving school at ten, he became an errand boy for an ironmonger and later a journeyman bookbinder. From the seventies onward he was busy in the trade-union, co-operative, settlement-house, and educational movements. His modest but interesting autobiography gives a detailed account of the reading he managed to accomplish despite his long hours as a binder of account books and his manifold social-betterment activities. One of his special hobbies was the Elizabethan drama.

[20] Arch, *The Story of His Life*, pp. 8–9.

ville's father, finding the ragged book in his son's possession, was
dubious of its propriety, but "the genius of Burns subdued him.
He took that old volume from me, and read it again and again, his
grave countenance relaxing, and the muscles of his face curling into
a smile, and the smile widening to a broad laugh at certain passages, which having read to himself, he would read aloud, that we
might all laugh." Still, he could not wholly approve, and seeing
that his son insisted upon reading verse, the hard-working man
spent half a week's wages on a book of *Gospel Sonnets*, which, his
son says, "were received and read, but there was something want-
ing either in me or in them."[21]

In the autobiography of the geologist Hugh Miller, another
Scotsman, we read of a "literary cabinetmaker" who had between
eighty and a hundred books, chiefly of poetry, and who had won
local celebrity by composing a thirty-line poem on the Hill of
Cromarty; and of a carpenter who was "deeply read in books of all
kinds, from the plays of Farquhar to the sermons of Flavel; and as
both his father and grandfather . . . had also been readers and collectors of books, he possessed a whole pressful of tattered, hard-
working volumes, some of them very curious ones; and to me he
liberally extended, what literary men always value, 'the full freedom of the press.' " Miller's chief benefactor at Cromarty was one
Francie, a retired clerk and supercargo, whose books included, in
addition to some black-letter volumes on astrology, the planetary
properties of vegetables, and folk medicine, a generous number of
the British essayists, a handful of travels and voyages, and translations from German poetry and drama.[22]

As a young man Thomas Cooper had a friend named Henry
Whillock, a grocer's assistant. The two youths spent Sundays together, studying astrology and divination, but later turning to the
English essayists and Langhorne's *Plutarch*.[23] Later in the century,
Thomas Burt knew a whole coterie of fellow colliers with bookish
tastes: Sam Bailey, a specialist in science, Frank Bell, who "first
introduced me to Artemus Ward, Mark Twain, and other American humorists," and Joe Fairbairn, whose interests ran to poetry.
Burt and Fairbairn were drawn together by a common enthusiasm

[21] Somerville, pp. 12, 43–44.

[22] Miller, *My Schools and Schoolmasters* (Boston, 1869), pp. 48–53.

[23] Cooper, *Life*, pp. 47–49.

for P. J. Bailey's then famous poem *Festus*, and soon Fairbairn was teaching Burt to appreciate Wordsworth. The eventual result, many years later, was that Burt, who had risen to a seat in Parliament, often recited passages from Wordsworth to a knot of auditors gathered in a corridor near the House of Commons library.[24]

Occasionally, too, humane master artisans opened their shelves to their book-hungry apprentices. Thomas Carter's master, a woolen draper and tailor, gave him free run of his little collection, which included the most popular poetry, histories, and essays of the eighteenth century.[25] In like fashion Thomas Cooper's appetite for literature was fed by the shoemaker to whom he was apprenticed, a man who "spoke passionately" of Byron's poetry and lent Cooper his copy of Burns. Clark, the master, had gone often to the theater when he lived in London, and his frequent talk about Shakespeare on the stage sent Cooper back to the dramatist's pages with new understanding.[26]

In 1833 the Factory Commissioners heard that books were brought into the very factories and mills. Boys, they were told, sometimes read while waiting for their duties to begin, or while a machine was being repaired, and "the girls often bring books to the factories to read . . . not much else except religious books, except it be a song now and then. I never found any indecent book among them." Though the practice was ordinarily frowned upon —it was equivalent to a soldier poring over a pocket novel on the drill field—an occasional overseer, anxious to dissipate the growing public impression that all English factories were "dark, satanic mills," confided that "if the work is right we never notice it. I have read many a volume through when I was a spinner."[27] Since, however, he was now on the side of management, his evidence is not quite as credible as it might otherwise be. Life in a big noisy factory, regulated as it was on the model of a prison or barracks, was hardly conducive to reading during working hours. But in small establishments, especially where the master himself was a reader, books were tolerated and even encouraged. In some milli-

---

[24] Burt, pp. 124, 146, 274.

[25] Carter, *Memoirs*, pp. 74–75.

[26] Cooper, pp. 42–43.

[27] *First Report of the Central Board of His Majesty's Commissioners for Inquiring into the Employment of Children in Factories* (1833), C. 1, p. 87; D. 2, pp. 111, 125, 134.

ners' and tailors' shops it was customary for one worker to read
aloud to the others, who made up out of their own pockets the
money he or she thereby lost.

William Chambers, an Edinburgh bookseller's apprentice in the
1820's, earned a hot roll every morning by appearing at a bakeshop
at five o'clock to read to the baker and his two sons while they
kneaded their dough. "The baker was not particular as to subject.
All he stipulated for was something droll and laughable." So
Chambers chose the novels of Smollett and Fielding, which gave
his floury listeners "unqualified satisfaction." After two and a half
hours of such entertainment, Chambers would descend from his
perch on a folded sack at the window, dust his clothes, take his
roll, and go merrily off to work.[28]

An anecdote told by Somerville reveals that literature sometimes could be found even in the blacksmith's shop. The same
James Wilson who had introduced him to the delights of Burns
happened into a village smithy and found a copy of Anson's *Voyages*, which the smith had borrowed to read in snatches while his
iron was heating.[29] Wilson relayed the news to Somerville, who,
though extremely shy, determined to see that book. "The struggle
I had with the desire to go to the owner of Anson's *Voyages*
to borrow the book to read, and the shame of the thought that
a boy like me, who only wore corduroy clothes, nailed shoes with
thick soles, and a highland bonnet, should presume to go to the
house of those who had a back door and a front door, was a war of
thoughts that allowed me no peace for several weeks." But he
overcame his shyness, was lent the book, and read it during the
dinner recess in the turnip field where he was working. When his
fellow hoers came back, he told them of Anson's marvelous adventures, and from then on they brought their dinners to the field in
order to hear him read to them.[30]

So long as employers or overseers looked the other way, a youth

[28] Chambers, *Memoir of Robert Chambers*, pp. 94–95.

[29] Blacksmith shops were not the most likely places in the world for literary recreation,
but the one where the smith read Anson was not unique. Will Crooks, the Labour politician
who grew up in the London dock area in the sixties, recorded that when he was a
blacksmith's helper, aged about twelve, he often recited Shakespeare to his fellow workers
(George Haw, *From Workshop to Westminster: The Life Story of Will Crooks, M.P.* [1917],
p. 22).

[30] Somerville, pp. 45–47.

in almost any occupation could contrive to read a bit while nominally earning his wages. At the beginning of the century, Samuel Bamford, later a radical weaver-poet, was a combination office boy and porter in a Manchester calico-printing works. In the warehouse he fixed up a snuggery where, when his duties allowed, he repaired to read a wide variety of history and biography—as well as Cobbett's *Political Register.*[31] Several decades later another humble poet, Joseph Skipsey, who had gone to work as a little boy, learned to write by chalking on the mine trapdoor he tended. He not only read poetry behind the trapdoor but even made his first attempts at composing it.[32] In the late 1860's, but in the very different setting of a Gravesend draper's shop, an assistant named Henry Arthur Jones was deep in *Paradise Lost* when he was interrupted by a fussy woman intent on buying some ribbon. When she was not satisfied with the first boxes he got out, he collected every box and tray in the shop, spread them on the counter before her, and saying, "Make your choice, madam," returned to his Milton.[33] Jones did not go far in the drapery trade, but he became a highly successful dramatist.

Needless to say, reading at work often caused trouble, if not for others—though Skipsey's literary preoccupations at the mine entrance might easily have caused an accident—at least for the student himself. In his early teens, for instance, William Hone, later a writer and publisher of radical political squibs, lost a job because the room in which he worked was lined with unlocked bookcases and he could not resist temptation.[34] And when penny dreadfuls became the favorite reading matter of English boys, it was a standing complaint among employers that to get work out of office boys and errand runners was next to impossible. The number of dismissals caused by too overt or ill-timed an absorption in the latest instalment of *Black Bess* or *Tyburn Dick* must have been staggering.

Everywhere in the memoirs of lower-class readers are laments that in their youth good reading matter was hard to come by. The

---

[31] Bamford, *Early Days*, pp. 280–81.

[32] Robert S. Watson, *Joseph Skipsey: His Life and Work* (1909), pp. 17–19.

[33] Doris Arthur Jones, *Life and Letters of Henry Arthur Jones* (1930), pp. 32–33.

[34] F. W. Hackwood, *William Hone* (1912), pp. 46–47.

resources of the home shelf and those of friends or employers were soon exhausted, and, until mid-century at least, formidable obstacles were in the way of the reader whose appetite grew ever sharper. The next chapters will reveal how slow was the process that eventually brought book prices down to the reach of the masses. Even if new books had been reasonably cheap, only the reader in the larger towns, where there were bookshops, would have had access to a fair-sized selection. Elsewhere the best he could hope for was to be within trudging distance of a stationer's or draper's shop where a few books were sold as a side line. It was nothing for a boy to walk many miles to buy a book he coveted. The thirteen-year-old John Clare, rapturous after a chance encounter with a fragment of Thomson's *Seasons*, determined to possess the whole of that poem. One Sunday he got 18*d*. from his father and made his way to Stamford, the nearest town. "But when I got there, I was told by a young shop boy in the street (who had a book in his hand, which I found to be Collins' *Odes and Poems*) that the booksellers would not open the shop on a Sunday." Disappointed, he walked back home; but during the next week he paid another boy a penny to take over his chores and returned to Stamford, where he got his book and "clumb over the wall into Burghley Park, and nestled in a lawn at the wall side." There he had one of the great formative experiences of his life, poring over Thomson's pages.[35]

Secondhand shops, "the poor man's browsing ground," were particularly important sources of supply in the cities, and their small-scale equivalents were found at country fairs and markets, which sellers of the printed word had attended ever since the sixteenth century. The great trouble was that many, if not most, of the books thus made available to the poor reader were ill suited to his needs and capacities. The father of Jesse Collings, later a leading Birmingham politician and reformer, brought his son secondhand books from stalls in Exeter, "a strange medley," the son commented in retrospect.[36] John Passmore Edwards, the son of a Cornish carpenter and in later life a millionaire newspaper proprietor, bought used copies of Locke's *Essay on the Human Understand-*

---

[35] *Sketches in the Life of John Clare*, ed. Blunden (1931), pp. 58–59.

[36] *The Life of the Right Hon. Jesse Collings* [Part I by himself, Part II by Sir John L. Green] (1920), p. 13.

ing and Newton's *Optics* at Truro, only to find, on getting them home, that both works completely baffled him.[37]

Henry Mayhew, in one of the few authentic accounts of the secondhand book business during the nineteenth century, described the contents of the London street stalls he inspected. They were, of course, exceedingly miscellaneous. A regular practice in the middle of the century, as it had been for the past fifty years, was to break up sets of the collected *Spectator* papers or of a multi-volumed old novel like *Pamela;* sold a volume at a time, these went more quickly, and at better prices, than in sets. One street-seller told Mayhew that nothing sold better than eighteenth-century prose classics, from Addison to Goldsmith. The multiplicity of editions brought the prices of the English classic poets very low, with Shakespeare, Pope, Thomson, Goldsmith, Cowper, Burns, Byron, and Scott outselling Milton, Young, Prior, Dryden, and Gay. The poems of such nineteenth-century writers as Hood, Shelley, Coleridge, Wordsworth, and Moore, however, seldom turned up on the stalls.

A generation earlier, that is, about 1825, patrons of the secondhand trade had been offered a class of books that by the fifties had largely disappeared: Klopstock's *Messiah*, Walpole's *Castle of Otranto*, Clara Reeve's *Old English Baron*, Burke's *On the Sublime and Beautiful*, Hannah More's *Coelebs in Search of a Wife*. One more generation removed (about the end of the eighteenth century) the familiar titles on the stalls had been *The Whole Duty of Man*, *A Tale of a Tub*, Pomfret's *Poems*, and Richardson's novels.[38]

In the earlier nineteenth century, secondhand books were sold also in street auctions. The shade of Dr. Johnson, revisiting his favorite haunts, would have been startled to hear the following patter addressed to a group of idlers by a red-faced auctioneer in a dirty neckcloth: " 'The Rambler!' Now you rambling boys—now you young devils, that's been staring those pretty girls out of

---

[37] Edwards, *A Few Footprints* (1905), p. 6.

[38] A familiar title *underneath* the counter at that time was Tom Paine's *Age of Reason*, which could be obtained by any customer who was willing to buy some other book for three times the marked price. Mayhew's informant, relaying information he had picked up from an old street-seller long since dead, added, "A sly trade's always the best for paying, and for selling too. The old fellow used to laugh and say his stall was quite a godly stall, and he wasn't often without a copy or two of the 'Anti-Jacobin Review,' which was all for Church and State and all that, though he had 'Tom Paine' in a drawer."

countenance—here's the very book for you, and more shame for
you, and perhaps for me too; but I must sell—I must do business.
If any lady or gen'l'man 'll stand treat to a glass of brandy and
water, 'warm with,' I'll tell more about this 'Rambler'—I'm too
bashful, as it is. Who bids? Fifteen-pence—thank'ee, sir. Sold
again!" By Mayhew's time street auctions had been banished
from London because they obstructed traffic, but they were still
conducted in the provinces.

Secondhand vendors got their wares from the sources one would
expect: the "trade auctions" at which publishers got rid of their
unsold stock (the vendors taking the odds and ends that were left
after the larger dealers and remainder and reprint specialists like
Thomas Tegg had had their pick); general auctions; and individual
sellers. "It is not uncommon," Mayhew reported, "for working
men or tradesmen, if they become 'beaten-down and poor,' to
carry a basket-full of books to a stall-keeper, and say, 'Here, give
me half-a-crown for these.' "[39]

Thus, while the man who had access to a stock of cheap secondhand books was the most fortunate of all poor readers, his choice
still was restricted. The most easily obtained books were certain
standard classics and books that had been popular a generation or
more earlier. Recent publications, except those which had died on
the publisher's or retailer's hands, were much harder to get at
reduced rates. Until the cheap reprint was extensively developed
in the second half of the century, the impecunious reader who
wanted a library of his own had to content himself chiefly with
volumes that had gathered dust for years or decades on someone
else's shelves.

Before free libraries appeared in towns, some poor readers, as we
saw in the last chapter, borrowed from circulating libraries. In the
late eighteenth century the radical tailor Francis Place obtained a
book at a time from a small shop in Maiden Lane, Covent Garden.[40] Somewhat later, when Christopher Thomson of Edwinstowe
taught his innkeeper father to read and write, he was rewarded

---

[39] *London Labour and the London Poor*, I, 313–24.

[40] Graham Wallas, *Life of Francis Place* (3d ed.; New York, 1919), pp. 17–18.
Another stratagem by which Place obtained books was somewhat out of the ordinary.
His landlady, an elderly charwoman, surreptitiously "borrowed" books for him from the
rooms she cleaned in the Temple.

with a subscription to the village library.[41] Thomas Cooper was unusually fortunate in being able to read the new books and periodicals his friend at Gainsborough, Mrs. Trevor, obtained for the local gentry—the latest Scott novel, the poetry of Campbell, Moore, and Byron, the current numbers of the leading critical reviews and magazines. He considered himself additionally lucky in discovering a whole forgotten cache of books which a mercer had long ago left to his fellow townsmen. "I was in ecstasies," he writes, "to find the dusty, cobwebbed shelves loaded with Hooker, and Bacon, and Cudworth, and Stillingfleet, and Locke, and Jeremy Taylor, and Tillotson, and Bates, and Bishop Hall, and . . . a score of other philosophers and divines,—mingled with Stanley's *History of the Philosophers*, and its large full-length portraits —Ogilvy's *Embassies to Japan and China*, with their large curious engravings—Speed's and Rapin's folio histories of England—Collier's *Church History*—Fuller's *Holy War*—Foxe's *Book of Martyrs*, the first edition, in black letter, and with its odd, rude plates—and countless other curiosities and valuables."[42]

III. From the lists of titles given in many of the autobiographies upon which this chapter is based, it is possible to outline pretty precisely the sort of cultural and literary tradition the self-made reader inherited. The Bible, naturally, had immense influence; but in childhood, at least, it was read less as a book of divine revelation than as a treasury of memorable characters and stories, a substitute for the secular juvenile fiction which was so scarce, particularly below the middle class, in the earlier nineteenth century. As a child Joseph Barker, the future religious controversialist, read the Bible "chiefly as a book of history," and Thomas Carter, among many others, bore witness that it was the narrative and poetical portions of Scripture which claimed his attention. Next to the Bible came *Pilgrim's Progress*. The familiar assumption that Bunyan's book figured in the imaginative awakening of countless children is entirely correct. It too was read as a story. "I had no idea," wrote Barker, "that it was a parable or an allegory." And Thomas Burt echoed a half-century later: "Not as a dream or allegory, but as solid literal history did it present

[41] Thomson, *Autobiography of an Artisan*, pp. 65–67.

[42] Cooper, pp. 34, 51–52.

itself to my boyish mind. I believed every word of it. Perhaps it was the only book I ever read with entire, unquestioning acceptation." William Hone and Samuel Bamford left similar reports.[43]

Milton was incomparably the most influential in encouraging a taste for poetry. Not only did the religious element in his verse recommend him to readers in an era of revived Puritanism; his political attitudes appealed strongly to those who were affected by popular feeling first against the Tory state and then against middle-class Whiggism. It was as "the literary champion of the Commonwealth" fully as much as in his role of religious poet that Milton won a popular audience in the nineteenth century. Some readers initially found his works beyond their comprehension, or at least too rich for their still unsophisticated powers of enjoyment; but to the rescue often came Addison's appreciations or the influential essay of William Ellery Channing, the reading of which Thomas Burt, among others, celebrated as the real beginning of his veneration of Milton. Joseph Barker recalled that he "read . . . *Paradise Lost* at a gallop," which is perhaps not the most felicitous way of describing one's first looking into Milton's epic. Thomas Carter, however, confessed that the pleasure of reading *Paradise Lost* was "a good deal alloyed by the pain I felt at the catastrophe of the poem." Memorizing lengthy portions was a favorite pastime among studious young men. By the time he was sixteen Ebenezer Elliott, the Corn-Law Rhymer, knew three books by heart; Thomas Cooper, who had already learned the whole of *Hamlet*, memorized the first four books of *Paradise Lost* and would probably have memorized the remaining eight had his health not broken down.[44]

Of Shakespeare we hear somewhat less in these memoirs, probably because he was associated with the playhouse and most of the memoirists grew up in the strict atmosphere of dissent. Thomas Burt, for instance, first came upon the dramatist some years after he had mastered Milton. "Except in short tags, Shakespeare was then wholly unknown to me. Often had I heard him denounced from pulpits; often had I been warned not to read his plays, the preacher not infrequently, all unconsciously, quoting him, so completely had the great dramatist's words and phrases entered into

[43] Barker, *Life*, p. 53; Carter, p. 28; Burt, p. 115; Hackwood, p. 29; Bamford, pp. 40–41.

[44] Burt, p. 117; Barker, p. 80; Carter, p. 81; Ebenezer Elliott, "Autobiography," *Athenaeum*, January 12, 1850, p. 48; Cooper, p. 68.

the very texture of our language." The writers who record having read Shakespeare give somewhat mixed reports. Samuel Bamford confessed that "though deeply interested by his historical characters and passages, I never either then or since relished his blank verse, or that of any other poet." But Thomas Cooper, on the other hand, remembered that "the wondrous knowledge of the heart unfolded by Shakespeare, made me shrink into insignificance; while the sweetness, the marvellous power of expression and grandeur of his poetry seemed to transport me, at times, out of the vulgar world of circumstances in which I lived bodily," and Joseph Barker found Shakespearean plays a great relief from his regimen of religious books: "He had always a meaning in what he said, and you could easily see his meaning. . . . I felt quite delighted to read something that was rational, plain, stirring, and straightforward."[45]

Hardly less revered by the common reader was the poet Thomson, whose *Seasons* seems to have penetrated where few other books did. John Clare's delight, nestling behind a wall with his newly purchased copy, was shared by numerous other young readers. Thomas Carter found the poem "of great use to me in the way of preserving me from the depraved tastes and habits of those with whom my duty compelled me to associate. . . . With the exception of the Bible, I know not that I ever read any other book so attentively and regularly." Ebenezer Elliott's first attempt at verse was an imitation of "Thomson's blank-verse thunderstorm." And William Hone testified that "the just descriptions and noble sentiments in the *Seasons*, refined and elevated my mind. I saw nature with a new-born sight; in its quiet scenery I felt emotions of peaceful delight unknown to me before—my affections went forth to every living thing; my heart expanded with rapturous joy."[46]

The eighteenth-century poets generally were standard fare among the bookish young down into Victorian times: Goldsmith, of course, and Cowper; and Pope, Akenside, Gray, the "graveyard school" of Blair, Collins, and Young, even such now-forgotten worthies as Denham, Pomfret, and Falconer. These were the poets who were most frequently reprinted in cheap series and excerpted as space-fillers in the cheap religious and "instructive" magazines.

[45] Burt, p. 143; Bamford, p. 209; Cooper, p. 64; Barker, pp. 70–71.
[46] Carter, p. 75; Elliott, *loc. cit.*; Hackwood, p. 47.

Except for Shakespeare, of the poets before Milton we hear virtually nothing; their slowly reviving critical fame did not penetrate to the common reader until later in the century.

Robinson Crusoe was read (often in an abridgment) almost as much as *Pilgrim's Progress;* and the now-forgotten imitation of *Crusoe, Philip Quarll,* is mentioned as often in readers' reminiscences as Defoe's own book.[47] Then there was the whole great fund of eighteenth-century essays, whose sweet reasonableness and unexceptionable morality recommended them to every serious mind, and which were available in relatively cheap reprints and secondhand sets. The popularity of the eighteenth-century travelers and navigators—Anson, Cook, Byron—and even, sometimes, their Elizabethan sea-dog predecessors was considerable. So too was that of the historians, especially Smollett and Hume. Gibbon was somewhat less favored because of his doubtful religious tendencies; but, as Thomas Burt was able to point out to his father when the young man brought home the first volume of Bohn's edition, even so orthodox a biblical commentator as Albert Barnes praised the historian's scholarship and fairness. "Needless to observe," Burt wrote, "Gibbon won the day. . . . With youthful glee I read till a late hour. I slept but little that night; the book haunted my dreams. I awoke about four on the bright summer Sunday morning, and went into the fields to read till breakfast-time. The stately, majestic march of Gibbon's periods had some attraction for me even then; but the *Decline and Fall*, it must be admitted, was hard reading for an unlettered collier lad. Yet I plodded on until I had finished the book. . . ."[48]

Another powerful element in the early experience of nineteenth-century studious readers was the fund of theological and hortatory works bequeathed by the Puritan era and the eighteenth-century religious awakening. The contents of the Gainsborough cache

---

[47] In 1860 excavators for a railway line laid bare the remains of the tile-works Defoe had once run at Tilbury. When one of Defoe's biographers, who went to the scene, told the laborers, "These bricks and tiles were made 160 years since by the same man that made 'Robinson Crusoe'!" he "touched a chord that connected these railway 'navvies' with the shipwrecked mariner, and that bounded over the intervening period in a single moment. Every eye brightened, every tongue was ready to ask or give information, and every fragment became interesting. Porters, inspector, and station-master soon gathered round me, wondering at what was deemed an important historical revelation" (William Lee, *Daniel Defoe: His Life, and Recently Discovered Writings* [1869], I, 32). Ten years later an obelisk was erected over Defoe's grave with money 1,700 boys and girls gave to a fund started by a religious paper (*Publishers' Circular*, October 1, 1870, p. 589).

[48] Burt, pp. 118–19.

Thomas Cooper describes were typical of the ponderous, tough volumes the earnest young student willingly devoured. In addition, all sorts of works of secular instruction found an eager audience among those to whom knowledge was precious: books ranging from popularized compilations of miscellaneous facts (*A Thousand Notable Things, The Oddest of All Oddities*) through ordinary tattered schoolbooks strayed from the classroom (Bonnycastle's *Mensuration* and Fenning's *Arithmetic*) to the Cassell self-help library after the middle of the century.

History and travel to a great extent took the place of the classic fiction which for various reasons was not as easily available to the poor reader. It was only the occasional young man, and usually one of slightly superior station, who read widely even in the novels which had gone out of copyright and therefore could often be had more cheaply. Dickens owed much to his father's little collection of Smollett, Fielding, Goldsmith, and other standard fiction, purchased in one of the several reprint series then current. John Clare, on the other hand, said that he knew only *Tom Jones* and *The Vicar of Wakefield*.[49]

Perhaps the most significant fact to emerge from the published records of working-class reading is this: Until the latter half of the century brought cheap periodicals that printed the new work of outstanding writers, truly cheap reprints of contemporary literature, and free libraries, the masses had relatively little access to the best that was written in their own day. Few persons of Thomas Cooper's social position had his opportunity to keep up with the latest serious books and periodicals. The village libraries, the penny-a-day circulating libraries, the mutual improvement societies, the mechanics' institute libraries—all had, for one reason or another, failed to meet the needs of intellectually ambitious workmen who could not afford the outright purchase of new books. Only in the memoirs of men who had grown up after the middle of the century do we find frequent allusions to contemporary authors. By then it was possible for a sailor like Ben Tillett to buy, between voyages, the books of Huxley, Haeckel, Spencer, Darwin, Newman, and Carlyle.[50] The story of the cheapening of books is so important to our theme that it must now be told in some detail.

[49] Johnson, *Charles Dickens*, I, 20–21; J. W. and Anne Tibble, *John Clare: A Life* (New York, 1932), p. 88.

[50] Tillett, *Memories and Reflections*, p. 77.

CHAPTER 12 **The Book Trade 1800–1850**

I (1800–24). During the first quarter of the nineteenth century, conditions in the English book trade discouraged the spread of the reading habit. New books were more expensive than ever before: the usual price of an octavo rose to 12s. or 14s., and that of a quarto to as much as two guineas. The 12mo volume, commonly used for novels, went from the 2s.6d. or 3s. that had been standard in Smollett's and Fanny Burney's time to 5s. or 6s., and, as we shall see, was destined to go much higher as a result of Sir Walter Scott's phenomenal popularity.[1] It was with good cause that a printer told a committee of the House of Commons in 1818 that "books are a luxury, and the purchase of them has been confined to fewer people. In general, those who would be disposed to purchase books, have not the means of so doing, and are obliged to be frugal."[2]

Why were books so expensive? One reason was the traditional conservatism of the publishing trade, now intensified by the financial uncertainties of the war and the postwar era. None of the leading firms, the Rivingtons, Longmans, Murrays, and the rest, were willing to take chances. The bold, speculative spirit that made fortunes overnight in war commodities never touched Paternoster Row. Although Lackington's success as a remainder and second-hand dealer and the popularity of Bell's and Cooke's classic reprint series had revealed the existence of a wide market for moderately priced books, the "respectable" publishing firms were not interested in exploiting it. Charles Knight, who was often to wax bitter over what he deemed the obstinate shortsightedness of these houses, likened the prevailing practice to that of the wholesale

[1] Knight, *The Old Printer and the Modern Press*, p. 238.

[2] *Report from the Select Committee on the Copyright Acts* (1818), p. 67.

fishmongers in Billingsgate, who kept prices high by destroying their surplus. "The dealers in fish had not recognised the existence of a class who would buy for their suppers what the rich had not taken for their dinners; and knew not that the stalls of Tottenham Court Road had as many customers for a low price as the shops of Charing Cross for a high price. The fishmongers had not discovered that the price charged to the evening customers had no effect of lowering that of the morning. Nor had the booksellers discovered that there were essentially two, if not more, classes of customers for books—those who would have the dearest and the newest, and those who were content to wait till the gloss of novelty had passed off, and good works became accessible to them, either in cheaper reprints, or 'remainders' reduced in price."[3]

Knight and others often charged that there was a deliberate conspiracy among the tightly knit London publishers to maintain high prices. The charge was well founded, but the motives behind the policy could be interpreted in different ways. Advocates of cheap books alleged that publishers encouraged an artificial scarcity simply because there was more profit in selling small editions at high prices. The publishers, on the other hand, could make a plausible, if not wholly convincing, defense. For one thing, the class that had come into sudden wealth through manufacturing or trading in war supplies formed a lucrative market for luxury books. Valuing books primarily as conspicuous tokens of wealth, these people lined the shelves of their mansions with volumes whose costliness was obvious to the most casual beholder. The publishers would have been eccentric businessmen indeed if they had failed to cater to the vanity trade. Again, publishers complained that circulating libraries had reduced the bookshop trade. The typical middle-class family, its purchasing power reduced by wartime taxation, had become accustomed to renting books instead of buying them. By multiplying the number of readers a single copy would serve, the libraries profited mightily at the expense of the publishing and retail trades. Thus, to the extent that their burden fell upon the libraries, higher prices could be defended as the publishers' attempt to get a slice of that profit.[4]

---

[3] Knight, pp. 225–26.

[4] See the (unsigned) interpretation of R. English's chart of fiction prices in the *Author*, V (1894), 99.

Most important of all, book prices were high simply because costs were high. Printing-house compositors were the best-paid skilled workers in London; in 1801 they made 33*s.* a week, and in 1811 the rate went to 36*s.*, where it remained until 1832. (Newspaper compositors made even more—40*s.* in 1801, 48*s.* in 1810—which accounts in part for the high prices of newspapers at this period.)[5] Materials were even more expensive than labor. Two-thirds of a publisher's total outlay in issuing a 500-copy edition went for paper. During the Napoleonic Wars, England suffered an acute paper shortage; between 1793 and 1801 alone the price of paper doubled.[6] And to the maker's price was added a tax of 3*d.* a pound—by no means the least burdensome of the "taxes on knowledge" over which a great political battle was destined to be fought.

Technologically, the book trade was far behind most other British industries. The Earl of Stanhope's iron press, patented in 1798, while reducing the labor involved in printing, failed to improve the rate of production, which was about 250 impressions an hour. Steam was first used in printing when the *Times* of November 28, 1814, was produced on a machine newly invented by Frederick Koenig, but not until the 1840's did steam generally replace hand labor in book printing. The plaster-of-Paris method of casting stereotypes, which enabled a printer to distribute his type and yet to produce new impressions of a book whenever they were required, was perfected in 1802. But because there were relatively few books, such as Bibles and schoolbooks, whose prospects for continued sale warranted the expense of plate-making, stereotypes did not come into general use for two decades.[7]

The effect of Scott's popularity upon English book-trade economics, and therefore upon the rate at which the reading public was to grow, can hardly be overestimated. The commercial success of his poems, and even more of his novels, seemed at the time to prove that exorbitant prices were no bar to large sales. *The Lay of the Last Minstrel* (1805), published, like his other volumes of poetry, in sumptuous format, sold 15,050 copies in three years at 25*s.*; *Marmion* (1808) went through four editions, totaling 11,000 copies, in the first year at 31*s.*6*d.*; and *The Lady of the Lake* (1810)

[5] Cole and Postgate, *The Common People*, p. 201.

[6] Plant, *The English Book Trade*, pp. 325–27.

[7] *Ibid.*, pp. 271–75; 301–303. See also Ellic Howe (ed.), *The London Compositor . . . 1785–1900* (1947), *passim*.

sold 20,300 copies in its first year at the even steeper price of 42*s.*
Scott's first novel, *Waverley* (1814), cost 21*s.*, at a time when the
customary price of a three-volume novel was 15*s.* or 18*s.*, and went
through eight editions (11,500 copies) in seven years. As the public
appetite for Scott's fiction increased, so did the cost of indulging
it. *Ivanhoe* (1820) was published at the virtually unheard-of figure
of 30*s.* the set, and *Kenilworth*, issued the following year, cost
31*s.6d.*[8]

Thirty-one shillings sixpence: a fateful figure. In the beginning,
it reflected the premium readers had to pay if they could not do
without Scott's latest romance. Only here and there was a protest-
ing voice raised. But the evil that best-sellers do lives after them,
and to apply Scott prices to new fiction in general, as the trade
proceeded to do, was an error whose consequences were felt to the
end of the century. In 1823 there were only a handful of guinea-
and-a-half novels, but by 1840 fifty-one out of fifty-eight new novels bore this price, which was all the more exorbitant because none
of them bore the magic name of Scott.[9] The result was that fiction-
lovers flocked, not to the bookshops (31*s.6d.* for one novel), but to
the circulating libraries (only a half-guinea more for a full year's
supply), and the libraries became more firmly established as the
publishers' best customers. Publishers could afford to be indifferent to the fact that they had priced their wares out of the individual buyer's reach; so long as libraries took a substantial part of an
edition, their profit was safe.

Thus the old practice of issuing high-priced books in small editions was reaffirmed on a new basis. The average edition of a serious book was around 750 copies.[10] If a book caught on, editions
might rapidly follow one another, but their individual size was
still limited, mainly because publishers were unwilling to tie up
large quantities of precious paper. Only in very exceptional instances, such as Scott's novels, did editions in the early nineteenth

[8] J. G. Lockhart, *Memoirs of the Life of Sir Walter Scott* (Boston, 1861), II, 175, 294;
III, 100; IV, 174–75. Prices are from the *English Catalogue, 1801–36.* To avoid cluttering
up these pages with too many statistics, figures relating to nineteenth-century best-sellers,
from Scott onward, have been gathered in Appendix B.

[9] On the whole topic of Scott's influence on the price of novels, and subsequent developments, see Morton, "News for Bibliophiles," pp. 330–32; Pollard, "Commercial Circulating Libraries and the Price of Books"; and [English], "The Price of the Novel, 1750–1894."

[10] See Theodore Besterman (ed.), *The Publishing Firm of Cadell & Davies* (1938),
p. xxxi. This figure is supported by the testimony of John Murray and Owen Rees before
the 1818 Copyright Committee, pp. 12, 60.

century run to 6,000 copies. Throughout the century, the ordinary circulating-library novel seldom had an edition of more than a thousand or 1,250 copies.

Thus in the first half of the century the common reader who could not afford to subscribe to a good circulating library had relatively little access to "copyright works"—a category that included almost all recent books by English authors, fiction and non-fiction alike. Fortunately, however, books continued to be available to the reader of modest means in two forms that had flourished during the later eighteenth century: number-publications and classic reprint series.

Since number-publications were usually reprints (or remainders in a new guise), and classic reprint libraries, on the other hand, were often issued in numbers, the houses that produced the two types constituted, in effect, a single branch of the book trade. Its size is suggested by the fact that in 1819 its members asserted their inventory was worth a million pounds.[11]

In this period perhaps the most successful specialist in number-publications was Thomas Kelly, who began humbly in Paternoster Row in 1809 and ended up as Lord Mayor of London. A French visitor who saw him in the days of his eminence characterized him, wonderingly, as "a thriving bookseller, yet a perfectly honest man." In the course of his career he is said to have disposed of 230,000 Bibles, 20,000 histories of the French Revolution, and 100,000 copies of a life of Christ.[12] In the provinces, where, in lack of regular bookstores, the number trade found most of its customers, several men made a good thing of such publications. One of them, Edward Baines of Leeds, is reported to have taken over a two-volume *History of the Wars of the French Revolution* whose original edition had already been sold for wastepaper, reprinted it in sixpenny parts, and sold 20,000 copies through hawkers.[13]

Most number-publications actually were far from cheap. The

[11] *Hansard*, Ser. 1, XLI (1819), col. 1319. The statement was made in a petition to Parliament, urging that number-publications be exempted from the proposed comprehensive tax on newspapers and certain types of periodicals (see chapter 14). The resultant law exempted number-publications from the tax if their contents had been printed at least two years before their first appearance in number-form.

[12] Curwen, *History of Booksellers*, pp. 364–71; R. C. Fell, *Passages from the Private and Official Life of the Late Alderman Kelly* (1856), especially pp. 135–36, 155.

[13] Thomas Constable, *Archibald Constable and His Literary Correspondents* (Edinburgh, 1873), III, 364.

total cost of some of Kelly's greatest successes in number-books is startling. One of his Bibles, issued in 173 numbers, cost £5 15*s*., his edition of Hume's *History of England* £4 10*s*., and his history of the French Revolution £3.[14] We can assume that few of the purchasers who endured to the end of a serial issue counted up what they had spent; or, if they did, they failed to reflect that by determinedly saving sixpence or a shilling a week, rather than giving it to the canvasser, they might have had their completed book sooner and much more cheaply.

The appeal of many number-publications resided as much in their illustrations as in their literary content—at least in the beginning. All too often, however, subscribers were disillusioned on both accounts after the first few issues. John Kitto, the heroic self-taught Bible scholar, recalled that when he was a youth, about 1816, a canvasser visited his parents' room. "Oh! how my heart was delighted by the display of magnificence and varied wealth which this man's portfolio contained. There were various bibles, various histories, various poems. There was John Bunyan's 'Pilgrim;' 'Robinson Crusoe;' 'The Arabian Nights;' 'Drelincourt on Death;' 'Hervey's Meditations;' 'Pamela, or Virtue Rewarded;' 'The History of Henry, Earl of Moreland;' and many more that I do not now remember. . . ." Dazzled by the colored plate in the first shilling number of a history of the French Revolution, the boy rashly agreed to subscribe. But he soon rued his impulse, because "no previous reading had prepared me to be interested in the rather dry details about parliaments and 'beds of justice,' which the first number of this history comprehended: I also discovered that every number would not contain one of those fine plates which had formed so great an attraction in the first number. I learned that these plates would be few and far between; and as the letter-press was in large type and loosely printed, I could not but think it a hard bargain to go on paying a shilling for it without the pictures. . . ."[15]

[14] Fell, p. 155. Curwen (p. 370) gives even higher figures.

[15] "A Poor Student's Literary Expenditure," *Penny Magazine*, IV (1835), 227–28; attributed to Kitto in *St. Paul's Magazine*, XII (1873), 544. However profuse or sparse the illustrations were, they still provided the most powerful incentive to buying the numbers of a work as issued. What the innocent eye of the purchaser lighted upon among these woodcuts or engravings was sometimes remarkable. One working-class reader recorded that a Bible he pored over at this time had a picture of "two men, one of whom was depicted as having a small splinter of wood sticking in his eye, and the other as in the act of

The fact that working-class politicians were especially given to issuing their propaganda in cheap numbers shows how well fitted this practice was to the needs of readers who worked sixteen hours a day for two shillings or less, and who therefore could afford only a penny or two a week for printed matter. Working-class weekly papers abounded in advertisements of books in numbers, "almost exclusively directed to the united object of inspiring hatred of the Government and contempt of the Religious Institutions of the Country."[16] John Wade's *Black Book*, a storehouse of factual ammunition for the use of radical agitators, containing data on the revenues of the aristocracy and clergy, public finance, and other sources of popular grievance, came out in 2*d.* sheets or 6*d.* fortnightly parts and sold 10,000 copies of each issue. An anonymous account of the Peterloo Massacre, issued in 2*d.* parts, had a similar sale.[17] William Cobbett constantly relied on cheap numbers to circulate his works. He reissued his book, *Paper against Gold*, an attack on paper money, in fifteen 2*d.* numbers; and his *Cottage Economy, History of the Protestant "Reformation,"* and *The Poor Man's Friend* all were first published in 2*d.* or 3*d.* parts.[18]

Series of non-copyright fiction were available at a wide range of prices. Among the cheaper were two fiction-reprint libraries that began appearing in 1823, when the price of new fiction was reaching its peak. One was Whittingham's Pocket Novelists, a 16mo series in over thirty volumes, the individual volumes ranging from 2*s.* to 5*s.6d.*[19] A rival series was issued by John Limbird, a retail stationer in the Strand and publisher of the first long-lived cheap periodical, the twopenny *Mirror of Literature.* Limbird offered certain shorter fictions for as little as 6*d.*, *The Mysteries of Udolpho* for 3*s.6d.* (half of Whittingham's price), and *The Vicar of Wakefield* for 10*d.* Like Limbird's other ventures in cheap publishing, this series met fierce opposition from the bigger firms. Boycotted by most country booksellers, who had to keep peace with their chief

---

attempting to pull it out, although a fair-sized beam was protruding from his own," and another of St. Paul regaining his sight, a pair of balances falling from his eyes (Carter, *Memoirs of a Working Man*, pp. 20–21).

[16] Knight, *Passages of a Working Life*, I, 234.

[17] Wickwar, *The Struggle for the Freedom of the Press*, pp. 67, 103.

[18] Pearl, *William Cobbett*, pp. 92, 120, 134–36, 143–44, 147–48.

[19] Sadleir, *XIX Century Fiction*, II, 175–76.

suppliers, Limbird was forced to sell his wares through whatever outlets he could find. In Manchester the only person who handled his books was a tinman.[20]

There were also fresh experiments in the reprinting of standard essayists and poets. Limbird's helter-skelter collection of British Poets and British Classics—a "complete" Goldsmith at 8*d.* and a Franklin at 1*s.*2*d.*—competed with Whittingham's Cabinet Library, pocket-sized volumes selling from 2*s.* to 4*s.*6*d.* Also bidding for the shillings of the modestly circumstanced booklover were John Sharpe, with his Works of the English Poets in 2*s.* parts, and John Fowler Dove, whose large series of miniature classics embraced such diverse items as *The Compleat Angler* and Pope's *Poetical Works*.

While none of these reprint libraries achieved wide circulation, the persistence of a number of small publishers in starting them and in keeping prices as low as possible indicates that these men, at least, sought to cater to the common readers' market for literature. Although one finds fewer tributes to these books from readers whom they delighted than to the fondly remembered Bell and Cooke reprints of an earlier decade, they played their part in encouraging an interest in literature among those who could afford neither the more expensive editions of the classics nor the high-priced books of recent seasons.[21]

II (1825–32). Thus during the first twenty-five years of the nineteenth century the (relatively) "cheap" market was left almost entirely to small publishers who lacked the resources necessary to produce copyright books for the well-to-do public. These men were regarded by the moguls of British publishing much as a modern custom tailor regards a credit clothier. Only in 1824 did a leader of the book trade begin to mull over the possibilities of exploiting the growing mass public. In May of the following year, at Scott's Abbotsford, Archibald Constable portentously unveiled the results of his deliberations.

While Scott pushed the bottles around the table, the red-faced

[20] On Limbird, see the *Bookseller*, November 30, 1859, pp. [1326–27], and January 5, 1884, p. 6.

[21] Another important source of cheap books during this period, as well as later, was the remainder and reprint specialist, Thomas Tegg. His activities will be discussed below, pp. 284–85.

publisher announced that "printing and bookselling, as instruments for enlightening and entertaining mankind, and, of course, for making money, are as yet in mere infancy. Yes, the trade are in their cradle." He "sucked in fresh inspiration" (as his host's biographer, Lockhart, describes it) and proceeded to argue that hundreds of thousands of British subjects who paid luxury taxes never bought a book. Take the single item of hair powder, he said: even though it had gone out of style, the number of people who still used it, and paid the tax on it, "are an army, compared to the purchasers of even the best and most popular of books."

Scott remarked that no laird in the Abbotsford neighborhood spent ten pounds a year on reading matter. "No," said Constable, "there is no market among them that's worth one's thinking about. They are contented with a review or a magazine, or at best with a paltry subscription to some circulating library forty miles off. But if I live for half-a-dozen years, I'll make it as impossible that there should not be a good library in every decent house in Britain as that the shepherd's ingle-nook should want the *saut poke*. Ay, and what's that? why should the ingle-nook itself want a shelf for *the novels?*" Constable's excitement mounted as he contemplated the multitude of lower-class readers who might be served. "I have hitherto been thinking only of the wax lights," he said, "but before I'm a twelvemonth older I shall have my hand upon the tallow."

And so "the grand Napoleon of the realms of print," as Scott then dubbed him, planned his campaign of Marengo: "a three shilling or half-crown volume every month, which must and shall sell, not by thousands or tens of thousands, but by hundreds of thousands—ay, by millions! Twelve volumes in the year . . . so good that millions must wish to have them, and so cheap that every butcher's callant may have them, if he pleases to let me tax him sixpence a-week!"

"Such were," observes Lockhart, ". . . the first outlines of a daring plan never destined to be carried into execution on the gigantic scale, or with the grand appliances which the projector contemplated, but destined, nevertheless, to lead the way in one of the greatest revolutions that literary history will ever have to record."[22] A few months later (January, 1826), Constable, the Napoleon of print, met his Waterloo in a bankruptcy that shook the whole British publishing world. Constable's Miscellany, as the

[22] Lockhart, VII, 126–30.

new brain child was named, was extricated from the ruins in January, 1827, when its first volume, a reprint of Captain Basil Hall's *Voyages*, appeared. A new volume, priced at 3*s*.6*d*., came out approximately every three weeks. In the Miscellany there was something for every serious taste: Chambers' *History of the Rebellion*, Lockhart's *Life of Burns*, Gilbert White's *Natural History of Selborne*, Wilson and Bonaparte's *American Ornithology*, and Archdeacon Wrangham's *Evidences of Christianity*. But the vision of its projector, a sale of millions, did not materialize, because both the intellectual tone and the price were too high for most of the intended audience. "The millions," Charles Knight later remarked, "were not ready to buy such books at a shilling, nor even at sixpence."[23] The Miscellany's main importance is that it was the first noteworthy attempt to pull down the price of new or recent nonfiction from the heights to which it had climbed in the past several decades.

Meanwhile, in 1826, another scheme for the production of cheap non-fiction was taking shape. The projector this time (not surprisingly) was Henry Brougham. There was little point, said Brougham, in the schoolmaster's being abroad if he were not followed by the vendor of wholesome reading matter. So he and his disciples formed the Society for the Diffusion of Useful Knowledge, to serve the same public for which the mechanics' institutes were then being founded—skilled workingmen and their families.[24] In the spring of 1827, hard on the heels of Constable's Miscellany, the society began to issue its Library of Useful Knowledge. Fortnightly parts were 6*d*. each, the thirty-two closely printed pages being advertised to contain as much text as a hundred ordinary pages. The subjects were almost exclusively scientific and utilitarian—differential and integral calculus, the art of brewing, the calculation of annuities and reversions, and "animal mechanics." During the first eighteen months, thanks to enthusiastic notices in the always helpful *Edinburgh Review* and the formation of local committees to stimulate distribution, each issue sold between 22,350 and 27,900 copies.[25]

Late in 1829, as if already aware that "useful knowledge" had a

[23] *The Old Printer and the Modern Press*, p. 243.

[24] The fullest firsthand account of the Useful Knowledge Society is in Knight, *Passages of a Working Life*, Vol. II.

[25] Webb, *The British Working Class Reader*, p. 69.

limited appeal, the society undertook a companion series, the Library of Entertaining Knowledge, issued in 2s. parts, or in complete volumes at 4s.6d. The weightiness of the subjects treated in this series merely demonstrates that "entertaining" is a relative term. Typical titles included *Egyptian Antiquities, The Elgin Marbles, Insect Architecture, Pompeii, Secret Societies of the Middle Ages, Vegetable Substances* (in three volumes), and *The Menageries* (in four).

Under Charles Knight's vigorous direction as superintendent of publications, the society branched out into other lines. Its *British Almanac* helped drive from the market the superstitious and sometimes obscene almanacs that had been common for centuries. In 1832–33, with the society's blessing, Knight established the *Penny Magazine* and the *Penny Cyclopaedia*, both of which will appear later in these pages. Each new venture involved the society, and Knight, in deeper financial complications. In the mid-forties they finally bit off more than they could chew: a biographical dictionary undertaken on so ambitious a plan that seven half-volumes were used up by the letter *A* alone, at a loss of £5,000. When contributors were invited to suggest names for inclusion under *B*, and one man sent in over two thousand, the society voted to disband.[26]

Brougham encouraged contemporary Britain to credit the society with having made cheap literature a reality.[27] In a sense, this was true. Its publications were genuinely inexpensive according to the prevailing standards. But one may question whether Müller's *History of Greek Literature* (a "useful" book) or Lane's *Manners and Customs of Modern Egyptians* (an "entertaining" one) gladdened many humble chimney corners. And though it was doubtless a fine thing for the society to give the world a shilling reprint of Bacon's *Novum Organum*, such readers as the book found were not mechanics.

The truth was that the Useful Knowledge Society expected the

[26] Curwen, p. 263.

[27] At least some of the *Edinburgh Review's* encomiums of the society's work were from Brougham's own pen; see Arthur Aspinall, *Lord Brougham and the Whig Party* (Manchester, 1927), pp. 235, 259–60. For a later paean of self-congratulation, see Brougham's address, "The Diffusion of Knowledge," *Transactions of the National Association for the Promotion of Social Science* (1858), pp. 25–42. A slashing contemporary attack on the society is "Useful Knowledge," *Westminster Review*, XIV (1831), 365–94. Webb, pp. 66–73, 85–90, 114–22, provides an admirable antidote to previous historians' uncritical acceptance of the society's claims.

common reader, whose formal education likely had ended at twelve or fourteen, if not much earlier, to relish a home university course. Not only were the topics of the books too difficult for all but the most ambitious or brilliant students; the manner of treatment was undeviatingly dull. While the authors may not have been "literary Gibeonites," to use Carlyle's phrase,[28] some of them were professors at the new London University, and that was just as bad. The didactic prose of the era seldom was very lively, but in the hands of the men commissioned by the society it became positively leaden. Although some improvement is discernible in the *Penny Magazine* and the *Penny Cyclopaedia*, for the most part the prose published in behalf of the diffusion of useful knowledge cannot be conceived of as having quickened the appetite for reading among the masses.[29]

Brougham's further claim, that the society had been "eminently conducive to allaying the reckless spirit which, in 1830, was leading multitudes to destroy property and break up machines,"[30] is hardly borne out by history. The society had done its best to promote a brighter view of industrialization than was then common among the Cobbett-agitated working class; among its books were such works of reconciliation as Charles Knight's *Results of Machinery* and *Rights of Industry*. But the popular upheavals of the late thirties and early forties are proof enough that the society's message failed to reach, or at all events to impress, the great majority of workers.

What the Useful Knowledge Society did achieve was the publicizing of the *idea* of cheap, enlightening literature. The desirability of cheap books with "healthy tendencies"—to combat the notorious twopenny trash—had occasionally been discussed in various quarters, but now, for the first time, it became the subject of an

[28] *Correspondence between Goethe and Carlyle*, ed. C. E. Norton (1887), p. 169.

[29] Only those who have glanced through typical volumes of the Libraries of Useful and Entertaining Knowledge can appreciate the full extent of Brougham's self-delusion, when in 1852 he told his long-time coadjutor, Matthew D. Hill, that they had innocently been responsible for the degeneracy of popular taste: "This influence of romance-writers is getting to be a crying evil—for nothing else is now-a-day [*sic*] read but novels. I fear we of the Useful Knowledge Society are a little to blame because we made science entertaining, and so tended to spoil people's appetite" (Rosamond and Florence Davenport-Hill, *The Recorder of Birmingham: A Memoir of Matthew Davenport Hill* [1878], p. 332). The society's treatises may well have stimulated readers' desire for fiction, but not in the way Brougham thought.

[30] Knight, *Passages of a Working Life*, II, 310.

intensive propaganda campaign and, even more important, an avowed goal of reformers. From 1826 onward, the topic was recurrently debated in the press, on the platform, and in Parliament. The society's activities and the publicity it received were not, however, an unmixed blessing to the cause of cheap literature. Brougham and his co-workers were attacked from many sides. The commercial publishers accused them of trying to set up a monopoly and "threatening to destroy the legitimate thrones and dominions of the empire of books." Rumors were spread that the idea of the *Penny Cyclopaedia* had been stolen from a poor man struggling to maintain his family and that the writers employed for it were all hacks, lifting their material from books in the British Museum.[31] The society was frequently accused of questionable business practices.[32]

Nor was commercial jealousy the only reason for opposition. Everyone who disliked Brougham as a person or utilitarianism as a doctrine joined the outcry. Carlyle, although he told Goethe in 1830 that the society's treatises were "really very meritorious," later echoed the current jest that the society was really dedicated to "the 'Confusion' of useful Knowledge," and complained to John Stuart Mill of the "triumphant quackle-quackling of the Diffusion Society intent only on sine and cosine."[33] In his *Crotchet Castle* Thomas Love Peacock managed a diverting scene in which Dr. Folliott's cook, a greasy and highly inflammable subject, took to bed with her the "Steam Intellect Society's" sixpenny pamphlet on hydrostatics, written by a "learned friend"—obviously Brougham— "who is for doing all the world's business as well as his own, and is equally well qualified to handle every branch of human knowledge." The cook fell asleep, the candle overturned and set

[31] *Ibid.*, II, 236.

[32] Harriet Martineau recorded that a member of the society's committee on publications invited her to write a life of John Howard, the prison reformer, and promised her a fee of £30. She turned in her manuscript, but received no payment. Later she found that "half-a-dozen or more Lives of Howard had been ordered in a similar manner, by different members of the Committee; . . . my manuscript was found, after several years, at the bottom of a chest,—not only dirty, but marked and snipped,—its contents having been abundantly used without any acknowledgment,—as was afterwards admitted to me by some of the members. . . ." Nor, she added, was she the only writer to endure such shabby treatment (*Autobiography* [Boston, 1877], I,107).

[33] Letter to Goethe cited above, n. 28; *Correspondence of Thomas Carlyle and Ralph Waldo Emerson*, ed. C. E. Norton (Boston, 1884), I, 24; *Letters of Thomas Carlyle to John Stuart Mill, John Sterling and Robert Browning*, ed. Alexander Carlyle (1923), p. 118.

the curtains ablaze, and tragedy was averted only by the opportune arrival of the footman, who, Dr. Folliott supposed, had come to the cook's bedroom to help her study hydrostatics. "Sir," said Mr. Firedamp, the meteorologist, "you seem to make very light of science." "Yes, sir," rejoined Dr. Folliott, "such science as the learned friend deals in: every thing for every body, science for all, schools for all, rhetoric for all, law for all, physic for all, words for all, and sense for none. . . . I wish the learned friend, for all his life, a cook that will pass her time in studying his works; then every dinner he sits down to at home, he will sit on the stool of repentance."[34]

While the flippant ridiculed the society, the sober-sided took a graver view. When Charles Knight was traveling from town to town, organizing local committees to carry on the good work, he was warned that people still were fearful of "Corresponding Societies, Carbonari, Tugendbund, Jesuits, and other frightful images."[35] He had to explain very carefully to prospective subscribers that the elaborate organization of the society implied no sinister conspiracy against church or state. The press, this time, was to be used for the most benign of purposes, the confirming of the established order.

Constable's Miscellany and the Library of Useful Knowledge together touched off one of the most exciting periods in English publishing history and, in the long view, one of the most fruitful. In April, 1829, John Murray brought out his Family Library, composed of biographies, histories, and travel narratives, closely followed by other non-fiction series: Lardner's Cabinet Library, the Edinburgh Cabinet Library of Oliver and Boyd, and Colburn and Bentley's National Library—all priced initially at 5s. At the same time, and at the same price, William Pickering issued the first dainty volumes of the older poets in his famous Aldine series.

But most momentous of all, in view of the increasing popular appetite for novels, was the attention given to the recent-fiction reprint. In June, 1829, Thomas Cadell, who had bought Constable's huge stock of Scott's works following the crash, issued the

---

[34] *Crotchet Castle*, chap. ii.

[35] *Passages of a Working Life*, II, 93. Nothing better epitomizes the spirit of the age than Knight's reply to the fellow "bagmen" he met on his journeys: "Pray, sir, what do you travel in?" "In Useful Knowledge, sir" (*ibid.*, II, 76).

"Author's Edition of the Waverley Novels" in five-shilling volumes, full-length novels occupying two or more volumes. Thus, ironically, did Constable's dream come true under the auspices of the man who salvaged his ruins; and thus, too, did Scott's works, which had led the price of fiction to the highest level in history, start it downward once again.

Less than two years later—in February, 1831—began Colburn and Bentley's famous and long-lived series of Standard Novels at 6s., most of which, in contrast to Cadell's Waverley, contained complete works in a single volume. The forbiddingly expensive three-decker at 31s.6d. now had a rival in the 5s. or 6s. reprint.[36] The price was only a half or a third of what had been paid for a complete novel even before the Scott-inspired inflation had set in, and less than a fifth of what a fashionable novel now cost in its original edition.[37]

Between 1827 and 1832, therefore, London and Edinburgh publishers behaved as if they stood on a peak in Darien, beholding for the first time a vast sea of common readers. Suddenly—and belatedly—the prosperous artisan or clerk with a few shillings to spend loomed more important than the gentleman with a guinea or two. Contributing to the excitement over the potentialities of cheap reprint publishing was an unusual dearth of good new books, a situation which always turns publishers' minds toward reviving their back lists, and the political crisis, which deterred the trade, still convalescing from the panic of 1826, from sinking capital in new copyrights so long as the times were unsettled.

In 1831 it was not unusual to find that over half the titles issued in a given week, whether reprints or originals, belonged to one cheap series or another.[38] A lively anthology might be made of journalistic comments on the craze. In general, it was the "useful knowledge" aspect, rather than the cheapening of reprinted fic-

---

[36] For the next two decades, however, apart from one or two abortive efforts by other houses, only Bentley and Colburn made a regular practice of reissuing current fiction at reduced prices. After the middle of the century such reprints became much more common.

[37] For a detailed account of the cheap series, 1827–32, see Sadleir, II, 91–94.

[38] The word *library* became, and was to remain, a favorite term in the publishers' merchandising vocabulary. Its use was increasingly elastic, denoting not only a formal series but also any miscellaneous collection of titles whose sale a firm hoped to promote by suggesting that a reader who bought one should eventually buy them all. Cobbett, who never overlooked a promising trick of the trade, promptly christened his own highly diversified list of writings "The Cobbett Library."

tion, that received the greater attention. "This is the age of sub-division of labour," remarked the *Athenaeum:* "four men make a pin and two men describe it in a book for the working classes."[39]

In the pages of *Blackwood's*, the worthies of the "Noctes Ambrosianae" raised what is, for our purposes at least, the most crucial question concerning the first great burst of cheap "wholesome" books. "The people," remarked Christopher North, "appear to me to want bread rather than books."

"Let them hae baith," said James Hogg, the Ettrick shepherd.

"But bread first, James," replied North.

"Shurely—for wha can read to ony purpose on an empty stamach?"[40]

This was one matter, at least, on which the *Blackwood's* coterie and Cobbett saw eye to eye. Cobbett acidly remarked that the workingmen who kept the middle class well fed and well clothed were paid in water porridge, potatoes, and "ample *food for their minds*." "It is a curious fact," he added, "that, within these four or five years, no less than four corn mills in the neighbourhood of Uxbridge, and several in the neighbourhood of Maidstone, have been turned into paper mills! One would think that the poor souls had actually taken to eating the books."[41]

Such comments at once place in perspective the celebrated "cheapness" of the books that flooded the market in the late twenties and early thirties. Cheap the books were, when measured against standard trade prices. The purchaser got his money's worth, if not in physical comeliness (for the type was small and the margins narrow, and every other aspect of the "economy book" was present), at least in actual amount of printed matter.

But how many could afford them? Not as many, certainly, as the sanguine publishers thought. After reaching a level of 187 in 1813, the cost-of-living index (using 1790 as a base of 100) had come down to 109 by 1832.[42] But if commodities were relatively

[39] *Athenaeum*, September 28, 1833, p. 650; see also its issues for July 24 and September 25, 1830, pp. 449, 593.

[40] *Blackwood's Magazine*, XXVIII (1830), 847.

[41] Quoted in Collins, *The Profession of Letters*, p. 267.

[42] This is the Silberling index, based chiefly on the cost of living among the urban lower-middle class and therefore applicable particularly to the social group from which the majority of new readers were drawn at this period; see Cole and Postgate, *The Common People*, pp. 85, 198.

cheap, wages were also low. Farm workers were worse off, indeed, than they had been a generation earlier. Except for certain favored groups of skilled artisans, especially in London, industrial workers, the victims of a glutted labor market, lived constantly on the edge of starvation. A skilled London worker in the thirties earned about 30s. or 33s. a week; hence a volume of the Library of Entertaining Knowledge (4s.6d.) would have cost him almost a day's wages. The cost, reckoned in terms of labor, would have been far higher to a Glasgow carpenter, who made 14s. a week in 1832, and unthinkable to a handloom weaver, whom the blessings of machinery had reduced to a weekly income of 5s.6d.[43]

It was merely fanciful, therefore, to regard the great majority of literate workers as forming an eager public for so-called cheap books. Like the Reform Bill which coincided with it, the cheap-book movement was of immediate benefit primarily, if not exclusively, to the middle class. The buying power of this widening social stratum must not, however, be exaggerated. A family was thought to be "respectable" if it had a weekly income of 48s., or roughly £125 a year; a beneficed clergyman lived well, if hardly in splendor, on £300 or £400; an officer of the line could marry on £200 to £400. In 1834 Trollope began his clerkship at the General Post Office at £90 a year and after seven years made £140. Browning's father, after forty-nine years of service, earned only £275 a year as a clerk at the Bank of England.[44] Meanwhile five shillings —the price of a reprinted novel—would buy five pounds of butter, or ten pounds of meat; and seven shillings would provide a family of five with good table beer for a month.[45] Hence the middle-class booklover of moderate means, though able to patronize a bookshop occasionally, could not afford to buy many volumes even at the reduced rates of the early thirties. Books remained a minor luxury.

The important thing, however, is that the class of readers who

---

[43] *Ibid.*, pp. 136–38, 199–202. Typical budgets for early Victorian families belonging to various income groups are given, along with the prices of specific commodities, in G. M. Young (ed.), *Early Victorian England* (1934), I, 104–108, 126–34.

[44] Young, I, 107–108, 126–27; Anthony Trollope, *Autobiography*, ed. B. A. Booth (Berkeley, Calif., 1947), pp. 30, 43; Betty Miller, *Robert Browning: A Portrait* (New York, 1953), p. 20.

[45] Young, I, 127.

had a little money to spend for books grew so markedly in the period following the advent of Knight, Cadell, Bentley, and other innovators that it could never again be neglected by publishers. By 1850 about 110,000 families had an annual income of over £150. Of these, by far the greater portion belonged to the middle or lower-middle class: 39,500 families reported a taxable income of £150–£200, 29,400 an income of £200–£300, and 14,400 an income of £300–£400.[46] These families, willing to spend five or six shillings on a book but seldom more, constituted the prime market for cheap books in the era between the first Reform Bill and the middle of the century.

III (1833–50). Although the tide of cheap books receded temporarily after 1832, leaving many small publishers high and dry, it deposited on the beach some ideas and innovations which in the long run were destined to revolutionize English publishing. Conspicuous among them were technological advances in bookmaking. Only as the market expanded were mass-production techniques found practicable; but once they were introduced, they brought down costs, and the cheapening of books, by further enlarging the market, encouraged the search for still better manufacturing methods. It was fitting that the books of the Useful Knowledge Society, which extolled the benefits of industrialism, were among the first to be printed on the new steam presses. By 1839 the society's printer, William Clowes, had nineteen such presses at work, each capable of turning out a thousand sheets an hour. Taking full advantage of steam printing and stereotypes, he was the great pioneer of mass-produced books and periodicals. In the 1830's and 1840's steam replaced hand operations throughout the book-printing trade.[47]

Meanwhile paper, the shortage of which had been partly responsible for the high prices of books earlier in the century, declined somewhat as a major factor in production costs. Handmade paper was replaced, for ordinary purposes, by the product of machines. As prices fell, however, the paper duty, even though halved in

[46] Levi, *Wages and Earnings of the Working Classes*, p. 48.

[47] Plant, *The English Book Trade*, pp. 275–79. For the comparative hourly output of the early mechanical presses, see *The History of "The Times,"* I, 119. An article, "The Printer's Devil," *Quarterly Review*, LXV (1839), 1–30, gives a detailed description of Clowes's establishment at this time.

1837, became proportionally more burdensome, and there was growing agitation to abolish it entirely.[48]

The substitution of cheaper bindings for leather helped reduce book costs in the century's second quarter. Boards were first used extensively by the cheap series of 1828–32. Just at this time, also, Archibald Leighton put on the market a cloth specially made for bookbinding, and within a few years the cloth-bound book was commonplace. To avoid the slow, expensive operation of sewing the binding around the sheets (a grave handicap in days when wholesalers raced one another to supply circulating libraries with novels hot from the press) the publisher's casing, a pre-made case into which the folded sheets were glued, was invented. This quickly replaced old-fashioned bindings as the normal garb of moderate-priced books.[49]

Though the 12mo or 16mo pocket volume dates from as far back as the time of Aldus Manutius and the Elzevirs, this was the period when it achieved the great popularity it has since retained. As reading habits changed, larger formats became distinctly inconvenient; one of the reasons why the eighteenth-century novel was issued in handy 12mo size was that it was read by so many women. When reading ceased to be confined to its traditional indoor locale and was practiced outdoors and in public vehicles, pocket-sized volumes became more and more necessary. And there was, obviously, the matter of cost. "Men," said John Murray, as reported by the bibliophile Dibdin, "wished to get for *five*, what they knew they could not formerly obtain for *fifteen*, shillings. The love of quartos was well nigh extinct. . . . There was no resisting the tide of fashion. . . . The dwarf had vanquished the giant—and . . . Laputa [*sic!*] was lording it over Brobdignag."[50] The effect was circular: the diversification of the reading audience and therefore of the circumstances under which reading was done, as well as the low price, had brought the small book into esteem, and its added convenience in turn made reading a more appealing and practical pastime than ever before.

Returning from the printing house and bindery to the pub-

---

[48] Plant, pp. 329–33.

[49] *Ibid.*, pp. 343–53; Michael Sadleir, *The Evolution of Publishers' Binding Styles, 1770–1900* (New York, 1930), pp. 31–32, 61–62.

[50] [T. F. Dibdin], *Bibliophobia* (1832), p. 31.

lisher's office, another great occurrence of the thirties and forties was the first formidable challenge to the supremacy of the guinea-and-a-half three-decker as a vehicle for the original publication of fiction. When, early in 1836, Chapman and Hall first laid plans for the book that became *The Posthumous Papers of the Pickwick Club*, they had in mind the sort of thing that had become popular with William Combe's *Dr. Syntax's Tours* (1812–21) and Pierce Egan's *Life in London* (1820–21)—a picture book issued in parts, with just enough letterpress to give continuity to the entertaining illustrations. But by a course of events famous in literary history, the *Pickwick Papers* turned out to be something quite different. After a discouragingly slow start, what began as a routine publishing venture turned into a sensation. By Part 15 the sale was a phenomenal 40,000 copies per issue. Young Dickens found himself even more famous than Scott and Byron had been in their time; *Pickwick* became a popular fad; and the part-issue of new fiction won an acceptance it was to enjoy until the seventies, when the competition of magazine serialization and cheap one-volume reprints finally proved too much for it. Dickens, Thackeray, Ainsworth, Lever, and Trollope issued many of their novels in numbers, sometimes simultaneously with magazine serialization.[51] During the first decades after *Pickwick*, the monthly parts of a new novel were usually priced at a shilling. This method of publication had several great advantages for the purchaser. Like number-issues in general, it spread the cost of a book over a long period, thus appealing to the great body of middle-class readers who could afford to spend a shilling every month but not to lay out a cool guinea or a guinea and a half at a time. And it actually reduced the price in two ways. Had *Pickwick*, for instance, made its original appearance in book form, almost certainly it would have cost 31*s*.6*d*. But its total price in parts was 20*s*., and upon completion of the part-issue it was published in bound form at only a shilling more.[52] Nor was this all. Most books published in parts were, like

---

[51] For a contemporary review of the influence of the part-issue, see *Publishers' Circular*, November 1, 1866, pp. 649–50.

[52] In general, only novels that first appeared in parts subsequently came out in book form at less than the customary price. Fiction serialized in half-crown periodicals like *Bentley's Miscellany* usually reappeared as "library" novels at 31*s*.6*d*. or 21*s*. This was true also of the novels serialized in the shilling magazines that supplanted the half-crown miscellanies after 1860.

Pickwick, expansive affairs; so that for his guinea—a third less than the price of an ordinary three-decker—the purchaser received not merely a novel of three-decker length but a considerably longer one.

Now English readers began to resume the habit of buying books rather than borrowing. It took a degree of self-discipline few men possessed to listen to one's friends speculating on what would happen in Mr. Dickens' next number and yet delay one's own reading of the book until, long months in the future, it was complete, bound, and available in the circulating library. And Dickens' novels, unlike run-of-the-mine fiction, were books to be kept on the household shelf, to be read over and over again. The immense sale of Dickens' works revealed to the early Victorian publishing trade the size of the public that would—if the author were sufficiently popular and the price were right—patronize bookshop as well as library. Not that the circulating libraries suffered as a consequence of Dickens' vogue; their heyday, indeed, was yet to come. But in the enlarged market of the period there was plenty of room for both buyers and subscribers.

Meanwhile, fresh attention was given to the cheapening of non-fiction. In Edinburgh, William and Robert Chambers, brothers who had read Lackington's memoirs with profit, became imbued with the idea of furnishing cheap wholesome literature to the multitude. Their first major venture in that direction, *Chambers's Edinburgh Journal*, of which an account will appear in a later chapter, was so successful that they decided to use its large-scale production and distribution channels for other purposes. Beginning in 1833–35 with *Information for the People*, in fortnightly numbers at $1\frac{1}{2}d.$, they published an extensive assortment of nonfiction serials—the *Miscellany of Useful and Entertaining Information, Papers for the People*, the *Pocket Miscellany*, and the *Repository of Instructive and Amusing Tracts*. All these publications were devised on the shrewd theory that most readers disliked reading too long upon a single subject; therefore they resembled magazines more than books, offering potpourris of science, geography, history, literature, fireside amusements, and other material with popular appeal. The *Papers for the People*, for instance, included informative pieces, written by reputable journalists, on such subjects as "The Sepulchres of Etruria," "Ebenezer Elliott," "The

Sanitary Movement," "Francis Jeffrey," "Arctic Explorations," "Every-day Life of the Greeks," "Sir Robert Peel," and "The Science of the Sunbeam."[53]

A second leading publisher of "improving" literature in the period 1830–50 was Charles Knight. Knight merits remembrance for his own sake, and not merely as the publisher for the Society for the Diffusion of Useful Knowledge. His *Passages of a Working Life* is one of the most readable and continuously interesting of Victorian autobiographies. It reveals him—and all contemporary evidence substantiates this impression—as an attractive person, energetic, idealistic (though without the stridency of the typical Victorian zealot), resilient (as he certainly had to be), and thoroughly in love with life.[54] In his own time he was looked upon as the very symbol of the cheap-book movement, and he fully deserved this distinction; for no one worked harder, and at greater personal sacrifice, for this cause in which he passionately believed. Furthermore, as his comments which have occasionally been quoted in these pages suggest, there was no more level-headed student of the whole problem of the mass reading public. He clung to some illusions, it is true, and he made some mistakes, but on the whole he had a refreshingly sane conception of what obstacles delayed the spread of the reading habit, what the people really wanted to read, and how a publisher should go about fulfilling their wishes—at the same time doing his bit to improve their taste.

Knight's leading motive, first as a journalist and then as a publisher, was to make decent the popular reading matter of the time. He was for Constitution and God, though not a fanatic on either account, and he was profoundly disturbed by the irreligious and seditious quality of the printed matter available to the masses, especially before the countermovement began in the late twenties. Unlike many of his fellow workers in the cheap-literature field, he was a moderate, tolerant man who wished simply to make the printed page the agent of peace, justice, and pleasure. One may well believe (and in his memoirs he sometimes hints as much) that

[53] Two small books by William Chambers, *Memoir of Robert Chambers* and *Story of a Long and Busy Life*, are the principal sources of material on the firm. Additional information is scattered through the files of *Chambers's Edinburgh Journal.*

[54] At the end of a cozy evening together, Knight asked his friend Douglas Jerrold to propose an epitaph for him. "Good (K)night," replied Jerrold (*Publishers' Circular*, March 17, 1873, pp. 177–78).

he was often uncomfortable in the company of some of the members of the Useful Knowledge Society, whose views were at once more dogmatic, narrower, and more impractical than his own.

Perhaps his most influential contribution to the education of the common reader, apart from the *Penny Magazine*, was the *Penny Cyclopaedia*, issued in weekly parts beginning in 1833. Unlike some encyclopedias which sold for more, it was no scissors-and-paste job, but a collection of original articles commissioned from experts. Special efforts were made to keep the writing as clear as possible, and its substance was solid, many articles comparing well with the corresponding ones in the *Britannica*. Nor did it have the narrowly utilitarian bias that blighted most of the society's other publications. Generous space was given to articles on the fine arts, for example, and on literature; in the latter department the contributors included such writers as George Lillie Craik, George Henry Lewes, and J. R. Planché.

The completion of the *Cyclopaedia* in twenty-seven volumes, in the spring of 1844, was celebrated by a "sumptuous entertainment" at the Albion Tavern, with Brougham in the chair and Knight as honored guest. The celebration was well deserved, because to bring the work to a triumphant conclusion had involved a heroic struggle on Knight's part. He had to bear the entire burden of financing, and his loss at the end was £30,788. In addition to the £42,000 expended for text and illustrations, he had had to pay £16,500 in paper duty. It is little wonder that he was conspicuous among the crusaders for the abolition of the taxes on knowledge.[55]

However costly and harassing his connection with the Useful Knowledge Society was, it never diverted Knight from his lifelong goal. The losses he sustained on the society's publications seem to have been offset, at least in part, by his success with the books he issued independently. His *Pictorial Shakespeare, Pictorial History*

---

[55] Knight, *Passages of a Working Life*, II, 200–204, 308, 331–36. The case of the *Penny Cyclopaedia* was Exhibit A in the last stages of the campaign for the total repeal of the paper duty, which was widely alleged to stand in the way of really cheap literature. When the Chambers brothers brought one of their miscellanies to a close, they sometimes explained that it had been "absolutely choked to death by the [paper] tax." Thomas Frost, the ex-Chartist who wrote for *Papers for the People*, said that that publication was discontinued despite its popularity simply because the Chamberses wanted to dramatize the iniquity of the duty (Chambers, *Story of a Long and Busy Life*, pp. 93–94; Frost, *Forty Years' Recollections*, pp. 195–96). The effectiveness of this sort of propaganda, however, must have been somewhat dulled by the firm's constant readiness to start a new series, paper tax or no paper tax.

of England, and *Pictorial Bible* were superior examples of number-publications, though their cost limited their sale to the fairly well-to-do. Using the profits from this side of his business to keep solvent, he continued to experiment with books for the million. Within weeks after the *Penny Cyclopaedia* was completed, and while the society's ill-fated biographical dictionary was still coping with the letter *A*, he launched his Weekly Volumes, pocket-sized books costing a shilling in paper, 18*d*. in cloth, and prepared with special attention to durability, so that they could be passed from reader to reader. This was in June, 1844, three years before complete novels became available at the same low price. The list of titles included such items as *The Civil Wars of Rome*, *The History of the Dog*, *The Dutch in the Medway*, Miss Martineau's *Feats on the Fiord*, and *Mind amongst the Spindles*, a selection from the *Lowell Offering*. Many of the volumes were collections of material already printed in the *Penny Magazine* and other publications whose copyright Knight owned. A distinguishing feature of the series was the sprinkling of volumes devoted to literary subjects—Lamb's *Tales from Shakespeare*, G. L. Craik's *Literature of England*, John Saunders' condensation of *The Canterbury Tales*, and Knight's own study of Caxton.

Knight considered the venture a success, mainly because it did not lose him any money. Although it enjoyed much prestige (the queen, for example, commanded that copies be placed in each of her palaces) sales averaged less than 5,000 copies per title, and not more than twenty titles sold as many as 10,000. "The volumes," wrote Knight, "were not cheap enough for the humble, who looked to mere quantity. They were too cheap for the genteel, who were then taught to think that a cheap book must necessarily be a bad book."[56] Again, Knight knew that his books had to fight a grim and really foredoomed battle with fiction in cheap periodicals and in the brand-new "railway novels," which were as cheap as the Weekly Volumes and, to the common run of readers, a great deal more entertaining.

Among the pioneers of cheap books in the first half of the century, Knight was held in perhaps highest respect; he had ideals, but he never made a fortune. At the opposite pole from him was

[56] Knight, *Passages of a Working Life*, II, 311–22; III, 11–17. See also his "Book-Clubs for All Readers," *Penny Magazine*, XIII (1844), 179–80.

Thomas Tegg, the undoubted monarch of a race whom Carlyle once categorized as "extraneous persons." Tegg had few discernible ideals, and Parliament was informed in 1840 that he had made a fortune of £200,000.[57] For whatever evil repute cheap books had among the genteel, Tegg and his kind were largely responsible.

Such information as comes down to us about Tegg—most of it strongly prejudiced—suggests more a myth than a man. There is no reason, however, to doubt the main outlines of his story.[58] A runaway apprentice from Dalkeith, he turned up in London in 1796 with the traditional few shillings in his pocket. He worked briefly at the Minerva Library, then started a bookselling business upon receipt of a £700 legacy, went bankrupt, started over again, and went bankrupt again—but this time his creditors thought it more prudent to let him remain in business. Perhaps in this young man, who always carried Franklin's *Essays* in his pocket, they discerned, and rightly so, an eye riveted upon the main chance. In any event, his practice was to buy large quantities of remainders, equip them with new title pages, and sell them at cut rates. "The broom that swept the booksellers' warehouses," as he described himself, he acquired the Ballantyne Novelist's Library after the crash of 1826. A few years later he bought the 100,000 remaining copies of Murray's Family Library for a shilling a volume and resold them for 3s.6d.

He was always on hand, like the secondhand clothes dealer after a funeral, when a publishing firm was fighting off creditors or on the sheer verge of extinction. Nor was he ever one to miss an expiring copyright in which some prospect of profit remained. He early discovered that a lucrative side line to his scavenging activities could be the reprinting in cheap form of books just out of copyright, or of popular abridgments of standard works. Up to 1840, he boasted, he had published under his own imprint 4,000

[57] Carlyle, *Critical and Miscellaneous Essays* (Centenary ed.; New York, 1896–1901), IV, 207; *Hansard*, Ser. 3, LI (1840), col. 1254.

[58] This account of Tegg is based on: *Bookseller*, September 1, 1870, pp. 756–57, reproducing material from Tegg's autobiography; Curwen, *History of Booksellers*, pp. 379–98 (unlike the next two items, a *nil nisi bonum* treatment); [James Grant], *Portraits of Public Characters* (1841), II, 24–46; Henry Vizetelly, *Glances Back through Seventy Years* (1893), I, 89; James S. Bain, *A Bookseller Looks Back* (1940), p. 137; Sadleir, *XIX Century Fiction*, II, 92, 94.

such works. Many stories circulated in the trade about his cavalier treatment of old authors. According to one, a printer who was running off a cheap *Paradise Lost* reported that the paper Tegg had given him was insufficient to complete the job. "How far can you go with what you have?" Tegg asked. "To the end of the Tenth Book," the printer said. "That will do," Tegg replied. "When you have come to the end of Book Ten put 'Finis,' and print no more." A variant of this story had it that his custom in reprinting old classics was simply to tear out as many pages at the end of the printer's copy as would reduce the book to his preordained dimensions. If the last remaining page ended in the midst of a sentence, the printer was directed to end at the last full stop.

Whether or not such stories were true, Tegg's reprints were notorious for their slovenly text and miserly format. But poor students were not finicky, and Tegg's books, whether remainders from some embarrassed publisher's warehouse or penuriously contrived reprints, made available hundreds of works that otherwise were beyond their reach. Tegg may have been execrated and ridiculed by the more respectable publishers, but it is likely that the many readers who could afford nothing better than his wares did not begrudge him the country house and carriage with which he crowned his career.

While Tegg had to be content with wealth and to forego honor, his successor as the nation's leading reprint specialist won both. Henry Charles Bohn, twenty years his junior, entered the literary salvaging trade in the early forties. Like Tegg, he soon began to publish under his own name the titles he acquired at auction or in the public domain. In 1846, in direct and (according to contemporary accounts) unscrupulous competition with David Bogue's European Library which was then beginning, Bohn issued the first volumes of his Standard Library, a highly miscellaneous non-fiction series priced at only 3*s*.6*d*., which was joined within a decade by eight other Bohn Libraries, at the uniform price of 5*s*. The Bohn Libraries as a group were one of the century's two or three most famous cheap reprint enterprises. Acquired by Bell and Daldy in 1864 for a reputed £40,000, they eventually ran to over seven hundred titles, the majority being standard texts in the various fields of the humanities which were otherwise available, if at all, only in expensive editions. The serious reader owed a substantial debt to these compact editions. In Victorian times they were valued as highly as the Cooke and Bell series had been fifty years earlier, and as the Everyman and World's Classics editions would be in the twentieth century.

IV. Thanks, therefore, to enterprise in certain areas of the trade, books were less expensive at mid-century than they had been during the first cheap-book movement of 1828–32. Between 1828 and 1853, according to Charles Knight's computation, the average price of a complete book declined from 16*s*. to 8*s*.$4\frac{1}{2}d$., or, in terms of single volumes, from 12*s*.1*d*. to 7*s*.$2\frac{1}{2}d$.[59] But the benefits of this reduction continued to be limited to the relatively prosperous minority—a steadily expanding minority, to be sure, but still only a fraction of the population. So far as the masses of people were concerned—the daily wage-earners and their families—George Dawson, a veteran mechanics' institute lecturer, did not seriously exaggerate when he told a committee of Parliament in 1849: "The fact is, we give the people in this country an appetite to read, and supply them with nothing. For the last many years in England everybody has been educating the people, but they have forgotten to find them any books. In plain language, you have made them hungry, but you have given them nothing to eat; it is almost a misfortune to a man to have a great taste for reading, and not to have the power of satisfying it."[60] The provision of cheap books still lagged far behind the spread of literacy.

True, the workman was somewhat better off economically than he had been two decades earlier. Though wages had risen little if at all, commodity prices had fallen, so that the purchasing power of the shilling had increased. Shillings nevertheless were still too precious, especially in an era of recurrent and widespread unemployment, to be spent on books. In 1850 London shipwrights made 36*s*. a week, builder's laborers 20*s*. Ironfounders had a weekly wage of 27*s*.6*d*. The average weekly wage in the Lancashire and Cheshire cotton factories was only 9*s*.6*d*.[61] In the light of such facts, Charles Knight was simply being realistic when, in projecting his Weekly Volumes a few years earlier, he patiently explained

[59] Knight, *The Old Printer and the Modern Press*, p. 261.

[60] Public Libraries Committee, Q. 1308.

[61] Cole and Postgate, pp. 296–97.

how his intended customers, these ordinary working people, could contrive to buy books costing a shilling. By laying aside a penny a week, he said, a family could purchase four such volumes in a year's time. Or twelve neighbors, or fellow workmen, or school-mates could club together, each contributing a penny a week, and thus could buy each volume as it came out.[62]

Knight and Dawson were entirely right in assuming that the book-buying capacity of the worker was still to be reckoned in pennies, not shillings. But their further assumption—that the man with only a few pence to spend would naturally prefer a good book, if good books were priced so low—was more dubious. Though the literacy rate was rising, the state of education among the masses was still dreadfully low. Only the existence of a strong spirit of self-education in these years justified the belief that even a small proportion of workers and their families would read the sort of books accounted "good" by educated middle-class standards.

As the forties drew to a close, the reformers' cry for truly cheap *wholesome* literature grew ever more urgent. And with good reason; for while the publishers who might have provided such fare stood fastidiously aloof from the penny market, the semiliterate masses were being amply supplied from the squalid fringes of the trade, the sensation-mongers of Salisbury Square and Holywell Street. The audience for sensational reading matter, whose unprecedented increase about the middle of the century deeply affected the future of the mass public, was itself not new; it was, in fact, as old as the ballad and the news broadside. How large it had already become somewhat earlier in the century is indicated by the success of James Catnach, whose electrifying chapbooks, ballads, and broadsides supplied the place yet unfilled by the popular newspaper.[63] No newsworthy event—no gory murder, no well-attended execution, no contested election, no marriage or death in the royal family—went uncommemorated by one or more of Catnach's "Seven Bards of Seven Dials," a stable of seedy authors who earned shillings for gin by composing to order. When times were dull, Catnach kept his presses busy by issuing fictitious accounts ("cocks")

[62] Knight, *Passages of a Working Life*, II, 313–14.

[63] On Catnach, see Hindley, *The Life and Times of James Catnach* and *The History of the Catnach Press;* and Ted Peterson, "James Catnach: Master of Street Literature," *Journalism Quarterly*, XXVII (1950), 157–63.

of murders, fires, and fearful accidents which were vended in the
streets, the hawkers' patter altering the scene of the event to suit
the neighborhoods in which they were working.

One of Catnach's most spectacular feats was the issue of a "Full,
True and Particular Account of the Murder of Mr. Weare by John
Thurtell and His Companions" in 1823. It is said that by working
four presses day and night, he produced a quarter-million copies
within a week. When Thurtell came to trial, even this record fell.
Catnach put two more printers to work, and in eight days they
turned off 500,000 copies of the trial proceedings. In 1828 he reputedly sold 1,166,000 copies of the "Last Dying Speech and Confession" of William Corder, the murderer of Maria Marten. This
astounding number itself was eclipsed by Catnach's last great
achievement in 1837, when the several "execution papers" called
forth by the expiation of James Greenacre and his paramour,
Sarah Gale, for the murder of Hannah Brown sold 1,650,000
copies. This figure might have gone even higher, according to a
veteran "running patterer," had not Greenacre's crime followed so
close upon another, equally sensational one. "That took the beauty
off him. Two murderers together is no good to nobody."[64]

Even after allowing generously for exaggeration, the sale of
Catnach's most successful productions is an impressive clue to the
size of the semiliterate public in his day. And Catnach, we must
remember, was but the most famous of the many printers who
supplied thrills by the pennyworth to the manual laborers, factory
hands, and domestic servants of London and the large industrial
towns. While he specialized in (more or less) factual horror, others
dealt in reading matter which, though no less terrifying, was
avowedly fiction. The most characteristic product of this branch
of the hole-in-the-wall book trade down to the thirties was the poor
man's Gothic novel, a crude sixpenny leaflet, bound in blue covers,
which abridged into thirty-six pages or so all the heart-stopping
excitements contrived by the school of Clara Reeve and Monk

[64] Homicides that came too close together to be commercially profitable were but one
of the hazards of this branch of the publishing trade. Another was the last-minute reprieve.
Accounts of executions and "last dying speeches" customarily were prefabricated so that
hawkers could be selling their wares in outlying districts practically at the moment the
trap was dropped. When the execution did not come off as scheduled, and news of the fiasco
reached the spot where a hawker was at work, some embarrassment naturally resulted.
Did Catnach give his unlucky hawkers an allowance on the unsold copies they brought
back to Seven Dials? (Tinsley, *Random Recollections of an Old Publisher*, I, 11.)

Lewis. These capsule entertainments were complete in themselves, but at the same time a thriving trade was developing in serial fiction adapted to the humble taste and pocketbook. In the 1820's, for instance, reprints of sensational or (less frequently) salacious fiction could be bought in numbers, priced at from 2d. to 6d., under such titles as *The French Novelist, The Story Teller,* and *Legends of Terror; and Tales of the Wonderful and the Wild.*

It was this kind of literature, no less than radical propaganda, that the cheap-book crusade of 1828–32 was intended to eradicate. The hope proved vain. Instead of withering away, the sensational-fiction industry flourished as never before, profiting by the publicity given the reading habit among the masses and by the widening popularity of the cheap serial.[65] The Salisbury Square publishers—John Clements, J. Cunningham, John Cleave, Edward Lloyd, and the rest—were to the bottom level of the reading public what Knight and the Chambers brothers were to the lower-middle class. Year after year in the thirties and forties, they stepped up their production of the various kinds of fiction that appealed to the man in the back street. The neo-Gothic novel retained its hold on popular affection; such works as *The Black Monk, or The Secret of the Grey Turret; Almira's Curse, or The Black Tower of Bransdorf; The Ranger of the Tomb, or The Gypsy's Prophesy;* and above all *Varney the Vampire, or The Feast of Blood* chilled the marrows of countless workingmen and their families, transporting them from their dingy world into the dungeons of sinister castles hidden in German forests, or convents where nuns found recreation in flogging screaming novices. Life was much easier to endure when one could read, with mounting horror, of the evil deeds of werewolves and vampires, specters and hags.

A near relative of the Gothic novel, the novel of sensational crime, came into great popularity during early Victorian days. This, connoisseurs agree, was one of the golden ages of English

[65] The ensuing discussion is based for the most part upon Turner, *Boys Will Be Boys,* chap. i—the whole book being an uncommonly diverting study of sensational literature from early Victorian days to our own; Montague Summers, *A Gothic Bibliography* (1942); Frost, pp. 86–95; testimony before the Public Libraries Committee and the Newspaper Stamp Committee; "The Literature of Vice," *Bookseller,* February 28, 1867, pp. 121–23; *Publishers' Circular,* December 31, 1866, p. 988; and W. Roberts, "Lloyd's Penny Bloods," *Book Collectors' Quarterly,* No. XVII (1935), 1–16. On the audience for sensational literature among the London poor, see the evidence in Mayhew, *London Labour and the London Poor,* I, 27, 467; III, 398–99.

crime, and current literature always has a healthy tendency to follow the headlines, if only by reviving classic analogues. In the
early thirties Bulwer produced *Paul Clifford* and *Eugene Aram;*
within a few years Dickens portrayed the fearful chiaroscuro of the
London underworld in *Oliver Twist;* and during the same period
Ainsworth was writing his popular Newgate novels. And if hunger
was great in Belgravia for such recitals of criminal adventure,
whether set in the present or in some past age, it was infinitely
greater in Bethnal Green. What Ainsworth brought to the drawing-room audience, the hacks of Salisbury Square manufactured
for the tenements.

Rivaling the Gothic romance and the crime novel in popularity
was the violently sentimental, or domestic, novel. Filled with
pathetic seductions, villainous fathers, suffering mothers, cruelly
treated children, and misunderstandings all around, these stories,
of which *Fatherless Fanny, or The Mysterious Orphan* was perhaps
the most famous, wrung floods of tears from the common reader.
In addition, there were rousing sea stories, concocted, as often as
not, by men whose maritime experience hardly extended beyond
the London docks, and filled with the adventures of pirates and
smugglers. Typical of them was the capaciously titled *The Death
Ship, or The Pirate's Bride and the Maniac of the Deep.* And during
the early phase of Dickens' vogue, Edward Lloyd, the future
owner of the *Daily Chronicle*, laid the basis of his publishing fortune, and evoked Dickens' almost apoplectic wrath, by supplying
the penny market with imitations under such transparent titles
as *The Penny Pickwick, Oliver Twiss, Nickelas Nicklebery,* and
Martin Guzzlewit.

The authors who toiled in the literary sweatshops of the period
are almost all forgotten now. Thomas Peckett Prest, who is credited with contriving the Dickens imitations for Lloyd, was the
creator of the immortal Sweeney Todd, the mad barber of Fleet
Street, and of countless other tales. The younger Pierce Egan, son
of the author of *Boxiana* and *Life in London,* specialized in Ains-
worthian sagas of crime and punishment. James Malcolm Rymer,
author of *Varney the Vampire*, is said to have kept ten serial stories
going at the same time. But he was a lackadaisical worker compared with G. W. M. Reynolds, the most successful of all Salisbury
Square romancers, of whom more in a moment.

The forms of publication adopted by the Salisbury Square firms closely imitated the modes formerly or currently popular in the more reputable precincts of the trade. Serial publication at weekly or fortnightly intervals was the ordinary practice, though a penny (or sometimes a halfpenny and sometimes twopence) was the standard price instead of the shilling charged for an instalment of middle-class reading matter. The serializing of reprint fiction under a generic title was continued in Salisbury Square long after it had dropped from fashion elsewhere. *The Romancist, and Novelist's Library*, about 1840, offered old novels in 2*d.* weekly parts, and whole batches of completed tales subsequently were bound up in volumes, primarily for the tiny lending libraries that catered to slum dwellers. In this diversified series Shelley's *Zastrozzi* and *St. Irvyne* and Walpole's *Castle of Otranto*—high-powered Gothic novels—stood side by side with Lamb's *Rosamund Gray* and *The Vicar of Wakefield*, fictions of quite a different flavor. About the same time, a similar serial, *The Novel Newspaper*, devoted itself to printing instalments of German Gothic novels and piracies of such popular American romancers as Cooper, Bird, and Paulding.[66]

When in 1836 the *Pickwick Papers* established the fashion of issuing *new* novels in parts, the slum publishers were quick to follow suit. Again, when monthly miscellanies like *Fraser's* and *Bentley's* came on the market, they soon had their crude counterparts in penny or twopenny periodicals which offered not only an instalment of a novel but an assortment of other features.[67] The output of both penny parts and cheap miscellanies was, according to the standards of the time, staggering. In 1845 it was said that half a million copies were sold weekly.[68] Early on Sunday mornings the narrow streets in the vicinity of Salisbury Square and Paternoster Row were crowded with hawkers taking away heavy bundles of the week's issue for sale on the sidewalks and in the tiny

[66] Sadleir, *XIX Century Fiction*, II, 142–44, 163–67.

[67] It is almost hopeless to draw a firm line of bibliographical distinction between the penny part-issue of an individual novel and the cheap miscellany; they were both serials, and, so to speak, blood brothers. Perhaps the future historian of early Victorian popular literature might adopt the inclusive term used by the "unlettered mother of a voracious reader of that kind of literature"—"prodigals" (Brown, *Some Account of Itinerating Libraries*, p. 16). For our purposes it will be convenient, if admittedly arbitrary, to postpone to chapter 14 our discussion of the sensational miscellany, which was a true periodical rather than a book issued in slices.

[68] Keefe, *A Century in Print*, p. 7 n.

shops patronized by the poor. Sunday was the day upon which the laboring classes read, and for their Sabbath edification they preferred "the foulest filth of all literary matter [in which] robbery was represented as merely a skilful sleight of hand, murder as nothing else but heroism, and seduction and prostitution as being anything else but blameable."[69]

The longevity of the "penny dreadful" serial novels was remarkable. One of the most popular, *Black Bess*, ran to 2,067 pages and was issued over a span of almost five years, after which—the market giving no evidence of satiety—a sequel was begun.[70] G. W. M. Reynolds' *Mysteries of London*, an enterprise designed to exploit the vogue of Eugène Sue's *Mysteries of Paris*, was another highly successful marathon fiction, running to four series. Only the first two, however, were from Reynolds' own pen, for after a disagreement with his publishers he started a rival romance, *Mysteries of the Court of London*, which itself comprised four series. The two novels together occupied him for twelve years, or, to reckon as his faithful readers did, 624 penny numbers. And while he wrote the *Mysteries* with his right hand, with his left he was turning out an endless supply of thrilling fiction for *Reynolds' Miscellany*.[71] Most of his colleagues were similarly ambidextrous, the penny-number trade and the cheap periodicals forming a gluttonous market for their wares, which took the form, usually, of an eight-page leaflet, large octavo size, printed in double columns of eye-straining type, minion or brevier. The letterpress was accompanied by one or more wood engravings, which were as dramatic as the narrative itself.

Despised though they were by the regular firms, these pariah publishers in London's lower depths were the shrewdest businessmen the trade had ever known. At least one of them, Edward Lloyd, pre-tested his manuscripts by having them read by a servant or a machine boy.[72] Their promotional schemes deserve much credit for spreading the reading habit among the semiliterate. When a new serial began, two numbers were sold for the price of

[69] Newspaper Stamp Committee, Q. 1265.

[70] Keefe, p. 7 n.

[71] The fullest collection of data on Reynolds is in Summers, pp. 146–59. See also *Times Literary Supplement*, January 24, 1924, p. 56.

[72] Frost, p. 90.

one, and with the connivance of wholesalers free samples were inserted into copies of cheap periodicals. Posters and handbills at news vendors' helped carry the message, as did advertisements on the wrappers of other serials issued by the same publisher. When a romance drew to a close, its last number sometimes was accompanied by a complimentary copy of its successor's first number. Some serials were reissued every six months or so, no more for a new audience than for the former purchasers, who in the interim had forgotten most of what they had read and were eager to relive their week-to-week excitement. When the sale of a certain fiction failed to satisfy the publisher, it was not unusual for him to start it off again under a new title and hope for a better reception the second time around.[73]

This, then, was the sort of literature favored by a large portion of the audience which the expanding system of elementary education had brought into being. Despite the high-minded efforts of men like Charles Knight to improve their tastes, the semiliterate public remained stubbornly faithful to the rousing products of Lloyd and Reynolds. The rate at which sensational fiction was selling around 1850 gave deep concern to all public-spirited citizens. Some interpreted the phenomenon as proof that popular education did more harm than good; others, more sanguine, maintained that the cure lay in improving education and abolishing the taxes which, they alleged, prevented the dissemination of a higher quality of literature. One thing, however, was certain: for better or worse, in the period from the first Reform Bill to the Great Exhibition the reading habit had spread among the English masses as never before. The demand for cheap books had already begun a transformation, reluctant but inevitable, in publishers' outlook and publishers' practices. But the full impact of the democratic audience upon the English book trade was reserved for the decades still to come.

[73] *Bookseller*, February 28, 1867, p. 122.

CHAPTER 13 { *The Book Trade*
1851–1900

I (1851–60). A good case could be made for viewing the 1850's as the great turning-point in the history of the English book trade's relations with the mass public. The conflicting forces we saw at work in the last chapter—on the one hand, loyalty to traditional attitudes and policies; on the other, the tempting commercial possibilities inherent in a vastly enlarged market—came to a crisis in this decade. The resolution of the crisis, however, occupied the rest of the century.

At mid-century the conservatism that had always governed the old established houses persisted, hale and hearty. It was against these publishers, rather than innovators like Knight and the Chamberses, that the advocates of cheap literature concentrated their attack. The average price of a book may well have declined 40 per cent between 1828 and 1853, as Knight maintained; but the 1828 level had been abnormally high, and in any event the reduction had occurred preponderantly among reprints of various kinds, not among new books. Now, when the free-trade philosophy was in the ascendant, the old protest against the publishers' alleged conspiracy to keep prices high acquired fresh vigor. In 1852 Gladstone told the House of Commons that from 90 to 95 per cent of new publications had a sale of five hundred copies or less. "The purchase of new publications is scarcely ever attempted by anybody. You go into the houses of your friends, and unless they buy books of which they are in professional want, or happen to be persons of extraordinary wealth, you don't find copies of new publications on their tables purchased by themselves, but you find something from the circulating library, or something from the book-club."[1]

This was patently an exaggeration, overlooking, for one thing,

[1] *Hansard*, Ser. 3, CXXI (1852), col. 596.

the great sales of a novelist like Dickens. But it could not be denied that the cost of most original publications was indefensibly high: the result, critics said, of many firms' unhealthy reliance upon the circulating library for the bulk of their business. They were content with, or at least resigned to, a situation they had themselves created when they priced original fiction out of the individual purchaser's reach. The publishers countered with a cliché not peculiar to that era (it is still flourishing a century later): the public, they asserted, simply refused to acquire the book-buying habit. Actually, both parties were right; each merely viewed the vicious circle from a different angle. The circulating libraries bought large quantities of newly published books; the publishers charged prices established in the inflationary 1820's (and gave the libraries big discounts). The publishers found it more profitable to supply, say, five hundred copies of a new book to a few reliable customers, either directly or through jobbers, than to dispose of them one by one through the bookshops. And so prices were kept high, the reader who wished to keep up with current literature was driven to the libraries, the libraries flourished and bulked larger than ever in publishers' views of their market.

The tyranny of the circulating libraries was symbolized by the figure of Charles Edward Mudie, who, though he had begun to rent books from his shop ten years earlier, came to full eminence when he set up his famous headquarters in New Oxford Street in 1852.[2] Compared with his, the older libraries were small, ineffectual operations. He charged only one guinea for a year's subscription, as against his competitors' two. He advertised extensively; he set up branch libraries in various parts of London and used eight vans in a metropolitan pickup and delivery arrangement; he gave country customers speedy and efficient service, and installed a large export department. In a word, he turned the circulating library into big business. But he did not, as is sometimes assumed, monopolize the trade. Some rivals, to be sure, he drove under: Hookham's, for instance, and Booth's in Regent Street, and an upstart firm called the Library Company, Limited, which offered subscriptions at half Mudie's rate and ended up in a resounding bankruptcy. Others,

[2] The present account of Mudie is derived from Curwen, *History of Booksellers*, pp. 424–30, and Colby, " 'The Librarian Rules the Roost,' " where references to further material may be found.

however, managed not only to survive but to prosper in the face of Mudie's aggressive methods—Cawthorn and Hutt of Cockspur Street, Day's of Mount Street, Miles of Islington, and the Grosvenor Gallery Library.[3] And in the early sixties W. H. Smith and Son, whose proposal to act as Mudie's agents at their railway bookstalls had been turned down, went into the book-lending trade on their own account and soon did a volume of business which approached Mudie's.

Hence the figures given of Mudie's book purchases do not represent the total amount of trade between publishers and libraries. But the scale of Mudie's own buying was impressive enough. In the ten years 1853–62 he added to his stock about 960,000 volumes, almost half of which (416,706) were novels; works of history and biography accounted for 215,743 more, and travel and adventure 125,381.[4] He took 2,400 copies of the third and fourth volumes of Macaulay's *History of England* (and had to set aside a special room for handling them); 2,000 of *The Mill on the Floss;* 2,500 of *Enoch Arden;* and 500 of *Adam Bede,* in addition to several reorders.[5]

By astute business methods, and above all by achieving a reputation as the watchdog of contemporary literary morals, Mudie did much to encourage reading among the class that could afford a guinea for a year's subscription. He throve upon the role of the mid-Victorian Mr. Grundy: "What will Mudie say?" was the invariable question that arose in publishers' offices when a new novel was under consideration. Mudie paid the piper, and on behalf of his large clientele he called the tune.

In his own time, however, it was not primarily his enforcement of Evangelical standards that called forth criticism; in his role of censor, after all, he had most readers solidly behind him. Rather, as the leader of circulating-library proprietors he was attacked, along with the subservient publishers, for discouraging the pur-

[3] On some of Mudie's rivals, see Tinsley, *Random Recollections,* I, 64–74, and Waugh, *One Hundred Years of Publishing,* p. 102.

[4] "The Circulation of Modern Literature," *Spectator,* supplement to issue of January 3, 1863, p. 17. Considerably more than a third of this total (391,083) was bought in the period from January, 1858, to October, 1860—a good measure of how Mudie's business grew during the fifties. The breakdown for this period was 165,445 volumes of fiction, 87,210 of history and biography, 50,572 of travel and adventure, and 87,856 "miscellaneous" (Mudie's own figures, in a letter to the *Athenaeum,* October 6, 1860, p. 451).

[5] Cruse, *The Victorians and Their Reading,* pp. 315–16, 330; Curwen, p. 428.

chase of books by maintaining the price of newly published fiction at 10*s.*6*d.* a volume and clinging to the anachronistic and wasteful three-volume form. In 1854 a writer in the *Times*, after demolishing the publishers' stock argument that cheap books could not return a decent profit, struck a note that was to be echoed again and again in the next decades: "We simply ask, on behalf of all classes, but especially in the interest of the great masses of the people, that the old and vicious method of proceeding shall be reversed—that, instead of commencing with editions of a guinea, and gradually coming down in the course of years to cheap editions of 5*s.*, all good books on their first appearance shall appeal to the needy multitude, while the requirements of the fortunate and lazier few are postponed to a more convenient season."[6]

Occasionally a publishing firm that was heavily dependent on library patronage made a halfhearted effort to meet criticism. In 1845–46 Chapman and Hall had experimented, unsuccessfully, with publishing original fiction in 3*s.* monthly parts, the novel being completed in four parts.[7] In the same period, the ultra-conservative house of Murray issued the Home and Colonial Library, a series which, in the words of the firm's historian, "would contain nothing offensive to morals or good taste, and would appeal . . . to heads of families, clergymen, school-teachers, and employers of labour." Priced at 2*s.*6*d.* a volume, the series was laden with travel books, a house specialty; among them were Melville's *Typee* and *Omoo*. But in 1852 John Murray III told Gladstone the venture was a failure.[8] Nevertheless, his firm embarked on another venture,

[6] Reprinted in *Living Age*, XLIII (1854), 122; for a later barrage of criticism, see *Publishers' Circular*, February 1, 1872, pp. 69–70.

[7] On these experiments, see E. P. Morton, "News for Bibliophiles," pp. 331–32, and Sadleir, *XIX Century Fiction*, II, 132–33, 170–71.

[8] "George Paston" [i.e., Emily Morse Symonds], *At John Murray's, 1843–1892* (1932), pp. 39, 114. In 1861 the series was "reissued" at cut rates. The unctuous trade-journal advertisement heralding this public-spirited gesture is typical of those that sought to disguise publishers' efforts to liquidate an unlucky speculation as a contribution to the grand cause of cheap literature: ". . . a fresh class of readers has arisen, and the establishment of Literary Institutions, School and Village Clubs, Book-Hawking Societies, Parochial and Lending Libraries, has become so general, that it appears to the Publisher a good opportunity to disseminate these Volumes, at a rate which shall place them within reach of the less wealthy classes. By removing the impediment of price, he hopes to throw open these attractive and useful Works to the Million; so that having hitherto been the delight of the Parlour and Drawing-room, they may now do equally good service in the Factory and Workshop—in the Cottage of the Peasant and Log-hut of the Colonist—in the Soldier's Barrack and the Sailor's Cabin" (*Publishers' Circular*, November 1, 1861, p. 498).

the Library of Railway Readings—an attempt to supply the new race of train-readers with superior literature. The initial volume, in fact, was a selection of reviews and articles from the *Times*. It appears that literature for any but the passengers in first-class carriages was not the firm's forte. As John Wilson Croker wrote Murray, "You are not, and cannot be a cheap book-seller. . . . It would require a large return of profit to reconcile me to your making your venerable establishment into a kind of old-clothes shop, in which worn-out garments are furbished up for second-hand prices."[9]

This was, however, exactly what some equally dignified firms now did, though the garments in many cases were scarcely worn out. Since 1832, the two London houses of Bentley and Colburn had been virtually alone in issuing 6s. reprints of novels which they had originally brought out at regular circulating-library prices. But from the middle of the century onward, the 6s. reprint was adopted by many houses, so that the middle-class reader who wished to buy rather than borrow was able to do so—provided he had enough patience. The interval between the original, high-priced edition and the first cheap reprint varied considerably. As a rule, so long as demand for the original edition continued at the libraries and the booksellers', a reprint was out of the question; and even when a book was no longer called for at the libraries, reprinting was delayed until the unwanted copies found buyers in the secondhand market. Some more aggressive houses, though, exploited the initial success of a book by issuing a less expensive reprint within a year or two, as happened with George Eliot and Trollope. In Thackeray's case, the interval was three to five years; in Dickens', substantially longer. It was this delay, lasting in many instances until public interest in a book had largely evaporated, that caused the crusaders for cheap literature to regard the 6s. reprint with very tempered enthusiasm.[10]

The firms which now unbent sufficiently to issue 6s. reprints undoubtedly did so in an effort to fill the yawning gap in the price

[9] "Paston," pp. 106–107.

[10] Often it was the author, rather than the publisher, who had to take the initiative in getting out a cheap reprint. Only when John Stuart Mill, moved by frequent pleas from workingmen, offered to forego his half-share of the profits, did Longmans agree to issue a cheap People's Edition of his works (Michael St. John Packe, *Life of John Stuart Mill* [1954], p. 448; Mill, *Autobiography* [New York, 1944], p. 195).

scale between the 31*s*.6*d*. original edition and the new "railway novel" at 1*s*. or 1*s*.6*d*.[11] In 1846 the Belfast firm of Simms and McIntyre issued the first monthly volume of its Parlour Novelist series at the virtually unheard-of price of 2*s*. in wrappers and 2*s*.6*d*. in cloth. A year later, in April, 1847, the same firm reduced prices even further with its Parlour Library, which offered monthly volumes at 1*s*. in boards and (a little later) 1*s*.6*d*. in cloth. The success of this daring venture was immediate and overwhelming. After trying for two years to maintain their old price, both Bentley and Colburn cut their reprint series first to 3*s*.6*d*. and then to 2*s*.6*d*. In deliberate imitation of the Parlour Library came George Routledge's shilling Railway Library, which "bestrode the bookstall market for decades" and by 1898 piled up a total of 1,300 titles. Routledge, who had begun as a remainder specialist, soon became the leading figure in a crowded field.

Cheap railway novels (or "yellow-backs" as they were called after 1855, when their characteristic binding—glazed colored paper laid over boards, with an eye-catching picture on the front and advertisements on the back—was established) were the most inspired publishing invention of the era. For one or two shillings a volume, the scores of "libraries" that sprang up offered a tremendous selection to suit every taste but the crudest and the most cultivated. G. P. R. James, Marryat, Mayne Reid, Ainsworth, James Payn, Miss Braddon, Charles Lever, Samuel Lover—the catalogues of the various series were veritable rosters of Victorian bestsellerdom. The firms that specialized in such books sometimes paid large prices for reprint rights; Routledge, for instance, contracted to pay Bulwer-Lytton £2,000 a year for ten years' rights to his lucrative literary property.

Though most of the yellow-backs were novels or collections of tales, they also included a good portion of non-fiction, especially topical books—narratives of the Crimean War, for instance, and the Indian Mutiny, and the War of Italian Liberation—and the various sorts of "comicalities" that were the delight of Victorian readers embarking on a long railway journey or a holiday by the

[11] The most detailed studies of the yellow-backs and other cheap fiction series are in Sadleir, *XIX Century Fiction*, Vol. II, and in Sadleir's earlier essay in Carter (ed.), *New Paths in Book Collecting*, pp. 127–61; see also Carter and Sadleir, *Victorian Fiction*, pp. 10–13. On Routledge's yellow-backs, see Mumby, *The House of Routledge*, pp. 61–62, 120–22, 139–41.

sea. Nor were they all reprints. Some series had a sprinkling of "originals" by popular journalists like Augustus Mayhew, Edmund Yates, Douglas Jerrold, and G. A. Sala; and one or two libraries, like Routledge's Library of Original Novels, were devoted to new works. The latter, however, were not successful. But the very fact that *some* books made their first appearance, apart from serialization, at one or two shillings helped undermine the position of the publishers who thought only in terms of expensive first editions.

One of the difficulties in yellow-back publishing was that there were not enough copyrights to go around, for some firms withheld the reprint rights to their most popular authors, and in any case a publisher working on a small profit margin could not afford to spend much money for either original or reprint book rights. There remained, however, contemporary American literature, which seemingly was as vast as the continent and as profitable as a California lode, and which until 1891 was largely unprotected under British law. It was up to the individual publisher's conscience whether he would follow the gentleman's course of compensating the American author or the pirate's device of appropriating the work without any payment whatsoever. Some settled the matter one way, some the other. Routledge, who was especially fond of reprinting American books, usually preferred the latter alternative.[12]

For various reasons, among them the fact that cheap publishing was more advanced in the United States than in Britain, the American author had learned more quickly than his English cousin how to write for a democratic audience. Thus, when the cheap series began in the late twenties, and even more when the stream swelled to a flood in the fifties, no English reprint publisher had to be at a loss for titles suitable for his market. Had books by such writers as Cooper, Irving, Willis, Longfellow, and Lowell not been freely available, the cheap reprint series would have appealed far less to popular taste, and their expansive influence upon the reading audience would have been much smaller.[13]

The place of the American book in English life was dramatically

[12] American publishers faced the same moral issue in the case of English books, which were equally unprotected under American law—and they solved it in the same ways.

[13] Gohdes, *American Literature in Nineteenth-Century England*, chap. i.

illustrated in 1852, when *Uncle Tom's Cabin* touched off the biggest sensation the publishing trade had yet known. In a single fortnight in October of that year, at least ten different editions came out. Six months after publication, the book had sold 150,000 copies, and within a year, according to one account, the total sales in England and the colonies had reached a million and a half.[14]

Inseparable from the vogue of the yellow-back, for "railway reading," was another influential trade development of the fifties, the multiplying of retail outlets, most conspicuously in railway stations. During the first years of their existence, English railways had leased their bookstall concessions to injured employees or their widows, who vended an unappetizing stock of newspapers, magazines, beer, sandwiches, and sweets to jaded travelers. As journeys became longer, thanks to the network of lines left by the speculative frenzy of the 1840's, novels were added to the wares for sale. But these were not only cheap but nasty, predominantly translations from the French; it was said, in fact, that people went to railway stations for the books they were ashamed to seek at respectable shops. In response to widespread criticism, the railways decided to lease their stalls to reputable firms. The firm which soon won a virtual monopoly throughout the country was that of W. H. Smith and Son, the nation's leading wholesale news agents.

The head of the house at this period was the founder's son, the very model of a pious businessman—the sort of person who consulted the chained Bibles that were installed in railway terminals.[15] William Henry Smith was hardly less strict in his literary principles than Mr. Mudie, and as a result the trash piles quickly vanished. As travelers passed through city stations and country transfer points, they never failed to see the familiar W. H. Smith stalls, efficiently managed, neatly arranged, and plastered with posters. No longer was it possible for people to avoid reading matter; everywhere they went it was displayed—weekly papers at a penny or twopence, complete books, enticing in their bright picture covers, at a shilling, and all fresh and crisp from the press. No

[14] *Ibid.*, pp. 29–31; Sabin, *Dictionary of Books Relating to America*, XXIV, 48. The various figures cited to illustrate the magnitude of the "*Uncle Tom* mania" are not always reconcilable.

[15] Later he entered politics and became First Lord of the Admiralty under Disraeli—a feat of incongruity commemorated by Gilbert and Sullivan in their character of Sir Joseph Porter.

wonder that the fifties, which saw the spread of Smith's stalls to almost every principal railway line in the country, were also the period when the sales of books and periodicals reached unprecedented levels.[16]

At the very time the yellow-back publishers, aided by Smith, were making books available to millions who previously had been indifferent to them, another firm was exploiting on a large scale the old practice of issuing standard and educational works in cheap parts. This was the house which was presided over, until his death in 1865, by John Cassell, and which still bears his name today. Since John Cassell's story has never been satisfactorily told, it must be pieced together from a number of fragmentary and not always reliable sources.[17] According to a malicious contemporary account, in his youth he was a drunken carpenter who, on the road from Manchester to London, discovered his aptitude for lecturing as a reformed sinner before temperance gatherings. Under the auspices of his teetotal sponsors (so this story goes), he set up as a dealer in coffee heavily adulterated with chicory and then drifted into publishing. Other narratives of his earlier days are silent concerning both his affection for the bottle and the purity of his coffee. It is indisputable, at least, that in the 1840's he had a national reputation both as a temperance orator and as a dealer in coffee and tea. Sir Newman Flower, long an official of the Cassell publishing firm, has described how this dual role led to the third one of publisher. At a time when tea was normally sold in forty-pound cases, Cassell got the idea of putting it up in shilling packets. To print labels for the packets, he bought a small press; and this he used in the evenings to produce the first of the many Cassell periodicals, the *Teetotal Times* (a modest success) and the *Standard of Freedom* (a failure—not least because its title was scarcely appropriate in 1848, the year when Britons were uneasily watching European thrones toppling right and left). These were followed,

---

[16] The fullest source of information on W. H. Smith and Son in the nineteenth century is Sir Herbert Maxwell, *Life and Times of the Rt. Hon. W. H. Smith* (1893), Vol. I, chaps. ii, iii. A recent article, based on this and other sources, is Robert A. Colby, "That He Who Rides May Read."

[17] Henry Vizetelly, *Glances Back through Seventy Years* (1893), II, 52–53; Sir Newman Flower, *Just As It Happened* (1950), pp. 50–59; G. Holden Pike, *John Cassell* (1894); Curwen, pp. 267–74; *Publishers' Circular*, October 15, 1886, p. 1234, and January 13, 1894, pp. 50–53; *Le Livre*, VI (1885), 164–73.

though presumably not from the same little press, by the *Working Man's Friend*, a serious penny publication with a strong temperance bias, one of whose features was a continuing prize contest for essays sent in by working-class readers. In 1851, the year after it began, its circulation was 50,000. Thus encouraged, Cassell rapidly branched out into other publishing activities. In 1852 he launched the first of the almost innumerable part-issues for which his name was to be a Victorian by-word: *Cassell's Popular Educator*, an encyclopedic self-instruction course which sold for a penny a number. It had hardly begun before a witness told a parliamentary committee on education that "Mr. John Cassell is doing more at the present time than any other individual to supply the increasing demand by the operative classes for useful knowledge, and in supplying works peculiarly adapted to their circumstances and condition. His popular mode of education is receiving an extended and an extraordinary circulation, and is highly estimated by a large number of the operative classes."[18] He achieved, in brief, what the Useful Knowledge Society had set out to do—to "popularize" knowledge. The *Popular Educator's* contribution to Victorian culture is suggested by the number of subsequently distinguished men who learned from its pages. Thomas Hardy taught himself German from the *Popular Educator;* Thomas Burt, the labor politician, used it for English, French, and Latin lessons; and with its aid the future great philologist, Joseph Wright, atoned for his almost complete lack of formal education. "The completed book," said Wright, "remained my constant companion for years. I learned an enormous lot from it."[19]

After the *Popular Educator* came, also in cheap instalments, the *Illustrated Family Bible* (which sold 350,000 copies in six years), the *Illustrated History of England*, illustrated volumes of natural history, Shakespeare, *Don Quixote*, Dante, Bunyan, Goldsmith— the profusion was endless. In 1862 the Cambridge meeting of the British Association heard that Cassell sold between 25,000,000 and 30,000,000 copies of his penny publications annually.[20] In addition

[18] *Report from the Select Committee on Manchester and Salford Education* (1852), Q. 2261*.

[19] Flower, p. 55; Burt, *Autobiography*, p. 120; Elizabeth M. Wright, *Life of Joseph Wright* (1932), I, 38.

[20] Henry Roberts in *Report of the 32nd Meeting of the British Association* (1862), p. 174.

to part-issues of educational and literary works, the firm produced regular tradebooks, juveniles, and periodicals, the latter including such familiar appurtenances to Victorian domestic life as *Cassell's Family Magazine*, the *Quiver*, and *Little Folks*. In the 1890's it had eight monthly magazines and nearly fifty other serials running simultaneously.

Cassell's success was due both to a shrewd sense of popular taste and to the absolute blamelessness of the house's productions. Already associated in the popular mind with tea and temperance, the name of Cassell on a penny part or a cheap fireside paper was sufficient guarantee of its fitness for the strictest household. During Cassell's lifetime, at least, the pages of his publications were never sullied by mention of liquor. Since the name was so valuable an asset, it was exploited in the most extensive advertising campaigns yet seen in English publishing. On hoardings, in magazine advertisements, in posters at railway bookstalls, the magic word CASSELL's was kept ceaselessly before the reading public.

In the same year (1852) that saw Mudie opening his Great Hall in New Oxford Street, W. H. Smith setting up his stalls along the British railway lines, and Cassell beginning his *Popular Educator*, occurred still another event of profound consequence to the development of the mass public. The underselling practice—retailing new books below the advertised price—had been plaguing the trade ever since the days of Lackington. In 1829, the leading publishers had formally agreed to drive undersellers out of business by cutting off their supply of books. This boycott had proved fairly effective for the next two decades, but with the founding in 1848 of a new Booksellers' Association, dedicated to the same ends, a real fight began. In 1852 the bookseller John Chapman, never a man to conform when there was profit or publicity in doing otherwise, ran afoul of the organization. He aired his case in the *Westminster Review*, and to his support came many of the leading authors of the day (who, unlike their publishers, felt that their interest lay in the widest possible circulation of books), the *Times* and the *Athenaeum*, and Gladstone. By clinging to protectionism at a time when free-trade sentiment was at its peak, publishers gave fresh substance to the belief that theirs was the most reactionary of businesses.

The barrage of publicity forced the Booksellers' Association to the wall, and in April, 1852, it agreed to submit the issue to the arbitration of Lord Campbell, Henry Milman (the Dean of St. Paul's), and George Grote, the historian. William Longman and John Murray were chosen to present the protectionists' case. But they were no match for the eloquence of leader-writers in the liberal press and Gladstone in Parliament. Lord Campbell's committee quickly decided in favor of free trade in books, and the Booksellers' Association thereupon was dissolved.[21]

Hence during the next fifty years an English bookbuyer expected, and in most cases received, a discount of 2*d.* or 3*d.* on the shilling. A 6*s.* reprint could be bought for as low as 4*s.*6*d.* cash, a 3*s.* book for 2*s.*3*d.*, and a 6*d.* paper-bound volume for 4½*d.* Only a few booksellers, especially those having the closest ties with the publishers, refused to give the discount. No further steps were taken to regulate retail prices until the nineties, but the publishers and the more conservative booksellers never ceased to grumble. Year after year, the trade journals were filled with their complaints. Underselling, they maintained, was ruining the book business. "In country towns," Alexander Macmillan told Gladstone in 1868, "few live by bookselling: the trade has become so profitless that it is generally the appendage to a toyshop, or a Berlin wool warehouse and a few trashy novels, selling for a shilling, with flaring covers suiting the flashy contents."[22]

Though Macmillan and his fellow publishers probably exaggerated the ruinous effect of underselling upon regular bookshops, there is no question that as the profit margin was reduced, bookselling as such became a less attractive occupation. The result was that the old custom of selling books as a side line in shops devoted chiefly to other commodities became much more widespread. Thus the tendency promoted by the W. H. Smith bookstalls—the placing of books in the main-traveled roads of Victorian daily life— received simultaneous impetus from another direction. Whatever its effect upon the professional booksellers, the discount system encouraged the reading habit both by reducing actual prices and by increasing the availability of books.

[21] Chapman's manifesto was "The Commerce of Literature," *Westminster Review*, N.S., I (1852), 511–54: a valuable document on book-trade economics at the time. See also Gordon S. Haight, *George Eliot and John Chapman* (New Haven, 1940), pp. 50–53, and the columns of the *Athenaeum* and other papers for 1852.

[22] Charles L. Graves, *Life and Letters of Alexander Macmillan* (1910), p. 286.

II (1861-90). Between 1860 and 1890 the history of the book trade followed the lines already suggested. The three great requisites of a mass reading public—literacy, leisure, and a little pocket-money—became the possession of more and more people. Though there were temporary setbacks, particularly during the serious depression of the mid-seventies, the period as a whole was one of remarkable economic progress. The number of families with an income of over £150 a year more than trebled in thirty years. In 1850-51, 83,300 families were in the £150-£400 bracket; in 1879-80 there were 285,100. Meanwhile the average income of a lower-middle-class family rose from £90 in 1851 to £110 in 1881.[23] This rise in money income was accompanied, especially in the period 1874-96, by sharply falling prices, so that real income increased faster than wages. During the half-century, the average family's real income rose by 70 or 80 per cent. But "the total flow of wealth to the different segments of the population continued to be very disadvantageous to the working class"; it was still the middle class, far more than the workers, who benefited from the prosperous times.[24]

Even the workers, however, were somewhat better off than they had been. A working-class family who in 1851 made 20s. a week, or £52 a year, earned 32s. a week, or £83 annually, thirty years later.[25] Their extra pennies and shillings, translated into a wider consumers' market for printed matter, did much to stimulate the book trade's quest for cheaper materials and more efficient manufacturing techniques. About 1860, esparto, a North African grass, was successfully introduced as a cheap substitute for rags in papermaking, and by the eighties the development of chemical and mechanical methods of preparing wood pulp helped satisfy the demand for a paper suitable for cheap books and periodicals. In 1861 the paper duty was repealed.[26]

The printing process itself was constantly improved. Introduced from America in the sixties, the high-speed Hoe press was designed primarily for printing newspapers and mass-circulation periodicals, but toward the end of the century it was used, as similar

---

[23] Levi, *Wages and Earnings of the Working Classes*, pp. 48, 52.

[24] Cole, *Short History of the British Working-Class Movement*, pp. 126, 266-67; Lynd, *England in the Eighteen-Eighties*, pp. 48-53.

[25] Levi, p. 53.　　　　　[26] Plant, *The English Book Trade*, pp. 334-40.

presses are today, to turn out enormous quantities of paper-bound books. The making of illustrations, a vital feature of books and periodicals appealing to the mass audience, was facilitated by innumerable inventions, culminating in techniques for the quick and accurate reproduction of photographs. One major phase of bookmaking which remained unaffected by mechanization until the end of the century was typesetting. Although composing machines were used by provincial newspapers from the late sixties onward, and by the (non-union) London *Times* from 1879, book type was composed by hand until the introduction of the Monotype machine early in the twentieth century.[27]

Apart from composition, therefore, manufacturing costs stood less and less in the way of cheaper books; and the average price of books continued to decline. As if to make a second reparation for inflating the price of new fiction in the 1820's, Scott's novels led the way as they had when Cadell issued his 5*s*. edition in 1829. The property of A. and C. Black following Cadell's death in 1849, they were issued in successively cheaper reprints, culminating in a shilling-a-volume edition in 1862–63. Then, as their copyrights expired, they were reissued by other publishers in cutthroat competition. John Camden Hotten brought out complete novels at 6*d*., and a few years later even this sensationally low price was halved by John Dicks. Waverley novels at 3*d*. were a far cry from the 31*s*.6*d*. form in which they had first appeared.[28]

From the late sixties onward, 6*d*. was a common price for books bound in paper and printed in strenuously small type, usually in double columns. In the late seventies several of Dickens' early books, printed from plates acquired from Chapman and Hall, appeared at 6*d*. in Routledge's Caxton Novels, a series which eventually included about eight hundred titles.[29] In the purlieus of the

[27] *Ibid.*, pp. 279–86, 307–20; Ellic Howe (ed.), *The London Compositor* (1947), pp. 492–93.

[28] Curwen, pp. 138–39, 150–51; *Publishers' Circular*, October 1, 1866, p. 587; *Bookseller*, January 3, 1874, p. 4.

[29] Mumby, *The House of Routledge*, pp. 139–40. Trollope wrote in 1879 of a tea dealer ordering 18,000 volumes of Dickens to be given away to customers who bought a specified amount of his product. The bookseller deferentially wondered if another author might not be equally acceptable, but the tea man insisted that "the tea-consuming public preferred their Dickens." In any event, the use of novels as commercial premiums is a good sign of the hold the reading habit had among the masses at this time ("Novel-Reading," *Nineteenth Century*, V [1879], 32–33).

trade, John Dicks prospered for years on the sale of a seemingly endless list of sixpenny thrillers dominated by the productions of G. W. M. Reynolds, whose publisher he had become following Reynolds' break with the *Family Herald*. The popularity of Dicks's books reflected the humble reader's continuing appetite for sensational literature. The competition of cheap weekly papers specializing in such fiction did little to stem the flood of old-fashioned penny parts. In 1887 a writer in the *Edinburgh Review* reported, on the customary "good authority," that the sale of sensational novels in serial form exceeded two million copies a week, with individual titles selling from ten to sixty thousand each.[30] While these thrillers, the equivalents of modern "pulps" and "comic" books, appealed primarily to a juvenile audience, compassing the social gamut from public-school boys to errand-runners, we may safely assume that the taste for such reading hardly ended with adolescence. In the late Victorian age there were, as today, millions of readers whose literary preferences were immutably fixed before they reached man's estate.

The enduring popularity of literature of adventure and crime disheartened many who had welcomed the repeal of the newspaper and paper taxes as the dawn of an era of improved public taste. A more hopeful sign was the increased demand for cheap books of an altogether higher level. In the latter half of the century there were some eighty or ninety inexpensive series consisting chiefly, if not exclusively, of reprints of the English classics. One reason for this phenomenon was that classics, being out of copyright, were cheaper to publish; another was that the inclusion of English literature as a subject in competitive examinations, and then in the schools themselves, created a large market for standard classics.

In the 1840's cheap reprints of English masterpieces were to be had from only a handful of publishers, among them Tegg and Chambers. Beginning in 1847, however, the success of Bohn's Libraries encouraged one firm after another to add series of standard works to their lists. Bohn's prices, 3s.6d. and 5s., remained the customary ones for books of this sort for at least two decades. But in the late sixties and the seventies, because these prices compared unfavorably with the shilling or two charged for reprints of copy-

---

[30] "The Literature of the Streets," *Edinburgh Review*, CLXV (1887), 43, 47. The whole article (pp. 40–65) is an indignant description of the penny-dreadful output at the time.

right works in the railway libraries, many firms went still lower. John Dicks brought out a shilling Shakespeare, a 473-page illustrated Byron at 7*d*., and a dozen other classic authors at similarly low prices. The well-known Aldine edition of the poets, originally issued (1830–44) at 5*s*. a volume, came down to 1*s*.6*d*. in 1870. In the eighties, an exciting duel between two great publishing houses brought the price of the rival National and World Libraries (Cassell's and Routledge's, respectively) down to 3*d*. in paper and 6*d*. in cloth. And not only were prices cut: the selection of titles was greatly enlarged, the old standbys—Pope, Milton, Cowper, Thomson, Burns, Goldsmith, and the rest—being joined by many other authors who had seldom if ever appeared in cheap editions. The serious reader with only pennies to spend was served as he had never been served before.

Inevitably, price-cutting was accompanied by corner-cutting. In many cases, cheapness was a synonym for shoddiness. The amount of text provided from series to series varied tremendously; often volumes which were put forth as the "works" of a certain great author, or which bore simply the name of a famous masterpiece, in reality were nothing but haphazard selections. Seldom did a cheap series have the benefit of responsible editorial supervision, and sometimes this was exerted mainly in behalf of bowdlerization. All too often the physical format was both ugly and flimsy. The paper was the cheapest obtainable; the wrappers soon became soiled and dog-eared, and tore off; the sewing gave way. And, worst of all, the type was small and worn. These defects were of course not peculiar to reprints of the classics; they were just as common in every other kind of cheap book. On the other hand, they were not inevitable, and they did not necessarily multiply as the price went down. Some of the cheap Victorian libraries of classics were attractive, convenient books. But oftener than not, the aesthetic pleasure the reader derived from them was confined to the text itself—whatever it was worth.

This was the background against which Matthew Arnold, in 1880, added his magisterial voice to the perennial chorus of protest against the high prices of new works: "As our nation grows more civilised, as a real love of reading comes to prevail more widely, the system which keeps up the present exorbitant price of new books in England, the system of lending-libraries from which books are hired, will be seen to be, as it is, eccentric, artificial, and unsatisfactory in the highest degree. It is a machinery for the multiplication and protection of bad literature, and for keeping good books dear. . . . True, old books of surpassing value are to be bought cheap; but there are good new books, too, and good new books have a stimulus and an interest peculiar to themselves, and the reader will not be content to forego them. . . . The three-shilling book is our great want . . . [not] a cheap literature, hideous and ignoble of aspect, like the tawdry novels which flare in the bookshelves of our railway-stations, and which seem designed, as so much else that is produced for the use of our middle-class seems designed, for people with a low standard of life."[31]

Arnold's strictures were occasioned by the recent publication of the report of the royal commission which in 1876–77 had conducted lengthy hearings on all aspects of copyright. Insofar as book publishing specifically was concerned, the issue was the old one between protectionism and free trade. In the extreme liberal view, copyright was an insidious form of monopoly, as it reserved to one owner the profits from a literary property for a term of forty-two years or the author's lifetime plus seven years, whichever was longer. One proposal extensively canvassed by the commission was to limit absolute copyright to a year or so, after which time a book could be reprinted by any publisher who agreed to pay the copyright owner a legally fixed royalty rate. The hoped-for result of this form of free trade in books would be issuing of competitive editions which would appease the public hunger for current works at low prices.

Faced with so radical a scheme, the "monopolists" took refuge in evasiveness or outright hostility to the commission and its aims. When Anthony Trollope, one of the commissioners, asked William Longman, "Have you ever considered whether the public is or is not entitled to extremely cheap editions of [Macaulay's] works?" the publisher curtly replied, "I do not think that the public are at all entitled to them." Although the old-guard publishers desired the legal protection of their property which copyright afforded, they bitterly resented governmental interference such as was represented by the commission's airing of complaints against them. "It seems to me," said John Blackwood, "that publishers and au-

[31] "Copyright," *Fortnightly Review*, N.S., XXVII (1880), 327–28.

thors must conduct their business as best they may, and name their own prices for the books." In particular, the allegedly unholy alliance between publishers and libraries was not a matter for public discussion. "You may rely upon it," Blackwood remarked at another point in his testimony, "that the publishers and authors have considered the subject [of the circulating-library system] thoroughly, and act according to the best of their light." But it was left to Herbert Spencer to put into a few blunt words the philosophy to which publishers like Longman and Blackwood still subscribed in 1876: "Whereas, at present, the poorer class of readers are inconvenienced by having to wait for a cheap edition a certain number of years, they shall, by this arrangement [restricting absolute copyright to a year], be advantaged by having a cheap edition forthwith; which is to say that people with smaller amounts of money shall have no disadvantages from their smaller amounts of money. It is communistic practically: it is simply equalising the advantages of wealth and poverty."[32]

Although one would expect that such reactionary attitudes as these would have decisively tipped the balance in favor of the cheap-book party, the copyright inquiry had no immediate practical results. The situation remained for another decade as it had been described in the course of the commission's hearings. New novels, still pegged at 10s.6d. a volume, were accessible to few but library subscribers and the members of book clubs. The somewhat cheaper part-issue of new fiction, though used by Dickens to the end of his career and by Trollope for several of his novels between 1864 and 1871, was virtually extinct by 1880. The major forms of copyright reprints already established in the fifties—the cloth-bound volume at 6s. or 7s., issued usually by the original publisher, and the railway edition of more popular works at 1s. or 2s.—flourished. But many readers who were willing to pay 6s. for a current book resented having to await the publisher's pleasure before it became available at this price. There were many more who would pay 3s. or less, but not 6s. And there were many too who, like Arnold, found no delight in either the format or the contents of the yellow-back. It was this swelling band of discontented readers, whose wants were vigorously championed in the press and by men like Sir Charles Trevelyan in testimony before the Copy-

[32] Copyright Commission Report (1878), Qq. 329, 832, 915, 5236.

right Commission,[33] that finally overthrew the last proud citadel of high prices—the expensive first edition.

III (1890–1900). In 1885, George Moore wrote one more of the century's numerous assaults on the circulating-library system, a pamphlet called *Literature at Nurse, or Circulating Morals*. This was accompanied, as earlier blasts sometimes had been, by the actual publication of a new novel at a reduced price— in this case, Moore's *A Mummer's Wife*. Instead of proving futile, as previous defiant gestures had, this one started a new trend: one house after another began to issue new books at 6s. In the late eighties and early nineties the "library novel" still made its appearance, like an ancient dowager tottering to the ball, but its doom could be read in the fact that the publishers, responding to pressure from the libraries, often cut its list price to 5s. or 6s. a volume. In the middle of 1894, Mudie's and Smith's informed the trade that henceforth they would refuse to buy fiction for more than 4s. a volume, less discount, and even then only on condition that cheaper reprints of books sold to libraries be delayed for at least a year. Few firms saw fit to accept the ultimatum, and the much-abused partnership between publishers and libraries was at an end.[34]

In 1894 the Authors' Society estimated that the existing libraries together had 60,000 subscribers, or, reckoning four adult members to an average household, some 240,000 actual readers.[35] At Mudie's death (1890) his own library was said to have about 25,000 subscribers, and in 1894 W. H. Smith and Son's library division had 15,000.[36] While no evidence has been discovered on the number of subscribers the circulating libraries enrolled in their mid-Victorian prime, these figures must represent a sharp decline from the peak. This is not to say, however, that the book-borrowing habit was on its way out. Far from it. In 1898 the *Publishers' Circular* estimated that of 50,000 copies of a successful "society

[33] *Ibid.*, Qq. 1–94.

[34] The decline and fall of the three-decker can be studied in minute detail in the files of the *Publishers' Circular* and the *Bookseller*, especially for the year 1894.

[35] *Publishers' Circular*, July 28, 1894, p. 80.

[36] *Ibid.*, November 1, 1890, p. 1418; May 5, 1894, p. 465.

novel," 10,000 reached the public through the libraries.[37] The great difference was that the subscription- and rental-library trade itself was being re-established on a more popular basis. Mudie's steadily declined after the nineties, though the firm clung to life until 1937. In its place sprang up cheaper libraries, the most famous of which was (and is) the Boots Book-lovers' Library, begun in 1900 in connection with the already thriving Boots chain of cash chemists. In the next thirty years, this library alone is said to have bought an average of almost one million new books yearly.[38] By the middle of the twentieth century, the two great subscription libraries had almost 1,000 branches between them, with a total issue of about fifty million books a year, and the so-called "twopenny" rental libraries were so numerous that no accurate count was possible. The largest chain had 120 branches.[39]

On the whole, the end of the expensive library novel in the mid-nineties was deplored only by sentimentalists and those who had a financial stake in its survival.[40] Most publishers and authors were too busy catering to the new buyers' market to shed more than a perfunctory farewell tear. For the six-shilling novel was being bought in huge quantities; first editions of works by popular novelists were scores of times larger now than they had been when they were destined principally for a handful of libraries. In 1900, for instance, Marie Corelli's *The Master Christian* had a pre-publication printing of 75,000 copies.[41]

The whole price structure was revised downward. Now that first editions cost 5*s.* or 6*s.*, cloth-bound reprints of recent fiction, hitherto priced at that figure, came out at 2*s.6d.* or 3*s.6d.* Paper-bound reprints of copyright works, formerly the specialty of a few firms like Dicks, were adopted by many of the leading houses.[42] In 1889 Macmillan brought out a million-copy edition of Kingsley's

---

[37] *Ibid.*, October 8, 1898, p. 423.

[38] James Milne, "A Library of To-day," *Cornhill Magazine*, CL (1934), 444.

[39] B. Seebohm Rowntree and G. R. Lavers, *English Life and Leisure: A Social Study* (1951), pp. 307–308.

[40] See the correspondence columns of the *Publishers' Circular* in 1894–95 (particularly Miss Braddon's letter to the press, quoted in the issue of September 28, 1895, p. 334), and Tinsley, *Random Recollections*, I, 53.

[41] *Publishers' Circular*, August 4, 1900, p. 93.

[42] There had been a flurry of sixpenny copyright reprints from "respectable" firms in 1882, but after the first excitement was over they proved not to have caught on.

works at 6*d.* a volume,[43] and within a few years reprinted Marion Crawford and other popular authors at the same price; rival firms reprinted for the sixpenny market the novels of such writers as Hall Caine, Clark Russell, William Black, and Richard Blackmore. As a result, the shilling railway novel disappeared from the scene.

The general realignment of prices naturally affected the noncopyright reprint, which was now often reduced to 3*d.* At this price Routledge, for example, issued the novels of Bulwer-Lytton, Hugo, Marryat, Lover, and other old-time romancers. At the bottom of the scale remained the hardy penny leaflets, usually running to thirty-two pages and inclosed in a garish wrapper. Some of these leaflets were penny bloods, pure and simple; but in response to a renewed clamor in the press against cheap thrillers, some firms made a brave show of promoting more wholesome literature for the masses. Side by side with the familiar shockers, therefore, were to be found such items as Miss Braddon's heroic condensations of Scott's novels into pennyworths, and excerpts from Dickens vended under such titles as "Joe the Fat Boy," "Mr. Winkle's Wooing," "The Artful Dodger," and "Bardell *v.* Pickwick." The sales of these pamphlets remained enormous. One firm alone advertised that between 1887 and May, 1892, their Penny Stories for the People (*Through Weal and Woe, The Rightful Heir, Mary, the Poacher's Wife, Thrown to the Lions, The Smuggler's Doom,* etc.) sold 18,250,000 copies.[44]

In the last years of the century, a penny bought a great deal more in both quality and quantity. W. T. Stead's Penny Novelist volumes (which *Punch* inevitably dubbed "Penny Steadfuls") abridged into 30,000 or 40,000 words novels which originally were six or eight times as long. A trade journal ironically complimented Stead upon relieving great novels of "all verbiage, all flowers of the imagination, all fine speeches—all superfluities, in short," but Stead's editors might have retorted that all they did, in behalf of the impatient multitude, was let the excess air out of stories which had been inflated to abnormal proportions to fill the three volumes favored by the old genteel, leisured public. There could be no more pregnant comment on the transformation the reading public had

[43] Morgan, *The House of Macmillan,* p. 136.

[44] *Publishers' Circular,* May 14, 1892, p. 528.

undergone between Scott's time and that of Rider Haggard (whose *She* sold 500,000 copies in Stead's abridgment).

Stead—who, it is interesting to note, had formed his taste for books by reading Dicks's penny-number Shakespeare as an office boy in Newcastle—issued also a generous series of Penny Poets, whose first number, Macaulay's *Lays of Ancient Rome*, sold 200,000 copies. During the brief life of the series, the total sales of the Penny Poets approached 5,000,000 copies, and that of the Penny Novelists, 6,500,000.[45]

The crowning refinement in penny books occurred in 1896, when George Newnes introduced his Penny Library of Famous Books, composed of unabridged texts of favorite tales and novels: Goldsmith, Poe, Scott, Reid, Marryat, Reade, Dickens, translations of Dumas, Sue, and Mérimée. Each book contained from 80 to 120 closely printed pages; some of the longer novels therefore had to be spread over two or three volumes. Despite all the current activity in this cheapest of cheap-book fields, Newnes found that the market still was not saturated. The first forty-four weekly numbers of his series sold an average of 96,587 copies.[46]

Thanks to the restless enterprise of men like Stead and Newnes, the perfection of large-quantity printing methods, and the use of news agents for distribution, books had become so cheap by the end of the century that seemingly the only step remaining was to give them away. But these paperbacks were a credit to the bookmaker only in a strictly technological sense. Aesthetic appeal and durability had been almost wholly sacrificed to economy.

It was time, therefore, for a radical improvement in cheap bookmaking. This was brought about by J. M. Dent, since 1867 a London bookbinder. Like Charles Knight (the story of whose career deeply influenced his own ambitions), Dent was a man with a mission. His goal was to publish for the mass audience books whose physical appearance matched their literary excellence. In 1894-96 he issued the Temple Shakespeare, which reproduced the scholarly Cambridge text of the plays and sold for a shilling a volume. For some time the series sold 250,000 volumes a year, and by 1934 its

---

[45] *Ibid.*, November 30, 1895, p. 619; December 21, 1895, p. 697; *Newsagents' Chronicle*, November 7, 1896, p. 30; Frederic Whyte, *Life of W. T. Stead* [1925], II, 228-31.

[46] Sadleir, *XIX Century Fiction*, II, 61-62; *Newsagents' Chronicle*, November 21, 1896, p. 1.

total sale had reached five million copies. It was immediately followed by the popular Temple Classics, which, though not overlooking the standard masterpieces, made a special point of including neglected works like Ben Jonson's *Timber*, Caxton's translation
of *The Golden Legend*, and Wordsworth's *Prelude*. In 1906 Dent's
career was climaxed by the founding of Everyman's Library,
whose story, however—a fascinating one of hectic planning, editorial work, and production—falls beyond the scope of this book.[47]
Once again, after many decades of indifference to physical attractiveness, English publishers began to make the classics available
to the common reader in a cheap form that was dainty yet sturdy,
convenient to the pocket, and printed on good paper in readable
type.

Thus the 1890's saw the ultimate victory of the cheap-book
movement. Only one event counteracted, to some extent, the gains
that had been made. Despite the constant opposition of publishers
and a few regular booksellers, since 1852 the practice of allowing
the retail buyer a discount from list price of as much as 25 per cent
had become almost universal. In 1890, however, Frederick Macmillan came forth with a fresh proposal to end underselling. New
books, he said, should be divided into two categories: "net books,"
upon which no discount was to be allowed by the bookseller, and
"subject books," upon which the bookseller was free to allow a discount if he wished. The Macmillan firm gingerly tried out the idea,
followed by a few other firms. Throughout the decade the "net
book" scheme was argued back and forth, the chief opposition
coming from the booksellers, who, while approving the plan in
principle, insisted that they were at the mercy of their discount-
giving competitors, especially drapers and department stores. Finally, in 1899, the trade as a whole took the plunge: 1,106 out of
1,270 booksellers in the United Kingdom agreed to allow no discount on books priced at over 6s.[48] The net book agreement, how-

---

[47] Dent, *Memoirs, passim;* Ernest Rhys, *Everyman Remembers* (New York, 1931),
pp. 230–42; Rhys, *Wales England Wed* (1940), pp. 163–69; Frank Swinnerton, *Swinnerton:
An Autobiography* (New York, 1936), pp. 65–85.

[48] Morgan, pp. 178–81; *Publishers' Circular* and *Bookseller*, 1890–99, *passim.* At the
same time the Council of the Publishers' Association recommended that its members
convert their existing books into "net books" by reducing their list price by a sixth—an
admission that during the long regime of underselling, publishers' prices were deliberately
inflated in order to make up for the anticipated retail discount.

ever, did not wholly end the discount practice, even in respect to books costing over 6s. There were recurrent squabbles, the bitterest being occasioned in 1906 by the *Times* Book Club's offering to its members, at sharp reductions, books which the Publishers' Association maintained were protected under the terms of the 1899 pact.[49]

Even with the return of price regulation, the fact remained that the common reader in the last days of Victoria was more amply supplied with books than ever before. And the new century saw constant fresh efforts in that direction; in 1907, for instance, Nelson and Collins simultaneously issued 7d. cloth-bound editions of copyright works, which sold many millions. Reprint series at 6d. or 1s. continued to multiply, and as the second World War began, the welcome given the Penguin and Pelican series was dramatic new evidence that the ordinary reader was eager for truly good books if they were priced within his reach. Though the inflation resulting from both great wars inescapably affected book prices, in general the gains achieved during the latter half of the nineteenth century have lasted to the present time. Through countless vicissitudes, and against great odds, the cause of cheap books had triumphed; and, as the *Publishers' Circular* remarked editorially in 1886, "in the social history of the country there can be no chapter more striking in its importance."[50]

[49] *History of "The Times,"* III, 831–34.

[50] *Publishers' Circular,* October 1, 1886, p. 1055.

CHAPTER 14 } *Periodicals and Newspapers 1800–1850*

I. Great as was the increase in book production between 1800 and 1900, the expansion of the periodical industry was greater still. This was only natural, for of all forms of reading matter, periodicals—including newspapers—are best adapted to the needs of a mass audience. They can be produced and sold much more cheaply than books. They appeal to millions of men and women who consider the reading of a whole book too formidable a task even to be attempted. They can be read straight through in an hour or two, or picked up for a few minutes at a time; for on the whole they do not require sustained attention, having been dedicated from their earliest days to the principle of variety. Again, periodicals cater best to one of the most compelling motives behind the reading habit, the desire to keep up with the world. The topicality of the newspaper and many weekly and monthly publications has always recommended them, over other forms of printed matter, to the common reader.

Viewed in long perspective, the relationship between the development of a mass audience in the nineteenth century and the rise of the cheap periodical was simple: the growth in the number of readers made periodical publishing an increasingly attractive commercial speculation, and the more papers that were issued for popular consumption, the more the reading habit spread. But examined more closely, the process proves to have been no clear circle of cause and effect. Here once more the accidents of history repeatedly intervened to complicate matters.

Early in the nineteenth century the largest audience seemingly was attained by several denominational magazines, at least two of which had circulations as high as 18,000 in 1807. Next to these were the newly founded critical quarterlies; the *Quarterly* and the

Edinburgh each sold about 12,000 or 13,000 in their heyday. The older critical periodicals and the new-style magazines, such as *Blackwood's* and *Fraser's*, ranged from 3,000 to 8,000, seldom exceeding the latter figure.[1] At the beginning of the century the leading reviews, the *Critical* and *Monthly*, cost 2s.; general magazines, such as the *Gentleman's*, the *Monthly*, the *Universal*, and the *European*, were 1s.6d.; and specialized magazines—the *Lady's*, the *Commercial*, the *Sporting*, the *Zoological*—were a shilling. The cheapest periodicals were those subsidized by the various religious denominations. The *Evangelical, Gospel,* and *General Baptist* magazines were priced at 6d.[2] Periodicals shared in the general rise of prices during the next decades. In 1834, the *Edinburgh* and *Quarterly* reviews cost 6s., or three times as much as their monthly predecessors in the critical field. Some leading magazines, such as the *New Monthly*, the *Metropolitan*, the *Court*, and the *Lady's*, were 3s.6d., and the rest, the *Monthly, Blackwood's, Tait's,* and *Fraser's* among them, were 2s.6d.[3] Such prices of course placed them out of the reach of most buyers; they were publications distinctly intended for the drawing-room in town and country, and for the subscription reading-rooms whose very existence was evidence that many readers on the cultural level to which these periodicals appealed could not afford to buy them outright.

Serious-minded readers who could ill afford 2s.6d. or 3s.6d. for a monthly magazine or from 6d. to a shilling for a weekly were, therefore, provided for only in the most desultory way. Apart from the sixpenny denominational monthlies, there was virtually nothing but the catchpenny miscellaneous papers put out by small proprietors. None of these short-lived cheap papers had a definite plan; they consisted for the most part, as William Chambers wrote, "of disjointed and unauthorized extracts from books, clippings from floating literature, old stories, and stale jocularities."[4]

---

[1] In order to reduce arithmetical interruptions to a minimum, circulation figures for individual periodicals and newspapers have been tabulated in Appendix C. When, as will be the case occasionally, figures are cited also in the text, the authority for them will be given at the appropriate place in the notes to that appendix.

[2] The prices of some twoscore periodicals published about 1800 are given in Timperley, *Encyclopaedia of Literary and Typographical Anecdote,* p. 805.

[3] The prices of numerous periodicals in the Reform Bill era are quoted in *Chambers's Journal,* III (1834), 1.

[4] *Memoir of Robert Chambers,* p. 209.

The very names of most of them are known only to specialists, and few files, comprising in most cases only a volume or two, are extant.

Typical of such papers, though motivated by a somewhat loftier purpose than lay behind most of them, was one begun in 1813 by the East Lothian printer George Miller. Miller, alarmed by "the shocking scenes that disgraced the streets of Edinburgh at the commencement of last year, and their melancholy consequences,"[5] and adopting as his motto "It is better to prevent crimes than to punish them," began publishing the *Cheap Magazine*, a fourpenny monthly printed on cheap paper and embellished with woodcuts unusually crude even for that age. Subtitled "The Poor Man's Fireside Companion," it printed "stories of the primitive passions, the lessons of which were made painfully evident in almost every paragraph," Watts-like poems, "papers on the industrial arts and the commoner sciences, hints on etiquette," and miscellaneous information. Although Miller boasted that 21,000 copies of the first number were issued, including reprinted editions, the paper died after two years.[6] According to Alexander Somerville, its religious readers "took alarm at it, because it aimed at popularizing philosophical and purely literary subjects, and did not give a predominancy to religion. This defection and opposition sealed its fate; and after several years of heavy struggles, mental and pecuniary, George Miller left off publishing, a poorer man in purse and reputation than he began."[7]

A more successful enterprise—indeed, the only one that lasted for more than a few seasons—was John Limbird's *Mirror of Literature, Amusement and Instruction*, which began late in 1822 and continued until 1849. The *Mirror*, a sixteen-page weekly, printed on good paper and adorned with one or two woodcuts, cost 2*d.* Its miscellaneous contents were snipped from books and other periodicals and pasted together by John Timbs, Limbird's shopman, who later became one of the most prolific of Victorian compilers. The *Mirror* met with great approbation among the clergy and "respectable classes," and with decidedly less among the established

[5] Quoted from the first issue, in the Newberry Library.

[6] W. J. Couper, *The Millers of Haddington, Dunbar and Dunfermline: A Record of Scottish Bookselling* (1914), pp. 119–21.

[7] *Autobiography of a Working Man*, p. 48.

booksellers and wholesale houses, who would have nothing to do with a periodical that cost but twopence and on which therefore the discount was negligible. But the public liked the *Mirror*. Brougham reported, two years after it began, that some numbers sold "upwards of 80,000." When Limbird died in 1883, an obituary writer called him with some justification "the father of our periodical literature."[8] In a way he was to the mass-audience periodical of the nineteenth century what Addison and Edward Cave had been to the middle-class periodicals of the preceding century.

The Stamp Act of 1819, though directed specifically against the radical press, placed a formidable barrier in the way of the cheap press in general.[9] Ironically, one of its provisions gave official blessing and an unquestionable advantage to a class of periodicals which, though innocent of dangerous political tendencies, were certainly not calculated to improve the cultural level of the people. As we noted in an earlier chapter, Parliament exempted from the 4*d*. duty all part-issues of works which had originally been published in book form. While this concession allowed the reprinting in cheap numbers of all sorts of books, including "standard literature," in practice it primarily benefited the already flourishing Gothic fiction trade.[10] Encouraged by the unequivocal language of the act, the proprietors of such number-publications proceeded to the logical next step, the issuing of cheap papers dedicated to the serialization of sensational tales. These found great favor among those sections of the mass public unaffected by the evangelical horror of imaginative indulgence. Dickens, for example, recalled that as a schoolboy he used to buy the *Terrific Register*, "making myself unspeakably miserable, and frightening my very wits out of my head, for the small charge of a penny weekly; which, considering that there was an illustration to every number in which there was always a pool of blood, and at least one body, was cheap."[11]

So far as periodicals generally were concerned, then, the situa-

[8] *Bookseller*, November 30, 1859, pp. [1326–27], and January 5, 1884, p. 6.

[9] For the terms of this law, see below, pp. 327–28.

[10] Again ironically, this provision also had the effect of exempting weekly or fortnightly part-issues of the very sort of literature it was designed to eradicate, since it covered the works of Paine and other radical thinkers—especially the French rationalists—which had earlier been issued in volumes.

[11] John Forster, *Life of Charles Dickens*, I (13th ed., 1873), [vi].

tion down to 1832 was only mildly conducive to the spread of interest in reading among the masses. Publications like Limbird's *Mirror*, penny helpings of terror, religious papers, and the various
short-lived miscellaneous papers, whether grave or gay, did give
the impecunious reader something on which to sharpen his eyes.
The selection, however, was not large, and since only stamped
papers could be carried by post, the circulation of these cheap
papers was limited to London and the provincial towns.

But where they failed to penetrate, the newspaper press, and to
a much greater degree the press of radical comment, did; and it is
in that direction we must look to understand the true place of the
periodical in the era before the first Reform Bill. The excitement of
the times, as reflected in the newspapers and in turn intensified by
popular response to the radical journalists' message, turned hundreds of thousands of Englishmen into readers.

II. As we saw in chapter 2, down to the time
of Pitt the newspaper's appeal and influence were limited chiefly to
the upper and the urban commercial classes. As organs of opinion
the daily papers were simply the hired mouthpieces of one party or
the other. Not until the nineteenth century was decades old would
the increasing value of newspapers as advertising mediums allow them gradually to shake off government or party control and
to become independent voices of public sentiment.

But in the era of the Napoleonic Wars, newspapers won more and
more readers. When disastrous or triumphant dispatches from the
Peninsula or the Nile, reports of political crises in Paris or Westminster, and rumors of invasion were the stuff of life to the average
Englishman, he came to need newspapers as never before. He still
could not buy them outright; increasing taxation had sent their
price to 6*d.* by 1800, and after 1815 they rose to 7*d.*—a price prohibitive even to most middle-class families with an income of less
than, say, £300 a year. Most copies of a daily paper in the first
third of the century passed through a dozen or even scores of
hands. The coffeehouses in every town took in the papers as a
matter of course; without the latest news, they would have lost
most of their customers. In most towns, too, there were subscription reading-rooms for the middle class, where, for a guinea or a
guinea and a half a year, one could have access to a selection of

London and provincial papers as well as to the current magazines and reviews.[12] Such a reading-room, started in the 1820's at 192 Strand, was the first venture of W. H. Smith and Son; there a subscriber could find 150 newspapers a week.[13] Nor was it only the relatively well-to-do who hungered for the news. In "Cayenneville," the Scottish mill town described in John Galt's *Annals of the Parish*, the local bookseller "took in a daily London newspaper for the spinners and weavers, who paid him a penny a week apiece for the same, they being all greatly taken up with what, at the time, was going on in France."[14]

The hiring-out of newspapers, though illegal, was widely practiced. A London newsman might make seventy or eighty lendings of the morning's *Times* in a day, at a penny an hour, after which he would post the used copies to subscribers in the country who paid him 3*d.* for a copy mailed the day of publication or 2*d.* for one mailed the day following.[15] In 1830 Charles Lamb, living at Enfield, had William Hone send him day-old copies of the *Times*.[16] Once arrived in the country, the paper continued its travels. In a Devon town in 1799, the London *Courier* went first to the surgeon, then successively to a French emigré, the Congregational minister, the druggist, and the undermaster of a local school. The next day it went to another citizen, who sold it to a sergemaker who in turn sent it among the common people. Another copy of the same paper went through fifteen pairs of hands before it ended up with a parson, who, it was reported, used it to "poison the honest countrymen."[17] This informal method of circulating newspapers gave rise to "newspaper societies" composed of six or a dozen families who clubbed together to subscribe to a London or a provincial paper, or sometimes both. In 1821 a writer in the *Monthly Magazine* asserted that there were "not less than 5,000" such groups, "serving with mental food at least 50,000 families."[18]

[12] Aspinall, *Politics and the Press*, p. 25. Chaps. i and ii of this work gather much information on the devices by which newspapers found their readers at this period.

[13] Waugh, *A Hundred Years of Publishing*, p. 100.

[14] *Annals of the Parish*, chap. xxxi.

[15] *History of "The Times,"* I, 275, 435–36.

[16] Lamb, *Letters*, ed. Lucas (New Haven, 1935), III, 282.

[17] E. S. Chalk, "Circulation of XVIII-Century Newspapers," *Notes & Queries*, CLXIX (1935), 336.

[18] *Monthly Magazine*, LI (1821), 397–98.

By these various means the newspapers of the early nineteenth century entered the daily lives of a steadily greater number of the middle class and even to some small extent of the working class. The new audience, however, was concentrated for the most part in the cities and towns. There was a provincial newspaper press, but the circulation of the individual journals was small and their news was meager and stale, for no daily papers were to be published outside London until after 1855. Hence comparatively fresh and detailed national and world news was available to rural readers only if they had access, at second or third hand, to copies of London papers sent down through the post. And in any event, among artisans and laborers in both town and country it was not the newspaper but the weekly paper of political comment—in effect, a weekly pamphlet—that was most instrumental in initiating and confirming the reading habit.[19]

At the end of the eighteenth century the Pitt government had effectively silenced the radical press. But with the coming of peace in 1815—an event accompanied by widespread unemployment and actual starvation—radical journalism revived under the leadership of William Cobbett, whose *Political Register*, begun in 1802 as a Tory paper, now was firmly on the side of the people. The *Register*'s price was a shilling halfpenny, far beyond the reach of most individuals, and its weekly circulation in 1816 was only between one and two thousand; but workingmen clubbed together to buy it and read it aloud in the alehouses.[20] Hence, despite the price, its message reached scores of thousands of the economically oppressed. Here was a new kind of journalism, which trenchantly commented on domestic events and prescribed remedies for the desperate state in which the workers found themselves. It was a journalism which struck home, as none had done since the days of Paine, even to village-bound men who had remained indifferent to all papers so long as they merely reported news from faraway places, whether London or Austerlitz, in which they had no slightest interest.

For some time, however, Cobbett had been hearing that the

[19] For a more detailed treatment of the radical press of this era, see, in addition to the sources given in the following notes, Webb, *The British Working Class Reader*, chaps. i–iii.

[20] Unless otherwise specified, material on Cobbett is taken from G. D. H. Cole's *Life*.

publicans at whose houses the *Register* was being read aloud were in danger of losing their licenses if the practice continued; the laws enacted by the Pitt government, designed to eliminate public houses as centers of seditious discussion, were still in effect. The only alternative was for Cobbett to enable men to read the *Register* at home instead. On November 2, 1816, he issued the *Register* not only in its customary form but as a twopenny pamphlet, the latter omitting the news contained in the expensive edition (which subjected it to the stamp duty) but printing in full his newly written "Address to the Journeymen and Labourers." The novelty of this plan of enabling the workingman to acquire political enlightenment by the fireside may be gauged by the pains to which Cobbett went to spell out its advantages: "Two or three journeymen or labourers cannot spare a shilling and a half-penny a week; but they can spare a half-penny or three farthings each, which is not much more than the tax which they pay upon a good large quid of tobacco. And, besides, the expense of the thing itself thus becomes less than the expense of going to a public-house to hear it read. Then there is the time for reflection, and opportunity of reading over again, and of referring to interesting facts. The *children* will also have an opportunity of reading. The expense of other books will be saved by those who have this resource. The wife can sometimes read, if the husband cannot."[21] If the appearance of the twopenny *Register* proved to be a turning point in English political history, it was no less revolutionary a development in the history of the reading public.

Within a few months the circulation of the twopenny *Register* leaped to forty or fifty thousand, and perhaps as high as seventy thousand, thus completely eclipsing every other journal of the day. The timeliness of this weekly political tract had a great deal to do with its success, but just as important was Cobbett's ability both as a businessman and as a writer. He set up an efficient system of distribution throughout the country, sending bundles of each week's *Register* by coach to agents in every town. The discount he allowed was enough to give a decent living to a man with a small family, and even to encourage his agents in the towns to hire hawkers to carry the paper through the countryside. One man, it is said, made 75*s.* in two or three weeks by selling 1,800 copies of the

[21] *Political Register*, November 16, 1816, p. 611.

Register.[22] It took no extraordinary sales ability to dispose of the paper, for Cobbett, stimulated by the presence of an audience larger than any political writer had had since Paine, quickly mastered the art of writing for the working class. His pungent, vigorous paragraphs set a model for popular journalism—a model which many sought in vain to imitate. Here at last, at a crucial moment in the history of the English common people, was a writer on political matters who "tried to speak to the people instead of speaking for them, to lead them instead of patronising them, and to educate them instead of lecturing their unheeding Government."[23]

Early in 1817 the government, which had failed to find any specific grounds upon which to prosecute Cobbett, seized the opportunity offered by the suspension of habeas corpus to threaten him with arrest. He therefore chose to flee to America, but behind him he left a newly energized journalism of protest. In the next two years, at least a score of radical papers were started, and Parliament and the "respectable" press resounded with ominous accounts of the people's absorption in radical propaganda. Whenever a new issue of Wooler's *Black Dwarf* or Hone's *Register* arrived in town alehouse or at country crossroads, crowds would gather to hear one of their number read its contents aloud.[24] The weekly circulation of the *Black Dwarf*, 12,000 in 1819, could without straining the ruling class's imagination be translated into twelve thousand seditious assemblages throughout England. Farm laborers, mill hands, miners, handloom weavers, soldiers—all who had cause to be disaffected—were reading now or listening to someone else read. They had discovered that the printed word was capable of uses far different from those with which they had come to associate it. It was not merely a soporific dose anxiously administered by clergymen and ladies: it was a means through which they found leadership and inspiration, and above all a prescription for escaping from their present enslavement. Jobless, starving, often homeless, their blind, furious demonstrations met by the rifles of the soldiery, they looked upon the printed word as a new revelation, one which was infinitely more applicable to their immediate situa-

[22] Aspinall, pp. 30–31.

[23] Wickwar, *The Struggle for the Freedom of the Press, 1819–32*, p. 54.

[24] Aspinall, p. 29.

tion than the Scriptural precepts expounded in religious tracts. No wonder, then, that great numbers of men now learned to read for the first time, and that many more groped back to the long-past days of their schooling to retrieve the art they had once fleetingly possessed.

The government's frantic attempts to suppress the printed utterances of the radical leaders whetted the popular appetite still more. The English worker, even at this black moment in national history, was not so tyrannized out of all resemblance to a human being that he failed to covet something all the more because it was denied him. In 1818 the radical bookseller Richard Carlile brought out a thousand-copy edition of Paine's *Age of Reason*. Despite his advertising in the newspapers and on placards, he sold only a hundred copies in the first month. But then the Society for the Suppression of Vice started a prosecution; the news got into the Sunday papers; and in another month the edition was sold out. A second edition, of 3,000 copies, was printed, and in six months two-thirds of it was gone. The publicity given Carlile's trial helped sell 10,000 copies of the verbatim proceedings of the first day. Since *The Age of Reason* had been read into the record during that day, as the basis of the case against him, it was incorporated into these pamphlets and thus given additional distribution. Carlile relished the irony of the situation: the more he was persecuted, the more both his business and his cause flourished. While he was in prison, his wife continued his bookselling business and was promptly arrested in turn. In his *Republican* he wrote: "I take this opportunity of repeating my thanks to the Vice Society for the extensive circulation they are again giving my publications. I hear from London that the prosecution of Mrs. Carlile produces just the same effect as my prosecution did—it quadruples the sale of all her publications."[25]

The ruling class's boldest attempt to cut off the supply of this sort of reading matter from the rebellious masses was the act of Parliament known as 60 George III c.9 (December, 1819), one of the notorious "six acts." This law defined as a newspaper, and thus as subject to the tax (which had been raised to 4*d.* in 1815), every periodical containing news or comments on the news that was pub-

[25] "Religious Prosecutions," *Westminster Review*, II (1824), 13; Wickwar, pp. 82, 94–95, 206–207.

lished oftener than every twenty-six days, printed on two sheets or less, and priced at less than 6*d*. exclusive of the tax.[26]

The framing of the act left no doubt as to its purpose. It was legislation shrewdly designed to wipe out antigovernmental, antireligious papers. It was not a tax upon news alone, as earlier newspaper-stamp enactments had been, but upon views; and not upon all views, but specifically upon those of radical demagogues. To avoid implying that all cheap papers were dangerous (if that were so, pertinently inquired a Newcastle pamphleteer, "how are we to defend our Cheap Religious Tract Societies?"[27]) the act went on to exempt from taxation papers "containing only matters of devotion, piety, or charity."[28] No further proof was needed of the particular end that Parliament had in view, and the new public that the radical press had called into being in the past several years was not slow to recognize it.

Superficially, the Act of 1819 was a success. Prosecution of offending printers, booksellers, and hawkers was swift, and the sentences handed down upon conviction were severe. Many radical papers died, and the rest, including the *Black Dwarf*, Carlile's *Republican*, and Cobbett's *Political Register*, went up to 6*d*. Inevitably, their circulation fell off. But the excitement of the 1820's —the swelling demand for parliamentary reform, the trial of Queen Caroline, the controversy over Catholic emancipation—forbade that the popular interest in current events which they had aroused should die away. The day had passed forever, indeed, when the rank and file of the English population could remain indifferent to the course of political events. Now that the radical press had again been temporarily muted, the demand for regular newspapers grew, despite their prohibitive cost to individual purchasers. In London, in the industrial Midlands, even in small country towns, cheap subscription reading-rooms sprang up in imitation of those supported by the middle class. Workingmen, upon the payment of a

[26] For the text of this all-important act, see *Hansard*, Ser. 1, XLI (1819), cols. 1678–90. On the events leading up to its passage, and on its consequences, the books of Wickwar and Aspinall and the earlier article by J. Holland Rose, "The Unstamped Press, 1815–1836," are especially informative.

[27] Quoted in Wickwar, p. 81.

[28] Cobbett, whose impudence was matched only by his resourcefulness, named his new series of radical propaganda pamphlets "Cobbett's Monthly Religious Tracts"—changed after the third number to "Cobbett's Monthly Sermons" (Pearl, *William Cobbett*, p. 117).

small sum, could have free access to as many papers as they desired. These newsrooms were looked upon, and rightly, as beehives of seditious activity, but not much could be done to suppress them. As a modern student has observed, they were "more important agencies for the dissemination of newspaper information than either public meetings or Radical Reformist Societies."[29] In addition to the communal reading facilities offered by individuals or organizations devoted to spreading radical opinions, more and more non-political coffeehouses were begun, all of which attracted their patrons by a generous selection of newspapers. "Now no man," remarked a writer in 1829, "or no man who can read (and how few are there of those who go to coffee-shops who cannot read), thinks of calling for his cup of coffee without at the same time asking for a newspaper."[30]

In 1829 newspaper circulation had reached a level previously unattained except during a few critical moments of the Napoleonic Wars. The seven London morning papers together circulated 28,000 (an increase of 5,000 in seven years), and the six evening papers 11,000. But the dailies were far overshadowed by the Sunday newspapers, which had an aggregate sale of 110,000 a week.[31] The growing popularity of the Sunday press was the chief evidence of the spread of the newspaper-reading habit in the decade before the Reform Bill. Taking up where the victims of the Act of 1819 had left off, the Sunday newspaper (which was duly stamped) became the principal organ of radical sentiment. At the end of the decade it was calculated that the radical Sunday papers outsold the conservative ones at a ratio of almost ten to one.[32] It was not only their political tone, however, which won them a place in the lives of those who did not mind encouraging shopkeepers and hawkers to break the Sabbatarian laws. Besides political news and opinions, these papers dished up generous helpings of the week's scandal and crime, garnished with all the titillating or gruesome details, and some of them devoted substantial space to sporting news. Newspapers were becoming more and more interesting to the common reader.

In summary, the political and social turmoil of the years be-

[29] Aspinall, p. 27.

[30] Merle, "Weekly Newspapers," p. 476.

[31] *Ibid.*, pp. 469, 475, 477.   [32] *Ibid.*, p. 470.

tween Waterloo and the passage of the first Reform Bill greatly
enlarged the audience for periodicals. In Great Britain as a whole
during the period 1800–30, the annual sale of newspaper stamps
had virtually doubled, from sixteen million to thirty million,[33]
while the population had grown half as fast, from ten and a half
million to sixteen million. Furthermore, an individual paper probably passed through more hands than it had earlier. Although the
journalist Gibbons Merle may have exaggerated when he assumed
in 1829 that "every newspaper is read by thirty persons,"[34] certainly the increase of subscription reading-rooms and coffeehouses
was responsible for a much greater spread of the reading habit than
is suggested on the face of the stamp returns.

However, in the excitement and apprehension that the appearance of the new public generated in the 1820's, it was only natural
that its size and social comprehensiveness should have been exaggerated. Statements like those uttered by frightened politicians
pushing for the Newspaper Stamp Act of 1819, one of whom
averred that every miner in the northern collieries carried a *Black
Dwarf* in his hat,[35] give the impression that practically everybody
was reading radical papers.[36] Actually, of course, only a relatively
small proportion of the total population *read* any kind of paper,
though the custom of reading the newspaper aloud to a group of
listeners meant that far more people came into indirect contact
with the printed word than would appear from any circulation figures. Although many unskilled laborers joined the reading public
under the influence of the Cobbett-Wooler-Hone-Carlile school of
violent journalism, they fell away for the most part after the
Stamp Act limited its circulation. It was rather from the class of
artisans and small shopkeepers that the periodical-reading public
received most of its permanent recruits at this period.

What was to be done with this startling new force in English
life, whose political potency was being demonstrated as the drama

[33] Aspinall, "The Circulation of Newspapers in the Early Nineteenth Century," p. 29 n.

[34] Merle, p. 477.

[35] Wickwar, p. 57.

[36] One estimate of the size of the reading public at this time was that of Sydney Smith:
"Readers are fourfold in number compared with what they were before the beginning of
the French war. . . . There are four or five hundred thousand readers more than there were
thirty years ago, among the lower orders" (Sydney Smith, *Letters*, ed. Nowell C. Smith
[Oxford, 1953], I, 341, 343).

of Reform Bill agitation swept to its climax? Experience had shown that it could not be legislated out of existence. But in the eyes of the conservatives and the more moderate liberals, it posed a standing threat to the peace of the nation, for it was a force which every demagogue could manipulate at will. They were convinced that if the spread of interest in reading among new sections of the population endangered English institutions, it did so only because the new readers had fallen into the wrong hands. Put them into the right hands, and the reading habit could be transformed from an instrument of evil into one of unlimited good.

Two things had to be done. One was to open the way for the establishment of cheap respectable newspapers. Since the hunger for news had grown to so great proportions, the ordinary man should be enabled to have his own paper for home consumption. It was not healthy for him to be forced to read his paper in a place of public resort, where discussion could so easily get out of hand and indignation work up a dangerous head of steam. Again, making cheap newspapers commercially practicable would encourage men with venture capital (and therefore, presumably, men of dependable political views) to enter the field, thus driving out the demagogues. But such a step could not be taken until the "taxes on knowledge" were reduced or abolished. The 4*d.* newspaper duty, the tax on advertisements (3*s.*6*d.* each), and the paper tax combined to make cheap journalism a decidedly unattractive field for the profit-seeking enterpriser.

The other great goal of the reformers was the establishment of cheap family periodicals. There was no reason why the common reader's attention should be confined to the news. Too great absorption in problems of the day, especially as those problems were interpreted by radical journalists, was, to say the least, unwholesome. What the new reading community needed was papers of general information and entertainment, papers which would quietly direct the reader's thinking along lines approved by the responsible part of the nation. Such cheap general papers as existed were crude, rag-tag-and-bobtail affairs without plan or direction. What an opportunity there was for a venturesome publisher! "The Lower orders," a correspondent wrote to Archibald Constable in 1825, "at present are somewhat in the same situation in which the higher and middling ranks were at the time when Mr.

Addison and the other authors of the *Spectator*, etc., took them in hand, and contributed so much to their improvement by dealing out to them constant doses of religious, moral, philosophical, critical, literary sentiment and information, and may be said almost to have formed the minds of the better orders of the people for successive generations." He therefore proposed to Constable, who was then dreaming of reaching the millions through his Miscellany, a paper that should address the lower orders "in a tone of perfect confidence and equality—should encourage them in every liberal and enlightened study—should show them how differences in rank have arisen in the world, and in what way alone men can rise advantageously from a lower rank to a higher," and calling them, "with a voice of authority, to abandon low and brutal vices, and to go on in the grand course of industry, virtuous contentment, and the ambition of knowledge and improvement."[37] This was the program of the day, but it remained for other hands than Constable's to carry it out.

III. Between 1827 and 1832 Britain, as we have seen, went through its first great cheap-literature craze. Cheap books—or relatively cheap ones—led the way: Constable's Miscellany, the Libraries of Useful and Entertaining Knowledge, Murray's Family Library, Cadell's cut-rate Scott, and the rest. The assumptions that inspired the production of these series were also applied to family periodicals. Early in 1832 appeared two cheap "wholesome" papers whose success had much to do with the character of journalism for the middle class (not, to be sure, the class for which they were designed) in the approaching Victorian era. *Chambers's Edinburgh Journal* was launched on February 4; Charles Knight's *Penny Magazine* on March 31.

The aims of the two new ventures were essentially the same. In his "Address to His Readers" William Chambers promised that his three-halfpenny weekly would have something of interest and value for everyone: "Literary and Scientific subjects, including articles on the Formation and Arrangements of Society; short Essays on Trade and Commerce; observations on Education in its different branches . . . ; sketches in Topography and Statistics,

[37] Thomas Constable, *Archibald Constable and His Literary Correspondents* (Edinburgh, 1873), II, 450–51.

relative to Agriculture, Gardening, Planting, Sheep-farming, the making of Roads, Bridges, and Canals; the establishment of Ferries, the best means of Conveyance by Land and Water; Increase of Population; the Uses of Machinery to simplify Human Labour, Manufactures, &c"—to say nothing of information on emigration, articles for artisans, young ladies, boys, "men who reflect deeply on the constitution of man," and so on almost indefinitely.[38]

The *Penny Magazine* offered an equally panoramic program of instruction, with even greater emphasis upon practical knowledge. In the first volume Knight introduced also many features of less demonstrably "useful" value—articles on literature, the fine arts, history, and other topics of cultural interest—but these were dropped from succeeding volumes with a suddenness that suggests an enforced change of policy. For the *Penny Magazine*'s sponsors, the publications committee of the Society for the Diffusion of Useful Knowledge, were, Knight himself later remarked, "as opposed to works of imagination, as if they had been 'budge doctors of the Stoic fur,' whose vocation was to despise everything not of direct utility."[39]

It had taken some persuasion to get the society to undertake a periodical for the lower orders in the first place. Some members felt that the publication of a penny magazine was beneath the dignity of such a group; during the preliminary discussions, one "old gentleman of the Whig school" kept muttering over and over, "It is very awkward."[40] Chambers, on the other hand, was a free agent. Unlike Knight, who could print no fiction, he leavened his loaf of utilitarian instruction with a weekly short story—"a nice amusing tale," as he put it, "either original, or selected from the best modern authors—no ordinary trash about Italian castles, and daggers, and ghosts in the blue chamber, and similar nonsense, but something really good."[41] This was the great point of difference between the two periodicals, and it had much to do with the fact that the *Penny Magazine* went under in 1845 while *Chambers's*

[38] *Chambers's Journal*, I (1832), 1.

[39] Knight, *Passages of a Working Life*, II, 315. This book contains (II, 179–94) the fullest available history of the *Penny Magazine*. Webb, *The British Working Class Reader*, pp. 77–80, gives a good critical account of both it and *Chambers's Journal*.

[40] Knight, II, 181.

[41] *Chambers's Journal*, I (1832), 1.

Journal prospered down to the end of the century and beyond—indeed, to our own time.

Affiliation with the Useful Knowledge Society handicapped the *Penny Magazine* in other ways. The fact that Brougham and his clique were its sponsors disturbed middle-class Tories on two counts, political and religious.[42] Commercial publishers resented the intrusion into their preserve of a non-profit organization, bent, they feared, on cornering the cheap-periodical market. Many working-class readers reacted to the magazine as they did to every other scheme hatched by the Brougham faction.

Chambers's Journal again was more fortunate in that it was frankly a commercial enterprise, and though its underlying purpose duplicated that of the *Penny Magazine*, it had no connection with controversial parties like Brougham's. Chambers was resolved that neither Church nor Dissent, neither Tories nor Whigs, and least of all radicals, would affect its policy. Thus the paper was welcomed by many who would have rejected one sponsored by, say, the Church of England or by a group of men notorious for their liberal sympathies. But this studied independence had its own unhappy side. Chambers was acutely conscious that he was walking on eggs; as a man who staked his fortune on the success of the paper, he could afford to offend no one. This cautiousness led him to steer away from most, though not all, controversial subjects and to exercise tireless vigilance over the paper's prose. "Numberless topics and expressions," he said, "which the conductors of hardly any other periodical work would think objectionable, are avoided by us, and . . . we hardly ever receive a contribution from the most practised writers, which does not require purification before we deem it fit for insertion."[43] Inevitably, blamelessness shaded into innocuousness; in his zeal to avoid giving offense on any side, Chambers kept from the *Journal* the qualities necessary to win working-class readers accustomed to the hard-hitting commentary of the political press and the melodrama of both the Sun-

[42] Dr. Arnold of Rugby was one of those who, while deeply in sympathy with the program to educate the people through a cheap press, felt that the society "should take a more decided tone on matters of religion." He went so far as to send the magazine some contributions designed to help "Christianize" it. Arnold objected also to the "ramble-scramble" character of the *Penny Magazine*, taking the position that the masses would be enlightened through cheap newspapers rather than miscellanies (A. P. Stanley, *Life and Correspondence of Thomas Arnold* [1898], I, 262, 277, 299).

[43] *Chambers's Journal*, IV (1835), 1.

day newspapers' surveys of crime and the penny numbers of Gothic fiction.

Both papers, in conspicuous contrast to Limbird's *Mirror* and the more ephemeral household periodicals which had preceded them, commissioned their main articles from professional writers. Much of the *Penny Magazine*'s material, however, was written by men close to the Useful Knowledge Society, who as a rule had far less command of the style required by a popular periodical than did Chambers' contributors. The *Penny Magazine* at best was never light reading.

Whatever the deficiencies of the *Penny Magazine*'s text, it had a great edge over its rival in respect to pictures. *Chambers's* was not illustrated in the early years; Knight, on the other hand, went to great trouble and expense to obtain good woodcuts. Like the publishers of number-books, he seems to have consciously intended this emphasis upon pictures as a means of bringing printed matter to the attention of a public unaccustomed to reading. Even the illiterate found a good pennyworth of enjoyment in the illustrations each issue of the *Penny Magazine* contained. And these, perhaps more than the letterpress, were responsible for the affection with which many buyers thought of the magazine in retrospect.[44]

Whatever the comparative merits of the two periodicals, each had a dazzling initial success—so starved was the mass public for reading matter of the quality and quantity now set before it for a penny or three halfpence. Within three months after *Chambers's Journal* began, its fame had spread from its native Edinburgh to London, where, for the sake of quick distribution in England, a second edition was printed. By the end of the first year, the combined circulation was 50,000. As for the *Penny Magazine*, though the evidence is conflicting, at some time during the first three or four years the circulation, according to Knight himself, reached 200,000. This record circulation, which was more than twice that achieved by *Chambers's Journal* at the very height of its prosperity, did not last long. Near the end of its career, in the mid-forties, the *Penny Magazine* was selling only 40,000 copies, "which number," Knight said, "was scarcely remunerative"[45]—a significant indication of how radically the economics of cheap-periodical pub-

[44] See, for example, Frederic Harrison, *Autobiographic Memoirs* (1911), I, 6–7.

[45] Clowes, *Charles Knight*, pp. 225–26.

lishing had changed in the course of a few years. In an attempt to win back readers, Knight reduced the stress on natural history, engineering, astronomy, mineralogy, and geography in order to make room for Mrs. Jameson's series on great Italian painters and John Saunders' popularization of *The Canterbury Tales*. But it was then too late to save the magazine, and this abrupt liberalizing of policy may well have hastened its end.

Who bought these papers? At first, Chambers believed that his audience was the thoroughly democratic one he had intended it to be. On the *Journal's* second anniversary, he described how "one shepherd, upon a tract of mountain land, receives his copy, perhaps, from an egg-market-man or a travelling huckstry-woman. When perused, he takes it to the extremity of his walk, and places it under a certain stone, where the shepherd of the adjacent farm soon after receives it. By this person, again, it is taken, after perusal, to another place of appointment, to be there received by his neighbour." At the other end of the social scale, Chambers was "given to understand that it reaches the drawing-rooms of the most exalted persons in the country, and the libraries of the most learned. . . . In short, it *pervades the whole of society*."[46]

In a Cambridgeshire village, five poor boys clubbed together to get a communal copy of the *Journal* every week: three contributed a halfpenny each (which they had been given to drop in the missionary box) and the other two walked seven miles to the nearest bookseller to get the paper.[47] In a certain cotton mill near Glasgow, eighty-four copies of the *Journal* were purchased every week. Its reception among the country people was described by a bookseller writing only a year after the paper began: "Chambers," he said, "has done what others could not do, not even the Tract Societies. . . . Not many years ago, I drew £30 annually for trashy ballads, and still more trashy pamphlets, such as *John Cheap the Chapman, Paddy from Cork*, &c. . . . I no longer keep such trash in my shop." The news of *Chambers's Journal*, he continued, flashed through the countryside, and now, "if you only choose to watch, on certain days, the milk-boys returning seated on donkeys or

[46] *Chambers's Journal*, III (1834), 2; IV (1835), 1 (italics in the original).

[47] Chambers, *Story of a Long and Busy Life*, pp. 34–35. By a typically Victorian instance of causality, two boys grew up to be headmasters of schools, a third became a clergyman, and the other two prospered as a builder and a New Zealand sheep-farmer, respectively.

donkey-carts, you will discover that almost every urchin among them is thumbing Chambers in place of a ballad, and reaping the benefit of a partial perusal earlier than either his master or mistress. . . . Chambers has done more to wean the people from trash, cultivate their minds, and excite curiosity, than all the Tract Societies that ever existed."[48]

This evidence of *Chambers's* initial popularity among the workers comes from the proprietor's memoir and the pages of the paper itself; hence, while not necessarily untrue, it is subject to some discount. But now and then one finds in working-class reminiscences more independent testimony to the appeal that both *Chambers's* and the *Penny Magazine* had for some workers and their children. Christopher Thomson, the autobiographical housepainter of Nottinghamshire, having seen the first volume of the *Penny Magazine*, resolved to do without sugar in his tea in order to buy each new number as it came out.[49] In London, meanwhile, a candlemaker's son was enchanted by the magazine's woodcuts; by the highly miscellaneous nature of the articles which opened up many new intellectual interests simultaneously; and by the allusions to noteworthy examples of art and architecture which led him to go out and see them for himself. The magazine, he wrote many years later in an extended appreciation, was "an image of the mighty world."[50]

But after the first intoxication of success had worn off, even Chambers was forced to admit that his paper did not reach as far down into the multitude as he had at first thought. It *was* read, he said in 1840, by "the *élite* of the labouring community; those who think, conduct themselves respectably, and are anxious to improve their circumstances by judicious means. But below this worthy order of men, our work, except in a few particular cases, does not go. A fatal mistake is committed in the notion that the lower classes read. . . . Some millions of adults of both sexes, in cities as well as in rural districts, are till this hour as ignorant of letters as the people were generally during the middle ages."[51] Eleven years

[48] *Chambers's Journal*, IV (1835), 1; II (1833), 296.

[49] Thomson, *Autobiography of an Artisan*, p. 319.

[50] "The Penny Magazine," *St. Paul's Magazine*, XII (1873), 542–49. The article, one of a series of autobiographical papers from the same pen, was signed "An Irreconcileable." The author has not been identified.

[51] *Chambers's Journal*, XI (1840), 8.

later (1851), when a committee of Parliament was inquiring into reading tastes among the masses, one witness said flatly that he never knew of a poor man taking in the *Penny Magazine*, and as for *Chambers's Journal*, its sale had been "almost exclusively confined to the middle classes . . . chiefly among small shopkeepers, not among those dependent upon weekly wages; not certainly among any portion of the working classes earning less than 16s. a week."[52]

The initial popularity of these two periodicals resulted in an unprecedented boom in the field of cheap journalism. Within a few months were born the *Half-Penny Magazine*, the *Christian's Penny Magazine*, the *London Penny Journal*, the *Girl's and Boy's Penny Magazine*, the *True Half-Penny Magazine*, *Dibdin's Penny Trumpet*, the *Penny Comic Magazine*, the *Penny Story Teller*, and the *Penny Novelist*. As their titles suggest, these periodicals ran the whole gamut of popular taste. At one extreme were religious sheets that were hardly more than weekly tracts; at the other were comic (and not infrequently coarse) papers and Gothic fiction serials. In every case the undertaker followed close at the heels of the midwife. A gentleman in London, emulating the George Thomason who during the Commonwealth made a matchless collection of current ephemeral literature, accumulated a large pile of first numbers of periodicals which died at birth.[53] "These little strangers," wrote Bulwer, "seem, Pigmy-like, of a marvellous ferocity and valour; they make great head against their foes—they spread themselves incontinently—they possess the land—they live but a short time, yet are plenteously prolific."[54]

The "Noctes Ambrosianae" coterie were amused by the whole furor.

"A penny paper," Christopher North remarked, "fills the empty stomach with wind—or lies in it, in the shape of a ball; and 'tis hard to say which is the worser, flatulence or indigestion."

"I doubt," commented Timothy Tickler, "if any man, earning wages by ordinary hand-work, ever continued such subscription through a twelvemonth."

"Never," North rejoined. "They almost all give in within the

[52] Newspaper Stamp Committee, Qq. 3248–51.

[53] Chambers, *Memoir of Robert Chambers*, p. 211.

[54] *England and the English* (1833), II, 114.

quarter; for they either get angry with themselves, on finding that they are not one whit the wiser from studying the Tatterdemalion —or, growing conceited, they aspire to write for it—and a rejected contributor will not condescend to be an accepted subscriber."[55]

Though faultily conceived in some respects, the *Penny Magazine* and *Chambers's Journal* were landmarks in the development of popular journalism. Their sedulous respectability enabled them to be distributed through the regular channels; news agents and shopkeepers handled them without embarrassment, and thus wholesome reading matter was brought to the attention of many who never before had had access to it. Again, they elevated taste and broadened cultural interests, accomplishing a great deal that had been left undone during the brief formal schooling of most of their readers. They were responsible, perhaps more than any other single factor, for whatever smattering of culture the class of shopkeepers and skilled artisans possessed during the early Victorian age.

Thus they at least partially, though temporarily, cleansed cheap journalism of the odium that had been attached to it when it connoted rabble-rousing politics and crude sensationalism almost exclusively. They encouraged people in the upper reaches of society to regard cheap periodicals, not with disgust and apprehension, but with hope—hope that, under the right auspices, the popular press could be made to contribute to the settling of society. After 1832, therefore, the way was cleared for further attempts to provide respectable reading matter for the new public.

IV. Meanwhile, agitation for the other great goal of the reformers—the creation of a cheap newspaper press— gathered momentum. In July, 1831, the opening gun in the historic "War of the Unstamped Press" was fired, as Henry Hetherington, a radical printer, issued the first number of his *Poor Man's Guardian*, an unstamped penny weekly deliberately meant to defy the law of 1819. Within a few months Hetherington's paper was joined by a number of others, all radical and all blatantly unstamped, which the Grey government sought to crush by wholesale arrests and convictions. Within three and a half years, over eight hundred vendors of these papers were arrested, and five hundred were fined or jailed or both—many on the charge of "ob-

[55] *Blackwood's Magazine*, XXXII (1832), 853.

structing the public thoroughfare."[56] The editors and proprietors suffered also, Hetherington himself serving three prison terms. But persecution simply fanned the enthusiasm of all who sympathized with the aims to which it was giving such satisfactory publicity, and for a time their surreptitious distribution of the forbidden papers resembled a high-spirited game. Hetherington once sent into the streets a corps of porters groaning under heavy bundles of wastepaper, to be pounced upon by the waiting police, while the true copies of that week's *Poor Man's Guardian* were spirited out the back door and across the rooftops.[57] Finally, in 1834, the government, tiring of arraigning Hetherington before ordinary magistrates, brought him instead before Lord Lyndhurst and a special jury in the Court of the Exchequer. With Lyndhurst's approval, the jury decided that the *Poor Man's Guardian* was not a newspaper within the meaning of the law, and the first victory in the campaign for an untaxed periodical press was won.[58]

Between the popular hysteria over the Reform Bill and the publicity given to the government's dogged efforts at suppression, radical journalism in 1831–36 enjoyed a hectic prosperity. Roebuck told Commons in 1834 that 130,000 copies of unstamped papers were sold every week—an estimate that a writer in the *London Review* shortly afterward raised to 200,000.[59] In 1836 the Chancellor of the Exchequer said that on one raid the government's agents seized 40,000 copies of the forthcoming issue of a radical paper, and if the raid had occurred two days later—on a Saturday, when the press run would have been complete—the total would have been much higher.[60]

While the stamp authorities and the radical publishers were locked in combat, several attempts were made in Parliament, led by Spring-Rice and Bulwer, to reduce or abolish the stamp duty. Finally, in 1836, after a typically obscurantist controversy, the tax

[56] On at least one occasion a magistrate sentencing a boy to prison for hawking a radical paper recommended that on his release he could find safer employment selling the *Penny Magazine* and similar wholesome works (Bourne, *English Newspapers*, II, 59; see also Newspaper Stamp Committee, Qq. 923–24). This did not greatly endear such periodicals to the people, for a boy selling the *Poor Man's Guardian* obstructed the pavement no more than one selling the *Penny Magazine*—and if it were a question of the stamp, according to the strict letter of the law the *Penny Magazine* was as taxable as any radical print.

[57] Rose, "The Unstamped Press," p. 720.   [58] Bourne, II, 56–58.

[59] *Hansard*, Ser. 3, XXIII (1834), col. 1208; *London Review*, II (1835), 345.

[60] *Hansard*, Ser. 3, XXXIV (1836), col. 627.

was lowered to a penny a sheet. But generous as the concession appeared on the surface, the new act was immediately recognized as a fresh obstacle in England's progress toward a cheap newspaper press. It was so framed, and above all so enforced, that it became primarily a means of preserving the journalistic monopoly of the moneyed publishers. So far as the small publisher was concerned, the penny duty was as onerous as the fourpenny one had been. His expenses in having his paper stamped and the loss he sustained on unsold copies, whose stamps were not redeemable, virtually equaled the cost of the stamp itself. In addition, since the news vendor got a 25 per cent discount on the total price of each paper, the publisher in effect had to pay a premium on the penny tax. Finally, the increased stringency of the "security" provisions of the newspaper stamp law, requiring heavy bonds to be posted against the printing of criminal libel, placed an impossible burden upon the resources of the small publisher.[61]

After the unsatisfactory compromise of 1836, therefore, the campaign against the "taxes on knowledge" was intensified. In an interesting reversal of the usual process seen in these pages, the crusade for the unobstructed circulation of news and political opinion became not a by-product but a direct cause of new agitation in the broader political sphere. It was an organization founded specifically to pay the fines of convicted editors and printers, William Lovett's London Working Men's Association, which, by expanding its objectives, became the fountainhead of the Chartist movement. Now the repeal of all the taxes on knowledge—stamp tax, advertisement duty, paper duty—was an integral, not an incidental, part of the radical prescription for improving the condition of England.

The lowering of the tax brought the price of the London dailies down to 5*d*. in most cases, 6*d*. in the rest—a negligible reduction. Hence all the devices that had been used for generations past to multiply the usefulness of a single copy of a paper were kept in play. In 1851 the Newspaper Stamp Committee of Commons was told that the re-transmission of papers was "carried on to a most enormous extent." Once a paper was stamped, it enjoyed the

[61] Collet, *History of the Taxes on Knowledge*, I, 52–58, 63–75. This work gives a detailed narrative of the various stratagems—public meetings, lobbying, tactical maneuvering in Parliament, and so forth—employed in behalf of the repeal of the taxes on knowledge from 1836 onward.

privilege of free postage for the rest of its natural life. There was nothing in the law or the post office regulations to prevent a bundle of old newspapers as big as a diving bell from riding in the mails until doomsday.[62] Newsrooms and coffeehouses continued to multiply. London alone, by 1840, had between 1,600 and 1,800 coffeehouses. One of them attracted from 1,500 to 1,800 customers a day with a selection of forty-three copies of the dailies (half-a-dozen copies of a single paper were received), as well as several provincial and foreign papers, twenty-four magazines, four quarterlies, and eleven weeklies. Although this establishment was frequented by all classes (the quarterlies obviously appealed only to intellectuals), its proprietor said that the majority were artisans.[63] In the provinces, also, the habit of going to newsrooms grew. In Manchester, for instance, an establishment attached to the bookshop of the radical reformer and trade-union leader John Doherty took in ninety-six different papers a week.[64] There were some disadvantages to this method of keeping up with the world—the papers soon were torn and blotched with coffee stains, and not everyone relished the rank tobacco smoke that filled the room—but it was the only cheap way, costing but the price of a cup of coffee or a pint of beer, or, if one was not in need of refreshment, a flat halfpenny an hour for the privilege of sitting and reading.[65]

While daily papers were thus made accessible to the ordinary townsman in places of public resort, the private reading of most workers and their families was largely confined to weekly papers. At the very beginning of the 1840's, the field was still dominated by the old established Sunday papers. In a London parish inhabited by domestic servants and laborers, a survey revealed that of the 616 families who read newspapers (823 other families did not), 283 read *Bell's Weekly Dispatch*, 79 the *Sunday Times*, 23 *Bell's Life in London*, 15 the *Penny Sunday Times*, and 13 the

[62] Newspaper Stamp Committee, Qq. 1678, 1773–75, 2832–33.

[63] Aspinall, *Politics and the Press*, p. 28. In 1838 the newly formed London Statistical Society gathered information on the periodicals found in some 40 coffeehouses, 250 public houses, and 20 eating houses in the parishes of St. George, St. James, and St. Anne Soho. Most of these places provided only newspapers. Twenty-five had *Chambers's Journal*, twenty-one Limbird's *Mirror*, and ten the *Penny Magazine*. Such magazines as *Blackwood's*, *Tait's*, and *Fraser's* were found in only four or five coffeehouses, and the leading quarterlies in only three (*Journal of the Statistical Society*, I [1838], 486).

[64] Aspinall, *Politics and the Press*, p. 26.

[65] *Publishers' Circular*, Christmas number, 1896, p. 3.

Weekly Chronicle.[66] During this period the *Weekly Dispatch* had an average weekly circulation of about 55,000, and three others, the *Sunday Times, Bell's Life in London,* and the *Weekly Chronicle,* sold between 17,700 and 21,000.[67]

The multiplication of weekly papers, attended by unremitting competitive efforts to give the increasingly democratic public what it wanted, threw popular journalism into a lively ferment.[68] New papers were launched every year, and while the mortality rate was high, the most successful soon left the older papers far behind. Of the five weekly newspapers with the greatest circulations in 1850, four—the *Illustrated London News,* the *News of the World, Lloyd's Weekly Newspaper,* and the *Weekly Times*—were less than ten years old. The 49-year-old *Weekly Dispatch,* foremost in 1843, had fallen to fifth place.

In the long view, the most influential novelty during this period was the growing emphasis upon illustrations. In the mid-thirties newspaper pictures of current events had been still something of a novelty. To be sure, James Catnach, who issued "extras" long before there were cheap newspapers to do so, had adorned his accounts of murders and executions with woodcuts, but these, following a practice common in broadside production since Elizabethan days, were merely taken from his dusty stock, not made for the immediate event. Only on special occasions had newspapers gone in for pictures. William Clement had sometimes used them with gratifying effects upon the circulation of his *Observer, Bell's Life in London,* and the *Morning Chronicle.* The illustrated edition of the *Observer* at the time of George IV's coronation (1821) sold 60,000 at 14*d.* Later the *Weekly Chronicle* adopted the practice, and during the Greenacre murder sensation in 1836–37 its illustrations helped send its sale to 130,000 copies an issue.[69] The *Penny Sunday*

[66] *Journal of the Statistical Society,* VI (1843), 21.

[67] Newspaper Stamp Committee, Appendix 4.

[68] The following discussion of cheap papers in the 1840's is based principally upon Hammond, *The Age of the Chartists,* pp. 317–22; Kellett, "The Press," pp. 59–71; Bourne, II, 119–25; and Dodds, *The Age of Paradox,* pp. 107–28. The first three of these rely to a greater or less extent upon Frost, *Forty Years' Recollections,* pp. 82–90; and none is without some inaccuracies.

[69] Shorter, "Illustrated Journalism," pp. 483–85. Meanwhile, other types of cheap periodicals had used pictures quite regularly. Limbird's *Mirror*—whose first issue, in 1822, is said to have sold 150,000 copies largely because of the fascination of its picture of a treadmill recently set up at the Brixton workhouse (*Bookseller,* November 30, 1859, pp. [1326–

Times (1840) pleased its semiliterate public with crude illustrations depicting the murders, child kidnappings, armed robberies,
and other violent occurrences with which its columns were filled.
But the sixpenny *Illustrated London News*, begun two years later,
was the first to make a policy of subordinating text to pictures.
Although the cheaper papers that directly adopted the formula
soon died or were absorbed by its originator, from this time onward a generous supply of pictures became an almost indispensable
adjunct to text in the journals that sought to exploit the working-
class market.

The 3*d*. weekly newspapers that sprang up in the forties took
over the basic pattern of their older rivals, in most cases covering
the general news of the week as well as running dramatic and literary reviews and other conventional features. But their success was
due primarily to a more intensive exploitation of several lines of
interest that appealed particularly to the artisan- and working-
class audience. Certain of the older general papers had made profitable specialties of "criminal intelligence," and one or two other
papers had printed little else, but the comprehensive reporting of
recent crimes and disasters now became a staple of the cheap newspaper. The waywardness of man and Providence was a double
blessing to early Victorian popular journalism, for not only was the
supply of such material inexhaustible; so too was the common
man's appetite for it.

Like their predecessors, most of the new Sunday papers were
left-wing in their political sympathies, ranging from the relatively
decorous liberalism of the Manchester school to violent republicanism. It is hard to decide which motive—principle or policy—was
the stronger. The men behind the leading popular weeklies, most
notably Edward Lloyd and G. W. M. Reynolds, were active in
such current radical causes as anti-corn-law agitation and Chartism, and it would have been remarkable if their papers had not
voiced their personal views. But they were also shrewd businessmen, well aware of the commercial value of radical propaganda.

27])—and its later rivals in the family periodical field, such as the *Penny Magazine*, relieved the monotony of their letterpress with cuts. Grisly illustrations helped sell penny
numbers of sensational fiction, and drawings were a feature of the shoal of short-lived
comic papers that preceded *Punch* (1841). The systematic illustration of current events,
however, seems not to have been attempted until the early forties.

Exposés of governmental corruption, ministerial obstinacy, the stupidity or knavery of politicians, the greed of employers, and the sexual immorality reputedly endemic in the ruling class had a powerful appeal to multitudes who cared little for their specific political implications but relished their sensationalism.

Thus the new mass-circulation newspapers never pulled their punches as they offered fresh evidence of the social, economic, and political inequities which divided England into the two nations of Disraeli's phrase. If they caused somewhat less alarm on the higher levels of society than had their predecessors in the field of working-class journalism, it was chiefly because the accidents of history had provided them with respectable company. Many of the complaints and proposals they voiced were echoed by the middle-class faction that had crystallized around the Anti-Corn-Law League.[70]

Much more objectionable, from the middle-class viewpoint, were the penny weeklies issued for factory hands, unskilled laborers, street Arabs, and the like in the early forties. Some of these tried to combine in four or, at the most, sixteen pages every conceivable attraction, as the catch-all title of *Bell's Penny Dispatch, Sporting and Police Gazette, and Newspaper of Romance, and Penny Sunday Chronicle* well illustrates. Others were satisfied to concentrate upon only one or two features. But the element common to all of them was crude sensationalism. Some editors, who liked to live dangerously, gave their readers budgets of crime news while staying just outside the reach of the newspaper stamp authorities. Others printed only high-powered stories and serial romances. Edward Lloyd did both; first he brought out his *Penny Sunday Times and People's Police Gazette,* and then he added to it a "Companion," or supplement, which contained thrilling tales and nothing else. The initial success of this venture led at once to his start-

---

[70] Of the cheap weekly newspapers originating in the 1840's, *Lloyd's Weekly Newspaper* enjoyed the longest prosperity. Begun in 1842 as a direct imitation of the *Illustrated London News,* it ran afoul of the stamp law, and Lloyd was forced to revamp it and to raise its price from 2*d.* to 3*d.* Assisted by energetic advertising—Lloyd pressed the queen's coinage into his service by stamping every penny that came into his till with "Lloyd's Weekly Newspaper" on one side and "Purchase Number One of Lloyd's Last Penny Publication" on the other (Newspaper Stamp Committee, Q. 971)—the paper's circulation climbed to 350,000 in 1863. To print these enormous editions, Lloyd installed the first Hoe presses in England. Douglas Jerrold was its editor from 1852 to 1857; according to a contemporary, he found the paper "in the gutter and annexed it to literature" (Walter Jerrold, *Douglas Jerrold: Dramatist and Wit* [n.d.], II, 158). While many deplored its radicalism and what they considered its violent tone, the paper had solid virtues.

ing a *Penny Weekly Miscellany* and a *Penny Atlas and Weekly Register of Novel Entertainment*.

None of these papers lasted more than a few seasons. But by demonstrating the semiliterate audience's thirst for vicarious excitement, they established sensational fiction as a prime requisite in cheap journalism. General weekly newspapers began to serialize romances; as early as 1841 the *Sunday Times* ran Ainsworth's *Old St. Paul's*. And even more important, these early experiments pointed the way for three cheap periodicals which achieved and long retained immense circulations on the strength of their melodramatic fiction: the *Family Herald* (1842), the *London Journal* (1845), and *Reynolds' Miscellany* (1846). The popularity of such papers did not give conspicuous comfort to those who, a few years earlier, had felt that the welcome given the *Penny Magazine* and *Chambers's Journal* was a sure sign that the reading tastes of the masses were improving.

But there was even more deplorable evidence of the depths to which cheap journalism could descend. From the middle thirties into the sixties at least, there was a thriving trade in scandalous or pornographic papers and periodical guides to London low life: the *Town*, the *Fly*, the *Star of Venus: or Shew-Up Chronicle*, the *London Satirist*, *Paul Pry*, *Peeping Tom*, the *Fast Man*, and so on. What their circulations were, we have no way of knowing. Some were blackmail sheets; all were so scurrilous and licentious that even the most liberal-minded apologist for popular taste could not defend them. Thackeray's comment in 1838, after surveying a half-crown's worth of such sheets, epitomizes the disgust they aroused among all but their constant readers: ". . . the schoolmaster is abroad, and the prejudices of the people [against wickedness] disappear. Where we had one scoundrel we may count them now by hundreds of thousands. We have our penny libraries for debauchery as for other useful knowledge; and colleges like palaces for study—gin-palaces, where each starving Sardanapalus may revel until he die."[71] To all who denied the wisdom of spreading cheap literature among the masses, the existence of these papers— or, after they disappeared, their evil memory—was more than sufficient to strengthen their bleakest convictions.

On the other hand, grounds for optimism could be found in the

[71] "Half a Crown's Worth of Cheap Knowledge," *Fraser's Magazine*, XVII (1838), 290.

growing popularity of papers which, far from catering to base instincts, provided wholesome instruction and harmless entertainment. Admittedly, one of their prize exhibits, the *Penny Magazine*, succumbed in 1845 to the competition of the weekly newspapers and the increasing preference for fiction. But its coeval, *Chambers's Journal*, continued to purvey an assortment of banal short stories and serials, factual articles, thumb-nail biographies, little visits to famous landmarks, and similar instructive miscellany. Periodicals like *Eliza Cook's Journal, Howitt's Journal,* and the *People's Journal*, offering the same sort of varied diet, along with liberal political opinions in the case of some, enjoyed substantial prosperity in the late forties.

On a higher level of literary interest was Dickens' *Household Words*, which began its career in 1850 with a (short-lived) circulation of 100,000. Though sometimes banal and oversentimental, at 2*d.* it was a remarkable bargain. The writing and editing were done by competent professionals; controversial issues were treated forthrightly; general articles were not merely patronizing rehashes of useful information; and the fiction was something more than the customary circumspect "family" narrative, whose perfunctory morality did not wholly conceal a yawning emptiness of ideas. *Household Words* was primarily a middle-class paper, with little appeal to the average working-class reader, and as such it could not match the circulation of such sheets as the *London Journal* and the *Family Herald.* Its great importance is that through the excellence of its contents and the prestige of Dickens' name it helped to break down further the still powerful upper- and middle-class prejudice against cheap papers. A modest price, in this instance at least, could not be construed as a guarantee of shoddy writing and sensational, salacious, or seditious notions. Instead, every middle-class reader who wished to keep up with his Dickens was forced to buy *Household Words* every week, because *Hard Times* was serialized there alone; and the constant variety of other features, fiction and non-fiction, which flowed in from well-known and highly reputable writers made a regular reading of the periodical, however cheap, a necessity in cultivated households.

This, then, was the situation when the problem of the mass reading audience, especially as it applied to the cheap periodical press, engaged the attention of Parliament once more.

CHAPTER 15 } *Periodicals and Newspapers*
1851–1900

I. The campaign against the taxes on knowl-
edge, which dated from the time of Hetherington's *Poor Man's
Guardian* and the London Working Men's Association, had languished in the forties while its middle-class liberal leaders had
fought the greater evil of the Corn Laws. When that battle was
won, they returned with fresh determination to the fight for a
cheap newspaper press, and in 1851 a select committee of Commons was appointed to receive testimony on the subject. The
tendency of the evidence was mixed. Some of the witnesses must
have seriously embarrassed Cobden and his associates; and in the
friendly testimony, special pleading was more than usually obvious. But, when due allowance is made for the prejudices that
such inquiries always bring into the limelight, the record of the
committee's hearings is among the most instructive documents we
possess on the mass reading public at mid-century and on the
state of opinion in regard to it.

The Cobdenites' immediate objective was to reduce the power of
conservative journalism, especially as manifested by the *Times*'s
supremacy in the London daily press. Abolition of the penny tax,
it was believed, would encourage the rise of a press more favorable
to the Manchester school. This practical aim, however, was disguised, so far as the inquiry itself was concerned, by a more disinterested one: that of making newspapers, with their capacity for
public enlightenment, available to all.

Although recent innovations had enhanced the popular appeal
of the weekly press and the sales of leading weekly newspapers
were mounting, their circulation in 1850 was still small in proportion to the total potential audience. Daily papers, which were published only in London, still cost 5*d.* "Who below the rank of a

merchant or wholesale dealer," demanded Cobden, "can afford to take in a daily paper at fivepence? Clearly it is beyond the reach of the mechanic and the shopkeeper."[1] The common reader saw a daily newspaper only in his coffeehouse or public house. In many country parishes a daily paper was seldom encountered, and the only weekly that was received—to the extent of one or two copies —was the Tory farmer's old standby, *Bell's Weekly Messenger.* In 1855 Nathaniel Hawthorne wrote in his diary, "In Leamington, we heard no news from week's end to week's end, and knew not where to find a newspaper; and here [in the Lake District], the case is neither better nor worse. The rural people really seem to take no interest in public affairs; at all events, they have no intelligence on such subjects. . . . If they generally know that Sebastopol is besieged, that is the extent of their knowledge."[2]

In urging the repeal of the newspaper tax, the Cobdenites found themselves in an embarrassing position. With the exception of the *Illustrated London News,* the most popular weekly newspapers were all to the left of center politically. In this field "cheap" and "radical" were to many people synonymous, as they had been since the day of Cobbett's "twopenny trash," and there was a cer- tain easy (if not necessarily flawless) logic in the conservatives' assertion that if papers became cheaper, they would necessarily become more radical. The proposition could almost be reduced to the flat claim that a penny paper would be at least three times more violent in its radicalism than a threepenny one. In reply, the liberal faction dodged the question of whether or not papers like *Reynolds'* and *Lloyd's* were in fact dangerous, for these organs sup- ported them on the tax-abolition issue as they did on some other issues that affected the welfare of the working class. It would have been impolitic of the Cobdenites to disavow their support; on the other hand, it could not be alleged that such papers were models of what popular journalism would be like when the penny duty was abolished.

Hence the liberals were forced to take the vaguer line that the people's taste and political sagacity had greatly improved in recent years, and that the new journalism which would follow re-

---

[1] John Morley, *Life of Richard Cobden* (1883), p. 571.

[2] Nathaniel Hawthorne, *English Notebooks,* ed. Randall Stewart (New York, 1941), p. 163.

peal was bound to be moderate in tone. If repeal would prove a boon to the cheapest kind of inflammatory journalism—which nobody could deny—it would also foster the development of competing papers which would give the humble reader what he wanted even more, a sober, well-balanced panorama of current events; and by an inversion of Gresham's law, in which reformers expressed great faith, the "good" publications would soon drive the "bad" from circulation. The editor of the *Liverpool Journal* was perhaps the most emphatic on this point. Asserting that "if newspapers were sold at low prices there would be few or no bad publications issued," he told the committee of inquiry that "good is always preferred by the multitude; in a theatre, for instance, and even the speeches delivered in Parliament reported in newspapers, and in literature of every description their taste is natural; in other and more educated ranks of course the taste is to a great extent artificial—conventional; it may be bad or it may be good; but the taste of the people I apprehend is always correct."[3]

The reasoning involved in such a view will not bear too close scrutiny. If the people's taste was so sound, why did they buy hundreds of thousands of copies a week of sensational papers costing 2*d*. or 3*d*., while at the same time there seemingly was no demand for more sedate newspapers at the same price? Why was it assumed that with the repeal of the duty, the populace would miraculously switch to the sort of journals of which right-thinking men in Parliament could approve?

Such questions went unanswered. The Cobdenites' great object was to convince the nation that neither its internal security nor its morality would be jeopardized by lowering the prices of newspapers. To this end, a parade of witnesses—clergymen, reformers, educators, leaders of the periodical trade—appeared before the committee of inquiry. For our particular purposes, the most instructive witness was Abel Heywood, a Manchester bookseller, publisher, and wholesale news agent, who presented a mass of facts and then rationalized them to the satisfaction of the liberal party.[4]

---

[3] Newspaper Stamp Committee, Qq. 598, 601.

[4] Heywood's career is a striking measure of the progress of liberal thought in the Victorian era. As a young man in the 1830's, he was imprisoned for vending radical literature. Later he became a prosperous businessman and was twice made Lord Mayor of Manchester. In no more than twenty years the one-time defier of governmental thought-control had become a respected citizen, and this without greatly modifying his views.

Maintaining that he handled 10 per cent of the whole national issue of popular publications, he gave the committee a full account of his current sales. Unfortunately, he did not make clear in some cases whether the figures he gave were for his own sales alone or for the whole of the Manchester news-agent trade. In any event, these are the salient figures:[5]

Family papers

Chambers's Journal........................	3,000*
Chambers's Papers for the People............	1,200
Eliza Cook's Journal......................	600
Cottage Gardener ⎫	
Family Friend ⎬	1,800
Family Tutor ⎭	
Home Circle.............................	600
Household Words.........................	600
Cassell's *Working Man's Friend*.............	1,800

Weekly newspapers

News of the World........................	3,500
Weekly Times............................	4,000

Sensational fiction weeklies

Family Herald...........................	14,000*
London Journal..........................	14,000*
Reynolds' Miscellany......................	4,500

Religious papers

Catholic papers, total......................	22,000
Cassell's *Pathway*........................	700

Political and free-thinking papers

Christian Socialist........................	70
Friend of the People	
(formerly the *Red Republican*)............	250
[Oastler's] *Home* (protectionist).............	450
Robert Owen's Journal (co-operationist)......	250
[Holyoake's] *Reasoner* (free-thinking)........	400

* Total for Manchester.

[5] Newspaper Stamp Committee, Qq. 2481–2551. Curiously, there are some quite wide discrepancies between these figures and another set Heywood gave to Henry Mayhew only a year or two earlier (see Dodds, *The Age of Paradox*, pp. 125–28). The differences seemingly are too great to be accounted for by the normal fluctuations of popular demand. Must we suspect that Heywood doctored his figures for the occasion?—For a similar account of periodical sales in Leicester in 1850, see A. Temple Patterson, *Radical Leicester* (Leicester, 1954), p. 380.

With these figures may be compared the weekly sales of cheap part-issues of various types of literature:

Lloyd's penny numbers of sensational fiction: sixteen titles then current, total sale	3,400
Reynolds' *Mysteries of the Court of London*	1,500
Reprint of Southey's *Wat Tyler*	450
The London Apprentice	400
Shakespeare in penny numbers	150

From these statistics Heywood was able to conclude that of all types of papers sold in Manchester, "considerably the larger proportion are of a good tendency," and it was the wholesome papers which were then enjoying the greatest increases in circulation.[6]

Looking back over his twenty years as a Manchester news agent, he saw a remarkable improvement in popular taste. Granting his own criteria, he was probably right. In 1835 a committee of the Manchester Statistical Society had found that the working classes in that city were addicted to the reading of unstamped radical papers, reprints of Tom Paine, pamphlets on "Malthusianism" (birth control), Cobbett's *Legacy to Parsons*, the *Penny Story Teller*, and similar "immoral and irreligious publications." It was true that 1,600 copies of the *Penny Magazine*, the S.P.C.K.'s *Saturday Magazine*, the *Dublin Penny Journal*, and *Chambers's Journal* also were sold every week in Manchester, but the committee could not ascertain that these respectable periodicals were distributed among workingmen.[7]

If Heywood had access to this report, he would have welcomed its statistical confirmation of his own views. Other witnesses' testimony was more impressionistic, but nearly all of it was to the same effect: that the masses, having proved their discriminating tastes by preferring wholesome periodicals to unsettling ones, could be trusted to read cheap (untaxed) newspapers without any danger of political disaffection, and that indeed it was the lack of such pa-

---

[6] Heywood's comments on Reynolds' famous and interminable *Mysteries* deserve quoting. It "draws scenes of profligacy as strongly as it is possible for any writer to do, and the feelings are excited to a very high pitch by it," but "it is not in reality an indecent publication, because I do not believe that any words appear that are vulgar. . . . A great many females buy the 'Court of London,' and young men; a sort of spreeing young men; young men who go to taverns, and put cigars in their mouths in a flourishing way" (Newspaper Stamp Committee, Qq. 2490, 2517).

[7] Ashton, *Economic and Social Investigations in Manchester*, pp. 18–19.

pers which prevented the further improvement of popular taste. One "old educationist" submitted that only access to newspapers could insure that boys who had learned the rudiments of reading at school would not soon relapse into total illiteracy. He had himself tried to keep up their interest with *Chambers's Journal* and selected penny magazines—obviously he did not bring a Lloyd or Reynolds paper to their attention—but to no avail. "The only effectual thing to induce them to keep up or create the habit of reading was some local newspaper. If you began in that way, by asking them to read an account of somebody's rick that was burnt down, you would find that you would succeed."[8]

Inevitably, the relation of the cheap press to the cause of temperance came up. It was asserted once more that penny newspapers, by making it unnecessary for the workingman to repair to a public house for a draft of the latest events and opinions, would be of immense assistance in his resolve to keep sober. John Cassell argued that if he were allowed by law to add "general intelligence" as a leavening influence in his *Working Man's Friend,* which was "crammed from one end to the other with entirely temperance news," he could quadruple his circulation. "A man makes a resolve that he will be temperate," said Cassell, "and he has a great deal to contend with in the workshop, and it requires something in the shape of a periodical to stimulate his zeal, and keep him up to high-water mark."[9] No matter if mechanics' institutions and every other stratagem yet employed to lure the workers away from the public houses had failed to do so; faith was strong that something would turn the trick, and why not penny newspapers?

Finally, Herbert Spencer's social-reformer uncle, Rev. Thomas

[8] Newspaper Stamp Committee, Q. 3240. His example was injudiciously chosen, as he immediately discovered when his interrogator demanded whether accounts of murders and rick-burnings were "exactly the subjects which are best calculated to humanise the mind and affections, and most conducive to the formation of moral habits." The witness stuck to his guns. Far from putting mischievous ideas into the heads of members of the lower orders, "the paper would perhaps inform them that they would do the farmer, after all, no mischief, because his stacks were insured; readers are not rioters; readers are not rick-burners." The logic displayed here deserves attention, no less than the affirmation of the Victorian reformer's faith in the reading habit as the moral regenerator of man. A generation earlier, rick-burning was widely construed as the direct result of perusing radical papers. In 1851 many persons still clung to that view and thus feared for the safety of the nation if newspapers became more accessible to the common man.

[9] *Ibid.,* Qq. 1313, 1320-21.

Spencer, whose occupancy of the witness stand was the most diverting part of the whole inquiry, let it be known that God intended man not to be satisfied with the Bible and *Chambers's Journal*. "It is the will of the Almighty," he said, "that a man should know the things that concern himself; the taxes of the day, and the laws concern him. . . . The Bible contained news some thousands of years ago; it contains excellent precepts, but as to the news part of it, the history of the Kings and the Chronicles of old times, that may not affect so much a man at this day, yet it gives him a right to expect to know the events of the present day; and whatever else a man reads, he will desire to know that."[10]

Four years later (1855) the proposal to abolish the newspaper tax once more reached the floor of Commons. Introducing the measure, the Chancellor of the Exchequer said that the die-hards who identified the spread of reading with the rise of Demos were still vocal. He had heard from "many quarters" that the measure "will open the floodgates of sedition and blasphemy, and . . . will inundate the country with licentious and immoral productions, . . . will undermine the very foundations of society, and scatter the seeds of revolution broadcast over the land."[11] The *Times*, on the other hand, was converted. The duty, it thundered, was "a tax on knowledge . . . a tax on light, a tax on education, a tax on truth, a tax on public opinion, a tax on good order and good government, a tax on society, a tax on the progress of human affairs, and on the working of human institutions."[12] No radical reformer had ever denounced the newspaper stamp in more comprehensive terms. After long debate, the government's bill was passed, and the stamp (except for postal purposes) was no more. In 1861 the only surviving "tax on knowledge," the paper duty, was removed, and for the first time since the reign of Queen Anne the press was completely free of fiscal restrictions.

At last daily newspapers came down in price. The *Daily Telegraph* was reduced to a penny in 1856, followed by the *Standard*

[10] *Ibid.*, Qq. 2384, 2387.

[11] *Hansard*, Ser. 3, CXXXVII (1855), col. 782. For two critiques of the Cobdenite position on the newspaper stamp, see *Fraser's Magazine*, XLIV (1851), 339–54, and the *Edinburgh Review*, XCVIII (1853), 488–518.

[12] Quoted in *Hansard* as just cited, col. 811.

(1858), and at greater distance by the *Daily News*, the *Daily Chronicle*, the *Pall Mall Gazette*, the *St. James's Gazette*, and the venerable *Morning Post*. Nor did the cheapening process end there. In 1868 appeared Cassell's *Echo*, at the unheard-of price of a half-penny, and thirteen years later the *Evening News* came out at the same price.

No longer, therefore, were daily newspapers beyond the reach of the great body of middle-class buyers. In the sixties the *Times*, which in 1850 had sold four times as many copies as the three other "senior" London dailies put together, was overtaken by its livelier competitors. While the *Times*'s sales hovered between 50,000 and 60,000 (rising to the neighborhood of 100,000 on such occasions as the wedding of the Prince of Wales and the death of the Prince Consort), the *Daily News*'s circulation reached a steady 150,000 at the time of the Franco-Prussian War, and the *Daily Telegraph*, attaining 200,000 in the early seventies, was able to compliment itself on the largest circulation in the world.[13]

But events did not substantiate the liberals' contention that it would be the working classes who would profit most from lowering the price of daily newspapers. Whether or not they really wanted daily papers, as had been alleged during the campaign against the tax, workers did not buy them for some thirty or forty years after the penny daily came into being. The papers themselves made no great effort to attract lower-class readers. They remained what they had always been, papers for the upper and the substantial middle classes, giving most of their space to weightily reported political news and devoting relatively little attention to such topics of mass interest as sport and crime. Only in the 1890's, when the Harmsworth influence began to make itself felt, notably with the *Daily Mail* (1896), did the daily newspaper begin to circulate widely among workingmen.

Meanwhile, the mass audience remained faithful to the Sunday papers it had grown up with. In 1880 a writer in the *Quarterly Review* divided these into two categories. The ones he deemed "re-

[13] On daily journalism in the mid- and late-Victorian periods, see Ensor, *England, 1870–1914*, pp. 143–45, 310–16; *The History of "The Times,"* Vol. II, chap. xiv, and Vol. III, chap. iv; and Bourne, *English Newspapers*, Vol. II, *passim*. As in the preceding chapter, documentation for circulation figures will be given in connection with Appendix C.

spectable" were the *Observer*, the *Sunday Times*, which had a well-balanced menu of general news and comment on drama, sport, music, and letters, and, despite their radical politics, the *News of the World* and the *Weekly Times*, which enjoyed great favor among artisans and small tradesmen. The remaining three popular weekly newspapers were "distinguished chiefly by the violence and even brutality of their tone": the *Weekly Dispatch* ("very strong writing . . . somewhat gross personalities"), *Lloyd's Weekly Newspaper* ("the staple of the leading articles is discontent . . . with everything . . . which is not of the lowest workingman level") and *Reynolds' Weekly Newspaper* ("even worse than *Lloyd's*").[14] These were, of course, the judgments of a writer in a review never remarkable for its popular sympathies, and the papers condemned were politically not as reprehensible, or at least as inflammatory, as the comments suggest; "radical" is an elastic term, and in late Victorian days it might mean nothing more than fervent Gladstonianism.

One of the greatest effects of the abolition of the newspaper tax was to spread the newspaper-reading habit throughout the provinces. Immediately after 1855 daily papers were published for the first time in Manchester, Sheffield, Liverpool, and other cities. In Manchester alone, by 1876, the total circulation of daily papers was around 125,000.[15] The impetus thus supplied to local journalism resulted in a striking increase in periodical publishing generally. By 1873, 889 periodicals of all descriptions, including newspapers, were being issued in the provinces, in addition to 144 in Scotland and 59 in Wales.[16] The mass-circulation London weekly newspapers had to meet growing competition from local ones, especially with the introduction of the syndicate system by firms like Tillotson's of Bolton, which provided stereotypes of serial fiction on a subscription basis. Starting in 1873, Tillotson's "Fiction Bureau" bought serial rights from some of the most popular novelists of the time, among them Wilkie Collins, Trollope, Miss Braddon, Mayne Reid, Mrs. Lynn Linton, and Charles Reade. Nearer the end of the century this agency syndicated work by Hardy, Kip-

[14] "The Newspaper Press," *Quarterly Review*, CL (1880), 498–537.

[15] *Publishers' Circular*, April 1, 1876, pp. 245–46.

[16] *Chambers's Journal*, Ser. 4, X (1873), 285–87.

ling, Bennett, Barrie, Conan Doyle, and H. G. Wells.[17] The result
was that the weekly paper, with its agreeable combination of serial
fiction and local news, became more and more appealing to readers
in provincial towns and the countryside.

II. As the figures given in Appendix C show,
by 1855 at least a half-dozen weekly newspapers and cheap miscellanies had attained a circulation of more than 100,000. When the
tax on newspapers was repealed, records fell right and left. One
new paper, Henry Vizetelly's twopenny *Illustrated Times*, started
off with a circulation of 200,000. In 1858 the sale of three fiction
papers, the *Family Herald*, the *London Journal*, and *Cassell's Family Paper*, was said to total 895,000, and Wilkie Collins estimated
that the audience for such periodicals was at least three million
people.[18]

The repeal of the paper duty in 1861 benefited all periodicals
alike. The conjunction of a greatly expanded mass audience and
lower costs threw the publishing and printing trades into a happy
uproar. So overburdened were the printers' facilities that a type
famine occurred, during which the old-fashioned ſ, disused for
more than half a century, was brought back from retirement until
the type-founders could catch up with the demand.[19] This temporary reversion to old practice was the more picturesque because
the bustling plants in which mass-circulation periodicals were produced were each year looking less and less like the modest establishments where the *Gentleman's Magazine* and the *Times* were
turned out by hand sixty years earlier. With the introduction of
rotary presses and, toward the end of the century, typesetting machines, periodical printing became one of the most highly mecha-
nized of all English mass-production industries.

In 1864, John Francis, publisher of the *Athenaeum*, supplied a
set of figures to Edward Baines, M.P., which the *Publishers' Circular*, one of the two leading trade journals, regarded as an accurate reflection of the current situation. Weekly newspapers are not

[17] Graham Pollard, "Novels in Newspapers," *Review of English Studies*, XVIII (1942),
73; Malcolm Elwin, *Charles Reade* (1931), p. 333.

[18] Collins, "The Unknown Public," p. 218.

[19] Keefe, *A Century in Print*, p. 46.

included, nor are the host of periodicals appearing in the provinces or Scotland; the figures are for London publications alone:[20]

Description	Number	Price	Copies per Month
Monthly			
Religious	84	½d.–5d.	1,500,000
Religious magazines	22	6d. up	400,000
Temperance	20	½d.–3d.	800,000
Useful, entertaining, educational	19	1d.–6d.	350,000
Magazines and serials of a higher class	54	1s.–2s.6d.	250,000
Serials issued by the great publishing firms, embellished and illustrated	..	1s.–3s.6d.	350,000
Weekly			
Religious	15	1d.–1½d.	500,000
Useful, educational, entertaining*	32	1d.–3d.	750,000
Journals containing novels, tales, etc.	13	½d.–1d.	1,050,000
Romances exciting wonder and horror	8	1d.	200,000
Immoral publications	..	1d.	9,000†
Free-thinking publications	..	....	under 5,000

* Including "serial publications of standard works" put out by a handful of London publishers for sale in the country by "travelling commission agents," the Victorian equivalent of the old hawkers.

† Reputedly a drop of 43,500 since 1861. If, as Baines said, "immoral" papers circulated 52,500 or more in that year, the testimony of certain witnesses before the Newspaper Stamp Committee a decade earlier, that such publications had almost ceased to exist, would seem to have been somewhat premature.

These figures are a good measure of what had happened in the past generation. The increase in circulation is so apparent as to require no further comment. In addition, periodicals were much cheaper than ever before; in only three of Francis' categories, all relating to monthly publications, do prices reach above 6d., whereas before 1836 only unstamped radical papers, tax-excused "wholesome" papers of the *Penny Magazine* class, religious papers, and the motley crew of penny-fiction serials had sold for less.[21] Obviously the greatest increase in periodical-buying occurred among the lower-middle class and the working class. In the same year that the *London Journal* sold close to half a million copies an issue, *Punch*, addressed to an upper- and middle-class audience, circulated 40,000 and the *Athenaeum* only 7,200.

Between the *London Journal's* uncultivated audience and the intellectual one of the *Athenaeum* there lay a growing public

[20] *Hansard*, Ser. 3, CLXXV (1864), col. 296; *Publishers' Circular*, May 16, 1864, pp. 267–69.

[21] Although the estimates were made on a different basis, it is interesting to compare the figures for 1864 with those Charles Knight compiled in 1837. According to him, in the earlier year there were about forty-eight weekly papers (exclusive of newspapers), of which twenty-one were priced at 1d., eight at 1½d., and the remainder at 2d. or above, and some 236 monthlies, whose average price was 1s.11½d. In 1837, the sale of the "more important" weeklies was about 200,000 copies and that of the monthlies 500,000 (*Penny Magazine*, VI [1837], 507; Knight, *The Old Printer and the Modern Press*, p. 263, where the year is given as 1833).

which, until the sixties, had been inadequately cared for, largely because of the rush to accommodate the semiliterate millions. This was the middle-class audience of superior education but relatively little spending money: the people who disdained cheap weeklies, with a few exceptions like *Household Words*, but who could not spare the two shillings or half-crown at which the principal monthly magazines were priced. To their rescue came the shilling monthly. Within three months of each other, in the winter of 1859–60, *Macmillan's Magazine* and the *Cornhill Magazine* were launched. The first number of the latter sold an astounding total, considering its price, of 120,000 copies. This was one of the most heartening events in the whole history of English periodicals, for the *Cornhill*, with its unmatched array of talent—Trollope (*Framley Parsonage*), Thackeray (*Roundabout Papers*), Mrs. Browning, and Ruskin all contributed to the first volume—was a first-class magazine. That it could attract so many purchasers seemed proof that the audience of serious readers had expanded almost apace with that of the entertainment seekers.

The *Cornhill's* initial success, however, was short-lived. Many of its first readers were attracted by its novelty but soon were repelled by its quality. They wanted shilling magazines, but they also wanted more fiction and a lighter literary tone than the *Cornhill* gave them. Hence they transferred their patronage to the numerous "popular" monthlies that sprang up in the *Cornhill's* wake. But, as William Tinsley, who started *Tinsley's Magazine* in 1867, wrote, "There were more magazines in the wretched field than there were blades of grass to support them."[22] Despite an occasional spectacular beginning (the *Broadway Magazine*, for example, sold 100,000 copies of its first issue in 1867), the leading monthlies of the class of *Temple-Bar*, *St. James's*, and *Belgravia* had an average circulation of 15,000 or less. So, at least, reported a writer in 1884.[23] The competition grew ever keener, especially when sixpenny magazines appeared on the scene.

Hence it appeared that the genuinely serious audience could not be measured in six figures, as had been mistakenly inferred from the *Cornhill's* first success. The periodicals that catered to this public—the *Fortnightly*, the *Contemporary*, the *Nineteenth Century*—all

[22] Tinsley, *Random Recollections*, I, 323–24.
[23] Charles E. Pascoe, "The Story of the English Magazines," pp. 372–74.

had small circulations. The fact that leading reviews of this type
had to be priced at a half-crown is proof enough that a wider market, which would have permitted a reduction of price, was not yet
in sight.

Meanwhile, the most widely circulated periodicals, apart from
the weekly newspapers, were the "family" papers meant for the
indifferently educated reader.[24] Among these, the two which had
led the field in the fifties retained their supremacy down into the
eighties. The staple of both the *Family Herald* and the *London
Journal* was short stories and full-length novels. These were always escapist: the masses never read, and evidently never cared to
read, about people in their own walk of life. Instead they avidly
consumed, year after year and decade after decade, fiction dealing
with the aristocracy of wealth or blood, whose lives were crammed
with crises and no little sin. There was a contemporary feeling that
the *Family Herald*'s fiction was a cut above that of the *London
Journal*. One critic, probably not intending the compliment to be
left-handed, deemed its stories better than the average run of
three-decker novels issued by the fashionable publishers.[25] The
London Journal, on the other hand, was partial to tales of a more
emphatically melodramatic sort. Its very name, indeed, became
associated with a certain genre of thrilling story which had been
developed by one of the most prolific and popular of Victorian
writers, J. F. Smith—long a mainstay of the *London Journal*—and
by such other figures as Mrs. E. D. E. N. Southworth, Mrs. Henry
Wood, Pierce Egan the younger, and Charles Reade.

Fiction was not, however, the exclusive preoccupation of these
family papers. They gave much space to "Answers to Correspondents," which dealt with every subject from the date of Frederick
the Great's death to the population of Tasmania, from how to prepare a cheap stew to what a girl should do when she was ogled in
church or fell in love with two married men at the same time. One
suspects that many of the queries, especially the ones which today
would be addressed to reference librarians, were concocted in the
editorial office; but to the extent to which the questions were genuine, the "Answers to Correspondents" columns provide an instruc-

---

[24] On the tone and content of the mass-circulation papers in the period 1850–1900, see
the articles listed in the Bibliography under Bosanquet, "Byways of Literature," "Cheap
Literature," Wilkie Collins, Hitchman, "The Literature of Snippets," "The Literature of
the Streets," March-Phillipps, Millar, Payn, Pennell, Salmon, Strahan, Thomas Wright.

[25] Hitchman, "The Penny Press," p. 390.

tive panorama of the humble Victorian reader's everyday perplexities, above all in connection with flirtation, courtship, and marriage. In addition, the weekly paper featured columns of short, scrappy variety, "pickings from *Punch* and Plato," as Wilkie Collins phrased it.[26] These supplied the element of "instruction" with which "entertainment" had to be complemented in the Victorian scheme of respectable popular journalism.

The *Family Herald* and the *London Journal* had to meet strong competition from younger rivals. Conspicuous among them was John Dicks's *Bow Bells*, which made a strong appeal to the women in the mass audience by supplementing its serial novels—including eight by Ainsworth—with music, needlework, and patterns. A number of these papers in later years widened their audience still further by printing monthly supplements devoted to a complete novelette or a dress pattern. Such innovations as these are good evidence of the stimulating effect which increasing rivalry had upon editorial ingenuity.

Of the 630 magazines current in 1873, 253 were published under religious auspices, either by the various denominational publishing societies themselves or by commercial houses with which they were linked.[27] Eight years later it was said that eight leading cheap religious weeklies circulated in the aggregate between 1,250,000 and 1,500,000 copies a week.[28] The best of these were hardly distinguishable, in level of writing and breadth of interest, from secular family papers like *Cassell's* and *All the Year Round*. Norman Macleod's *Good Words* had a list of contributors that included Trollope, Kingsley, Dean Stanley, Hardy (*The Trumpet Major*) and F. D. Maurice. The Religious Tract Society's *Leisure Hour*, like *Good Words*, mingled instruction and recreation, with special emphasis on travel and natural history. Du Maurier illustrated it before he went over to *Punch*, and among its contributors were Walter Besant, Mrs. Oliphant, Mrs. Henry Wood, and Stanley Weyman. The *Christian World* specialized in the sensational religious novel, thus offering its readers the best of both worlds, while the *Christian Herald* regularly published sermons by T. DeWitt Talmadge, the famous American preacher, and articles interpreting current events in the light of scriptural prophecy.

[26] Collins, "The Unknown Public," p. 221.

[27] *Chambers's Journal*, Ser. 4, X (1873), 285–87.   [28] Hitchman, p. 388.

Another phenomenon of cheap journalism after mid-century was the great prosperity of juvenile papers. Until that time, such children's periodicals as had existed had been produced by the religious societies and distributed mainly through Sunday schools. With the spread of elementary education, commercial interests realized their opportunity, and from the middle fifties onward, new juvenile papers came out almost every year: the *Boy's Own Magazine*, the *Boy's Own Journal*, the *Boy's Journal*, the *Boy's Penny Magazine*, and so forth. In conspicuous contrast to their saintly forerunners, the most popular of these papers went in for hair-raising adventure stories. To combat this flood of "pernicious literature," the Religious Tract Society in 1879 began the *Boy's Own Paper*, which tried "to illustrate by practical example the noblest type of manhood and the truest Christian devotion." Thanks to an unusually gifted editor, George A. Hutchison, who worked on the assumption that a juvenile paper under religious auspices would succeed only if it were written for boys rather than for their grandmothers, the periodical enjoyed a success which still continues. Among its writers were Jules Verne and Conan Doyle, as well as a corps of celebrated sports experts headed, in the cricket department, by the idolized W. G. Grace.[29]

Long before weekly or monthly periodicals had come to occupy an important place in English household life, the well-to-do class had been entertained at the Christmas season, and often for months thereafter, by gift-books—the "keepsakes" and "parlour albums" whose annual issue, in their period of greatest vogue during the 1820's and 1830's, had enriched publishers, printers, binders, writers, and illustrators. In one season, 1828, it was estimated that 100,000 copies were produced, at a retail value of over £70,000.[30] Smith, Elder's *Friendship's Offering*, priced at 12*s.*, alone sold between 8,000 and 10,000 a year.[31] These annuals, important though they are in Regency and early Victorian literary and cultural history, were priced too high to affect the mass audience. But with the

---

[29] *The Story of the Religious Tract Society* (1898), pp. 24–25. See also Hewitt, *Let the People Read*, pp. 62–63, and, on boys' papers generally, Turner, *Boys Will Be Boys*, *passim*. Like their American contemporaries, *St. Nicholas* and the *Youth's Companion*, some late nineteenth-century English children's periodicals have a solid claim to the literary historian's remembrance. *Young Folks*, for instance, published Stevenson's *Treasure Island*, *Kidnapped*, and *The Black Arrow*.

[30] *Monthly Repository*, Ser. 2, II (1828), 728.

[31] [Huxley], *The House of Smith, Elder*, p. 12.

coming of mass-circulation periodicals, the gift annual was transformed into the special Christmas number or supplement, bulging
with verse, stories, and pictures. From about 1860 to the end of the
century, activity in the periodical trade reached its feverish peak
in December. The sales of some of these annual supplements were
tremendous, eclipsing even the records set by the Christmas numbers of *All the Year Round* under Dickens' editorship. They were
admirably fitted to the tastes of those whose pocketbooks were
opened a little wider than usual under the mellowing influence of
the Christmas season, and their presence in English homes had a
powerful effect on the spread of reading interest.

The formula for popular periodicals as it developed in the last
quarter of the century was threefold: a price of 6*d.* or lower; plenty
of light fiction and amusing non-fiction; and as many illustrations
as possible.[32] But the formula alone would not have sent periodical
circulation to the dizzy heights achieved at the end of Victoria's
reign. It had to be applied, and improved upon, by editors with a
special genius for knowing what the great mass public—the readers
turned out in hordes each year by the new board schools—wanted.
And such men forthwith appeared, to usher in a whole new school
of popular journalism.

In 1880 George Newnes began *Tit-Bits*, a penny paper of sixteen
quarto pages which was a compilation of scraps from books, periodicals, and newspapers, and of contributions from readers. Within
a few years Alfred Harmsworth competed with *Answers to Correspondents*, a sheet which at first concentrated upon the old journalistic staple referred to in the title, but which soon was converted
to the *Tit-Bits* formula. In 1890, Cyril Pearson, formerly a clerk in
the *Tit-Bits* office (he won the job as a prize in one of the paper's
contests), started *Pearson's Weekly*. The three men together,
Newnes, Harmsworth, and Pearson, revolutionized the lowest
level of cheap journalism. Apart from circulation-boosting stunts
like prize contests and insurance schemes, their policy was to fill
their papers with anecdotes, jokes, excerpts, riddles—nothing
which required sustained attention on the part of their readers, let

---

[32] Genuine literary quality was not ruled out, as the roster of first-rank authors who contributed to the popular magazines attests. The *Graphic*, one of the first successful rivals of
the *Illustrated London News*, sold a quarter-million copies of its sensational "Tichborne
number" in 1874; but it also serialized *The Mayor of Casterbridge* and *Tess of the D'Urber-
villes*.

alone concentration.[33] More and more, as the years passed, people would be buying reading matter whose chief function was to keep their eyes busy while their brains took a rest.[34]

"Our caterers nowadays," observed Edward Dowden in 1889, "provide us with a mincemeat which requires no chewing, and the teeth of a man may in due time become as obsolete as those which can still be perceived in the foetal whale."[35] This, it seemed, was the final result of the great movement to which men so utterly different as Cobbett, Knight, the Chamberses, and G. W..M. Reynolds had contributed. The pessimism that permeated comment on popular journalism in the eighties and nineties offers an ironic postscript to the bright expectations of the men who struggled for an untaxed press. True, those expectations were in some respects justified. After mid-century the cheap periodical press seldom gave cause for alarm on political grounds and infrequently if ever, its critics admitted—though some portions of the clergy would have disagreed—did it tolerate an improper expression or an overtly salacious situation.

But now it was recognized that, while earlier apprehensions had proved groundless, the reading habit among the masses was contributing nothing to their cultural improvement. Reading had become a popular addiction; indeed, again ironically, the soporific exercise that the earliest advocates of cheap religious reading matter had intended. Women wore out their eyes following the scandalous doings of fictional lords and ladies, or the spicy peccadilloes of real ones. Men and boys in the factories devoured tons of hack-written adventure stories, compact of hair-breadth escapes, desperate villainy, and superhuman heroism. The cook in the kitchen let the joint burn as she pored over the *Family Herald*, the mill-hand sat on his doorstep of a Sunday morning, smoking his pipe and reviewing the week's outrages in the *Illustrated Police News*. The British masses had won their cheap periodicals.

---

[33] On a somewhat less elementary level, though almost equally deplored by critics who persisted in believing that the masses should have loftier aims in their reading, were other periodicals established in the nineties by this great trio of magnates: Newnes' *Strand Magazine*, Pearson's *Magazine*, the same proprietor's *Royal Magazine*, and the Harmsworth *Monthly Pictorial Magazine*. Allowing for a decidedly lighter tone, these occupied essentially the place that *Chambers's Journal* had had in the thirties and *Household Words* in the fifties, and they sold by the hundreds of thousands.

[34] On these developments, see Ensor, pp. 310–16, and *The History of "The Times,"* Vol. III, chap. iv.

[35] "Hopes and Fears for Literature," *Fortnightly Review*, N.S., XLV (1889), 169–70.

CHAPTER 16 } *The Past and the Present*

By 1900 the English reading public had attained substantially the size and character it possesses today. Since that time there have been few really new developments; the major tendencies in the past half-century were, for the most part, continuations of those already in existence. The reduction of the workweek increased the amount of leisure the average man had for reading—if he wished to read. Workers had more money for free spending than their fathers and grandfathers had possessed; they could use it for football pools, bets on greyhound races, beer, or books. The production and sale of cheap literature continued, in astute hands, to be a highly profitable form of commerce, though possibly the $22\frac{1}{2}$ per cent dividend declared on common shares of Harmsworth's *Answers* Publications, Limited, in 1896 was not often duplicated.[1] Public library patronage grew. By the 1950's only a tiny portion of the English people were without library service, and in 1953–54 the total number of books issued in British public libraries was 370,605,000—ten times the estimate for 1897.[2]

On the other side of the ledger, public education, while improved in efficiency and with regular attendance up to the minimum leaving-age enforced by law, had not yet made the English people fully literate. A study made in 1948 revealed that of pupils who left school at fifteen, 5.7 per cent had no more ability to read silently for comprehension than the average nine-year-old, and 24.4 per cent were classified as "backward"—that is, with a reading ability definitely inferior to the average for their age-group.[3]

[1] *Newsagents' Chronicle*, August 8, 1896, p. 8.

[2] *Library Association Record*, LVII (1955), 30.

[3] London *Times*, February 28, 1951, p. 6, summarizing the report of a committee set up in 1947 by the Minister of Education. See also Sir Cyril Burt, "The Education of Illiterate

This high incidence of semiliteracy was one reason why millions concentrated on papers like the *News of the World,* the *Sunday Pictorial,* and *Picture Post* almost to the exclusion of more substantial reading matter. Another reason was that until the Education Act of 1944 laid the basis for a more liberal policy, secondary schooling—the stage at which a certain amount of literary discrimination can be cultivated in readers—was largely restricted to children of upper- and middle-class families.

Putting aside the matter of popular taste, it was clear that reading, of whatever sort, did not occupy as important a place in everyday life as might have been predicted from the increase of leisure and spending money and the cheapening of printed matter.[4] The new century had brought additional forms of entertainment to compete with the number already in existence—first motion pictures, then wireless, and most recently television. During the second World War, however, the English people, deprived of many of their favorite recreations and seeking respite from often intolerable emotional and physical strain, turned to the printed word as they had never done before. Hampered by a severe shortage of paper and other essential materials as well as of labor, publishers could not possibly keep up with the demand for books and periodicals of every description. Reading played an important role in sustaining morale on the home front. At the same time, huge quantities of reading matter were shipped to the armed forces everywhere; and, just as it had done in the first World War, the *Times* issued selections from English literature, printed on single sheets of thin paper, to be enclosed in letters to the nation's fighting men. The printed word, whether in comic papers or precious dog-eared volumes of Trollope, was an indispensable part of everyone's life, from generals and aerial gunners to transplanted Cockneys working the Shropshire soil.

Yet these two world conflicts were not the first English wars in which the printed page had circulated in large quantities among men in uniform. That distinction belongs to the Crimean War, whose soldiers prized, tucked into their pocket Testaments, the

---

Adults," *British Journal of Educational Psychology,* XV (1945), 20–27, for a higher estimate of the extent of illiteracy and semiliteracy.

[4] For a general view of English reading habits at mid-century, see B. Seebohm Rowntree and G. R. Lavers, *English Life and Leisure: A Social Study* (1951), chap. xi.

little slips Tennyson had caused to be printed bearing his "Charge of the Light Brigade," and among whom Florence Nightingale distributed many thousands of copies of temperance papers.

This is but one small illustration of the way in which the history of the mass reading public in the nineteenth century anticipated that of the twentieth. Scores of additional instances have been scattered through the foregoing chapters, though their relevance to the present-day situation has intentionally not been made explicit. In these closing pages, however, it will be worthwhile to review the "problem" of the mass audience as it appeared to successive generations of the "superior" classes during the nineteenth century and to consider how far their attitudes still influence our thinking today.

In the first half of the century, the implications of a democratic audience for print, viewed from above, were mainly political. Coleridge's exclamation in 1810, "These are AWEFUL TIMES!"[5] epitomized the horror he and most conservatives felt at the spread of the reading habit into, and even beneath, the lower reaches of the middle class. The fear of demagogue-inspired rebellion was uppermost in their minds when, having failed to check the growing appetite for reading, they attempted to control what the new public should read—turning popular elementary education, in Hazlitt's disgusted view, into "a go-cart of corruption, servility, superstition and tyranny."[6] And it was also political and social considerations (though of a different variety) which determined the policy of the middle-class liberals who joined Brougham in his crusade to convert the people to their way of thinking.

Only when the revolutionary threat passed at the end of the forties and the liberals, who were inclined to regard the working class as their potential ally rather than their enemy, won a greater voice in national affairs, did these hopes and fears cease to mold public opinion concerning what had by then become a major force in English social life. After the first fifteen years or so of Victoria's reign, as a rule only the anachronistic ultra-Tories of the "farming interest" denounced the spread of reading on political or social (and, beneath it all, economic) grounds. Instead, people worried chiefly about the dangers of moral corruption associated with

[5] *Letters*, ed. E. H. Coleridge (Boston, 1895), II, 557.

[6] *Edinburgh Review*, XXVII (1816), 458.

popular reading. The Society for Pure Literature was as characteristic of the sixties as the Society for the Diffusion of Useful Knowledge had been of the thirties. This concern for morality in reading
was of course not new, as the constant eighteenth-century de-
nunciations of circulating-library fiction remind us. But during
mid-Victorian times it was uppermost in the minds of those who
watched the spread of the reading habit among the masses. Later,
as the evangelical spirit declined and men no longer took themselves so seriously as the keepers of their humbler brothers'
morals, this preoccupation in turn became less prominent, though
it has not yet entirely disappeared.

With the fading of the moral concern, the problem of the mass
reading public became predominantly one of literary culture. As
we leaf through the many discussions of the popular audience that
appeared from 1850 to 1900 we can see this new emphasis gradually evolving. What positive good was the reading habit once it
had been acquired by the millions whose schooling had been confined to a few years? How, if at all, did the spread of the printed
word contribute to the spiritual enrichment and intellectual enlightenment of the nation at large?

More people were reading than ever before; but in the opinion of
most commentators, they were reading the wrong things, for the
wrong reasons, and in the wrong way. What depressed these observers more than anything else was the apparent decline of serious
purpose in reading. Sharing the familiar human bent for idealizing
the past, they maintained that things were far different, and infinitely better, in the old days before reading had become democratized. The identical lament is heard today; but perhaps some
comfort can be found in remembering that Coleridge had felt the
same way in 1817, when interest in reading was only beginning to
appear among the masses. Nine-tenths of the reading public, he
wrote, confined their attention to periodicals, "a shelf or two of
Beauties, elegant Extracts, and Anas," and circulating-library
novels. The readers of the latter were "that comprehensive class
characterized by the power of reconciling the two contrary yet co-
existing propensities of human nature, namely, indulgence of sloth,
and hatred of vacancy." Their favorite "kill-time" Coleridge refused to dignify with the name of reading. "Call it rather a sort of
beggarly day-dreaming, during which the mind of the dreamer

furnishes for itself nothing but laziness, and a little mawkish sensibility." Such activity, he said, was on the same plane as "gaming, swinging, or swaying on a chair or gate; spitting over a bridge; smoking, snuff-taking; tête-à-tête quarrels after dinner between husband and wife; conning word by word all the advertisements of a daily newspaper in a public house on a rainy day, &c. &c. &c."[7]

Equally deplorable to Victorian commentators, as to Coleridge and to many in our own time, was the growing demand for information and entertainment in the easy-to-take, easy-to-digest form of condensations, summaries, and excerpts—the "Beauties, elegant Extracts, and Anas" of Coleridge's despair. "The impatience of the age," remarked the *Publishers' Circular* in 1890, "will not tolerate expansiveness in books. There is no leisurely browsing and chewing of the literary cud such as Charles Lamb describes with the gusto of an epicure. As a people we have lost the art of taking our ease in an inn, or anywhere else; assuredly we do not take it in the library or in a corner under the bookshelf. The world presses, and reading has to be done in snatches."[8]

There was little doubt that this rage for capsule literature could be attributed as much to the limitations of the ill-educated mass audience as to the increased pressure of daily life. Frederick Rogers, the London journeyman bookbinder, said that "the average workman, as I knew him, was not capable of sustained reading, and the short story and crisp paragraphs inaugurated by G. R. Sims [in the *Referee*] were much more to his palate than the long stories I loved." Not even the sketches of Washington Irving, short though they were, appealed to Rogers' fellow craftsmen. "It was not from dislike of literature, or lack of intellectual energy, it was rather custom and habit, which might be and was broken down when the time came to do so."[9] Meanwhile, as shrewd editors exploited the expanding market for penny periodicals, variety, simplicity, and brevity were the rule. The common reader's diet was measured out in paragraphs or, at the most, a few pages of thin gruel.[10]

---

[7] *Biographia Literaria*, chap. iii.

[8] *Publishers' Circular*, October 1, 1890, p. 1164.

[9] Rogers, *Labour, Life, and Literature*, p. 138.

[10] "Adjust your proposed amount of reading to your time and inclination," Dr. Arnold of Rugby had advised a former pupil many years before. "This is perfectly free to every man, but whether that amount be large or small, let it be varied in its kind, and widely

Where would it all lead, this overwhelming preference of the great public for vacuous and frivolous fiction, for knowledge enclosed in easily opened nutshells, for whatever printed matter would provide an antidote to boredom? Virtually all observers agreed that as reading became a more and more passive habit, universal atrophy of the mind would result. The eye would remain active, but the vital nerve that connected it with the brain would simply wither away from disuse. Once again Coleridge had spoken prophetically. "Reading made easy," he had warned in 1810, would give men "an aversion to words of more than two syllables, instead of drawing them *through* those words into the power of reading books in general. . . . Whatever flatters the mind in its ignorance of its ignorance, tends to aggravate that ignorance, and . . . does . . . more harm than good."[11]

Most Victorian writers who discussed the current state and future prospects of the reading habit shared Coleridge's pessimism. Nevertheless, the common reader was not without his apologists. A defense could even be found for the practice of reading to escape boredom and to divert the mind for an hour or two from the unpleasant realities of life. No one, perhaps, matched Dickens' explosiveness, in a letter to Charles Knight: "The English are, so far as I know, the hardest-worked people on whom the sun shines. Be content if, in their wretched intervals of pleasure, they read for amusement and do no worse. They are born at the oar, and they live and die at it. Good God, what would we have of them!"[12] But the same notion was set forth in many variations, some of them touched with unconscious humor. James Payn, for example, the editor of *Chambers's Journal* in the sixties, stressed the preciousness of books to people in trouble—watching by a deathbed, miserable at boarding school, jilted by a lover, waiting for an overdue train. "Books," he concluded, in no reproachful spirit, "are the blessed chloroform of the mind."[13]

---

varied" (A. P. Stanley, *Life and Correspondence of Thomas Arnold* [1898], II, 146). One questions, however, whether Arnold would have been very enthusiastic about *Answers, Tit-Bits, Rare Bits,* and the other papers of the Harmsworth-Newnes-Pearson school which encouraged the reader to follow his counsel.

[11] Letter cited in n. 5 above.

[12] *Letters* (Nonesuch ed.), II, 548.

[13] *Chambers's Journal,* Ser. 4, I (1864), 578.

It was argued, too, that the purposes for which the common people read and the nature of their reading (so long as it was not really immoral) were less important than the fact that they read at all. Half a loaf was better than none; and a man reading was a man saved from coarser amusements. He might not profit conspicuously from what he read, but at least while he had a book or paper before him he did not get drunk, commit a burglary, or beat his wife. Hence even the masses' addiction to novels was not necessarily a sign of national decadence.

But most important of all, the men of hope who followed in Sir John Herschel's train challenged the assumption that the common man was irrevocably committed to idle, aimless, and profitless reading habits. According to Herschel's view, of which Charles Knight was perhaps the most stubborn advocate despite the innumerable disillusionments he suffered, it was both illogical and inhumane to assume that the capacity for improvement which many Victorians believed to be almost universal in creation had somehow been omitted from humble men and women. Knight stoutly claimed to have seen this principle of progress reflected in the changes of popular reading taste during his own lifetime. "The scurrilous stage—the indecent stage—the profane stage—the seditious stage" had been passed. "Let us hope," said Knight, "that the frivolous stage . . . will in time pass on to a higher taste, and a sounder mental discipline."[14] And, in his incorrigible optimism, he believed that it would.

Those who shared this faith felt that the task of improving popular reading taste was one for educators and publishers. It was foolish to expect much progress so long as the great majority of children left school without being able or inclined to read anything more elevated than a penny dreadful. The first job, then, was to transform the child's early experience of the printed word from a stupid chore to a pleasure, and at the same time to inculcate the first germs of taste. But since under even the best conditions only a small beginning could be made during the child's few years in the classroom, the second responsibility was to attract adolescents to good books after their formal education had ended. This could be done only on Dr. Johnson's principle: "I would let [a boy] at first read *any* English book which happens to engage his attention; be-

[14] *The Old Printer and the Modern Press*, p. 300.

cause you have done a great deal when you have brought him to have entertainment from a book. He'll get better books afterwards."[15] Reading had to be proved palatable before it could be made nourishing. This, as we have seen, was the ground upon which some people insisted that light literature should not be barred from mechanics' institutes and free libraries. It was not an end in itself, but a means to a higher end.

But it was not enough to cultivate the desire to read good books; just as important was the necessity for showing the masses of people *how* to read. Wilkie Collins, in his perceptive article in *Household Words* (1858), pointed out quite correctly that the queries addressed to the "Answers to Correspondents" sections in various cheap periodicals reflected a terrible ignorance of "almost everything which is generally known and understood among readers whom circumstances have placed, socially and intellectually, in the rank above them."[16] Attempts to serialize books like *The Count of Monte Cristo* and *The Wandering Jew* in penny papers had resulted in serious losses of circulation, because readers were baffled by foreign titles and references to foreign manners and customs. Not until the common reader acquired a fund of elementary general knowledge could he read with fair comprehension any books of some literary merit.

Again, there was the question of guidance. Granted that the reader had a genuine desire to refine his taste and broaden his understanding: who would tell him what books to seek? Ernest Rhys, writing of the experience of a popular reprint series which asked readers to nominate new titles for the series, said that the mixed quality of the lists received revealed the pathetic need for advice among the mechanics and tradesmen, miners and peasants who sent them in.[17] The attempts made in this direction late in the nineteenth century—primers of literature, Sir John Lubbock's much publicized list of the hundred best books, the lists of the National Home Reading Union, the very occasional leaflets of suggestions distributed by public libraries—were all to the good, but they fell into the hands of only a few among the millions whom they conceivably could have benefited.

[15] Boswell, *Life of Johnson* (Hill-Powell ed.), III, 385.
[16] Collins, "The Unknown Public," p. 222.
[17] *Encyclopaedia and Dictionary of Education*, ed. Foster Watson (1921), I, 204.

The final problem was the availability of good reading matter. Not until the latter part of the century was there a wide selection of books of substantial literary merit priced so low as to compete with other commodities and entertainments for the workingman's little spending money. Even though the lowering of prices was accompanied by wider distribution, through news agents and drapers and other channels, this was not enough. As a writer in the *Nineteenth Century* in 1886 put it, "If the literature were lying on their [the workingmen's] table they would often read, but they seldom sally forth into the highways and byways of the literary world to discover what they shall purchase. Beyond doubt they have become possessors of thousands of cheap volumes, but the working men and women of England do not number thousands, but millions. . . . The working classes read the Sunday newspaper as largely as they do because it is left at their door. What religious organisations have done in the distribution of tracts which the working classes do not read, surely some other organisation might do for the distribution of works of a wholesome character and of abiding interest which they would read."[18]

Thus in all the hundreds of pages of discussion that the rise of the mass public evoked during the Victorian era, there are few, if any, notions which we do not find echoed in modern commentary. We have inherited the same two-sided attitude toward the common reader. On the one hand, pessimism: "People in general," said Dr. Johnson long before there was a large audience for print, "do not willingly read, if they can have any thing else to amuse them."[19] The belief that aversion to serious reading is ineradicably rooted in the human makeup has been strengthened every time a scheme for increasing people's interest in print has failed. Equally convenient "proof" has been found in the superior popularity of non-literary pastimes, whether the dancing casino in the 1840's or the cinema in the 1940's. The experience of the past (and, for that matter, the present) is read as a sure portent of the future. But behind this whole fatalistic attitude can be detected a survival of venerable social prejudice. Even those with an unswerving emotional and intellectual commitment to democracy as a political

[18] *Nineteenth Century*, XX (1886), 116.

[19] Boswell, IV, 218.

principle sometimes betray skepticism when democratic theory is applied to the problem of the reading audience. The capacities that qualify a man to vote intelligently are not the same, inferentially, as those which qualify him to be a devotee of books.

On the other hand, hope: the belief that the literary enfranchisement of the people only awaits discovery of the right formula. A conscious desire to read may be felt by comparatively few; certainly in the nineteenth century there was no widespread popular—proletarian—agitation to have books and periodicals made available to all. The average human being does not press for cultural advantages as he does for what he deems his political or social rights. But the capacity to find knowledge, inspiration, escape, and sheer delight in reading is latent in far more people than have ever become confirmed booklovers. And that capacity has nothing to do with social or economic status. The memoirs of self-educated men from the nineteenth-century English working class, as well as the experience, both then and now, of teachers, librarians, and publishers of inexpensive series of good books, prove that the desire and the ability to enrich one's life through reading are not contingent on occupation, weekly wage, or family background.

Education has enlarged the reading public, and to some extent enlightened it; but education has only begun the task, and it has, in fact, taken the wrong path at least as often as the right one. With the possible exception of newly published titles, publishers have made good books cheap enough; in neither Britain nor the United States can there any longer be complaint on that score. If the audience for books and relatively serious periodicals remains dishearteningly small, it is because people still have not been sufficiently schooled to value and use good literature and because facilities for distribution still are inadequate. Those who retain the faith of Herschel and Knight persist in believing that a mass market for the best literature, a market large enough to reward many enterprising publishers, can in time be created if every force of modern education is intelligently used: not only the classroom teaching of reading and its uses but all the devices of adult education, including the public library. They find comfort in the fact that the doom of the reading habit has been falsely prophesied ever since the invention of the pneumatic tire, which spelled the end of the fireside reading circle by putting the whole family on bicycles. The latest alarm, occasioned by television, seems so far to have proved unjustified, at least in respect to adults.

Nearly everybody reads something nowadays, but only a small minority read wisely or well. As George Gissing observed, "the public which would feel no lack if all book-printing ceased tomorrow, is enormous."[20] To turn a literate population into a people that is emotionally and intellectually strengthened by books remains today, as it has been for many decades, an impressive challenge to our social institutions. The challenge is all the more urgent as we contemplate the signs of the future. With the development of atomic power and automation, a new industrial revolution, perhaps even more shattering in its effects upon the social order than the earlier one, seems already under way. One consequence, it is generally agreed, will be a great increase in leisure for everyone; and thoughtful students of society are already pondering how that additional leisure can be put to constructive use.

The outlook is complicated by the fact that as an instrument of diversion and instruction the printed word now has more intense competition than ever before. The other so-called "mass communication media" may in time render Gutenberg's invention wholly obsolete. Yet there are many who believe that the experience of reading is in some respects unique—that the peculiar kinds of satisfaction derived from the printed page cannot be duplicated by any other medium. If this is so, then educators, editors, publishers, librarians—all who are charged with preserving and transmitting the heritage of print—are confronted by a mighty task. How, in the face of looming obstacles, can the reading habit be spread and made to serve both the happiness of the individual and the strength of society?

By no stretch of the imagination can the experience of the past, as narrated in this volume, be regarded as an infallible guide for the future. Yet beneath all the surface diversities there remains a strong link of continuity binding one age with another—our age with that of the Victorians and their fathers. By whatever different names we call them, and whatever novel guises they wear, the problems posed by the mass reading public of our day are essen-

[20] *Private Papers of Henry Ryecroft* (Modern Lib. ed.), p. 57.

tially those of the nineteenth century as well. A sense of realism forbids closing this book on the serene note with which Macaulay began his history: "No man who is correctly informed as to the past will be disposed to take a morose or desponding view of the present"—or, as far as that is concerned, of the future. But perhaps it is not unreasonable to hope that in this record of the mistakes that were made, the prejudices that were stubbornly cherished, the promising avenues that were left unexplored, may be found some clues to the fuller and wiser use of the printed word in the democratic society of the future.

APPENDIXES

APPENDIX A | Chronology of the Mass Reading Public 1774–1900

1774   House of Lords' decision in *Donaldson* v. *Beckett* abolishes concept of perpetual copyright and opens way for cheaper books.

1776   and after. Cheap editions of British classics by Cooke, Bell, etc.

1776   Newspaper tax raised from 1*d.* to 1½*d.* per sheet. (Subsequent increases, 1789, 1797, and 1815, bring tax to 4*d.*)

ca. 1780   Book prices begin to climb; peak to be reached *ca.* 1830.

1780   Organized Sunday school movement begins at Gloucester.

1791   "Jacobin" propaganda campaign begins with publication of Paine's *Rights of Man*, Part One. Government initiates repressive measures.

1795–98   Cheap Repository Tracts: start of large-scale publishing activities on part of religious groups.

1799   Religious Tract Society founded.

ca. 1801   Plaster-of-Paris method of making stereotypes perfected. Fourdriniers receive English patents for improved paper-making machine.

1804   British and Foreign Bible Society founded.

1808   British and Foreign School Society (interdenominational) founded.

1809   National Society for the Education of the Poor (Anglican) founded.

1814   First use of steam in printing (by the *Times*). Success of Scott's *Waverley* marks new era in fiction.

1816   Cobbett's twopenny *Political Register* leads outburst of radical journalism.

1817   Samuel Brown's "itinerating libraries" start in East Lothian.

1819   Newspaper Stamp Act freshly defines "newspaper" and converts tax into weapon of political censorship.

1821   Scott's *Kenilworth* sets standard price for new fiction: 31*s.*6*d.*

1822   Limbird's *Mirror:* first successful cheap weekly.

1824   Mechanics' institute movement begins.

1825   Binder's cloth begins to supersede leather.

1827   Great flurry of cheap "libraries" begins with Constable's Miscellany and the Library of Useful Knowledge.

1829   Cadell reissues Scott's novels at 5*s.* a volume.

1830   Colburn and Bentley issue reprinted fiction at 6*s.*

1831–36   "War of the Unstamped Press"; hundreds of prosecutions under the Act of 1819.

1832   *Chambers's Journal* and the *Penny Magazine* begin.

1833   First state aid (£20,000) for elementary schools.

1834   Select Committee on Education inquiry reveals deplorable state of schools.

1836   Newspaper tax reduced to 1*d.*

1836–37   Success of *Pickwick Papers* begins great vogue of fiction in shilling parts.

1837   Paper duty cut in half.

1839–40   "Moral-force" Chartism crusades for better educational provision. First official figures on literacy rate: males, 67 per cent, females, 51 per cent.

1840   Penny post introduced.

1840 and after.   Great increase in circulation of weekly newspapers and cheap part-issue fiction. Steam printing machines generally adopted.

1842   Beginning of Mudie's circulating library.

1847   McIntyre and Simms' Parlour Library: reprints selling for 1*s.*

1848   W. H. Smith and Son take first lease on railway bookstalls.

1849   Public Libraries Committee inquiry.

1850   Ewart's Public Libraries Bill enacted.

1851   Newspaper Stamp Committee inquiry.

1852   "Underselling" practice approved by Lord Campbell's committee. *Uncle Tom's Cabin* breaks all best-seller records.

1855   Newspaper tax repealed. First Hoe rotary press in England, installed for *Lloyd's Newspaper.*

1857   Cost of paper reduced by use of esparto as ingredient.

1860   First number of *Cornhill Magazine* sells 120,000 copies.

1861   Paper tax repealed.

1862   "Payment by results" system introduced into schools, with effect of intensifying pupils' dislike of books.

1870   Forster's Education Act.

1873   University extension courses begin.

1876   "English literature" introduced as a subject in elementary schools; increased demand for suitable textbooks.

1880   Elementary education made compulsory. Newnes' *Tit-Bits* starts new era in cheap journalism.

1880 and after.   Popular series of classics issued at 6*d.* or less. The sixpenny reprint novel adopted by leading publishers.

1886   Linotype machine introduced.

ca. 1894   End of the three-decker "library" novel.

1896   Harmsworth's *Daily Mail* makes the daily paper "popular."

APPENDIX B $\left\{ \vphantom{\Bigg|} \right.$ *Best-Sellers*

No comprehensive collection of nineteenth-century English best-seller figures seems to exist. The following list is not to be regarded as an attempt to supply the lack, for it is not the product of a systematic combing of possible sources. The figures given here are simply those encountered in the course of research for this book. Although unquestionably many books and pamphlets which attained extraordinary sales are missing—the section on juvenile literature especially is inadequate—as a whole the list gives a good idea of the types of books that achieved best-seller status and the figures that gave them that distinction at various epochs in the century. Both varieties of best-sellers, those which enjoyed immense short-term sales and those which sold steadily over a long span of time, are included. "Permanent" best-sellers such as Shakespeare and the Bible are, however, omitted, as are tracts and most other forms of religious literature. Though figures on the gross *output* of this latter kind of printed matter are available, the fact that much of it was given away, rather than sold, makes such statistics valueless as a measure of the purchasers' market.

Gathered as they are from all kinds of sources, these figures run the whole gamut of authenticity, from the reasonably accurate (Dickens' novels) to the extravagant (the crime broadsides). No attempt has been made to sift or check them, and they are presented here simply for whatever they are worth.

NONCE LITERATURE
(Political squibs and other propaganda, crime-and-expiation broadsides, etc.)

1816   Cobbett's "Address to the Journeymen and Labourers . . ." published in No. 18 of the *Political Register* (November 2, 1816) and reissued separately at 2*d*.: 200,000 in two months.[1]

[1] Pearl, *William Cobbett*, pp. 94–95.

1819-22   William Hone and George Cruikshank's "The Political House That Jack Built": 47 editions in a year, total 100,000 copies. The same team's "Queen's Matrimonial Ladder," 44 editions; their "Non Mi Ricordo," 31 editions. Total of all five Hone-Cruikshank squibs issued at this time, about 250,000.[2]

1821-22   Cobbett's [so-called] *Sermons:* "English circulation" by the end of the series, 150,000; by 1828, 211,000.[3]

1823   Catnach's "Full, True, and Particular Account of the Murder of Weare by Thurtell and His Companions," 250,000. Account of Thurtell's trial, 500,000.[4]

1824-26   Cobbett's *History of the Protestant "Reformation"* (propaganda for Catholic Emancipation rather than genuine history): original part-issue reached at least 40,000 per number. In 1828 the total issue by Cobbett alone totaled 700,000 copies of individual numbers. Many subsequent editions by Roman Catholic publishers.[5]

1828   Catnach's "Confession and Execution of William Corder," 1,166,000.[6]

1834   Bulwer's "A Letter to a Late Cabinet Minister on the Crisis," 30,000 in six weeks; about 60,000 in a later, cheaper reprint.[7]

1836-37   Catnach's several "execution papers" relating to the Greenacre-Gale murder case, total 1,650,000.[8]

1848-49   Broadsides, etc., issued in connection with the murder of Isaac Jermy and his son by James Rush, 2,500,000; in connection with the Mannings' murder of O'Connor, 2,500,000.[9]

1871   Rev. H. W. Pullen's "The Fight at Dame Europa's School," a 6*d*. pamphlet on the Franco-Prussian War, 192,000 copies. (At least 81 separate sequels and replies were issued.)[10]

1871   Sir George Chesney's "The Battle of Dorking," a *jeu d'esprit* narrating a successful invasion of England; propaganda for British Army reorganization, first published in *Blackwood's Magazine.* Reprint in pamphlet form sold 110,000 in a few months, and eventually, according to another account, 400,000. (At least twenty replies appeared.)[11]

1874   *Jon Duan* (the most radical of S. O. Beeton's Christmas annuals), 250,000 within three weeks of publication. (Part of the demand may

[2] Knight, *Passages of a Working Life*, I, 246; F. W. Hackwood, *William Hone: His Life and Times* (1912), pp. 194, 228.

[3] Pearl, p. 117.

[4] Hindley, *Life and Times of James Catnach* (1878), pp. 142–43.

[5] Pearl, pp. 135–37.   [6] Hindley (1878), p. 186.

[7] *Life of Edward Bulwer, First Lord Lytton*, by his grandson (1913), I, 434 n.

[8] Hindley (1878), p. 281.

[9] Hindley, *History of the Catnach Press* (1887), p. 92.

[10] *English Catalogue* for 1871, pp. 92–94.

[11] *Ibid.*, p. 94; *Publishers' Circular*, October 2, 1871, p. 607 (hereafter cited as "*P.C.*"). The higher figure is given by Joseph Shaylor, *The Fascination of Books* (1912), p. 154.

be attributed to the fact that W. H. Smith and Son's stalls bore placards announcing that the firm refused to handle the book.)[12]

FICTION

SCOTT

1813   *Rokeby:* 10,000 in three months.

1814   *Waverley:* first edition (1,000) sold in five weeks; total of 6,000 in six months. 11,000 copies in collected editions of Scott's romances, 1820–29. 40,000 copies in new edition, 1829–ca. 1836.

1815   *Guy Mannering:* 2,000 sold a day after publication. Total sale to 1820, 10,000; sale 1820–36, 50,000.

1816   *The Antiquary:* 6,000 in first six days.

1818   *Rob Roy:* 10,000 in fortnight; total to 1836, over 40,000.[13]

(Between 1829 and 1849 the Waverley Novels sold 78,270 sets; Lockhart's *Memoirs of Scott* [published 1837–38] 26,060; *Tales of a Grandfather,* 22,190. The People's Edition of the Works, including Lockhart's *Memoirs,* sold 8,518,849 weekly numbers beginning in 1855—a figure not easily translatable into volumes.[14] In the 1850's the novels fell out of copyright, one by one, and many publishers issued reprints to compete with A. and C. Black's edition, which, as it contained Scott's latest revised text and his illustrations and notes, was still copyright. The total sales of Scott after this time cannot therefore be computed.)

DICKENS   (original issues only, except where noted)

1836–37   *Pickwick Papers:* 40,000 copies per issue at the time Part 15 appeared.[15] Total sale to 1863 (in book form alone[?]), 140,000; to 1879, 800,000.[16]

(Chapman and Hall, the original copyright owners, reported in 1892 that despite the competition offered by eleven different publishers following the lapse of copyright, their own sales of *Pickwick Papers* in the past twenty years had amounted to 521,750. The firm had issued the book in at least ten separate editions, of which the most popular were the two-shilling editions [250,250 copies, 1865–91], the Charles Dickens edition [219,750 copies, 1867–91], and the Household Edition [118,000 copies, 1873–91].[17])

1838–39   *Nicholas Nickleby:* first number sold 50,000, a level sustained throughout the issue. Total sale to 1863 (in book form alone[?]), over 100,000.[18]

[12] H. Montgomery Hyde, *Mr. and Mrs. Beeton* (1951), p. 152.

[13] Lockhart, *Memoirs of Scott* (Boston, 1861), III, 264; IV, 174–75, 211, 290; V, 74.

[14] Curwen, *History of Booksellers,* p. 138.

[15] Johnson, *Charles Dickens,* I, 149.

[16] "The Circulation of Modern Literature," *Spectator,* supplement to issue for January 3, 1863, p. 17 (hereafter cited as "Circ. of Mod. Lit."); Trollope in *Nineteenth Century,* V (1879), 33.

[17] *P.C.,* July 2, 1892, p. 6; August 13, 1892.

[18] Johnson, *Dickens,* I, 219, 249; "Circ. of Mod. Lit.," p. 17.

1840–41   *Master Humphrey's Clock:* began at 70,000, then slumped badly, but recovered with the introduction of *The Old Curiosity Shop* and reached 100,000 before the issue was concluded.

1843–44   *Martin Chuzzlewit:* no higher than 23,000.

1843   *A Christmas Carol:* 6,000 sold first day; 15,000 in year.

1844   *The Chimes:* 20,000 "almost at once."

1845   *The Cricket on the Hearth:* 30,000–40,000(?)

1846–48   *Dombey and Son:* about 30,000(?)

1848   *The Haunted Man:* 18,000 first day.

1849–50   *David Copperfield:* 25,000.

1852–53   *Bleak House:* 35,000.

1855   *Little Dorrit:* began at 35,000 or more.

1864   *Our Mutual Friend:* Part 1 sold 30,000 in three days.[19]

1870   *The Mystery of Edwin Drood:* Part 1, 50,000.[20]

(In 1871, the "penny edition" of *Oliver Twist* [weekly numbers, monthly parts] sold 150,000 in three weeks; *David Copperfield* sold 83,000 in an equal period.[21] In 1882 it was reported that the total sale of Dickens' works, in England alone, in the twelve years since his death amounted to 4,239,000 volumes.[22])

AINSWORTH

1849   *Windsor Castle* (first issued in 1843): in cheap collected edition, 30,000 "in a short time."[23]

G. W. M. REYNOLDS

1852   *The Soldier's Wife:* first two numbers (1*d.* each) sold 60,000 on day of publication.[24]

1854   *The Bronze Soldier:* first two numbers (½*d.* each), 100,000.[25]

(Reynolds' sales in book form and penny instalments undoubtedly were enormous, the aggregate for his scores of romances running into millions. These, however, are the only specific figures I have seen.)

HARRIET BEECHER STOWE

1852   *Uncle Tom's Cabin:* probably the greatest short-term sale of any book published in nineteenth-century England. Ten different editions in two weeks (Autumn, 1852); within a year, forty editions. Sales, April–October, 1852, 150,000; total for first year (April, 1852—April, 1853) including colonial sales, 1,500,000.[26]

[19] Johnson, I, 297, 304, 453, 490, 497, 532, 567; II, 603, 656, 670, 752, 756, 759, 853, 1014–15.

[20] Waugh, *One Hundred Years of Publishing*, pp. 134–35.

[21] *P.C.*, July 15, 1871, p. 426, and December 9, 1872, p. 807.

[22] Mowbray Morris, "Charles Dickens," *Fortnightly Review*, N.S., XXXII (1882), 762.

[23] S. M. Ellis, *William Harrison Ainsworth* (1911), II, 174 n.

[24] Montague Summers, *A Gothic Bibliography* (1942), p. 508.

[25] Montague Summers in *Times Literary Supplement*, July 4, 1942, p. 336.

[26] Sabin, *Bibliotheca Americana*, XXIV, 48; Gohdes, *American Literature in Nineteenth-Century England*, pp. 29–31.

BULWER-LYTTON

1853   *Pelham* (first issued 1828): railway edition (Routledge), 46,000 in five years. Among other cheap editions of this novel, the Railway Library edition (*2s.*) sold 35,750 between 1859 and 1893; one at *3s.6d.* sold 21,250 from 1873 to 1893; the Shilling Pocket edition, 20,000 in one year (1886); and the Sixpenny Edition, 66,000 from 1879 to 1890.[27]

KINGSLEY

1855   *Westward Ho!*: 8,000 in two years. A *6d.* reprint (1889 and later) ran to 500,000 copies.[28]

READE

1856   *It Is Never Too Late To Mend:* 65,000 in seven years.[29]

JAMES GRANT

1856   *Romance of War* in a cheap reprint: 100,000 to *ca.* 1882.[30]

HUGHES

1857   *Tom Brown's School Days:* 11,000 in first 9 months; 28,000 to 1863.[31]

MRS. HENRY WOOD

1861   *East Lynne:* 430,000 to 1898.

1862   *The Channings:* 180,000 to 1898.

1862   *Mrs. Halliburton's Troubles:* 120,000 to 1898.

1869   *Roland Yorke:* 115,000 to 1898.

> (These are the four leading Wood titles among some twenty for which Macmillan's gave figures in 1898. The total sales of Mrs. Henry Wood's fiction, the firm advertised, had then reached "over two and a half million copies."[32] In all likelihood Mrs. Wood was hard pressed by several other popular female novelists, such as Miss Braddon, but figures are lacking.)

[27] Leavis, *Fiction and the Reading Public*, p. 306.

[28] Morgan, *The House of Macmillan*, pp. 42–43, 136.

[29] "Circ. of Mod. Lit.," p. 17.

[30] Mumby, *The House of Routledge*, p. 49.

[31] Edward C. Mack and W. H. G. Armytage, *Thomas Hughes* (1952), p. 90; "Circ. of Mod. Lit.," p. 17. It is interesting to compare the sales attained during the fifties by "popular" authors like Dickens, Reynolds, and Reade with those of two other great novelists whose books appealed to a more limited public. Thackeray sold no more than 7,000 of each monthly part of *Vanity Fair* (1847–48); 1,500 copies of the completed novel were sold immediately after publication. At the beginning of 1857, Thackeray estimated that he had an audience of 15,000 for his new works ("Lewis Melville" [i.e., Lewis S. Benjamin], *William Makepeace Thackeray* [Garden City, 1928], pp. 237, 283; *Letters and Private Papers of W. M. Thackeray*, ed. Gordon N. Ray [Cambridge, Mass., 1945–46], IV, 3). George Eliot's *Adam Bede* (1859) sold 3,350 in its original three-volume form and 11,000 in a cheaper two-volume form within the first year. Of *The Mill on the Floss* (1860), 6,000 were sold in three volumes within three months of publication. Soon after the original appearance of *Middlemarch* (1871), a cheaper edition at *7s.6d.* sold 5,250 in three months (Sadleir, *XIX Century Fiction*, I, 378; Mrs. Gerald Porter, *John Blackwood* [New York, 1898], pp. 52, 384–85).

[32] *P.C.*, Christmas number, 1898, p. 88.

"HUGH CONWAY" (Frederick John Fargus)

1883   *Called Back:* 400,000 to 1898.[33]

MRS. HUMPHRY WARD

1888   *Robert Elsmere:* total sale of three editions (31s.6d., 6s., 2s.6d.) to 1891,
         70,500. "Hundreds of thousands" more were sold later in 6d. and 7d.
         editions. Mrs. Ward's biographer says, however, that the furor over
         the book was much greater in America than in England.[34]

DU MAURIER

1894   *Trilby:* 80,000 in three months.[35]

R. D. BLACKMORE

1897   *Lorna Doone* (first published 1869): 6d. reprint: advance order,
         100,000.[36]

HALL CAINE

1897   *The Christian:* 50,000 in a month.[37]

MARIE CORELLI

1900   *The Master Christian:* 260,000 in a few years.[38]

POETRY

SCOTT

1805   *The Lay of the Last Minstrel:* 44,000 copies to 1830, including 11,000
         in collected editions of Scott's poetry.

1808   *Marmion:* 2,000 sold in first month; 50,000 to 1836.

1810   *The Lady of the Lake:* 20,300 in first year; 50,000 to 1836.[39]

         (Between 1829 and 1849, 41,340 copies of the poetical works were
         sold in collected editions.)[40]

BYRON

1812   *Childe Harold,* first two cantos: 4,500 in less than six months.

1813   *The Bride of Abydos:* 6,000 in first month.

1814   *The Corsair:* 10,000 on day of publication.

1814   *Lara:* 6,000 in a few weeks.[41]

KEBLE

1827   *The Christian Year:* 379,000 to expiration of copyright, 1873.[42]

---

[33] *Ibid.,* November 12, 1898, p. 577.

[34] Mrs. Humphry Ward, *A Writer's Recollections* (New York, 1918), II, 97; Janet Penrose Trevelyan, *Life of Mrs. Humphry Ward* (New York, 1923), pp. 64, 73.

[35] *P.C.,* October 26, 1895, p. 472.

[36] *Ibid.,* October 2, 1897, p. 371.

[37] *Ibid.,* January 15, 1898, p. 67.

[38] Shaylor, *The Fascination of Books,* p. 241.

[39] Lockhart, *Memoirs of Scott,* II, 175, 294; III, 100.

[40] Curwen, *History of Booksellers,* p. 138.

[41] Samuel Smiles, *A Publisher and His Friends* (1891), I, 215, 222, 223, 230.

[42] John Collins Francis, *John Francis* (1888), II, 193 n.

POLLOK
1827   *The Course of Time:* 12,000 in some 18 months; 78,000 to 1869.[43]
TUPPER
1838   *Proverbial Philosophy:* 200,000 to 1866; 50th edition, 1880.[44]
BARHAM
1840–47 *Ingoldsby Legends* (3 series): 52,000 to 1863.[45]
TENNYSON
1850   *In Memoriam:* 25,000 in first year and a half(?); 60,000 in a somewhat
         longer period.
1859   *Idylls of the King* (first four books): first edition, 40,000; 10,000 sold
         in first week.
1864   *Enoch Arden:* first edition, 60,000, of which 40,000 sold in a few weeks.
         Tennyson's most popular volume.
1869   *Idylls of the King* (new books): pre-publication orders, 40,000.

         (Between 1885 and 1888, Tennyson's collected editions sold about
         15,000 copies a year; in the next three years, they averaged 19,000.)[46]
MACAULAY
1862   *Lays of Ancient Rome* (first published in 1842): cheap edition sold
         46,000 within a year.[47]
LONGFELLOW
         Two of the chief firms that published Longfellow's poems—Routledge
         and Warne—together sold over 1,126,900 copies of Longfellow's
         various volumes to 1900. More than seventy different publishers had
         at least one Longfellow volume on their lists. In the fifties there
         were ninety-four editions or issues; in each of the four succeeding
         decades, between thirty-six and fifty-five.[48]

[43] Margaret Oliphant, *Annals of a Publishing House* (New York, 1897), II, 94; *P.C.*, January 16, 1869, p. 3.

[44] Derek Hudson, *Martin Tupper: His Rise and Fall* (1949), p. 40.

[45] "Circ. of Mod. Lit.," p. 17.

[46] The first figure for *In Memoriam* is based on the assumption that since both the first edition (June, 1850) and the fifth (November, 1851) consisted of 5,000 copies, the intervening editions were at least as large (Edgar F. Shannon, Jr., *Tennyson and the Reviewers* [Cambridge, Mass., 1952], pp. 146, 156). For the other figures cited here, see Sir Charles Tennyson, *Alfred Tennyson* (1949), pp. 248, 319, 351 (cf. *P.C.*, December 31, 1864, p. 882), 383, 524.

[47] "Circ. of Mod. Lit.," p. 17.

[48] Clarence Gohdes, "Longfellow and His Authorized British Publishers," *PMLA*, LV (1940), 1179; the same, *American Literature in Nineteenth-Century England*, pp. 106–107. Compared with the sales of giants like Tennyson and Longfellow, those of Browning were minuscule. The original edition (1868–69) of *The Ring and the Book*, Volumes 1 and 2, included 3,000 copies and lasted until 1882; that of Volumes 3 and 4 (2,000) until 1872. *Balaustion's Adventure* (1871) sold out the first edition of 2,500 in five months: "a good sale for the likes of me," remarked Browning (Louise Greer, *Browning and America* [Chapel Hill, 1952], p. 129; W. C. DeVane, *A Browning Handbook* [2d ed.; New York, 1955], p. 357).

TRAVEL, HISTORY, AND BIOGRAPHY

1831   Croker's edition of Boswell: 50,000 to 1891.[49]

1848–61   Macaulay's *History of England:* Vols. 1 and 2 (late 1848) sold 22,000 in a little more than a year. Vols. 3 and 4 (1855), 26,500 in ten weeks. Total sale of the whole work by 1863, 267,000 volumes. Total for Vol. 1 alone to 1875, 133,653.[50]

1855–56   W. H. Russell's *The War from the Landing at Gallipoli to the Death of Lord Raglan:* 200,000 in unspecified period.[51]

1855   Motley's *Rise of the Dutch Republic:* 17,000 in first year.[52]

1856   *Cassell's Illustrated History of England:* 250,000.[53]

1857   Smiles's *Life of George Stephenson:* 7,500 in first year; 25,500 to 1863; 60,000 to end of 1880's.[54]

1857   Livingstone's *Travels:* sales to 1863 of guinea edition, 30,000; of 6s. edition (1861), 10,000.[55]

1859   McClintock's *Voyage of the "Fox" in the Arctic Seas:* 12,000 to 1863.[56]

1861   Du Chaillu's *Explorations in Equatorial Africa:* 10,000 in two years.[57]

1861–62   Smiles's *Lives of the Engineers:* 6,000 in a year or less.[58]

1868   Queen Victoria's *Leaves from a Journal of Our Life in the Highlands:* 103,000 in 2s.6d. edition.[59]

1874   John Richard Green's *Short History of the English People:* 35,000 in first year.[60]

JUVENILE LITERATURE

1833   Favell Lee Bevan's *Peep of Day:* 250,000 to 1867.[61]

1850   "Elizabeth Wetherell's" (i.e., Susan Warner's) *The Wide, Wide World:* 80,000 sold by Routledge alone.[62]

1851   Capt. Mayne Reid's *The Scalp Hunters:* "over a million copies" sold in Great Britain alone to 1890.[63]

[49] Smiles, *A Publisher and His Friends,* II, 289.

[50] Trevelyan, *Life and Letters of Macaulay,* II, 278, 393, 413; "Circ. of Mod. Lit.," p. 17.

[51] Mumby, *The House of Routledge,* p. 86.

[52] O. W. Holmes, *John Lothrop Motley: A Memoir* (Boston, 1881), p. 80.

[53] Sir Newman Flower, *Just As It Happened* (1950), p. 55.

[54] Samuel Smiles, *Autobiography* (New York, 1905), p. 221; "Circ. of Mod. Lit.," p. 17.

[55] "Circ. of Mod. Lit.," p. 16.

[56] *Ibid.*

[57] *Ibid.*   [58] *Ibid.,* p. 17.

[59] [Huxley], *The House of Smith, Elder,* p. 149.

[60] Morgan, *The House of Macmillan,* p. 107.

[61] *P.C.,* April 1, 1867, p. 174.

[62] Mumby, *The House of Routledge,* pp. 56–57.

[63] Elizabeth Reid, *Mayne Reid: A Memoir of His Life* (1900), p. 144.

1852   "Elizabeth Wetherell's" *Queechy:* 62,000 by 1854. Routledge alone eventually sold 114,000.[64]

1858   Elizabeth Sewell's *Tales and Stories* (9 vols.): 68,000 to 1863.[65]

1865   *Alice in Wonderland:* 180,000 to 1898.[66]

1867–69   "Hesba Stretton's" (i.e., Sarah Smith's) *Jessica's First Prayer:* 1,500,000 in unspecified space of time; her *Little Meg's Children* (1868) and *Alone in London* (1869) together sold 750,000.[67]

1871   *Through the Looking Glass:* 60,000 to 1893.[68]

1877   Anna Sewell's *Black Beauty:* 180,000 to 1894.[69]

TEXTBOOKS, REFERENCE WORKS, ETC.

1795   Lindley Murray's *Abridged English Grammar:* 48,000 annually "for many years." Total to *ca.* 1826: one million.[70]

1818   Cobbett's *Grammar of the English Language:* 13,000 in six months. By 1834, over 100,000. Many pirated editions, and "at least twelve different editions after 1860."[71]

1843–44   *Chambers's Cyclopaedia of English Literature:* 130,000 in "a few years."[72]

1852   *Cassell's Popular Educator:* 1,000,000 by 1885.[73]

1855   Soyer's *Shilling Cookery for the People:* 250,000 copies "soon accounted for"; one million to 1900.[74]

1856   Webster's *Dictionary* (taken over in this year by Ward, Lock): 140,000 by early seventies.[75]

1858   J. G. Wood's *Common Objects of the Country:* 100,000 in first week.[76]

1861   Mrs. Beeton's *Book of Household Management:* in book form, over 60,000 the first year; 640,000 to 1898.[77]

[64] "Literature for the People," *Living Age*, XLIII (1854), 121; Mumby, *The House of Routledge*, p. 57.

[65] "Circ. of Mod. Lit.," p. 17.

[66] Derek Hudson, *Lewis Carroll* (1954), p. 147.

[67] Cruse, *The Victorians and Their Reading*, pp. 80–81.

[68] Hudson, *Lewis Carroll*, p. 181.

[69] *P.C.*, January 27, 1894, p. 104.

[70] Lindley Murray, *Memoirs* [York, 1826], pp. 254–55.

[71] Pearl, *William Cobbett*, pp. 105–107.

[72] Curwen, *History of Booksellers*, p. 247.

[73] *Le Livre*, VI (1885), 165.

[74] Mumby, *The House of Routledge*, pp. 84–85.

[75] Edward Liveing, *Adventure in Publishing* (1954), p. 22 n.

[76] Mumby, *The House of Routledge*, p. 78.

[77] Hyde, *Mr. and Mrs. Beeton*, pp. 89, 109; *P.C.*, December 31, 1898, p. 769.

MISCELLANEOUS

1821–22   Cobbett's *Cottage Economy:* "pretty nearly 50,000" by 1828.[78]

1830   Charles Knight's *The Results of Machinery:* 50,000 in unspecified time.[79]

1833–44   *Penny Cyclopaedia:* 75,000 per penny number at beginning, declining to 20,000 at the end of issue.[80]

1833–35   *Chambers's Information for the People:* 170,000 sets by 1872.[81]

1845–47   *Chambers's Miscellany:* average sale in penny weekly parts, 80,000.[82]

1859   Smiles's *Self-Help:* 20,000 in the first year; 55,000 to 1863; 258,000 to 1905.[83]

1860   *Essays and Reviews:* 20,000 in two years.[84]

1878   Herbert Spencer's *Education* (first published 1860): 7,000 of the regular edition, 42,000 of the 2s.6d. edition, 1878–1900.[85]

1881   Henry George's *Progress and Poverty* (6d. edition issued in 1882): total sale to 1885, 60,000.[86]

1882   Carlyle's *Sartor Resartus* (first published in book form in England, 1838), 6d. edition: 70,000.[87]

[78] Pearl, *William Cobbett*, p. 121.

[79] Knight, *The Old Printer and the Modern Press*, p. 248.

[80] Knight, *Passages of a Working Life*, II, 203.

[81] Chambers, *Memoir of Robert Chambers*, p. 236.

[82] Chambers, *Story of a Long and Busy Life*, pp. 93–94; Newspaper Stamp Committee, Q. 1346.

[83] Smiles, *Autobiography*, p. 223; "Circ. of Mod. Lit.," p. 17.

[84] "Circ. of Mod. Lit.," p. 17.

[85] Judges (ed.), *Pioneers of English Education*, p. 161 n.

[86] Lynd, *England in the Eighteen-Eighties*, p. 143.

[87] *Correspondence of Thomas Carlyle and R. W. Emerson*, ed. C. E. Norton (Boston, 1884), I, 15 n.

APPENDIX C $\Big\{$ *Periodical and Newspaper Circulation*

Conforming to the special emphasis of this book, stress is laid here on mass-circulation periodicals and newspapers, but a generous sampling of figures for "quality" periodicals is added for the sake of contrast. Complete figures on taxable papers can be obtained from the various governmental returns down to 1855; only a small selection, with the numbers rounded off to the nearest thousand, is given here.

Apart from official stamp returns (which are themselves not always an accurate indication of the true sales of a paper), the figures given below are drawn from sources whose reliability is seldom beyond challenge. Only a few, unfortunately, come from the private correspondence of publishers and others who not only were in a position to know the truth but had—at least in personal letters— no motive for distorting it. The rest have their origin in current trade rumor and long-term legend, paid advertisements, unpaid puffery, casual gossip, and outright speculation. The source is therefore specified in each case, so that the curious or skeptical may evaluate the information for themselves.

In some instances the totals given seem to represent the combined sales of a periodical in, say, weekly and monthly issues and in bound annual volumes, and in a few other instances they may represent the aggregate number of copies produced in successive impressions spaced over some length of time. Such figures therefore are not dependable measures of a periodical's *immediate* sale.

Thus the primary significance of this tabulation lies not in the circulation figures for individual periodicals but in its reflection of the magnitude of sales which various classes of periodicals had at various times in the nineteenth century. Here, for example, may be traced the growth of the daily newspaper from a circulation of a few thousands to one of a half-million; the rise of the cheap weekly newspaper and "family" miscellany; the development of the shilling and sixpenny magazine; and—with but a few momentary exceptions—the failure of the "intellectual" review even to match the sales the *Quarterly* and *Edinburgh* enjoyed in the first quarter of the century.

1797   *Monthly Magazine* and *Monthly Review*, 5,000 each; *Gentleman's Magazine*, 4,550; *British Critic* and *Critical Review*, 3,500 each; *European Magazine*, 3,250; *Universal Magazine*, 1,750.[1]

1303   *Morning Chronicle*, 3,000; *Morning Post*, 4,500.[2]

1807   (a) *Methodist Magazine* and *Evangelical Magazine*, 18,000–20,000 each.
        (b) *Edinburgh Review*, 7,000 (13,000 in 1814; 12,000 in 1818; 11,000 in 1824–26).[3]

1808   *Examiner*, 2,200.[4]

1810   *Quarterly Review*, 5,000 (12,000–14,000 in 1817–18; 9,000–10,000 in the 1830's).[5]

1816   Cobbett's *Political Register*, 2d. edition, 40,000–50,000—or as high as 70,000(?).[6]

1817   *Blackwood's Magazine* began at 3,700 (but the seventh number, containing the "Chaldee Manuscript,"* sold 10,000).[7]

1819   *The Black Dwarf*, 12,000.[8]

1821   *John Bull*, 10,000 in sixth week of publication.[9]

1822   (a) *Monthly Magazine*, 3,000–4,000. (b) Among newspapers the leaders were: [dailies] the *Times* and its evening edition, the *Evening Mail*, together 5,730; *Morning Chronicle*, 3,180; *Morning Herald*, 2,800; *Morning Post*, 2,000; [thrice weekly] *St. James's Chronicle*, 3,700; [weeklies] *Bell's Weekly Messenger*, 5,020; *John Bull*, 4,500; *Observer*, 6,860.[10]

[1] Timperley, *Encyclopaedia of Literary and Typographical Anecdote*, p. 795.

[2] Wilfred Hindle, *"The Morning Post": 1772–1937* (1937), pp. 82, 84.

[3] (a) *Edinburgh Review*, XI (1808), 341. (b) Samuel Smiles, *A Publisher and His Friends* (1891), I, 80, 101; II, 4; Nesbitt, *Benthamite Reviewing*, pp. 5, 186.

[4] Leigh Hunt, *Correspondence* (1862), I, 40.

[5] Smiles, *A Publisher and His Friends*, I, 188, 259, 366, 372, 383, 495; II, 39, 448.

[6] The figure of 40,000–50,000 for the *Political Register* is given in that paper's issue of April 10, 1830, p. 463. The higher figure is quoted from *Twopenny Trash*, July, 1830, in "Lewis Melville," *Life and Letters of William Cobbett* (1913), II, 79,

[7] *Blackwood's Magazine*, VIII (1820), 80.

[8] Wickwar, *The Struggle for the Freedom of the Press*, p. 57 n.

[9] *Ibid.*, p. 168; Bourne, *English Newspapers*, II, 5–6.

[10] (a) *Blackwood's Magazine*, XI (1822), 371. (b) *Literary Gazette*, May 18, 1822, pp. 312–13.

ca. 1823 Limbird's *Mirror of Literature,* 80,000 for some issues; first number, 150,000.[11]

1824 *Mechanics' Magazine,* 16,000.[12]

1828 *Blackwood's Magazine,* 6,500 (over 8,000 in 1831).[13]

ca. 1830 (a) *New Monthly Magazine,* 5,000; (b) *Athenaeum,* 500–1,000.[14]

1831 (a) *Fraser's Magazine,* 8,700; (b) Doherty's *Voice of the People,* 30,000.[15]

1832 (a) *Chambers's Edinburgh Journal,* 50,000; (b) *Penny Magazine,* 100,000 or 200,000(?).[16]

1833 (a) Carlile's *Gauntlet,* 22,000; Hetherington's *Poor Man's Guardian,* 16,000; six other unstamped radical papers, 5,000–8,000 each. (b) *Spectator,* 1,953 (3,038 in 1838).[17]

1835 Cleave's *Weekly Police Gazette,* 40,000.[18]

1837 *Bentley's Miscellany,* second number, 6,000.[19]

1838–39 Feargus O'Connor's *Northern Star* variously reported as 35,000, 48,000, and 60,000. (Stamp returns for 1840 and 1842 show 18,780 and 12,500, respectively.)[20]

[11] Brougham, *Practical Observations upon the Education of the People (Speeches* [Edinburgh, 1838], III, 107); *Bookseller,* November 30, 1859, pp. [1326–27].

[12] G. T. Garratt, *Lord Brougham* (1935), p. 182.

[13] Margaret Oliphant, *Annals of a Publishing House* (1897), II, 84, 88, 102.

[14] (a) S. C. Hall, *Retrospect of a Long Life* (New York, 1883), p. 182. (b) Leslie A. Marchand, *"The Athenaeum": A Mirror of Victorian Culture* (Chapel Hill, 1941), p. 24.

[15] (a) *Fraser's Magazine,* III (1831), 260. (b) Sidney and Beatrice Webb, *History of Trade Unionism* (1902), p. 109.

[16] (a) *Chambers's Journal,* II (1833), 1. The figure is for the combined Edinburgh and London editions. In his *Memoir of Robert Chambers* (p. 211), William Chambers asserted that the circulation of the first number was 50,000 copies, and that of the third number, 80,000; but Henry J. Nicoll (*Great Movements and Those Who Achieved Them* [1881], p. 168 n.) had Chambers' authority for saying that "the numbers in the *Memoir* should have been made to apply to the *second* and not to the first series of the *Journal.*" The second series began in 1844. See also the *Journal,* I (1832), 104, where it is said that of the eleventh number 31,000 copies had been printed. Beginning with the issue of April 28, 1832, a separate edition was published in London, and the total circulation rose steeply. Advertisements of the *Journal* in the *Athenaeum,* June 16, 1832, p. 390, and March 9, 1833, p. 160, support the 50,000 figure. (b) A similar confusion occurs in the record of the *Penny Magazine*'s initial circulation. In the Preface to the first bound volume of the magazine itself, Knight claimed that it had found 200,000 purchasers. Many years later he repeated this statement (*Passages of a Working Life,* II, 184). But in a letter to Alexander Duff Gordon, March 17, 1855, Knight said that, though the circulation did indeed pass 200,000 at one time, this figure was reached during the third and fourth years. "In the first year (1832) it sold about 100,000; in the second, 160,000" (Clowes, *Charles Knight,* pp. 225–26).

[17] (a) The *Standard,* September 10, 1833, cited by J. Holland Rose in *English Historical Review,* XII (1897), 720–21. (b) William Beach Thomas, *The Story of the "Spectator" 1828–1928* (1928), p. 41.

[18] *London Review,* II (1835), 350.

[19] Johnson, *Charles Dickens,* I, 188.

[20] Mark Hovell, *The Chartist Movement* (2d ed., 1925), pp. 152, 173 n., 269 n.

ca. 1840   *Early Days* [juvenile], 50,000.[21]

1842   *Ainsworth's Magazine*, first year, 7,000.[22]

1843   Leading weekly newspapers: *Weekly Dispatch*, 55,000; *Illustrated London News* (second year), 41,000; *Lloyd's Weekly Newspaper*, 21,000.[23]

1845   *Penny Magazine*, 40,000.[24]

1847   *Howitt's Journal*, first issues, 30,000.[25]

1849   *Family Herald*, 125,000; *Chambers's Journal*, 60,000–70,000; *Eliza Cook's Journal*, 50,000–60,000.[26]

1850   *Household Words* began at 100,000; average sale during its "best years," 40,000.[27]

1850–55   Leading weekly newspapers: *Illustrated London News* (67,000 in 1850; 123,000 in 1854–55); *News of the World* (56,000 and 110,000, respectively); *Lloyd's Weekly Newspaper* (49,000 and 96,000); *Weekly Times* (39,000 and 75,000); *Reynolds' Weekly Newspaper* (began August, 1850; 49,000 in 1855).[28]

1854–68   The *Times*, 50,000–60,000 (attained circulation of 90,000 to 108,000 on a few occasions in this epoch).[29]

1854   *Punch*, 40,000; *Athenaeum*, 7,200.[30]

1855–58   (a) *Family Herald*, 300,000 in 1855, 260,000 in 1858; *London Journal*, 450,000 and 350,000, respectively; *Cassell's Family Paper*, 250,000 and 285,000; *Reynolds' Miscellany*, 200,000 in 1855. (b) *Illustrated Times*, first number, 200,000; "Rugeley number" in 1856, 400,000.[31]

[21] Mathews, *Methodism and the Education of the People*, p. 173.

[22] S. M. Ellis, *William Harrison Ainsworth* (1911), II, 9.

[23] Newspaper Stamp Committee, Appendix 4. This report gives exhaustive figures for stamped newspaper circulation, 1837–50.

[24] Clowes, *Charles Knight*, p. 226.

[25] Carl R. Woodring, *Victorian Samplers: William and Mary Howitt* (Lawrence, Kansas, 1952), p. 129.

[26] Public Libraries Committee, Qq. 2787–90. In 1845 *Chambers's Journal* claimed sales of "not much under ninety thousand copies," of which 40,000 were of the monthly edition (N.S., III [1845], 1).

[27] Johnson, *Charles Dickens*, II, 706, 946.

[28] Figures for 1850 are from the Newspaper Stamp Committee, Appendix 4; for 1854–55, from House of Commons, Accounts and Papers, XXX (1854–55), 497–519. The latter represent the average circulation for the whole of 1854 and the first six months of 1855.

[29] *History of "The Times,"* II, 352, 358.

[30] *Hansard*, Ser. 3, CXXXVII (1855), cols. 781–83.

[31] (a) The 1855 figures are from a letter of Charles Knight (Clowes, *Charles Knight*, p. 226). It should be noted, however, that at this very time Parliament was being given different figures—510,000 a week for the *London Journal* and 240,000 for the *Family Herald* (*Hansard*, just cited). The 1858 figures are from an address by Brougham, *Transactions of the National Association for the Promotion of Social Science* (1858), pp. 28, 36. (b) Ralph Straus, *Sala: The Portrait of an Eminent Victorian* (1942), pp. 109–11.

1858 *Welcome Guest*, first year, 120,000.[32]

1859–69 (a) *All the Year Round* began at 120,000 (300,000 in 1869); Christmas numbers, 185,000 to 250,000, 1862–65. (b) *Once a Week* began (1859) at 22,000, then declined sharply.[33]

1860 (a) *Cornhill Magazine* began at 120,000; average during first two years, 84,000. (b) *Temple-Bar* began at 30,000.[34]

1862 (a) *Englishwoman's Domestic Magazine*, 60,000; *Boy's Own Magazine*, 40,000. (b) *British Workman* and *Band of Hope Review* (both temperance sheets), 250,000 each.[35]

1863 *Lloyd's Weekly Newspaper*, 350,000.[36]

1867 *Broadway Magazine* began at 100,000.[37]

1868 (a) *Illustrated Police News*, 100,000; (b) *Good Words*, 130,000.[38]

1869 *Academy*, first year, 16,000.[39]

ca. 1870 *Daily News*, 150,000; *Daily Telegraph*, 200,000.[40]

1872 (a) The *Graphic*, Christmas number, 200,000 ("European" [including British] sale); its "Tichborne number," 1874, 250,000. (b) *Fortnightly Review*, 2,500.[41]

ca. 1880 *Boy's Own Paper*, 200,000.[42]

1881 *Christian Herald*, 195,000; *Weekly Budget*, 500,000.[43]

1882 (a) The *Times*, 100,000; *Daily Telegraph*, 250,000. (b) *Cornhill*, down to 12,000 and then up (temporarily) to 47,000.[44]

1886 *Lloyd's Weekly Newspaper*, 750,000.[45]

[32] Straus, *Sala*, p. 132.

[33] (a) Johnson, *Charles Dickens*, II, 946–47, 1004, 1014, 1061. (b) William E. Buckler, "*Once a Week* under Samuel Lucas," *PMLA*, LXVII (1952), 938–39.

[34] (a) George M. Smith, "Our Birth and Parentage," *Cornhill Magazine*, N.S., X (1901), 9; *Publishers' Circular*, May 1, 1862, p. 199, quoting the *Cornhill*'s publishers. (b) G. A. Sala, *Life and Adventures* (New York, 1896), I, 358.

[35] (a) H. Montgomery Hyde, *Mr. and Mrs. Beeton* (1951), pp. 46, 53, 120, 124. (b) Henry Roberts in *British Association Reports* (1862), p. 174. The temperance papers, though bearing the nominal price of 1d. and ½d., respectively, were given widespread free distribution. See Keefe, *A Century in Print*, pp. 35–41.

[36] Bourne, *English Newspapers*, II, 254.

[37] The proprietors' claim: *Publishers' Circular*, September 2, 1867, p. 513.

[38] (a) *Ibid.*, April 15, 1868, p. 210. (b) *Ibid.*, December 10, 1868, p. 794.

[39] *Ibid.*, October 15, 1869, p. 642.

[40] *History of "The Times,"* II, 303, 354.

[41] (a) Malcolm Elwin, *Charles Reade* (1931), p. 244; *Publishers' Circular*, March 16, 1874, p. 166. (b) Edwin M. Everett, *The Party of Humanity* (Chapel Hill, 1939), p. 321.

[42] *Publishers' Circular*, March 12, 1898, p. 307.

[43] Hitchman in *Macmillan's Magazine*, XLIII (1881), 387, 396.

[44] (a) Lynd, *England in the Eighteen-Eighties*, p. 367. (b) [Huxley], *The House of Smith, Elder*, pp. 119–20, 128–29.

[45] Salmon in *Nineteenth Century*, XX (1886), 110.

1889   *Pall Mall Gazette*, 12,250.[46]

ca. 1890   *Review of Reviews*, first year, 300,000 (including export).[47]

1896   *Strand Magazine*, July number, 392,000 (including 60,000 to U.S.A.); *Woman's Life*, 200,000.[48]

1897   *Tit-Bits*, Easter Week, 671,000; each of the three leading papers of this class—*Tit-Bits, Answers, Pearson's Weekly*—sold 400,000 to 600,000. A prize contest once sent the last-named to 1,250,000.[49]

1898   *Harmsworth's Magazine* and the *Royal Magazine*, around 1,000,000 each; *Strand Magazine, Windsor Magazine,* and *Pearson's Magazine,* 200,000–400,000 each.[50]

1899   *Daily Mail*, 543,000.[51]

[46] Frederic Whyte, *Life of W. T. Stead* (1925), I, 288.

[47] *Newsagents' Chronicle* [supplement to *Publishers' Circular*], November 27, 1897, p. 8.

[48] *Ibid.*, August 8, 1896, p. 8.

[49] *Ibid.*, July 24, 1897, p. 8; November 27, 1897, p. 8.

[50] *Publishers' Circular*, October 22, 1898, p. 479.

[51] Ensor, *England, 1870–1914*, p. 312.

BIBLIOGRAPHY

Bibliography

The following list, though representing only a small fraction of the sources consulted for this volume, includes all books and articles that have proved to be of substantial usefulness to the student of the mass reading public in nineteenth-century England. It serves also as a register of materials, such as workingmen's memoirs, which are frequently cited in the reference notes. The place of publication is London unless otherwise specified.

Of the many bibliographies bearing upon one or more aspects of the subject, the following five are the most useful:

Cambridge Bibliography of English Literature, Vol. III. (See especially the sections on "Book Production and Distribution," "Education," and "Newspapers and Magazines.")

EBISCH, WALTHER, and SCHÜCKING, LEVIN L. "Bibliographie zur Geschichte des literarischen Geschmacks in England," *Anglia*, LXIII (1939), 1–64.

HEADICAR, B. M., and FULLER, C. *A London Bibliography of the Social Sciences.* 4 vols., 1932, and later supplements.

PEET, WILLIAM. "Bibliography of Publishing and Bookselling," in Mumby, *Publishing and Bookselling* (see below), pp. 379–421. (The fullest bibliography of the subject.)

WILLIAMS, JUDITH BLOW. *A Guide to the Printed Materials for English Social and Economic History, 1750–1850.* 2 vols. New York, 1926.

ACKLAND, JOSEPH. "Elementary Education and the Decay of Literature," *Nineteenth Century*, XXXV (1894), 412–23.

ADAMSON, J. W. *English Education, 1789–1902.* Cambridge, 1930.

———. "Literacy in England in the Fifteenth and Sixteenth Centuries," in his *"The Illiterate Anglo-Saxon"* (Cambridge, 1946), pp. 38–61.

ALDIS, H. G. "Book Production and Distribution, 1625–1800," *Cambridge History of English Literature*, Vol. XI, chap. xiv.

ALEXANDER, WILLIAM. "Literature of the People—Past and Present," *Good Words*, XVII (1876), 92–96.

ALLEN, W. O. B., and MᴄCLURE, EDMUND. *Two Hundred Years: The History of the Society for Promoting Christian Knowledge, 1698–1898.* 1898.

ALTICK, RICHARD D. "English Publishing and the Mass Audience in 1852," *Studies in Bibliography*, VI (1953 for 1954), 3–24.

ARCH, JOSEPH. *The Story of His Life, Told by Himself.* 1898.

ARCHER, R. L. *Secondary Education in the Nineteenth Century.* Cambridge, 1921.

ARNOLD, MATTHEW. *Reports on Elementary Schools, 1852–1882.* 1889.

ASHTON, THOMAS S. *Economic and Social Investigations in Manchester, 1833–1933.* 1934.

ASPINALL, ARTHUR. "The Circulation of Newspapers in the Early Nineteenth Century," *Review of English Studies*, XXII (1946), 29–43.

———. *Politics and the Press, c. 1780–1850.* 1949.

AXON, WILLIAM E. A. "Free Public Libraries of Great Britain," *Companion to the* [British] *Almanac for 1869*, pp. 23–40.

BAMFORD, SAMUEL. *Early Days.* 1849.

———. *Passages in the Life of a Radical.* 2 vols. 1844.

BARKER, JOSEPH. *Life of Joseph Barker, Written by Himself.* 1880.

BARNARD, H. C. *A Short History of English Education from 1760 to 1944.* 1947.

BARTLEY, GEORGE C. T. *The Schools for the People, Containing the History, Development, and Present Working of Each Description of English School for the Industrial and Poorer Classes.* 1871.

BECKWITH, FRANK. "The Eighteenth-Century Proprietary Library in England," *Journal of Documentation*, III (1947), 81–98.

BELJAME, ALEXANDRE. *Men of Letters and the English Public in the Eighteenth Century: 1660–1744*, ed. Bonamy Dobrée, trans. E. O. Lorimer. 1948.

BENNETT, H. S. "The Author and His Public in the Fourteenth and Fifteenth Centuries," *Essays and Studies by Members of the English Association*, XXIII (1938 for 1937), 7–24.

———. "Caxton and His Public," *Review of English Studies*, XIX (1943), 113–19.

———. *English Books & Readers, 1475 to 1557.* Cambridge, 1952.

———. "Printers, Authors, and Readers, 1475–1557," *Library*, Ser. 5, IV (1949), 155–65.

BINNS, HENRY BRYAN. *A Century of Education: Being the Centenary History of the British & Foreign School Society, 1808–1908.* 1908.

BIRCHENOUGH, CHARLES. *History of Elementary Education in England and Wales from 1800 to the Present Day.* 2d ed. 1927.

BLAKEY, DOROTHY. *The Minerva Press, 1790–1820.* 1939.

BOSANQUET, HELEN. "Cheap Literature," *Contemporary Review*, LXXIX (1901), 671–81.

BOURNE, H. R. Fox. *English Newspapers: Chapters in the History of Journalism.* 2 vols. 1887.

BOWLEY, ARTHUR L. *Wages in the United Kingdom in the Nineteenth Century.* Cambridge, 1900.

BREADY, J. WESLEY. *England: Before and After Wesley.* 1938.

BROUGHAM, HENRY. "Practical Observations upon the Education of the People" [1825], in his *Speeches* (Edinburgh, 1838), III, 103–52.

[BROWN, SAMUEL, JR.]. *Some Account of Itinerating Libraries and Their Founder.* Edinburgh, 1856.

BROWN, TAYLOR. "Samuel Brown and His Libraries," *Library Review*, No. 60 (1941), 125–29.

BROWNE, GEORGE. *The History of the British and Foreign Bible Society.* 2 vols. 1859.

BUNCE, OLIVER B. "English and American Book Markets," *North American Review*, CL (1890), 470–79.

[BURT, THOMAS]. *Thomas Burt, M.P., D.C.L., Pitman & Privy Councillor: An Autobiography.* 1924.

"The Byways of Literature: Reading for the Million," *Blackwood's Magazine*, LXXXIV (1858), 200–216.

CARTER, JOHN, and SADLEIR, MICHAEL. *Victorian Fiction: An Exhibition of Original Editions.* Cambridge, 1947.

[CARTER, THOMAS]. *Memoirs of a Working Man.* 1845.

Central Society of Education Publications. Vols. I–III. 1837–39.

CHAMBERS, WILLIAM. *Memoir of Robert Chambers with Autobiographic Reminiscences of William Chambers.* New York, 1872.

———. *Story of a Long and Busy Life.* Edinburgh, 1882.

[CHAPMAN, J. W.]. "The Commerce of Literature," *Westminster Review*, N.S., I (1852), 511–54.

CHAPMAN, R. W. "Authors and Booksellers," *Johnson's England*, ed. A. S. Turberville (Oxford, 1933), II, 310–30.

"Cheap Literature," *British Quarterly Review*, XXIX (1859), 313–45.

"The Cheap Movement in Literature," *Book-Lore*, IV (1886), 10–12.

CHESNEAU, ERNEST. "Les grands éditeurs anglais," *Le Livre*, VI (1885), 163–87, 292–311; VII (1886), 257–81.

"The Circulation of Modern Literature," *Spectator*, supplement to issue for Jan. 3, 1863, pp. 16–18.

CLAPHAM, J. H. *An Economic History of Modern Britain.* Vols. I–II. Cambridge, 1926–32.

["CLARENDON COMMISSION"]. *Report of Her Majesty's Commissioners Appointed To Inquire into the Revenues and Management of Certain Colleges and Schools.* 4 vols. 1864.

CLARKE, W. K. L. *A Short History of S.P.C.K.* 1919.

CLOWES, ALICE A. *Charles Knight: A Sketch.* 1892.

CLOWES, WILLIAM LAIRD. "The Cheapening of Useful Books," *Fortnightly Review*, LXXVI (1901), 88–98.

COLBY, ROBERT A. " 'The Librarian Rules the Roost': The Career of Charles Edward Mudie," *Wilson Library Bulletin*, XXVI (1952), 623–27.

———. "That He Who Rides May Read: W. H. Smith & Son's Railway Library," *ibid.*, XXVII (1952), 300–306.

COLE, G. D. H. *The Life of William Cobbett.* 1924.

COLE, G. D. H. *A Short History of the British Working-Class Movement, 1789–1947.* 1948.

COLE, G. D. H., and POSTGATE, RAYMOND. *The Common People, 1746–1938.* 1938.

COLE, MARGARET. *Books and the People.* 1938.

COLLET, COLLET DOBSON. *History of the Taxes on Knowledge.* 2 vols. 1899.

COLLINS, A. S. *Authorship in the Days of Johnson.* 1927.

———. *The Profession of Letters . . . 1780–1832.* 1928.

COLLINS, WILKIE. "The Unknown Public," *Household Words,* XVIII (1858), 217–24.

COOPER, THOMAS. *The Life of Thomas Cooper.* 1872.

Copyright Commission. The Royal Commissions and the Report of the Commissioners. 1878.

CRUSE, AMY. *The Englishman and His Books in the Early Nineteenth Century.* New York, 1930.

———. *The Victorians and Their Reading.* Boston, 1936.

CURTIS, S. J. *History of Education in Great Britain.* 1948.

CURWEN, HENRY. *A History of Booksellers, the Old and the New.* 1873.

DAICHES, DAVID. *Literature and Society.* 1938.

"A Day at the London Free Libraries," *All the Year Round,* Ser. 3, VII (1892), 305–309.

DENT, J. M. *The Memoirs of J. M. Dent, 1849–1926.* 1928.

DITZION, SIDNEY. "The Anglo-American Library Scene: A Contribution to the Social History of the Library Movement," *Library Quarterly,* XVI (1946), 281–301.

DOBBS, A. E. *Education and Social Movements, 1700 1850.* 1010.

DODDS, JOHN W. *The Age of Paradox: A Biography of England, 1841–1851.* New York, 1952. (Chaps. iii, ix.)

EDWARDS, EDWARD. *Free Town Libraries: Their Formation, Management, and History.* 1869.

———. "Libraries and the People," *British Quarterly Review,* XI (1850), 61–80.

EDWARDS, M. L. *After Wesley: A Study of the Social and Political Influence of Methodism in the Middle Period, 1791–1849.* 1936.

———. *Methodism and England: A Study of Methodism in Its Social and Political Aspects during the Period 1850–1932.* 1943.

ELLIOTT, GEORGE H. "Our Readers and What They Read," *Library,* VII (1895), 276–81.

ENGELS, FREDERICK. *The Condition of the Working-Class in England in 1844,* trans. Florence Kelley Wischnewetzky. 1892.

[ENGLISH, R.]. "The Price of the Novel, 1750–1894 [actually 1860]," *The Author,* V (1894), 94–99.

"English Journalism," *Nation* (New York), XXI (1880), *passim.*

ENSOR, R. C. K. *England, 1870–1914.* Oxford, 1936.

ESCOTT, T. H. S. *England: Her People, Polity, and Pursuits.* 2 vols. 1880.

———. *Social Transformations of the Victorian Age.* 1897.

"Everybody's Books: Popular Taste and Clever Enterprises," *Times Literary*

Supplement, May 1, 1937, pp. 328–29. (This "Victorian Centenary Number" contains other useful articles on the Victorian book trade.)

FROST, THOMAS. *Forty Years' Recollections: Literary and Political.* 1880.

GARDINER, DOROTHY. *English Girlhood at School: A Study of Women's Education through Twelve Centuries.* Oxford, 1929.

GATTIE, WALTER MONTAGU. "What English People Read," *Fortnightly Review*, LII (1889), 307–21. (Based on public library statistics.)

GILBOY, ELIZABETH W. *Wages in Eighteenth Century England.* Cambridge, Mass., 1934.

GOHDES, CLARENCE. *American Literature in Nineteenth-Century England.* New York, 1944.

GRAHAM, WALTER. *English Literary Periodicals.* New York, 1930.

GRANT, JAMES. *The Newspaper Press: Its Origin, Progress, and Present Position.* 3 vols. 1871–72.

GREENWOOD, THOMAS. *Greenwood's Library Year Book.* 1897.

———. *Public Libraries: A History of the Movement and a Manual for . . . Rate-Supported Libraries.* 4th ed. 1894.

GREGG, PAULINE. *A Social and Economic History of Britain, 1760–1950.* 1950.

GREGORY, BENJAMIN. *Autobiographical Recollections.* 1903.

GUÉRARD, ALBERT. *Literature and Society.* Boston, 1935.

HALÉVY, ÉLIE. *A History of the English People in 1815*, trans. E. I. Watkin and D. A. Barker. New York, 1924.

HAMLYN, HILDA M. "Eighteenth-Century Circulating Libraries in England," *Library*, Ser. 5, I (1946–47), 197–222.

HAMMOND, J. L. and BARBARA. *The Age of the Chartists: 1832–1854.* 1930.

———. *The Town Labourer, 1760–1832.* New ed. 1925.

HARRISON, JOHN POWNALL. "Cheap Literature—Past and Present," *Companion to the* [British] *Almanac for 1873*, pp. 60–81.

HERSCHEL, SIR JOHN. "Address to the Subscribers to the Windsor and Eton Public Library and Reading Room" [1833], in his *Essays from the Edinburgh and Quarterly Reviews* (1857), pp. 1–20.

HEWITT, GORDON. *Let the People Read: A Short History of the United Society for Christian Literature.* 1949. (On the Religious Tract Society.)

HILL, FREDERICK. *National Education: Its Present State and Prospects.* 2 vols. 1836.

HINDLEY, CHARLES. *The History of the Catnach Press.* 1887.

———. *The Life and Times of James Catnach* (*Late of Seven Dials*), *Ballad Monger.* 1878.

The History of "The Times" [1785–1912]. 3 vols. 1935–47.

[HITCHMAN, FRANCIS]. "Penny Fiction," *Quarterly Review*, CLXXI (1890), 150–71.

———. "The Penny Press," *Macmillan's Magazine*, XLIII (1881), 385–98.

HODGEN, MARGARET T. *Workers' Education in England and the United States.* 1925.

HOLE, JAMES. *An Essay on the History and Management of Literary, Scientific, and Mechanics' Institutions.* 1853.

HOLMAN, HENRY. *English National Education: A Sketch of the Rise of Public Elementary Schools in England*. 1898.

HUDSON, J. W. *The History of Adult Education*. 1851.

HUMPHERY, GEORGE R. "The Reading of the Working Classes," *Nineteenth Century*, XXXIII (1893), 690–701.

[HUXLEY, LEONARD]. *The House of Smith, Elder*. 1923.

INNIS, HAROLD A. "An Economic Approach to English Literature in the Nineteenth Century," in his *Political Economy in the Modern State* (Toronto, 1946), pp. 35–55.

"Institutes for Working Men," *Quarterly Review*, CXIII (1863), 34–59.

IRWIN, RAYMOND. "The English Domestic Library"; "The Economics of Writing and Reading"; "The English Domestic Library in the Nineteenth Century," *Library Association Record*, LVI (1954), 195–201, 283–88, 382–89.

JACKSON, MASON. *The Pictorial Press: Its Origin and Progress*. 1885.

JEVONS, W. STANLEY. "The Rationale of Free Public Libraries," *Contemporary Review*, XXXIX (1881), 385–402.

JOHNSON, EDGAR. *Charles Dickens: His Tragedy and Triumph*. 2 vols. New York, 1952.

JOHNSON, FRANCIS R. "Notes on English Retail Book-Prices, 1550–1640," *Library*, Ser. 5, V (1950), 83–112.

JONES, M. G. *The Charity School Movement: A Study of Eighteenth Century Puritanism in Action*. Cambridge, 1938.

———. *Hannah More*. Cambridge, 1952.

JUDGES, A. V. (ed.). *Pioneers of English Education*. 1952.

KAY, JOSEPH. *The Education of the Poor in England and Europe*. 1846.

KAY-SHUTTLEWORTH, SIR J. P. *Four Periods of Public Education as Reviewed in 1832, 1839, 1846, 1862*. 1862.

KEEFE, H. J. *A Century in Print: The Story of Hazell's, 1839–1939*. 1939.

KELLETT, E. E. *As I Remember*. 1936. (See especially chap. vii.)

———. "The Press," *Early Victorian England*, ed. G. M. Young (1934), II, 3–97.

KERR, JOHN. *Scottish Education, School and University from Early Times to 1908*. Cambridge, 1910.

[KNIGHT, CHARLES]. "Education of the People," *London Magazine*, Ser. 3, I (1828), 1–13.

———. "The Market of Literature," *The Printing Machine*, I (1834), 1–5.

———. *The Old Printer and the Modern Press*. 1854.

———. *Passages of a Working Life during Half a Century*. 3 vols. 1864–65.

LACKINGTON, JAMES. *Memoirs of the Forty-Five First Years of the Life of James Lackington*. 13th ed. 1810(?).

LANG, ANDREW, and "X," A WORKING MAN. "The Reading Public," *Cornhill Magazine*, N.S., XI (1901), 783–95.

LEAVIS, Q. D. *Fiction and the Reading Public*. 1932.

LEIGH, JOHN GARRETT. "What Do the Masses Read?" *Economic Review*, XIV (1904), 166–77.

LEVI, LEONE. *Wages and Earnings of the Working Classes*. 1885.

"Libraries for the People," *Meliora*, II (1860), 293–305.
"Literature and Democracy," *Macmillan's Magazine*, LXXXIII (1901), 401–409.
"Literature of Labour," *Meliora*, II (1860), 1–16.
"Literature for the People," *Times*, Feb. 8, 1854; reprinted in *Living Age*, XLIII (1854), 118–22.
"The Literature of Snippets," *Saturday Review*, LXXXVII (1899), 455–56.
"The Literature of the Streets," *Edinburgh Review*, CLXV (1887), 40–65.
"The Literature of Vice," *Bookseller*, Feb. 28, 1867, pp. 121–23.
LOVETT, WILLIAM. *Life & Struggles of William Lovett in His Pursuit of Bread, Knowledge, and Freedom*. 1920.
LOWNDES, G. A. N. *The Silent Social Revolution: An Account of the Expansion of Public Education in England and Wales, 1895–1935*. 1937.
LUDLOW, JOHN M., and JONES, LLOYD. *The Progress of the Working Class, 1832–1867*. 1867.
LYND, HELEN M. *England in the Eighteen-Eighties: Toward a Social Basis for Freedom*. 1945.
MACK, EDWARD C. *Public Schools and British Opinion*. 2 vols. New York, 1939–41.
MCKERROW, R. B., "Booksellers, Printers, and the Stationers' Trade," *Shakespeare's England* (Oxford, 1916), II, 212–39.
MCKILLOP, ALAN D. "English Circulating Libraries, 1725–50," *Library*, Ser. 4, XIV (1934), 477–85.
MARCH-PHILLIPPS, EVELYN. "Women's Newspapers," *Fortnightly Review*, N.S., LVI (1894), 661–70.
MARTIN, G. CURRIE. *The Adult School Movement: Its Origin and Development*. 1924.
MATHEWS, H. F. *Methodism and the Education of the People, 1791–1851*. 1949.
MAYHEW, HENRY. *London Labour and the London Poor*. 4 vols. 1861(?).
"Mechanics' Institutes," *Meliora*, II (1860), 209–25.
"Mechanics' Institutes and Infant Schools," *Quarterly Review*, XXXII (1825), 410–28.
"Mechanics' Institutions," in *Chambers's Papers for the People* (Philadelphia, 1851), III, 197–228.
"Mechanics' Institutions," *Westminster Review*, XLI (1844), 416–45.
[MERLE, GIBBONS]. "Weekly Newspapers," *Westminster Review*, X (1829), 466–80.
[MILLAR, JOHN HEPBURN]. "Penny Fiction," *Blackwood's Magazine*, CLXIV (1898), 801–11.
MINEKA, FRANCIS E. *The Dissidence of Dissent: The "Monthly Repository," 1806–1838*. Chapel Hill, 1944.
MINTO, JOHN. *A History of the Public Library Movement in Great Britain and Ireland*. 1932.
"Mischievous Literature," *Bookseller*, July 1, 1868, pp. 445–49.
"The Monster-Misery of Literature," *Blackwood's Magazine*, LV (1844), 556–60. (An attack on the circulating-library system.)
MORGAN, CHARLES. *The House of Macmillan (1843–1943)*. New York, 1944.

[MORLEY, HENRY]. "The Labourer's Reading-Room," *Household Words*, III (1851), 581–85.

MORTON, E. P. "News for Bibliophiles," *Nation* (New York), XCVI (1913), 305–306, 330–32. (On the prices of novels and books of poetry in the nineteenth century.)

MUMBY, F. A. *The House of Routledge, 1834–1934*. 1934.

———. *Publishing and Bookselling: A History from the Earliest Times to the Present Day*. New ed. 1949.

MUNFORD, W. A. *Penny Rate: Aspects of British Public Library History, 1850–1950*. 1951.

NESBITT, GEORGE L. *Benthamite Reviewing: The First Twelve Years of the "Westminster Review," 1824–1836*. New York, 1934.

"New and Cheap Forms of Popular Literature," *Eclectic Review*, LXXXII (1845), 74–84.

["NEWCASTLE COMMISSION"]. *Report of the Commissioners Appointed To Inquire into the State of Popular Education in England*. 6 vols. 1861.

"The Newspaper Press," *Quarterly Review*, CL (1880), 498–537.

["NEWSPAPER STAMP COMMITTEE"]. *Report from the Select Committee on Newspaper Stamps*. 1851.

OGLE, JOHN J. *The Free Library: Its History and Present Condition*. 1897.

OWEN, EVAN. "Workmen's Libraries in Glamorganshire and Monmouthshire," *Library*, VIII (1896), 1–14.

PASCOE, CHARLES E. "The Story of the English Magazines," *Atlantic Monthly*, LIV (1884), 364–74.

PAYN, JAMES. "Penny Fiction," *Nineteenth Century*, IX (1881), 145–54.

PEARL, M. L. *William Cobbett: A Bibliographical Account of His Life and Times*. 1953.

[PENNELL, E. R.]. "Popular English Papers," *Nation* (New York), LII (1891), 195–96.

PERIODICALS. In addition to the files of general periodicals dealing with topics of the day, such as the *Edinburgh*, the *Quarterly*, the *Westminster*, the *Athenaeum*, the *Fortnightly*, the *Nineteenth Century*, *Fraser's*, *Blackwood's*, etc., the following specialized journals have much material relevant to the particular purposes of this study: the *Bookseller;* the *Journal of the Statistical Society;* the *Library;* the *Publishers' Circular; Transactions of the National Association for the Promotion of Social Science*.

[PHILLIPS, SAMUEL]. "The Literature of the Rail," in his *Essays from "The Times,"* Ser. 1, 7th ed. (1855), pp. 311–25.

PHILLIPS, WALTER C. *Dickens, Reade, and Collins, Sensation Novelists*. New York, 1919. (See especially pp. 38–57, on the history of cheap books, 1800–1850.)

PLANT, MARJORIE. *The English Book Trade: An Economic History of the Making and Sale of Books*. 1939.

"The Poetry of Seven Dials," *Quarterly Review*, CXXII (1867), 382–406.

POLLARD, A. W. "Commercial Circulating Libraries and the Price of Books," *Library*, Ser. 4, IX (1929), 411–16.

POLLARD, GRAHAM, "Serial Fiction," in John Carter (ed.), *New Paths in Book Collecting* (1934), pp. 247–77.

PORTER, G. R. *The Progress of the Nation in Its Various Social and Economic Relations from the Beginning of the Nineteenth Century*. New ed. 1912.

PREDEEK, ALBERT. *A History of Libraries in Great Britain and North America*, trans. Lawrence S. Thompson. Chicago, 1947.

PRESTON, WILLIAM C. "Messrs. W. H. Smith and Son's Bookstalls and Library," *Good Words*, XXXVI (1895), 474–78.

———. "Mudie's Library," *ibid.*, XXXV (1894), 668–76.

"Public Free Libraries," *Meliora*, X (1867), 235–46.

"Public Libraries," *Westminster Review*, VIII (1827), 105–27.

["PUBLIC LIBRARIES COMMITTEE"]. *Report from the Select Committee of Public Libraries*. 1849. (Not to be confused with subsequent reports from this committee, dated 1850–52.)

QUINLAN, MAURICE J. *Victorian Prelude: A History of English Manners, 1700–1830*. New York, 1941.

R., C. "What the People Read," *Academy*, LII–LIV (1897–98), *passim*.

"Readers," *Blackwood's Magazine*, CXXVI (1879), 235–56.

RICH, R. W. *The Training of Teachers in England and Wales during the Nineteenth Century*. Cambridge, 1933.

ROBERTS, HENRY. "Statistics Showing the Increased Circulation of a Pure and Instructive Literature Adapted to the Capacities and the Means of the Labouring Population," *Report of the 32nd Meeting of the British Association for the Advancement of Science* (1862), "Notices and Abstracts of . . . the Sections," pp. 172–74.

ROBERTS, W. "The Free Library Failure," *New Review*, XIII (1895), 316–24.

ROGERS, FREDERICK. *Labour, Life, and Literature: Some Memories of Sixty Years*. 1913.

ROSE, J. HOLLAND. "The Unstamped Press, 1815–1836," *English Historical Review*, XII (1897), 711–26.

ROWNTREE, J. W., and BINNS, H. B. *A History of the Adult School Movement*. 1903.

SADLEIR, MICHAEL. *XIX Century Fiction: A Bibliographical Record Based on His Own Collection*. 2 vols. 1951.

———. "Yellow Backs," in John Carter (ed.), *New Paths in Book Collecting* (1934), pp. 127–61.

SALMON, EDWARD G. "What Girls Read," *Nineteenth Century*, XX (1886), 515–29.

———. "What the Working Classes Read," *ibid.*, XX (1886), 108–17.

SCHÜCKING, LEVIN L. *The Sociology of Literary Taste*, trans. E. W. Dickes. 1944.

Select Committee on the State of Education. 1834.

"Sensation Novels," *Quarterly Review*, CXIII (1863), 481–514.

SHAYLOR, JOSEPH. "Reprints and Their Readers," *Cornhill Magazine*, XCI (1905), 538–45.

SHORTER, CLEMENT K. "Illustrated Journalism: Its Past and Its Future," *Contemporary Review*, LXXV (1899), 481–94.

SMITH, D. NICHOL. "The Newspaper," *Johnson's England,* ed. A. S. Turberville (Oxford, 1933), II, 331–67.

SMITH, FRANK. *A History of English Elementary Education, 1760–1902.* 1931.

SOMERVILLE, ALEXANDER. *The Autobiography of a Working Man,* ed. John Carswell. 1951.

SPIELMANN, M. H. "The Rivals of *Punch,*" *National Review,* XXV (1895), 654–66.

SPINNEY, G. H. "Cheap Repository Tracts: Hazard and Marshall Edition," *Library,* Ser. 4, XX (1939), 295–340.

STEINBERG, S. H. *Five Hundred Years of Printing.* 1955. (Touches briefly on many of the topics covered in the present book.)

The Story of the Religious Tract Society. 1898.

STOTT, DAVID. "The Decay of Bookselling," *Nineteenth Century,* XXXVI (1894), 932–38.

STRAHAN, ALEXANDER. "Our Very Cheap Literature," *Contemporary Review,* XIV (1870), 439–60.

SULLIVAN, HELEN. "Literacy and Illiteracy," *Encyclopaedia of the Social Sciences* (New York, 1933), IX, 511–23.

SUTHERLAND, JAMES R. "The Circulation of Newspapers and Literary Periodicals, 1700–1730," *Library,* Ser. 4, XV (1934), 110–24.

———. *A Preface to Eighteenth Century Poetry.* Oxford, 1948. (See chap. iii.)

SYDNEY, WILLIAM CONNOR. *The Early Days of the Nineteenth Century in England, 1800–1820.* 2 vols. 1898. (See I, 226–40.)

———. *England and the English in the Eighteenth Century: Chapters in the Social History of the Times.* 2 vols. 1891. (See II, 131–42.)

["TAUNTON COMMISSION"]. *Report of the Commission To Inquire into the Education Given in Schools Not Comprised within Her Majesty's Two Former Commissions.* 21 vols. 1868–70.

TAYLOR, JOHN TINNON. *Early Opposition to the English Novel: The Popular Reaction from 1760 to 1830.* New York, 1943.

THOMSON, CHRISTOPHER. *The Autobiography of an Artisan.* 1847.

TILLOTSON, KATHLEEN. *Novels of the Eighteen-Forties.* Oxford, 1954. (Part I discusses writers, publishers, and readers of fiction during the decade.)

TIMPERLEY, C. H. *Encyclopaedia of Literary and Typographical Anecdote.* 1842.

TINSLEY, WILLIAM. *Random Recollections of an Old Publisher.* 2 vols. 1905.

TROLLOPE, ANTHONY. "Novel-Reading," *Nineteenth Century,* V (1879), 24–43.

TURNER, E. S. *Boys Will Be Boys.* 1948. (On juvenile thrillers.)

[VAUGHAN, ROBERT]. "Popular Education in England," *British Quarterly Review,* IV (1846), 444–508.

[WADE, JOHN]. *History of the Middle and Working Classes.* 4th ed. Edinburgh, 1842.

WARNER, WELLMAN J. *The Wesleyan Movement in the Industrial Revolution.* 1930.

WATT, IAN. *The Rise of the Novel.* 1957. (See chap. ii: "The Reading Public and the Rise of the Novel.")

WAUGH, ARTHUR. *A Hundred Years of Publishing, Being the Story of Chapman and Hall, Ltd.* 1930.

WEBB, ROBERT K. *The British Working Class Reader, 1790-1848: Literacy and Social Tension.* 1955.

———. "Literacy among the Working Classes in Nineteenth Century Scotland," *Scottish Historical Review,* XXXIII (1954), 100–114.

———. "Working Class Readers in Early Victorian England," *English Historical Review,* LXV (1950), 333–51.

WELLARD, JAMES HOWARD. *Book Selection: Its Principles and Practice.* 1937. (Chaps. i, iii, and v are on the nineteenth-century free library movement.)

WHITELEY, J. H. *Wesley's England: A Survey of XVIIIth Century Social and Cultural Conditions.* 1938.

WICKWAR, WILLIAM H. *The Struggle for the Freedom of the Press, 1819-1832.* 1928.

WOODWARD, E. L. *The Age of Reform, 1815-1870.* 1938.

"A WORKING WOMAN." "Do Public Libraries Foster a Love of Literature among the Masses?" *Chambers's Journal,* Ser. 6, III (1899), 134–36.

WRIGHT, C. HAGBERG. "Readers a Hundred Years Ago," *Nineteenth Century,* LXX (1911), 251–64.

WRIGHT, LOUIS B. *Middle-Class Culture in Elizabethan England.* Chapel Hill, 1935.

WRIGHT, THOMAS. "Concerning the Unknown Public," *Nineteenth Century,* XIII (1883), 279–96.

———. "On a Possible Popular Culture," *Contemporary Review,* XL (1881), 25–44.

SUPPLEMENTARY BIBLIOGRAPHY

Supplementary Bibliography

The place of publication is London unless otherwise specified.

ADAMS, J. R. R. "The Determination of Historical Popular Reading Habits: A Case Study," *Journal of Documentation*, XLV (1989), 318–26.

———. *The Printed Word and the Common Man: Popular Culture in Ulster, 1700–1900*. Belfast, 1987.

AKENSON, DONALD H. *The Irish Education Experiment: The National System of Education in the Nineteenth Century*. 1970.

ALDERSON, BRIAN. "Tracts, Rewards and Fairies: The Victorian Contribution to Children's Literature," in Briggs (ed.), *Essays in the History of Publishing* (below), pp. 247–82.

ALLRED, JOHN R. "The Purpose of the Public Library: The Historical View," *Library History*, II (1972), 185–204.

ALTHOLZ, JOSEF L. *The Religious Press in Britain, 1760–1900*. New York, 1989.

ALTICK, RICHARD D. "From Aldine to Everyman: Cheap Reprint Series of the English Classics 1830–1906," *Studies in Bibliography*, XI (1958), 3–24.

———. "Nineteenth-Century English Best-Sellers: A Further List," *Studies in Bibliography*, XXII (1969), 197–206. (Supplements the list in the present volume.)

———. "Nineteenth-Century English Best-Sellers: A Third List," *Studies in Bibliography*, XXXIX (1986), 235–41.

———. "The Reading Public in England and America in 1900," in Daiches and Thorlby (eds.), *The Modern World II* (below), pp. 547–68.

———. "Varieties of Readers' Response: The Case of *Dombey and Son*," *Yearbook of English Studies*, X (1980), 70–94.

ANDERSON, PATRICIA. "'Factory Girl, Apprentice and Clerk'—The Readership of Mass Market Magazines, 1830–60," *Victorian Periodicals Review*, XXV (1992), 64–72.

———. *The Printed Image and the Transformation of Popular Culture 1790–1860*. Oxford, 1991.

ANDERSON, PATRICIA, and ROSE, JONATHAN (eds.). *British Literary Publishing Houses, 1820–1880*. (Dictionary of Literary Biography 106) Detroit, 1991.

ANDERSON, R. D. *Education and Opportunity in Victorian Scotland: Schools and Universities*. Oxford, 1983.

413

———. *Education and the Scottish People, 1750–1918.* Oxford, 1995.

ANGLO, M. *Penny Dreadfuls and Other Victorian Horrors.* 1977.

ARMYTAGE, W. H. G. *Four Hundred Years of English Education.* Cambridge, 1964.

BAILEY, PETER. *Leisure and Class in Victorian England: Rational Recreation and the Contest for Control, 1830–1885.* 1978.

BALL, NANCY. *Educating the People: A Documentary History of Elementary Schooling in England, 1840–1870.* 1983.

BARNES, JAMES J. *Free Trade in Books: A Study of the London Book Trade since 1800.* Oxford, 1964.

BARRY, JONATHAN. "Literacy and Literature in Popular Culture: Reading and Writing in Historical Perspective," in Tim Harris (ed.), *Popular Culture in England, c. 1500–1850* (1995), pp. 69–94.

BAYLEN, JOSEPH O. "Stead's Penny 'Masterpiece Library,'" *Journal of Popular Culture,* IX (1975), 710–25.

BECKETT, J. C. "The Irish Writer and His Public in the Nineteenth Century," *Yearbook of English Studies,* XI (1981), 102–16.

BELL, BILL. "Fiction in the Marketplace: Towards a Study of the Victorian Novel," in Myers and Harris (eds.), *Serials and Their Readers* (below), pp. 125–44.

BENNETT, H. S. *English Books & Readers, 1558–1603: Being a Study in the History of the Book Trade in the Reign of Elizabeth I.* Cambridge, 1965.

———. *English Books & Readers, 1603–1640: Being a Study in the History of the Book Trade in the Reigns of James I and Charles I.* Cambridge, 1970.

BENNETT, SCOTT. "The Editorial Character and Readership of *The Penny Magazine:* An Analysis," *Victorian Periodicals Review,* XVII (1984), 127–41.

———. "John Murray's Family Library and the Cheapening of Books in Early Nineteenth Century Britain," *Studies in Bibliography,* XXIX (1976), 139–66.

———. "Revolutions in Thought: Serial Publication and the Mass Market for Reading," in Shattock and Wolff (eds.), *The Victorian Periodical Press* (below), pp. 225–57.

BERRIDGE, VIRGINIA. "Popular Sunday Papers and Mid-Victorian Society," in Boyce et al. (eds.), *Newspaper History* (below), pp. 247–64.

BLACK, ALISTAIR. *A New History of the English Public Library: Social and Intellectual Contexts, 1850–1914.* Leicester, 1996. (Exhaustive documentation.)

BLACK, JEREMY. *The English Press in the Eighteenth Century.* 1987.

BONNELL, THOMAS F. "John Bell's *Poets of Great Britain:* The 'Little Trifling Edition' Revisited," *Modern Philology,* LXXXV (1987), 128–52.

BOYCE, GEORGE, CURRAN, JAMES, and WINGATE, PAULINE (eds.). *Newspaper History from the Seventeenth Century to the Present Day.* 1978.

BRACKEN, JAMES K., and SILVER, JOEL (eds.). *The British Literary Book Trade, 1475–1700.* (Dictionary of Literary Biography 170) Detroit, 1996.

——— (eds.). *The British Literary Book Trade, 1700–1820.* (Dictionary of Literary Biography 154) Detroit, 1995.

BRAKE, LAUREL. "The 'Trepidation of the Spheres': The Serial and the Book in the 19th Century," in Myers and Harris (eds.), *Serials and Their Readers* (below), pp. 83–101.

BRAKE, LAUREL, JONES, ALED, and MADDEN, LIONEL (eds.). *Investigating Victorian Journalism.* New York, 1990.

BRANTLINGER, PATRICK. "The Case of the Poisonous Book: Mass Literacy as Threat in Nineteenth Century British Fiction," *Victorian Review,* XX (1994), 117–33.

BRATTON, J. S. *The Impact of Victorian Children's Fiction.* 1981.

BREWER, JOHN. *The Pleasures of the Imagination: English Culture in the Eighteenth Century.* New York, 1997. (Chap. iv: "Readers and the Reading Public," the most up-to-date and best overview.)

BRIGGS, ASA (ed.). *Essays in the History of Publishing in Celebration of the 250th Anniversary of the House of Longman 1724–1974.* 1974.

BROOKS, GREG, and PUGH, A. K. *Studies in the History of Reading.* Reading, 1984.

BROWN, LUCY. *Victorian News and Newspapers.* Oxford, 1985.

BURGESS, HENRY JAMES. *Enterprise in Education: The Story of the Work of the Established Church in the Education of the People Prior to 1870.* 1958.

BURNETT, JOHN (ed.). *Destination Obscure: Autobiographies of Childhood, Education and Family from the 1820's to the 1920's.* 1982.

———. *Useful Toil: Autobiographies of Working People from the 1820's to the 1920's.* 1974.

BURNS, JAMES. "'Polite Learning' and 'Useful Knowledge,' 1750–1850," *History Today,* XXXVI (1986), 21–29.

CAPP, BERNARD. *Astrology and the Popular Press: English Almanacs, 1500–1800.* 1979. (American title: *English Almanacs 1500–1800: Astrology and the Popular Press.*)

———. "Popular Literature," in Reay (ed.), *Popular Culture in Seventeenth-Century England* (below), pp. 198–243.

CARPENTER, KEVIN. *Penny Dreadfuls and Comics: English Periodicals for Children from Victorian Times to the Present Day.* 1983.

CASTELEYN, MARY. *A History of Literacy and Libraries in Ireland: The Long Traced Pedigree.* Aldershot, 1984.

CHARLTON, KENNETH. *Education in Renaissance England.* 1965.

CHILSTON, VISCOUNT. *W. H. Smith.* 1965. (Chaps. i–ii.)

CLAIR, COLIN. *A History of Printing in Britain.* New York, 1965.

COLE, RICHARD C. "Community Lending Libraries in Eighteenth-Century Ireland," *Library Quarterly,* XLIV (1974), 111–23.

COLLISON, ROBERT. *The Story of Street Literature: Forerunner of the Popular Press.* 1973.

CORRIGAN, PHILIP RICHARD. *Class Struggle, Social Literacy, and Idle Time: The Provision of Public Libraries in England as a Case Study in the Organisation of Leisure with Direct Educational Results.* Brighton, 1978.

CRANFIELD, G. A. *The Development of the Provincial Newspaper, 1700–1760.* Oxford, 1962.

———. *The Press and Society from Caxton to Northcliffe.* 1978.

CRESSY, DAVID. *Education in Tudor and Stuart England.* 1975. (Documents.)

———. *Literacy and the Social Order: Reading and Writing in Tudor and Stuart England.* Cambridge, 1980.

————. "Literacy in Context: Meaning and Measurement in Early Modern England," in John Brewer and Roy Porter (eds.), *Consumption and the World of Goods* (1993), pp. 305–19.

CUNNINGHAM, HUGH. *Leisure in the Industrial Revolution, c. 1780–1880.* 1980.

DAICHES, DAVID, and THORLBY, ANTHONY (eds.). *The Modern World II: Realities.* 1972.

DALZIEL, MARGARET. *Popular Fiction 100 Years Ago: An Unexplored Tract of Literary History.* 1957.

DARTON, F. J. HARVEY. *Children's Books in England: Five Centuries of Social Life.* 3d ed. rev. by Brian Alderson. Cambridge, 1982.

DAVIES, DAVID W. *An Inquiry into the Reading of the Lower Classes* [1800–1850]. Pasadena, Calif., 1970.

DAVIES, W. J. FRANK. *Teaching Reading in Early England.* 1973.

DICK, MALCOLM. "The Myth of the Working-Class Sunday School," *History of Education,* IX, No. 1 (March 1980), 27–41.

DIGBY, ANNE, and SEARBY, PETER. *Children, School and Society in Nineteenth-Century England.* 1981.

DONALDSON, WILLIAM. *Popular Literature in Victorian Scotland: Language, Fiction, and the Press.* Aberdeen, 1986.

DROTNER, KIRSTEN. *English Children and Their Magazines, 1751–1945.* New Haven, 1988.

DUFFY, EAMON. "The Godly and the Multitude in Stuart England," *The Seventeenth Century,* I (1986), 31–55.

DUGAW, DIANNE. "The Popular Marketing of 'Old Ballads': The Ballad Revival and Eighteenth-Century Antiquarianism Reconsidered," *Eighteenth-Century Studies,* XXI (1987), 71–90.

DUNAE, PATRICK A. "Penny Dreadfuls: Late Nineteenth-Century Boys' Literature and Crime," *Victorian Studies,* XXII (1979), 133–50.

EARLS, MAURICE. "The Dublin Penny Press, 1830–1850," *Long Room,* XXXII (1987), 7–26.

ELIOT, SIMON. "Bookselling by the Backdoor: Circulating Libraries, Booksellers and Book Clubs 1870–1966," in Myers and Harris (eds.), *A Genius for Letters* (below), pp. 145–66.

————. *Some Patterns and Trends in British Publishing, 1800–1919.* (Bibliographical Society Occasional Papers 8.) 1993.

ELLEGÅRD, ALVAR. *Darwin and the General Reader: The Reception of Darwin's Theory of Evolution in the British Periodical Press, 1859–1872.* (Gothenburg Studies in English 8.) Göteborg, 1958.

————. "The Readership of the Periodical Press in Mid-Victorian Britain," *Göteborgs Universitets Årsskrift,* LXIII, No. 3 (1957); Part II reprinted in *Victorian Periodicals Newsletter,* No. 13 (1971), 3–22.

ELLIS, ALEC. *Books in Victorian Elementary Schools.* 1971.

————. *Educating Our Masters: Influences on the Growth of Literacy in Victorian Working Class Children.* Aldershot, 1985.

————. *A History of Children's Reading and Literature.* Oxford, 1968.

ERICKSON, LEE. *The Economy of Literary Form: English Literature and the Industrialization of Publishing, 1800–1850.* Baltimore, 1996.

FEATHER, JOHN. "The Commerce of Letters: The Study of the Eighteenth-Century Book Trade," *Eighteenth-Century Studies,* XVII (1984), 405–24.

———. *A History of British Publishing.* 1988. (Replaces Mumby's *Publishing and Bookselling* as the standard authority.)

———. "The Merchants of Culture: Bookselling in Early Industrial England," *Studies on Voltaire and the Eighteenth Century,* CCXVII (1983), 11–21.

———. *The Provincial Book Trade in Eighteenth-Century England.* Cambridge, 1985.

———. "Technology and the Book in the Nineteenth Century," *Critical Survey,* II (1990), 5–13.

FERCH, DAVID L. "'Good Books are a Very Great Mercy to the World': Persecution, Private Libraries, and the Printed Word in the Early Development of the Dissenting Academies, 1663–1730," *Journal of Library History,* XXI (1986), 350–61.

FERGUS, JAN. "Eighteenth-Century Readers in Provincial England: The Customers of Samuel Clay's Circulating Library and Bookshop in Warwick, 1770–72," *Papers of the Bibliographical Society of America,* LXXVIII (1984), 155–213.

———. "Women, Class, and the Growth of Magazine Readership in the Provinces, 1746–1780," *Studies in Eighteenth-Century Culture,* XVI (1986), 41–56.

FINKELSTEIN, DAVID. "'The Secret': British Publishers and Mudie's Struggle for Economic Survival, 1861–64," *Publishing History,* XXXIV (1993), 21–50.

FLAVELL, M. KAY. "The Enlightened Reader and the New Industrial Towns: A Study of the Liverpool Library 1758–1790," *British Journal for Eighteenth-Century Studies,* VIII (1985), 17–35.

FLINT, KATE. *The Woman Reader, 1837–1914.* Oxford, 1993.

FORD, WYN. "The Problem of Literacy in Early Modern England," *History,* LXXVIII (1993), 22–37.

FOX, CELINA. *Graphic Journalism in England During the 1830s and 1840s.* New York, 1988.

FRANTZ, RAY W., JR. "The London Library Society: A Turning Point," *The Library,* Ser. 6, IV (1982), 418–22. (The first subscription library in the City, 1785.)

GARDNER, A. D., and JENKINS, E. W. "The English Mechanics' Institutes: The Case of Leeds, 1824–42," *History of Education,* XIII (1984), 139–52.

GARDNER, PHIL. *The Lost Elementary Schools of Victorian Britain: The People's Education.* 1984.

GETTMANN, ROYAL A. *A Victorian Publisher: A Study of the Bentley Papers.* Cambridge, 1960.

GLYNN, JENNIFER. *The Prince of Publishers: A Biography of George Smith.* 1986.

GOLBY, J. M., and PURDUE, A. W. *The Civilisation of the Crowd: Popular Culture in England 1750–1900.* 1984.

GOLDEN, CATHERINE. "Rekindling the Reading Experience of the Victorian Age," *Profession 1995,* 45–47.

GOLDMAN, LAWRENCE. *Dons and Workers: Oxford and Adult Education since 1850.* Oxford, 1995.

GOLDSTROM, J. M. *Education: Elementary Education, 1780–1900.* Newton Abbot, 1972.

———. *The Social Content of Education, 1808–1870: A Study of the Working Class School Reader in England and Scotland.* Shannon, 1972.

GOMERSALL, MEG. "Ideals and Realities: The Education of Working-Class Girls, 1800–1870," *History of Education,* XVII, No. 1 (March 1988), 37–53.

GOSDEN, P. H. J. H. *How They Were Taught: An Anthology of Contemporary Accounts of Learning and Teaching in England 1800–1950.* Oxford, 1969.

GOTTLIEB, GERALD. *Early Children's Books and Their Illustration.* 1975.

GRAFF, HARVEY J. (ed.). "Exaggerated Estimates of Reading and Writing as Means of Education (1867), by W. B. Hodgson," *History of Education Quarterly,* XXVI (1986), 377–93. (Reprints the document so titled.)

GRIEST, GUINEVERE L. *Mudie's Circulating Library and the Victorian Novel.* Bloomington, Ind., 1970.

HARRIS, BOB. *Politics and the Rise of the Press: Britain and France, 1620–1800.* 1996.

HARRIS, MICHAEL. "Astrology, Almanacks and Booksellers," *Publishing History,* VIII (1980), 87–104.

HARRIS, MICHAEL, and LEE, ALAN (eds.). *The Press in English Society from the Seventeenth to Nineteenth Centuries.* 1986.

HARRISON, J. F. C. *Learning and Living 1790–1960: A Study in the History of the Adult Education Movement.* 1961.

HARRISON, STANLEY. *Poor Men's Guardians: A Record of the Struggles for a Democratic Newspaper Press, 1763–1973.* 1974.

HARROP, S. A. "Adult Education and Literacy: The Importance of Post-School Education for Literacy Levels in the Eighteenth and Nineteenth Centuries," *History of Education,* XIII (1984), 191–205.

HEDGES, DAVID. "Charles Knight of Windsor," *Antiquarian Book Monthly Review,* XII (1985), 4–9.

HIND, ROBERT J. "Working People and Sunday Schools: England, 1780–1850," *Journal of Religious History,* XV (1988), 199–218.

HOGGART, P. R. "Edward Lloyd, 'The Father of the Cheap Press,'" *Dickensian,* LXXX (1984), 33–38.

HOGGART, RICHARD. *The Uses of Literacy: Aspects of Working-Class Life, with Special Reference to Publications and Entertainment.* 1957. (American subtitle: *Changing Patterns in English Mass Culture.*)

HOLLIS, PATRICIA. *The Pauper Press: A Study in Working-Class Radicalism of the 1830s.* 1970.

HOUSTON, R. A. *Literacy in Early Modern Europe: Culture and Education, 1500–1800.* 1988. (Many references to England and Scotland.)

———. "The Literacy Myth?: Illiteracy in Scotland 1630–1760," *Past and Present,* No. 96 (1982), 81–102.

———. *Scottish Literacy and the Scottish Identity: Illiteracy and Society in Scotland and Northern England, 1600–1800.* Cambridge, 1985.

HOWSAM, LESLIE. *Cheap Bibles: Nineteenth-Century Publishing and the British and Foreign Bible Society.* Cambridge, 1991.

———. "Sustained Literary Ventures: The Series in Victorian Book Publishing," *Publishing History,* XXXI (1992), 5–26.

HUGHES, LINDA K., and LUND, MICHAEL. *The Victorian Serial.* Charlottesville, Va., 1991.

HUME, ROBERT D. "Texts within Contexts: Notes toward a Historical Method," *Philological Quarterly,* LXXI (1992), 69–100.

HUMPHERYS, ANNE. "G. W. M. Reynolds: Popular Literature and Popular Politics," in Joel H. Wiener (ed.), *Innovators and Preachers: The Role of the Editor in Victorian England* (Westport, Conn., 1985), pp. 3–21.

HUNTER, J. PAUL. *Before Novels: The Cultural Contexts of Eighteenth-Century English Fiction.* New York, 1990. (See especially chap. iii: "Readers Reading.")

HURT, JOHN S. *Education in Evolution: Church, State, Society and Popular Education, 1800–1870.* 1971.

———. *Elementary Schooling and the Working Classes 1860–1918.* 1979.

IRWIN, RAYMOND. *The Heritage of the English Library.* New York, 1964.

———. *The Origins of the English Library.* 1958.

JACK, IAN. *The Poet and His Audience.* Cambridge, 1984.

JACKSON, MARY V. *Engines of Instruction, Mischief, and Magic: Children's Literature from Its Beginnings to 1839.* Lincoln, Nebr., 1989.

JACOBS, EDWARD. "Bloods in the Street: London Street Culture, 'Industrial Literacy,' and the Emergence of Mass Culture in Victorian England," *Nineteenth-Century Contexts,* XVIII (1995), 321–47.

JAMES, LOUIS. *Fiction for the Working Man 1830–50: A Study of the Literature Produced for the Working Classes in Early Victorian Urban England.* 1963.

———. "The Trouble with Betsy: Periodicals and the Common Reader in Mid-Nineteenth-Century England," in Shattock and Wolff (eds.), *The Victorian Periodical Press* (below), pp. 349–66.

———. "The View from Brick Lane: Contrasting Perspectives in Working-Class and Middle-Class Fiction of the Early Victorian Period," *Yearbook of English Studies,* XI (1981), 87–101.

———. Working-Class Literature in England," in Daiches and Thorlby (eds.), *The Modern World II* (above), pp. 529–46.

——— (ed.). *Print and the People 1819–1851.* 1976. (American title: *English Popular Literature 1819–1851.*)

[JOHNS, B. G.] "The Literature of Seven Dials," *National Review,* II (1883), 478–92. (On street ballads.)

JOHNSON, RICHARD. "'Really Useful Knowledge': Radical Education and Working-Class Culture, 1790–1848," in John Clarke, Charles Critcher, and Richard Johnson (eds.), *Working-Class Culture: Studies in History and Theory* (1979), pp. 75–102.

JONES, ALED. "Constructing the Readership in 19th Century Wales," in Myers and Harris (eds.), *Serials and Their Readers* (below), pp. 145–62.

———. *Powers of the Press: Newspapers, Power and the Public in Nineteenth-Century England.* Aldershot, 1996. (A magisterial study.)

JORDAN, JOHN O., and PATTEN, ROBERT L. (eds.). *Literature in the Marketplace: Nineteenth-Century British Publishing and Reading Practices.* Cambridge, 1995.

JOYCE, PATRICK. *Visions of the People: Industrial England and the Question of Class 1848–1914.* Cambridge, 1991. (Part 4.)

KAESTLE, CARL. "The History of Literacy and the History of Readers," *Review of Research in Education,* XII (1985), 11–53.

KATOH, SHOJI. "Mechanics' Institutes in Great Britain to the 1850s," *Journal of Educational Administration and History,* XXI (1989), 1–7.

KAUFMAN, PAUL. *Borrowings from the Bristol Library, 1773–1784: A Unique Record of Reading Vogues.* Charlottesville, Va., 1960.

———. "The Community Library: A Chapter in English Social History," *Transactions of the American Philosophical Society,* N.S., LVII, Part 7 (1967), 1–67.

———. *Libraries and Their Users: Collected Papers in Library History.* 1969. (Gathers seventeen previously published essays on eighteenth-century non-private libraries.)

———. "Readers and Their Reading in Eighteenth-Century Lichfield," *The Library,* XXVIII (1973), 108–15.

KAUSCH, DONALD. "George W. M. Reynolds: A Bibliography," *The Library,* Ser. 5, XXVIII (1973), 319–26.

KELLY, THOMAS. *Books for the People: An Illustrated History of the British Public Library.* 1977.

———. *Early Public Libraries: A History of Public Libraries in Great Britain Before 1850.* 1966.

———. *George Birkbeck: Pioneer of Adult Education.* Liverpool, 1957.

———. *A History of Adult Education in Great Britain.* Liverpool, 1962.

———. *A History of Public Libraries in Great Britain, 1845–1965.* 1973. (Sequel to *Early Public Libraries.*)

———. "The Origin of Mechanics' Institutes," *British Journal of Educational Studies,* I (1952), 17–27.

———. "Public Libraries and Public Opinion," *Library Association Record,* LXVIII (1966), 246–51.

KERNAN, ALVIN. *Printing Technology, Letters and Samuel Johnson.* Princeton, 1987.

KINTGEN, EUGENE R. *Reading in Tudor England.* Pittsburgh, 1996.

KLANCHER, JON P. *The Making of English Reading Audiences, 1790–1832.* Madison, Wis., 1987.

LANDON, RICHARD G. "Small Profits Do Great Things: James Lackington and Eighteenth-Century Bookselling," *Studies in Eighteenth-Century Culture,* V (1976), 387–99.

LANDRY, DONNA. *The Muses of Resistance: Laboring-Class Women's Poetry in Britain, 1739–1796.* Cambridge, 1990.

LAQUEUR, THOMAS. "The Cultural Origins of Popular Literacy in England 1500–1850," *Oxford Review of Education,* II (1976), 255–75.

———. "Literacy and Social Mobility in the Industrial Revolution in England," *Past and Present,* No. 64 (1974), 96–107. (See also Michael Sanderson, "A Rejoinder," *ibid.,* 108–12.)

———. *Religion and Respectability: Sunday Schools and Working Class Culture, 1780–1850.* New Haven, 1976.

———. "Toward a Cultural Ecology of Literacy in England, 1600–1850," in Daniel P. Resnick (ed.), *Literacy in Historical Perspective* (Washington, D.C., 1983), pp. 43–57.

———. "Working Class Demand and the Growth of English Elementary Education, 1750–1850," in Stone (ed.), *Schooling and Society* (below), pp. 192–205.

LAWSON, JOHN, and SILVER, HAROLD. *A Social History of Education in England.* 1973.

LEE, ALAN J. *The Origins of the Popular Press in England 1855–1914.* 1976.

LILLINGSTON, LEONARD W. "The Catnach Press," *Connoisseur,* III (1902), 180–86.

LINTON, DAVID, and BOSTON, RAY (eds.). *The Newspaper Press in Britain: An Annotated Bibliography.* 1987.

"The Literature of the Rail," *Times,* August 9, 1851, p. 7.

LIVEING, EDWARD. *Adventure in Publishing: The House of Ward Lock 1854–1954.* 1954.

LOWENTHAL, LEO. *Literature, Popular Culture, and Society.* Englewood Cliffs, N.J., 1968.

LOWENTHAL, LEO, and FISKE, MARJORIE. "Reaction to Mass Media Growth in 18th-Century England," *Journalism Quarterly,* XXXIII (1956), 442–55.

LOWERSON, JOHN. *Time to Spare in Victorian England.* Hassocks, Sussex, 1977.

MCALEER, JOSEPH. *Popular Reading and Publishing in Britain 1914–1950.* Oxford, 1992. (Chap. i: "Popular Reading and Publishing, 1870–1914.")

MCCALMAN, IAIN. *Radical Underworld: Prophets, Revolutionaries and Pornographers in London, 1795–1840.* Cambridge, 1988.

MCCANN, W. P. "Elementary Education in England and Wales on the Eve of the 1870 Education Act," *Journal of Educational Administration and History,* II, No. 1 (December 1969), 20–29.

MCDONALD, WILLIAM R. "Circulating Libraries in the North-East of Scotland in the Eighteenth Century," *Bibliotheck,* V (1968), 119–37.

MCKENZIE, D. F. *The London Book Trade in the Later Seventeenth Century.* Cambridge, 1976.

MAIDMENT, BRIAN E. "Essayists and Artizans—The Making of Nineteenth-Century Self-Taught Poets," *Literature and History,* IX (1983), 74–91.

———. "Magazines of Popular Progress and the Artisans," *Victorian Periodicals Review,* XVII (1983), 83–94.

MALCOLMSON, ROBERT W. *Popular Recreations in English Society, 1700–1850.* Cambridge, 1973.

MANDELBROTE, GILES. "From the Warehouse to the Counting-House: Booksellers and Bookshops in Late 17th Century London," in Myers and Harris (eds.), *A Genius for Letters* (below), pp. 49–84.

MANLEY, K. A. "The London and Westminster Libraries, 1785–1823," *The Library,* Ser. 6, VII (1985), 137–59.

MAX, STANLEY M. "Tory Reaction to the Public Libraries Bill, 1850," *Journal of Library History,* XIX (1984), 504–24.

MAYO, ROBERT D. *The English Novel in the Magazines, 1740–1815.* Evanston, Ill., 1962.

MICHAEL, IAN. *The Teaching of English: From the Sixteenth Century to 1870.* Cambridge, 1987.

MITCH, DAVID F. *The Rise of Popular Literacy in Victorian England: The Influence of Private Choice and Public Policy.* Philadelphia, 1992.

MITCHELL, JIM. "The Spread and Fluctuating of Eighteenth-Century Printing," *Studies on Voltaire and the Eighteenth Century,* CCXXX (1985), 305–21.

MITCHELL, SALLY. "The Forgotten Woman of the Period: Penny Weekly Family Magazines of the 1840's and 1850's," in Martha Vicinus (ed.), *A Widening Sphere: Changing Roles of Victorian Women* (Bloomington, Ind., 1977), pp. 29–51.

———. *The New Girl: Girls' Culture in England, 1880–1915.* New York, 1995.

MOUNTJOY, PETER ROGER. "The Working-Class Press and Working-Class Conservatism," in Boyce et al. (eds.), *Newspaper History* (above), pp. 265–80.

MUNFORD, W. A. *Edward Edwards 1812–1886: Portrait of a Librarian.* 1963.

MURISON, W. J. *The Public Library: Its Origins, Purpose, and Significance.* 2d ed., 1971.

MURPHY, PAUL THOMAS. *Toward a Working-Class Canon: Literary Criticism in British Working-Class Periodicals, 1816–1858.* Columbus, Ohio, 1994.

MYERS, MITZI. "'Servants as They are Now Educated': Women Writers and Georgian Pedagogy," *Essays in Literature,* XVI (1989), 51–69.

MYERS, ROBIN. *The British Book Trade, from Caxton to the Present Day.* 1973. (Bibliography.)

MYERS, ROBIN, and HARRIS, MICHAEL (eds.). *The Development of the English Book Trade, 1700–1899.* Oxford, 1981.

——— (eds.). *A Genius for Letters: Booksellers and Bookselling from the 16th to the 20th Century.* Winchester, 1995.

——— (eds.). *Sale and Distribution of Books from 1700.* Oxford, 1982.

——— (eds.). *Serials and Their Readers 1620–1914.* Winchester, 1993.

——— (eds.). *Spreading the Word: The Distribution Networks of Print 1500–1850.* Winchester, 1990.

NEUBURG, VICTOR E. *Chapbooks: A Guide to Reference Material on English, Scottish and American Chapbook Literature of the Eighteenth and Nineteenth Centuries.* 2d ed. 1972.

———. "Literature of the Streets," in H. J. Dyos and Michael Wolff (eds.), *The Victorian City: Images and Realities* (1973), I, 191–209.

———. *The Penny Histories: A Study of Chapbooks for Young Readers over Two Centuries.* Oxford, 1968.

———. *Popular Education in Eighteenth-Century England.* 1971.

———. *Popular Literature: A History and Guide.* Harmondsworth, 1977.

"Notes on the Unstamped Press," *Bookseller,* September 30, 1867, pp. 683–86.

"Notes upon Comic Periodicals," *Bookseller,* August 31, 1867, pp. 617–19.

NOWELL-SMITH, SIMON. *The House of Cassell 1848–1958.* 1958.

O'DAY, ROSEMARY. *Education and Society, 1500–1800: The Social Foundations of Education in Early Modern Britain.* 1982.

ORME, NICHOLAS. *Education and Society in Medieval and Renaissance England.* 1989.

PARR, LINDA J. "The Library of Halifax Mechanics' Institution 1825–1857." *Library History,* VII (1987), 177–86.

PEDERSON, SUSAN. "Hannah More Meets Simple Simon: Tracts, Chapbooks, and

Popular Culture in Late Eighteenth-Century England," *Journal of British Studies*, XXV (1986), 84–113.

PERKIN, H. J. "The Origins of the Popular Press," *History Today*, VII (1957), 425–35.

PETERSON, TED. "British Crime Pamphleteers: Forgotten Journalists," *Journalism Quarterly*, XXII (1945), 305–16.

———. "The Fight of William Hone for British Press Freedom," *Journalism Quarterly*, XXV (1948), 132–38.

———. "James Catnach: Master of Street Literature," *Journalism Quarterly*, XXVII (1950), 157–63.

POLLARD, GRAHAM. "The English Market for Printed Books," *Publishing History*, IV (1978), 7–48.

POLLARD, M. *Dublin's Trade in Books, 1550–1800*. Oxford, 1989.

Publishing, the Booktrade and the Diffusion of Knowledge. Cambridge, 1986. (Microfiches of over 700 books on these subjects, originally published between 1801 and 1900.)

RAVEN, JAMES. "Le commerce de librairie 'en gros' à Londres au XVIIIe siècle," in Frédéric Barbier et al. (eds.), *L'Europe et le livre* (Paris, 1996), pp. 157–71.

———. *The Commercialization of the Book*. (Forthcoming.)

———. *Judging New Wealth: Popular Publishing and Responses to Commerce in England, 1750–1800*. Oxford, 1992.

———. "The Noble Brothers and Popular Publishing, 1737–89," *The Library*, Ser. 6, XII (1990), 295–343.

———. "The Publication of Fiction in Britain and Ireland 1750–70," *Publishing History*, XXIV (1988), 31–47.

———. "Serial Advertisement in 18th-Century Britain and Ireland," in Myers and Harris (eds.), *Serials and Their Readers* (above), pp. 103–22.

RAVEN, JAMES, SMALL, HELEN, and TADMOR, NAOMI (eds.). *The Practice and Representation of Reading in England*. Cambridge, 1996.

REAY, BARRY. "The Context and Meaning of Popular Literacy: Some Evidence from Nineteenth-Century Rural England," *Past and Present*, No. 131 (1991), 89–129.

———. "Popular Literature in Seventeenth-Century England," *Journal of Peasant Studies*, X (1976), 255–75.

——— (ed.). *Popular Culture in Seventeenth-Century England*. 1985.

RICHARDSON, ALAN. *Literature, Education, and Romanticism: Reading as Social Practice, 1780–1832*. Cambridge, 1994.

RIVERS, ISABEL (ed.). *Books and Their Readers in Eighteenth-Century England*. Leicester, 1982.

ROBERTS, LEWIS C. "Disciplining and Disinfecting Working-Class Readers in the Victorian Public Library," *Victorian Literature and Culture*, XXVI (1998), 105–32.

ROBINSON, F. J. G., and WALLIS, P. J. *Book Subscription Lists: A Revised Guide*. Newcastle upon Tyne, 1975. (Continued by *Book Subscription Lists: First Supplement*, ed. C. Wadham [1976]; *Second Supplement*, ed. L. Menhennet [1977]; *Third Supplement* [1980].)

ROBSON, ANN. "The Intellectual Background of the Public Library Movement in Britain," *Journal of Library History*, XI (1976), 187–205.

ROGERS, PAT. *Literature and Popular Culture in Eighteenth Century England*. Brighton, 1985. (Chap. vii: "Classics and Chapbooks.")

ROSE, JONATHAN. "Rereading the English Common Reader: A Preface to a History of Audiences," *Journal of the History of Ideas*, LIII (1992), 47–70.

———. "Workers' Journals," in J. Don Vann and Rosemary T. Van Arsdel (eds.), *Victorian Periodicals and Victorian Society* (Toronto, 1994), pp. 301–10. (Review of research.)

ROSE, JONATHAN, and ANDERSON, PATRICIA J. (eds.). *British Literary Publishing Houses, 1881–1965*. (Dictionary of Literary Biography 112) Detroit, 1991.

ROYLE, EDWARD. "Mechanics' Institutes and the Working Classes, 1840–1860," *Historical Journal*, XIV (1971), 305–21.

SCHOFIELD, R. S. "Dimensions of Literacy, 1750–1850," *Explorations in Economic History*, X (1973), 437–54.

———. "The Measurement of Literacy in Pre-Industrial England," in Jack Goody (ed.), *Literacy in Traditional Societies* (Cambridge, 1968), pp. 311–25.

[SHAND, INNES]. "Contemporary Literature," *Blackwood's Edinburgh Magazine*, CXXIV (1878), 641–62; CXXV (1879), 69–42, 225–47, 322–44, 482–506, 678–703; CXXVI (1879), 235–56, 472–93.

SHATTOCK, JOANNE. "Spheres of Influence: The Quarterlies and Their Readers," *Yearbook of English Studies*, X (1980), 95–104.

SHATTOCK, JOANNE, and WOLFF, MICHAEL (eds.). *The Victorian Periodical Press: Samplings and Soundings*. Leicester, 1982.

SHAW, MARGARET. "Constructing the 'Literate Woman': Nineteenth-Century Reviews and Emerging Literacies," *Dickens Studies Annual*, XXI (1992), 195–212.

SHEPARD, LESLIE. *The Broadside Ballad: A Study in Origins and Meaning*. 1962.

———. *The History of Street Literature: The Story of Broadside Ballads, Chapbooks, Proclamations, News-Sheets, Election Bills, Tracts, Pamphlets, Cocks, Catchpennies, and Other Ephemera*. Detroit, 1973.

———. *John Pitts: Ballad Printer of Seven Dials, London 1765–1844, with a Short Account of His Predecessors in the Ballad & Chapbook Trade*. 1969.

SHEVELOW, KATHRYN. *Women and Print Culture: The Construction of Femininity in the Early Periodical*. 1989. (Chap. ii: "Early Periodicals and Their Readers.")

SILVER, HAROLD. *The Concept of Popular Education: A Study of Ideas and Social Movements in the Early Nineteenth Century*. 1965.

SILVER, PAMELA, and SILVER, HAROLD. *The Education of the Poor: The History of a National School, 1824–1974*. 1974. (On a school in Lambeth.)

SIMON, JOAN. *Education and Society in Tudor England*. Cambridge, 1966.

SKALLERUP, HARRY R. *Books Afloat & Ashore: A History of Books, Libraries, and Reading among Seamen during the Age of Sail*. Hamden, Conn., 1974. (Chaps. i–ii.)

SMELSER, NEIL J. *Social Paralysis and Social Change: British Working-Class Education in the Nineteenth Century*. Berkeley, 1991. (Includes large bibliography.)

SNAPE, ROBERT. *Leisure and the Rise of the Public Library*. 1995.

SNYDER, HENRY L. "The Circulation of Newspapers in the Reign of Queen Anne," *The Library*, Ser. 5, XXIII (1968), 206–33.

SPECK, W. A. *Society and Literature in England 1700–60*. Dublin, 1983. (Chap. vii: "Augustan Writers and Their Readers.")

SPRINGHALL, JOHN. "'Disseminating Impure Literature': The 'Penny Dreadful' Publishing Business Since 1860," *Economic History Review*, XLVII (1994), 567–84.

———. "'A Life Story for the People'? Edwin J. Brett and the London 'Low Life' Penny Dreadfuls of the 1860s," *Victorian Studies*, XXXIII (1990), 223–46.

SPUFFORD, MARGARET. "First Steps in Literacy: The Reading and Writing Experiences of the Humblest Seventeenth-Century Spiritual Autobiographies," *Social History*, IV (1979), 407–35.

———. *Small Books and Pleasant Histories: Popular Fiction and Its Readership in Seventeenth-Century England*. 1981.

SREBRNIK, PATRICIA THOMAS. *Alexander Strahan: Victorian Publisher*. Ann Arbor, Mich., 1986.

STEPHENS, W. B. *Education, Literacy and Society, 1830–70: The Geography of Diversity in Provincial England*. Manchester, 1987.

———. "Illiteracy and Schooling in Provincial Towns 1640–1870," in D. A. Reeder (ed.), *Urban Education in the Nineteenth Century* (1977), pp. 27–48.

———. "Literacy in England, Scotland, and Wales, 1500–1900," *History of Education Quarterly*, XXX (1990), 545–71.

———. "Schooling and Literacy in Rural England, 1800–1914," *History of Education Quarterly*, XXII (1982), 73–82.

STONE, LAWRENCE. "The Educational Revolution in England, 1560–1640," *Past and Present*, No. 28 (1964), 41–80.

———. "Literacy and Education in England, 1640–1900," *Past and Present*, No. 42 (1969), 69–139.

——— (ed.). *Schooling and Society: Studies in the History of Education*. Baltimore, 1976.

STORCH, ROBERT D. (ed.). *Popular Culture and Custom in Nineteenth-Century England*. 1982.

STURGES, R. P. "Context for Library History: Libraries in 18th Century Derby," *Library History*, IV (1976), 44–52.

———. "The Place of Libraries in the English Urban Renaissance of the Eighteenth Century," *Libraries and Culture*, XXIV (1989), 57–68.

STURGES, R. P., and BARR, ALISON. "'The Fiction Nuisance' in Nineteenth-Century British Public Libraries," *Journal of Librarianship and Information Science*, XXIV (1992), 23–32.

STURT, MARY. *The Education of the People: A History of Primary Education in England and Wales in the Nineteenth Century*. 1967.

SUTHERLAND, JOHN. "Publishing History: A Hole at the Centre of Literary Sociology," *Critical Inquiry*, XIV (1988), 574–89.

———. *Victorian Fiction: Writers, Publishers, Readers*. New York, 1995.

———. *Victorian Novelists and Their Publishers*. Chicago, 1976.

SWANTON, MICHAEL. "A Readership (and Non-Readership) for *Martin Chuzzlewit*,

1843–44," *Dickens Quarterly,* XI (1994), 115–26, 161–71. (Borrowers of a book-club copy.)

SYKES, PAUL. *The Public Library in Perspective: An Examination of Its Origins and Modern Role.* 1979.

THOMAS, KEITH. "The Meaning of Literacy in Early Modern England," in Gerd Baumann (ed.), *The Written Word: Literacy in Transition* (Oxford, 1986), pp. 97–131.

THOMPSON, ALASTAIR R. "The Use of Libraries by the Working Class in Scotland in the Early Nineteenth Century," *Scottish Historical Review,* XLII (1963), 21–29.

THOMPSON, E. P. *The Making of the English Working Class.* 1963.

THWAITE, MARY F. *From Primer to Pleasure in Reading.* 1963. (History of children's books.)

TWYMAN, MICHAEL. *Printing 1770–1970: An Illustrated History of Its Development and Uses in England.* 1970.

VARMA, DEVENDRA. *The Evergreen Tree of Diabolical Knowledge.* Washington, D.C., 1972. (Circulating libraries.)

VERNON, JAMES. *Politics and the People: A Study in English Political Culture, c. 1815–1867.* Cambridge, 1993. (Chap. iii: "The Medium and the Message: Power, Print, and the Public Sphere.")

VICINUS, MARTHA. *The Industrial Muse: A Study of Nineteenth Century British Working-Class Literature.* New York, 1974.

VINCENT, DAVID. *Bread, Knowledge and Freedom: A Study of Nineteenth-Century Working Class Autobiography.* 1981.

———. *Literacy and Popular Culture: England, 1750–1914.* Cambridge, 1989. (The best overall study of the subject.)

———. "Reading in the Working-Class Home," in John K. Walton and James Walvin (eds.), *Leisure in Britain 1780–1939* (Manchester, 1983), pp. 207–26.

WALLIS, PHILIP. *At the Sign of the Ship: Notes on the House of Longman, 1724–1974.* 1974.

WARDLE, DAVID. *English Popular Education, 1780–1975.* 2d ed. Cambridge, 1976.

WATT, TESSA. *Cheap Print and Popular Piety, 1550–1640.* Cambridge, 1991.

WEBB, R. K. "The Victorian Reading Public," *Universities Quarterly,* XII (1957), 24–44.

WEST, E. G. "Literacy and the Industrial Revolution," *Economic History Review,* XXXI (1978), 369–83.

WIENER, JOEL H. *The War of the Unstamped: The Movement to Repeal the British Newspaper Tax, 1830–1836.* Ithaca, N.Y., 1969.

——— (ed.). *Papers for the Millions: The New Journalism in Britain, 1850s to 1914.* New York, 1988.

WILES, R. M. *Freshest Advices: Early Provincial Newspapers in England.* Columbus, Ohio, 1965.

———. "Middle-Class Literacy in Eighteenth-Century England: Fresh Evidence," in R. F. Brissenden (ed.), *Studies in the Eighteenth Century* (Canberra, 1968), pp. 49–65.

———. "The Relish for Reading in Provincial England Two Centuries Ago," in Paul J. Korshin (ed.), *The Widening Circle: Essays on the Circulation of Literature in Eighteenth-Century Europe* (Philadelphia, 1976), pp. 85–115.

WILLIAMS, KEITH. *The English Newspaper: An Illustrated History to 1900.* 1977.

WILLIAMS, RAYMOND. *Culture and Society, 1780–1950.* 1958.

————. *The Long Revolution.* 1961.

————. "The Press and Popular Culture: An Historical Perspective," in Boyce et al. (eds.), *Newspaper History* (above), pp. 41–50.

WILSON, CHARLES. *First with the News: The History of W. H. Smith 1792–1972.* 1985.

WURZBACH, NATASCHA. *The Rise of the English Street Ballad, 1550–1650.* Cambridge, 1990. (Translation, by Gayna Walls, of the author's *Anfange und gattungstypische Ausformen der englischen Strassenballade 1500–1650,* Munich, 1981.)

YGLESIAS, ROY. "Education and Publishing in Transition," in Briggs (ed.), *Essays in the History of Publishing* (above), pp. 351–88.

INDEX

Index

[References in italics indicate pages containing sales or circulation figures.]